MW01002207

Integrated Care

Integrated
Care

Applying Theory to Practice

EDITED BY
Russ Curtis & Eric Christian

Routledge
Taylor & Francis Group
New York   London

Disclaimer: The views expressed in this text are independent of and do not necessarily reflect the views of Eric Christian's employer, Community Care of Western North Carolina, one of the Community Care of North Carolina networks.

Routledge
Taylor & Francis Group
711 Third Avenue
New York, NY 10017

Routledge
Taylor & Francis Group
27 Church Road
Hove, East Sussex BN3 2FA

© 2012 by Taylor & Francis Group, LLC
Routledge is an imprint of Taylor & Francis Group, an Informa business

International Standard Book Number: 978-0-415-89132-5 (Hardback)

Library of Congress Cataloging-in-Publication Data

Integrated care : applying theory to practice / [edited by] Russ Curtis & Eric Christian.
    p. cm.
    Summary: "This book provides pertinent and practical information about how to create, work, and thrive in an integrated care (IC) setting. Unlike other books on the subject, it focuses on the "nuts and bolts" of establishing an IC practice; it also covers material that is often missing from or insufficiently covered in the existing literature"-- Provided by publisher.
    ISBN 978-0-415-89132-5 (hardback)
    1. Integrated delivery of health care. 2. Mental health services. I. Curtis, Russ. II. Christian, Eric.

RA971.I478 2012
616--dc23

2011050699

Visit the Taylor & Francis Web site at
http://www.taylorandfrancis.com

and the Routledge Web site at
http://www.routledgementalhealth.com

Contents

Martha Teater, MA, LMFT, and Don Teater, MD, collaborating to provide optimal care for their patient.

Preface

Nina's primary care doctor urged her to seek counseling for the stress that was negatively affecting her health and quality of life, but Nina never acted on the advice. Some years later, however, Nina's doctor invited a friend and colleague, who was a licensed counselor, to lease office space within her practice. The doctor and counselor promptly began referring patients to one another, with patients' permission, and consulted with each other about how to provide each patient with the best comprehensive health care possible. During this time of collaboration between the doctor and counselor, Nina's doctor once again encouraged her to seek counseling and explained that a counselor was available in the room next door. This time Nina agreed. They walked to the counselor's office together, and the doctor introduced Nina and the counselor to one another. Nina began receiving counseling services the very next day.

What caused Nina to change her behavior? After years of refusing counseling, Nina was willing to explore the recommendation when a counselor became an integral part of her physician's practice. Nina explained why she changed her mind, "I trusted my doctor and knew she would not allow just anyone to share an office with her. I also felt more comfortable receiving counseling in my doctor's office because I'd been going there for years and I knew where to park; I knew and liked the office staff, and they knew and liked me. I also did not like the idea of having to go to a mental health center and sit in the waiting room where everyone would wonder what my problem was."

Removing the sense of stigma and the fear of the unknown helped Nina to accept the services that her doctor advised would improve her overall health. After just a few sessions, Nina reported feeling better. There were improvements in her utilization of health care services as well. Her pattern of presenting unexpectedly at her doctor's office with unexplained symptoms ceased. In the past, Nina was referred to the emergency room when she could not be seen by her physician. In the context of integrated care, however, the counselor was able to speak with Nina by phone or in person, and helped her to develop and use behavioral health strategies that enabled her to wait for a scheduled appointment with her physician rather than visit the ER.

The type of care that was so successful in helping Nina to comprehensively improve her health is called Integrated Primary Behavioral Health Care (IPBHC), commonly called *integrated care* (IC). IC is the dynamic collaboration between primary care physicians (PCPs) and behavioral health providers (BHPs), and it is quickly gaining national prominence as a promising new model for health care. Practicing BHPs and those aspiring to be BHPs should be aware of IC for its many advantages. There is strong evidence that indicates the effectiveness of treating patients' medical and mental health needs within one location, and emerging evidence that indicates the ability of integrated care to control, and in some cases reduce, health care costs.

This text will discuss the reasons why and ways in which IC is quickly becoming a leading model for treating those with mental health and/or emotional problems. There has been vast approval of IC among many leading mental health, substance abuse, and medical associations, and in reflection of this endorsement, IC initiatives are gaining momentum and increasing in number across the country. A change from older health care models to IC does meet with some resistance and present challenges, though. It is not uncommon for some mental health professionals to express reluctance toward the IC model of care, perhaps because it is so different from the traditional mental health care model taught in many graduate school programs. Indeed, adjusting the curriculum within graduate counseling, marriage and family, psychology, and social work programs to prepare future BHPs to work effectively within the context of IC is not a simple task. We firmly believe, however, that resistance to IC among mental health professionals will fade as they are educated in and recognize the extraordinary benefits the model brings, including but not limited to reaching patients who would not otherwise seek counseling, promoting health behavior change for chronic physical health conditions, reducing the cost of health care, and improving patients' quality of life.

The purpose of this text is to provide comprehensive and practical information about how to become a successful IC professional. To accomplish this we have reviewed current research, surveyed expert clinicians working within IC settings, and spent many hours meeting with and learning from IC physicians, behavioral health professionals, policy makers, and consumers. The following chapters represent a culmination of this work and serve to provide educators, and future and current IC practitioners, with a comprehensive and practical manual for learning how to succeed as professionals in IC settings.

A special feature included with this text is an instructional DVD, *Integrated Care in Action: Demonstrating Effective Strategies*. Role-play vignettes demonstrating common IC practices, such as warm handoff, brief assessment, counseling treatment modalities, and consultation, are included to exemplify how a behavioral health provider and physician collaborate to provide quality patient care.

Unique aspects exist within each chapter of this text that may not be reflected in each respective title. While it would require an extensive list to highlight all of the important subtopics found in this book, a few essential ones are listed here:

- Creating and growing an IC practice: Chapters 2, 9, and 13
- Screening for medication-seeking patients: Chapters 3, 5, and 9
- Peek's three worlds of health care: Chapters 1, 16, and 17
- Graduate students' internship experiences in an IC practice: Chapter 18
- Pharmacology for substance abuse treatment: Chapters 9 and 10
- Ethical issues in IC: Chapters 6, 7, 9, and 10
- Overview of health care policies: Chapter 16

We would like to thank all of the contributors to this text for generously making time in their busy schedules to share their knowledge and expertise. We owe an immeasurable debt of gratitude to Diana Christian for her tireless and gifted editing. A special thanks also goes to Dana Bliss and Christopher Tominich of Routledge for encouraging us and shepherding this project. Of course, this textbook would not be possible had it not been for the love, patience, and support of our families and friends. Finally, it is published in memory of Daisy (a great dog), who was my (Russ') constant companion throughout this process. We hope you learn a lot from this book and DVD, and we wish you all the best in IC!

Russ Curtis and Eric Christian
August 9, 2011

About the Editors

Russ Curtis, PhD, is a licensed professional counselor and associate professor of counseling at Western Carolina University, where he serves as the coordinator of the Clinical Mental Health Counseling program. For the past 10 years, Dr. Curtis has helped establish internship sites for students in integrated care practices throughout western North Carolina. Prior to becoming a counselor educator, Dr. Curtis worked in a community mental health center where he coordinated with medical providers to ensure optimal care for at-risk clients with comorbid mental and physical illnesses. During his doctoral studies, Dr. Curtis completed his final internship in a large regional hospital where he provided integrated care services to patients in the oncology unit. His dissertation focused on the psychosocial coping mechanisms of men diagnosed with prostate cancer.

Eric Christian, MAEd, LPC, NCC, is a licensed professional counselor and a nationally certified counselor who has been working as an integrated care coordinator in western North Carolina for the past 5 years, promoting the systemic spread of behavioral health integration into primary care settings to serve larger populations of patients with behavioral health needs. He works as the integrated care coordinator for Community Care of Western North Carolina where, among other efforts, he provides technical assistance and consultation to providers interested in integration. Mr Christian coordinated and managed one national integrated care conference as well as an annual state-level integrated care conference for several years. He also took part in designing and implementing regional telepsychiatry and consulting psychiatry models, and wrote ICare 102 as an online resource guide for implementing integration. Mr Christian earned his master's degree in school counseling at Western Carolina University and began his career in counseling as an outpatient therapist in a community setting. Before transitioning to integrated care work, Mr Christian was an outpatient and crisis counselor, a position that grew to include a supervisory role and later his appointment as clinical manager in the outpatient and crisis child and family services unit in a community mental health center.

About the Contributors

Andrea Auxier, PhD, is director of integrated services and clinical training at Salud Family Health Centers, a large Federally Qualified Health Center in Colorado. She is a senior clinical instructor in the Department of Family Medicine at the University of Colorado Denver School of Medicine and an associate editor for the *Journal of Translational Behavioral Medicine.*

MaryLynn Barrett, LCSW, MPH, is the director of behavioral medicine at the Mountain Area Health Education Center Division of Family Medicine, Asheville, North Carolina. Ms. Barrett completed dual master's degrees in social work and public health at the University of Washington in 1998 and 1999, respectively. She is fluent in Spanish having lived and studied in Buenos Aires, Argentina, during her undergraduate training. Areas of special interest include effects of trauma on the mind and body, specifically as it pertains to PTSD, anxiety, panic, depression, and chronic diseases such as IBS, fibromyalgia, and chronic fatigue.

Darren S. Boice, LCSW, is currently the practice manager for the Developmental Pediatrics, Child Abuse Prevention and Treatment, and Behavioral Health programs of Mission Children's Specialists, a group of pediatric subspecialists at Mission Children's Hospital in Asheville, North Carolina. Mr. Boice received his master of social work degree from the University of North Carolina at Chapel Hill in 1996. He worked for 13 years in community mental health as a case manager and therapist until he became a behavioral health provider in the Mission Hospital system in 2002. He has recently made the transition to administration, supervising other behavioral health providers as well as developing the behavioral health program, which integrates psychiatry, psychology, clinical social work, and case management into the pediatric subspecialty medical clinics.

Stephen E. Buie, MD, DFAPA, is a board-certified psychiatrist and managing shareholder of the Pisgah Institute, P.A., located in Asheville, North Carolina. Dr. Buie attended the University of North Carolina at Chapel Hill as an undergraduate on a Morehead Scholarship. He obtained his medical education at the UNC-Chapel Hill School of Medicine. He completed a residency in internal medicine at a Columbia University training hospital in New York and a psychiatry residency at Cornell Medical College, also in New York. He is a distinguished fellow of the American Psychiatric Association in recognition of his contributions in several areas of psychiatry. Dr. Buie is past president of the North Carolina Psychiatric Association. He provides medication management for all psychiatric conditions with particular interests in bipolar disorder, attention deficit-hyperactivity disorder (ADHD), depression, and anxiety disorders.

Claire DeCristofaro, MD, is an associate professor at Western Carolina University, College of Health and Human Sciences, in the graduate School of Nursing. Currently, she continues to see patients in the free-clinic setting in South Carolina, where she also mentors students and medical residents, and retains an appointment as clinical assistant professor at Medical University of South Carolina.

Susan Denny, MS, LPC, received her master's degree in community counseling from Western Carolina University. During her studies she completed an internship in integrated care at the Mountain Area Health and Education Center (MAHEC) Family Health Center. She is a licensed professional counselor in Ohio, where she works at Nationwide Children's Hospital on the community support, multisystemic therapy (MST) team.

Jennifer M. Hardin, MS, earned her master's degree in clinical mental health counseling at Western Carolina University in May 2011. She completed her graduate internship in integrated care at MAHEC Family Health Center and is currently working as a clinician with an Assertive Community Treatment (ACT) Team in Haywood County, North Carolina, through Meridian Behavioral Health Services.

Rodger Kessler, PhD, ABPP, is a clinical psychologist who has been doing research in the area of integration of primary health care and mental health care for the past 15 years. Dr. Kessler created a five-site medical practice where behavioral health clinicians can deliver evidence-based, integrated medical psychological care. Dr. Kessler's current research focuses on patient compliance with psychological referral in an integrated practice, and the impact of integrated medical psychological care on medical and cost outcomes. He is the research director of the Collaborative Care Research Network, a subnetwork of the AAFP's National Research Network. He is a fellow of the American Psychological Association and a past president of the Vermont Psychological Association.

Valerie Krall, MA, LPA, LPC, is a behavioral health provider with the MAHEC division of Family Medicine. She provides brief psychotherapy to patients of all ages, as well as consultation services to the physicians in the practice. She has also helped with the development of an integrated care internship for graduate-level counseling students and supervises BHP interns.

Angela L. Lamson, PhD, is a licensed marriage and family therapist in North Carolina and an associate professor at East Carolina University, where she serves as the program director for the master's program in marriage and family therapy and the doctoral program in medical family therapy.

Benjamin F. Miller, PsyD, is an assistant professor in the Department of Family Medicine at the University of Colorado–Denver School of Medicine, where he is responsible for integrating mental health across all three of the department's core mission areas: clinical, education, and research. He is also the associate director of research and primary care outreach for the University of Colorado–Denver's Depression Center. Professionally, Dr. Miller is actively involved in the governance of the Collaborative Family Healthcare Association (CFHA), where he is currently a board member representing organizational partnerships and was recently elected CFHA president for 2011–2012. In Colorado, Dr. Miller is on the board of the Colorado Psychological Association as the federal advocacy coordinator. He has been active within the American Psychological Association for Graduate Students (APAGS), where he held the elected position of Member at Large—Practice Focus from 2006 to 2008. During his tenure in APAGS, he focused on assessing the needs of practice-focused students while attempting to raise students' awareness of the role of psychology within the larger health care system.

Robin R. Minick, MS, is a national certified counselor and outpatient therapist for the Mobile Crisis Management Team of Appalachian Community Services, North Carolina.

Richard L. Munger, PhD, has spent 30 years as an administrator in public community mental health. He is a practicing child psychologist in North

Carolina and formerly associate professor of psychiatry, John A. Burns School of Medicine, University of Hawaii. He received his PhD in educational psychology from the University of Michigan.

Eric M. Pitts, MS, is a research assistant at the University of North Carolina at Asheville and a counselor with Jackson County Psychological Services. He earned his degree in clinical mental health counseling from Western Carolina University.

Keeley J. Pratt, PhD, is a licensed marriage and family therapist in North Carolina, a teaching instructor and supervisor at East Carolina University, and a postdoctoral research fellow at RTI International.

Phyllis Robertson, PhD, is an associate professor of counseling at Western Carolina University. She has been a counselor educator for 6 years and previously was a school counselor for 15 years. Her teaching and research focus encompasses cross-cultural counseling issues.

Glenda C. Sawyer, MS, LCSW, LPC, is a behavioral health provider working with the MedWest/Carolinas Health Care system in western North Carolina. She graduated from Western Carolina University with a bachelor's degree in psychology and a master's degree in counseling. She established her own practice, INTERFACE Counseling & Consulting, Inc., and has done counseling and consulting nationally and across North Carolina, especially with the U.S. Department of Defense providing behavioral health services to members of the military, veterans, and their families and significant others for over 30 years.

John J. Sherlock, PhD, is an associate professor of human resources and leadership at Western Carolina University. He has also taught at University of Maryland and George Washington University. He has published more than 30 articles and has presented at numerous conferences on human resource and leadership topics. Prior to academia, he worked in the wireless communications industry for 20 years in various management and executive capacities, overseeing functions including sales, finance, business development, and human resources. He received his doctorate in human resource development from George Washington University, MBA from the University of Maryland, and BS from James Madison University.

Don Teater, MD, is the medical director for Mountaintop Healthcare and the Good Samaritan Clinic in Waynesville, North Carolina. Dr. Teater is board certified in family practice. He graduated from Ohio State University

Medical School and completed his family practice residency at the Duke–Fayetteville Area Health Education Center program.

Martha Teater, MA, LMFT, is the director of mental health for Mountaintop Healthcare and the Good Samaritan Clinic in Waynesville, North Carolina. She is a licensed clinical addictions specialist and a licensed marriage and family therapist in North Carolina. She has a master's degree in counseling from Ohio State University.

Heather Thompson, PhD, is an assistant professor of counseling at Western Carolina University. Dr. Thompson earned her doctorate degree in counselor education and supervision from the University of Virginia. Her professional areas of interests include intimate partner violence, childhood sexual trauma, play therapy, group counseling, and supervision of counselors in training.

Tonya Friberg Warren, PsyD, is a clinical psychologist who has been working in primary care since 2006. She was director of behavioral medicine at MAHEC Family Health Center in Asheville, North Carolina. She currently practices integrated care at MidState Health Center in Plymouth, New Hampshire.

Doug Zeh, MS, is a licensed professional counselor and serves as director of psychosocial rehabilitation services at the Western North Carolina Community Health Services in Asheville, North Carolina. He has been affiliated with integrated care practice for 6 years.

Important Terminology and Abbreviations

VALERIE KRALL, ERIC CHRISTIAN, and RUSS CURTIS

Terms and Abbreviations Commonly Used in Integrated Care

AAP: American Academy of Pediatrics.

Algorithm: A decision-tree diagram that details treatment options depending upon clients' needs and concerns.

AMA: American Medical Association.

Anticipatory guidance: Information given to caretakers by medical providers regarding what to expect and prepare for as the child enters his or her next developmental stage.

APA: American Psychiatric Association.

ASQ: Ages and Stages Questionnaire.

BHP: Behavioral health provider (e.g., counselor, social worker, marriage and family therapist, or psychologist).

Biopsychosocial care: A term often used to describe the importance of addressing biological, psychological, and social factors when addressing the needs of a patient.

Calling a code: Announcement for a medical emergency and need for life-saving procedures.

Carve-outs: When medical care is managed or insured differently than mental health care. It is not uncommon for insurance companies to contract with other insurers to handle their clients' mental health or substance abuse needs.

CMS: Centers for Medicare and Medicaid Services.

Collaborative care: A term frequently used interchangeably with integrated care but which tends to refer to everything from referral to mental health counselors to more dynamic, co-located integrated care agencies.

Comorbidity: The existence of physical and mental health issues within the same individual.

Controlled substance: Drugs that have the potential to be abused or pose a risk of addiction and are regulated by the Drug Enforcement Administration (DEA) for public safety.

Controlled substance contract: An agreement signed between a patient and a medical provider that outlines rules patients must follow in order to be prescribed a controlled substance. In some practices, parents must sign a contract if their child is prescribed a stimulant medication.

Current procedural terminology (CPT) code: A number used to denote which billable medical service was provided at the visit.

DEA: Drug Enforcement Administration.

Differential diagnoses: A way of thinking about possible diagnoses that could explain a problem a patient is having, with the goal being to eliminate the less likely diagnosis and deduce what the diagnosis is that needs to be treated.

Head Start: A program sponsored by the U.S. Department of Health and Human Services to promote school readiness for economically disadvantaged children.

HEADSS assessment: Pneumonic to aid in assessing teen psychosocial issues (home, education, activities, drugs, sex, and/or suicide).

Horizontal integration: Used interchangeably with *nontargeted* care to mean integrated care services being offered to a wide population of clients regardless of issues.

Integrated care (IC): The seamless and dynamic interaction of PCPs and BHPs working within one agency to provide both counseling and traditional medical care.

Integrative care: The use of alternative and complementary strategies (i.e., massage therapy, tai chi, yoga, and acupuncture) in treating clients with medical issues. These services are often provided by people without medical or counseling backgrounds.

International Statistical Classification of Diseases, 9th edition (ICD-9): A system used to classify medical and mental health conditions in medical settings. ICD-10 has also been published and is in use in some settings. The ICD is published by the World Health Organization (WHO).

Medicaid: A state and federally funded health plan that children (and adults) may qualify for based on financial need.

MUS: Medically unexplained symptoms.

National Provider Identification (NPI) number: An individual number assigned to all providers of medical and mental health care that is needed in order for services to be billed to insurance companies.

It is assigned to providers by Centers for Medicare & Medicaid Services (CMS).

Parents' Evaluation of Developmental Status (PEDS): A developmental-behavioral screening tool used to assess pediatric issues in a primary care setting.

PCMH: Patient-centered medical home.

PCP: Primary care physician (e.g., medical doctor or doctor of osteopathy).

Population-based care: The act of identifying at-risk groups of patients (e.g., patients with diabetes or depression) and devising comprehensive strategies to meet their needs.

Pre-authorization of services (pre-auth): A step often required by insurance companies in which the provider must contact the insurance company to inform them of the services they believe are indicated for the patient. The insurance company then states whether they agree or disagree that the service is warranted.

Quality-adjusted life year (QALY): The cost of an intervention to produce one year of perfect health.

Screening, brief intervention, and referral for treatment (SBIRT): Process recommended for the identification, intervention, and referral for treatment; used for assisting patients who have substance abuse issues.

SIG E CAPS: Pneumonic for the symptoms of depression (sleep, interest, guilt, energy, concentration, appetite, and suicide; depressed mood is assumed).

Self-pay: Paying for services without the use of insurance benefits of any kind.

Sliding scale: A system of basing fees for services upon a patient's income level.

Third-party payer: The insurance company, if present, which is paying for the patient's medical or behavioral health care.

Verify benefits: A step that is often taken by physician offices in which a patient's insurance carrier is contacted in order to find out what medical or mental health benefits will be covered based on the patient's insurance plan.

Vertical integration: Used interchangeably with *targeted care* to mean integrated service protocols specific to one population (e.g., treating clients who experience depression).

Warm handoff: When a PCP calls a BHP into the examination room, or vice versa, to introduce and offer services to clients within the same visit.

Well child exam: Medical visits that are scheduled at various ages during infancy and childhood to help monitor the child's development and overall health.

Women, Infants, Children (WIC): A federally funded program that provides assistance to pregnant women and infants for nutritional needs.

Abbreviations Used in Medical and Behavioral Health Documentation

2/2: secondary to
A1C: average glucose levels over 3 months (in diabetes)
BMI: Body Mass Index
BP: blood pressure
CC: chief complaint
C/O: complains of
CPE: complete physical exam
CX: cancel
Depo: injected, slow-acting medication
Derm: dermatology
DNKA: did not keep appointment
DSS: department of social services
Dx: diagnosis
ED: emergency department
EENT: eye ear nose throat
ECG or EKG: electrocardiogram
EEG: electroencephalogram
ER: emergency room
ETOH: alcohol
FOB: father of baby
GI: gastrointestinal
GP: general practitioner
Gravida: total number times pregnant regardless of outcome
GYN: gynecology
HA: headache
H&P: history and physical
H/O: history of
HI: homicidal ideation
HPN: hypertension
HR: heart rate
Hx: history
IM: intramuscular
IV: intravenous
MSE: mental status exam
MVA: motor vehicle accident
NIC-U: neonatal intensive care unit
OB: obstetrics

OCP: oral contraceptive pill
OD: overdose
OTC: over the counter
Para: number and type of birth (term, preterm, abortions (Ab) or miscarriages, and living)
P: pulse
PCP: primary care provider
Peds: pediatrics
PIC-U: pediatric intensive care unit
PRN: as needed
PT: physical therapy
R/O: to "rule out" another diagnosis
ROS: review of systems
RTC: return to clinic
Rx: prescription
SA: substance abuse
SE: side effects
SI: suicidal ideation
SOB: shortness of breath
SNRI: selective norepinephrine reuptake inhibitor
SSRI: selective serotonin reuptake inhibitor
STAT: immediately
Sx: symptom
T: temperature
TCA: tricyclic antidepressant
Tx: treatment
UTI: urinary tract infection
WNL: within normal limits

Abbreviations Used by Physicians When Writing Prescriptions

i, ii, iii, iiii: the number of doses (1, 2, 3, 4)
ac: before meals
bid: twice a day
cap: capsule
hs: hour of sleep (take at bedtime)
mg: milligrams
ml: milliliters
q4h: every 4 hours
qam: every morning
pc: after meals
po: by mouth
prn: as needed

q: every
qd: every day
q3h: every 3 hours
qid: four times a day
Rx: prescription
Sig: directions on a prescription regarding how to take the medicine
tabs: tablets
tid: three times a day

PART I

Requisite Knowledge and Skills Needed to Begin Working in Integrated Care

CHAPTER 1

Introduction to Integrated Care

ERIC CHRISTIAN and RUSS CURTIS

Integrated systems, including Kaiser Permanente in California, Geisinger Health System in Pennsylvania, the public systems in Finland and New Zealand, and the Veterans Administration in the United States, can provide better care at 20% to 30% lower cost. Clearly, systemic problems require systemic solutions. (Christensen, 2010)

Introduction

Integrated care (IC), for the purposes of this text, can be described as the provision of behavioral heath services within primary care settings to attend to the overall health care needs and wide array of problems presented by patients to providers in these settings, which can vary in their degree of behavioral health programming. The inception of IC was at the grassroots level, implemented in primary care medical offices and hospitals throughout the country in an effort to address the escalating number of patients presenting in these settings with mental health, substance abuse, and other behavioral health issues (Gatchel & Oordt, 2003; Salovey, Rothman, Detweiler, & Steward, 2000). Four main reasons can be attributed to the rapid growth of integrated care: (a) the continuing struggle of the health care industry to identify effective treatments while curbing skyrocketing costs (Lubell & Sloan, 2007), (b) the increasing number of patients presenting to primary care offices and emergency rooms with mental health needs (Gatchel & Oordt, 2003), (c) the effectiveness of behavioral health care in treating patients with medical issues (Katon et al., 2002; Rasmussen et al., 2006; Sotile, 2005), and (d) research indicating the wide-scale efficacy of integrating medical and mental health care (Blount et al., 2007; Cummings, 2002).

Although countries with socialized medicine health care systems have long practiced IC as a way to control health care costs, the United States is just now embracing integrated care on a wider scale. The U.S. Air Force and Navy, for instance, inducted integrated care models, as did one of the largest health maintenance organizations in the country: Kaiser Permanente in northern California (Cummings, 2002; Strosahl, 2007). The integration of medical and mental health services dates back as far as 1979, as documented in the U.S. Surgeon General's report, *Healthy People: General's Report on Health Promotion and Disease Prevention* (U.S. Department of Health, Education, and Welfare, 1979), and more recently has been touted by the Substance Abuse and Mental Health Services Administration and the American Academy of Family Physicians, among other influential agencies (Blount et al., 2007). IC is gaining such national prominence that House Resolution 5176, the Community Mental Health Services Act, was introduced into the U.S. Congress in January 2008. Resolution 5176 not only encourages bolstering the mental health workforce but also supports the provision of more effective treatment for the mentally ill by increasing the number of primary care physicians (PCPs) working within mental health agencies (National Council for Community Behavioral Health, 2011). The primary care medical home (PCMH) movement is one in which primary care practices strive to meet core competencies which are considered to provide comprehensive, coordinated, patient-centered, accessible, and ongoing quality-based care, that involves input from the patient and all of their health care providers. In this way, the primary care clinic becomes the medical hub for each patient's overall health care, which may mean coordinating the various types of providers and services (U.S. Department of Health and Human Services, 2011). The PCMH concepts are also in support of proven best practices in IC, and experts believe that behavioral health is an essential component of primary health care (Mauer, 2009).

It is clear there is growing popularity and adaptation of IC in U.S. health care. The purpose of this text is to explore the rising trend of IC health care, the role of behavioral health providers (BHPs) in IC settings (primarily in primary care settings), and the tools necessary for thriving within this budding and expanding system of care. Specifically, this text will assist BHPs in acquiring the fundamental and requisite knowledge and skills essential to working within integrated primary care medical settings. The reader will learn about considerations for working as a BHP in primary care with general and specific populations, and about issues related to the efficacy, operation, evolution, and the promising future of IC as a prominent health care treatment model.

Overview of Integrated Care

To conceptualize the various permutations in which IC is practiced, Doherty, McDaniel, and Baird (1996) created an IC hierarchy delineating the different levels of collaboration ranging from minimally to fully integrated care; Peek (2009) refined these concepts further (see Table 1.1). In minimal collaboration constructs, the PCP refers patients with mental health needs to BHPs located in separate facilities. Midlevel collaboration is typically characterized by the presence of a BHP in a medical office, commonly referred to as "co-located," in which patients are referred back and forth between providers, but with consultation between the PCP and BHP maintained at a generally minimal level. A fully integrated care facility, which is considered optimal for providing comprehensive and effective health care (Strosahl, 2007), exists when the BHP and PCP consult frequently throughout the day, regularly see patients together in the examination room, and collaborate for optimal treatment.

Integrated primary care clinics with co-located PCPs and BHPs can provide behavioral health services that are both nontargeted, called *horizontally integrated*, and targeted, called *vertically integrated*. Horizontal integration refers to the method a clinic follows for providing behavioral health services to patients who present with a range of concerns, to the degree of support needed. Horizontally integrated psychosocial services in primary care are population based, in that a wide net is cast to help all patients to improve their overall health (O'Donohue, Byrd, Cummings, & Henderson, 2005). Vertical integration employs the use of protocols for working with specific subpopulations of patients, such as those who have depression. Providers in integrated primary care settings serving large populations may decide to streamline care by defining treatment protocols to target a few key conditions that frequently affect subpopulations of their patients. Examples of vertical integration established to provide comprehensive treatment for two common conditions are the design of care protocols for depression and chronic pain (O'Donohue et al., 2005). This practice allows a clinic to address the special needs of patients with these conditions within the context of a fairly prescribed protocol based on best practices.

Specialty medical settings such as cardiology or oncology clinics can horizontally integrate behavioral health services to address the stress, anxiety, and depressive symptoms typically associated with conditions treated in these clinics, and to assist patients in achieving the health behaviors that best support the prescribed medical treatment regimen. In these example

Table 1.1
A Range of Goals for Collaborative Practice: Levels or Bands of Collaboration

Model	1 Minimal Collaboration	2 Basic Collaboration From a Distance	3 Basic Collaboration On-Site	4 Close Collaboration in a Partly Integrated System	5 Close Collaboration in a Fully Integrated System
Doherty, McDaniel, and Baird (1995)*	Separate systems	Separate systems	Separate systems	Some shared systems	Shared systems and facilities in seamless biopsychosocial web
	Separate facilities	Separate facilities	Same facilities	Same facilities	Patients and providers have same expectation of a team
	Communication is rare	Periodic focused communication mostly by letter or phone	Regular communication, sometimes face-to-face	Face-to-face consultation, coordinated treatment plans	Everyone committed to biopsychosocial; in-depth appreciation of roles and culture
	Little appreciation of each other's culture; little influence sharing	View each other as outside resources	Some appreciation of each other's roles and general sense of larger picture, but not in depth	Basic appreciation of each other's role and culture; share biopsychosocial model	Collaborative routines are regular and smooth
		Little understanding of each other's culture or sharing of influence	Medical side usually has more influence	Collaborative routines are difficult—times and operations barriers	Conscious influence sharing based on situation and expertise
				Influence sharing—but with some tensions	

Handles adequately	Routine, with little biopsychosocial interplay and management challenges	Moderate biopsychosocial interplay (e.g., diabetes and depression with mgmt of each going reasonably well)	Moderate biopsychosocial interplay requiring some face-to-face interaction and coordination of tx plans	Cases with significant biopsychosocial interplay and management complications	Most difficult and complex biopsychosocial cases with challenging management problems
Handles inadequately	Cases refractory to tx or with significant biopsychosocial interplay	Significant biopsychosocial interplay; when care plan is not satisfactory to either MH or medical providers	Significant biopsychosocial interplay; those with ongoing and challenging management problems	Complex, with multiple providers and systems; tension, competing agendas, or triangulation	Team resources are insufficient or breakdowns occur in the collaboration with larger service systems
Seaburn et al. (1996)	Parallel deliver: clear division of labor not flowing into each other significantly	Informal consultation: MH professional helps physician deal with a clinical problem, but usually not contact with the patient	Formal consultation: MH professional has direct contact with pt. in typical relationship as a consulting specialist	Co-provision of care: patient care is shared and the professionals may see the patient or family together	Collaborative networking: provider team is extended to include family and other medical specialists, educators, and community resources

(continued)

Table 1.1 (continued)
A Range of Goals for Collaborative Practice: Levels or Bands of Collaboration

Model	1	2	3	4	5
	Minimal Collaboration	**Basic Collaboration From a Distance**	**Basic Collaboration On-Site**	**Close Collaboration in a Partly Integrated System**	**Close Collaboration in a Fully Integrated System**
Strosahl (1998) and Peek (1998)	Traditional referral-between-specialties models		Co-location models	Organization integration or "primary care mental health" models	
MH provider might say:	"Nobody knows my name."	"I help your patients."	"I am your consultant."	"We are a team in the care of our patients."	"Together, we also teach others how to be a team in care of patients and design of the care system."
Medical prov. might say:	"Who are you?"	"You help my patients, but not me."	"You help me as well as my patients."		

Source: Reproduced by permission from Peek, C.J. (2009). Collaborative Care: Aids to Navigation. White paper prepared for *Creating a Research Agenda for Collaborative Care*, a research agenda-setting conference of the Collaborative Care Research Network, Denver, CO, October. Also appears in Doherty, W. (1995). The why's and levels of collaborative family healthcare. *Family Systems Medicine, 13(3/4).*

specialty settings, treatment for major depression might also be vertically integrated for a subpopulation in need of targeted services, with an identified protocol that involves the nursing staff for screening of depression, physicians who assess motivation for treatment, and a BHP who provides treatment. Each provider thereby fulfills optimal roles for treating patients based on his or her area of expertise.

Although most IC settings today consist of BHPs working within medical offices, another permutation of IC exists, called *reverse co-location* (Collins, Hewson, Munger, & Wade, 2010). In this arrangement, a PCP works within a mental health agency. Studies have shown that patients who suffer from severe and persistent mental illness die 25 years earlier on average than the general population. The unmet physical health needs of these patients are by and large cardiovascular and pulmonary disease management, with an occurrence rate of 60% (Moran, 2007). The provision of co-located primary medical care delivered in close collaboration with mental health services results in an increase in the number of recommended primary care interventions and health outcomes when compared to patients receiving usual care (Druss, Rohrbaugh, Levinson, & Rosenheck, 2001).

An additional descriptive IC term with which to be familiar is *bidirectional integration*, which indicates the presence of either physical health providers in behavioral health settings or behavioral health service providers within physical health settings (Mauer & Jarvis, 2010). In either case, some level of co-located collaboration is present and ideally patients can be approached from a *biopsychosocial* perspective within which the health of the whole person is considered. Biomedical and psychosocial issues are interconnected and therefore their influence on a patient's health concerns must be considered simultaneously (Blount, 1998; Engle, 1977).

When BHPs approach the provision of behavioral health services in medical settings, they are often the first clinician of their type to have worked in this setting. Successful programming requires more than simply having the clinical skills necessary to treat patients with mental health and substance abuse issues. Peek (2008) described a "three world view" of healthcare, within which BHPs must incorporate a balance of clinical, operational, and financial factors into their integrated behavioral health program. Clinical factors include providing the right intervention to the patient at the right time with evidence of measurable clinical outcomes for target conditions, and may include the ability to provide brief interventions for health behavior change, and consultation to PCPs who may see the BHP as their in-house expert. Operational factors incorporate the way in which the BHP can most efficiently function within the complex routines of the medical clinic, such as functioning within evidence-based protocols, entering data in the shared electronic medical record in a timely manner, sharing pertinent information with other providers on a daily

The Four Quadrant Clinical Integration Model

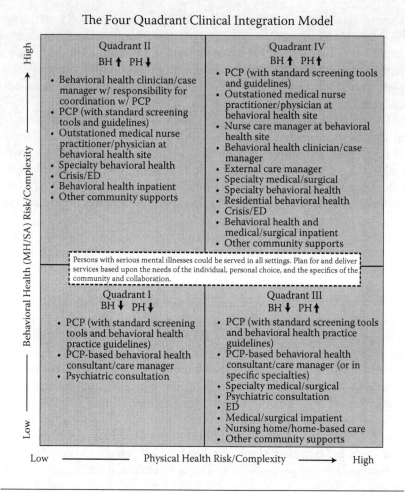

Figure 1.1 The four-quadrant clinical integration model. *Source*: Mauer (2009).

basis, and dynamically adjusting services based on the needs of the clinic. These clinical interventions and operational functions must also be fiscally responsible to the clinic, the BHP, insurers, and the patients receiving behavioral health services. See Chapters 16 and 17 for further detail on Peek's three-worlds view.

Mauer (2009), working with the National Council for Community Behavioral Healthcare, created a four-quadrant clinical integration model (see Figure 1.1) that specifies the types of services provided to meet patients' needs in different health care settings. In a 2009 webinar, Mauer described the model as a key part of current dialogue, as it helps to answer the question of where care should be delivered. It is a way of organizing thinking about care and working together in a community to think about the needs of the entire population. It also helps clarify the provider roles and activities within the subpopulations in each quadrant. The model is population based for system planning. Importantly, this is not a model to be used at the individual level; services should be person-centered for the individual (Mauer & Druss, 2009).

Quadrant One is composed of patients with low behavioral and medical health problems whose needs can most often be met in primary care settings. Quadrant Two includes patients with high behavioral health needs and low physical health concerns, whose needs are best met by behavioral health agencies, psychiatrists, and sometimes team-based approaches such as Assertive Community Treatment Teams (ACTT) that include clinicians, a case manager, a nurse, and a psychiatrist. Quadrant Three classifies patients with low behavioral health needs and high physical health needs, who are often seen in specialty medical settings such as a cardiology clinic, with care coordinated through a PCP or an internist acting as the patient's medical home. In this scenario, a care manager is sometimes made available to the patient to coordinate care with specialty medical and surgical professionals. Medical providers are able to screen for behavioral health issues, consider psychotropic medications, and refer as necessary. In the fourth quadrant, patients with high behavioral and medical needs are closely monitored by case managers to ensure seamless coordination between mental and physical health specialists. It should be noted that clinics serving patients who are best described by Quadrant Four encounter some of the most complex health care cases and often employ mental health and physical health providers who work closely together and are prepared for the challenges presented by this population. Integrated settings can utilize their in-house behavioral health resources to work with patients as they navigate their complex health care treatment needs, which often require a high level of health behavior change (Mauer, 2009).

Review of Current Literature

The need to investigate the efficacy of integrated care is paramount considering estimates that from 50% to as many as 70% of primary care visits are for psychosocial concerns (Gatchel & Oordt, 2003; Patterson, Peek, Heinrich, Bischoff, & Scherger, 2003; Robinson & Reiter, 2007; Salovey et al., 2000), and 50–90% of these patients don't follow through with mental health referrals to outside agencies (Escobar, Interian, Diaz-Martinez, & Gara, 2006). Fortunately, IC is documented to improve many of the key treatment variables, including reducing no-show rates (Reynolds, Chesney, & Capobianco, 2006), increasing PCPs' and BHPs' satisfaction with the care their patients receive (Kenkel, Deleon, Mantel, & Steep, 2005), and increasing patients' satisfaction with their medical and mental health care

(Kates, Crustolo, Farrar, & Nikolaou, 2001). In addition, emerging evidence suggests that IC can lower or stabilize health care costs (Katon et al., 2002) and, on a broader scale, decrease the societal economic cost by reducing employee absenteeism (Wang et al., 2007).

IC is proving particularly effective in treating two common problems faced by many patients seen in primary care: depression (Schulberg, Raue, & Rollman, 2002) and unexplained physical symptoms (Rasmussen et al., 2008). Managing depression ranks second in economic costs to society only to ischemic heart disease (Pincus et al., 1998), which is particularly disconcerting because depressed patients often seek help solely from their PCPs and not from mental health providers (Pincus & Petit, 2001). To examine the efficacy of IC in treating patients who have experienced depression, Katon et al. (2002) separated patients into three groups: two intervention groups and one control group. The two intervention groups, severely depressed and moderately depressed, received collaborative care from PCPs and BHPs. The control group consisted of depressed patients who received care from only PCPs. The collaborative intervention groups received a combination of education, counseling, and medication from both PCPs and BHPs, while the control group only received medication and consultation from PCPs. Results indicated that IC was effective for both intervention groups as evidenced by improved compliance with medication when compared to the control group, and the moderate-severity group showed continued improvement of depressive symptoms up to 2 years post treatment. Furthermore, results indicated that there were no significant differences in costs for delivery of care between the intervention groups and the control group (Katon et al., 2002).

In a study using telephone screening and care management targeting depressed patients, Wang et al. (2007) recruited 604 patients who met criteria for depression from 16 different businesses enrolled in the same health plan. Three hundred patients were assigned to usual care, and 304 were assigned to the intervention group. Patients within the intervention group received regular screening, counseling, medication monitoring, and case management services. Results at the 6- and 12-month assessments revealed that the intervention group scored significantly lower on the depression scales administered, and had significantly higher employment hours worked than did the usual care group. Researchers concluded that the cost savings from reduced absenteeism was estimated to far outweigh the cost of treatment (Wang et al., 2007).

In another study, Mims and Vinson (2007) examined the efficacy of IC within a community health center. All patients were screened for depression using the Patient Health Questionnaire (PHQ-9; Kroenke, Spitzer, Williams, 2001; Spitzer, Kroenke, & Williams, 1999). Patients who met the criteria for needing depression care completed another instrument, the 12

Item Short Form Health Survey (SF-12; Ware, Kosinski, & Keller, 1996), and were assigned a BHP who provided services ranging from education, medication monitoring, brief mental health counseling, and case management. These patients were followed for 8 months, and results indicated significant decreases in depression as well as significant increases in general health functioning following the IC intervention. The researchers also found evidence of cost savings, which was attributed to the reduction in both health center and emergency room visits by these patients (Mims & Vinson, 2007). The cost savings found in this study are particularly promising considering that most of the clientele were of lower socioeconomic status, a group that typically has higher rates of health problems and uses publically funded health care (Pampel & Rogers, 2004; Williams, 2003).

Patients with physically unexplained symptoms, health anxiety, and somatoform disorders consume a disproportionate amount of PCPs' treatment time, and the search for diagnoses and causes of ailments often requires expensive tests and procedures (Smith et al., 2003). Fortunately, research indicates that group therapy can significantly reduce patients' complaints and needs for excessive medical services. For example, Rasmussen et al. (2006) found that by providing supportive group therapy to patients with unexplained medical symptoms, costs were significantly reduced as evidenced by a decrease in the number of hospitalizations, inpatient days, and medication usage. The researchers did, however, find that the patients in this study had an increase in the number of physician visits.

In another study, patients were divided into a control group, and into a group consisting of patients who were taught cognitive-behavioral coping skills during group counseling sessions (Escobar et al., 2007). Results indicated that patients who received group therapy improved significantly more than the control group on the number and severity of symptoms experienced at the end of treatment. Notably, though, these positive results were not maintained 6 months post treatment and it was suggested that future studies should investigate brief booster sessions post treatment (Escobar at al., 2007). Another recent study, conducted by Graham, Manor, and Wiseman (2007), did, however, find a lasting effect of group therapy. Patients who received 24 sessions of supportive group therapy reported experiencing less symptoms post treatment and significantly decreased PCP visits 6 months post treatment.

Although the most rigorous studies to date have focused on using IC to treat depression and patients with unexplained medical symptoms, other promising treatment areas for IC exist as well. Using IC to treat women, for instance, can be an effective way to ensure that issues which occur at higher rates for women, such as physical and sexual abuse, anxiety, depression, and eating disorders, are all properly screened for and addressed within the primary care setting (Jarrett, Yee, & Banks, 2007). Evidence also exists suggesting the efficacy of using IC in treating patients with substance abuse disorders (Blount et al., 2007), and in pediatric and obstetric offices to identify and treat those with postpartum mood disorders (Curtis, Robertson, Forst, & Bradford, 2007).

State Initiatives in IC

Based upon the growing base of favorable IC research, states and municipalities are beginning to strengthen their IC initiatives. Texas, for instance, has created an IC program funded by the Hogg Foundation, which is housed at the University of Texas at Austin, in which IC is being provided to the many underserved children living along the Texas–Mexico border (Alexander, 2007). IC is also being successfully employed within agencies in Maine and within the Cherokee Health System in Tennessee (Cartwright, Mork, Korsen, & Boyack, 2007; Miller, Perry, & Wallace, 2007). In Gloucester, Massachusetts, efforts are underway to meet the needs of the many underserved people in the oldest seaport in the United States. The Integrated Care Consortium in Gloucester is currently renovating an older medical office to house both PCPs and BHPs, funded from a variety of sources including the United Way, the Office of Community Programs of Commonwealth Medicine at UMASS, and the Massachusetts Behavioral Health Partnership (Schott & Boardman, 2007). One of the more comprehensive IC initiatives is taking place in California, where in Proposition 63 of the year 2004, the Mental Health Services Act was passed allowing a 1% tax to be levied on any individual earning $1 million or more to be used specifically for improving mental health care in California. This act led to a $1.8 billion gain in revenue (Lurie, Bess, & Myers, 2007). A comprehensive IC program is being developed and tested in sites across California. Early data suggest strong client and provider satisfaction levels, including PCPs' recommendations that other primary care providers should move toward integrated models (Lurie et al., 2007).

Conclusion

In summary, the implementation of IC varies by the setting, target service population, interest in collaboration, financial implications, training, referral resources, practice resources, and the level of investment in the belief that collaboration can be impactful for improved patient outcomes. A thriving IC setting can be created when enthusiastic providers work to improve their work satisfaction by affecting greater change in their patients. The journey toward widespread integration may be a challenging one, but it has been pioneered and navigated by providers who have experienced the benefits of and success in working within the model, and who can share the value of their experiences and earned efficiencies.

Discussion Questions

1. How might a nonintegrated health system impede people from getting timely and effective care?
2. Who are the current health care stakeholders, and how might they help or hinder cost-effective care?
3. What has been your experience receiving care from your primary medical doctor?
4. Explain the differences between horizontally and vertically integrated behavioral health services. How would an IC practice decide which conditions warrant a vertical approach?
5. In what ways can IC improve client outcome and decrease costs?
6. What is the likelihood that you would have sought or would seek mental health care if it was integrated within your traditional medical care? Explain.

References

Alexander, L. (2007, November). Using collaborative care with children and adolescents in real-world settings: Lessons learned from a Texas initiative. Paper presented at the annual meeting of the Collaborative Family Healthcare Association, Asheville, NC.

Blount, A. (1998). *Integrated Primary Care: The Future of Medical and Mental Health Collaboration*. New York, NY: W.W. Norton & Company.

Blount, A., Schoenbaum, M., Kathol, R., Rollman, B. L., Thomas, M., O'Donohue, W., & Peek, C. J. (2007). The economics of behavioral health services in medical settings: A summary of the evidence. *Professional Psychology: Research and Practice*, 38(3), 290–297.

Cartwright, C., Mork, M. J., Korsen, N., & Boyack, C. (2007, November). It's all about the relationship: Developing partnerships between primary care and mental health. Paper presented at the annual meeting of the Collaborative Family Healthcare Association, Asheville, NC.

Collins, C., Hewson, D. L., Munger, R., & Wade, T. (2010). *Evolving models of behavioral health integration in primary care*. Milbank Memorial Fund. Retrieved from http://millbank.org

Curtis, R. C., Robertson, P., Forst, A., & Bradford, C. (2007). Postpartum mood disorders: Results of an online survey. *Counselling and Psychotherapy Research*, 7(4), 203–210.

Cummings, N. A. (2002). Are healthcare practitioners economic illiterates? *Families, Systems & Health*, 20(4), 383–393.

Doherty, W. J., McDaniel, S. H., & Baird, M. A. (October, 1996). Five levels of primary care/behavioral healthcare collaboration. *Behavioral Healthcare Tomorrow, 5*(5) 25–28.

Druss, B. G., Rohrbaugh, R. M., Levinson, C. M., & Rosenheck, R. A. (2001). Integrated medical care for patients with serious psychiatric illness. *Archives of General Psychiatry, 58,* 861–868.

Engel, G. L. (1977). The need for a new medical model: A challenge for biomedicine. *Science, 196,* 129–136.

Escobar, J. I., Gara, M. A., Diaz-Martinez, A. M., Interian, A., Warman, M., Allen, L. A., Woolfolk, R. L., Jahn, E., & Rodgers, D. (2007). Effectiveness of a time-limited cognitive behavior therapy-type intervention among primary care patients with medically unexplained symptoms. *Annals of Family Medicine, 5*(4), 328–335.

Escobar, J. I., Interian, A., Diaz-Martinez, A., & Gara, M. (2006). Idiopathic physical symptoms: A common manifestation of psychiatric disorders in primary care. *CNS Spectrum, 11*(3), 201–210.

Gatchel, R. J., & Oordt, M. S. (2003). *Clinical health psychology and primary care: Practical advice and clinical guidance for successful collaboration.* Washington, DC: American Psychological Association.

Graham, J., Manor, O., & Wiseman, S. (2007). Introducing humanistic group counseling for somatisation in a primary care practice: Preliminary findings. *Counselling and Psychotherapy Research, 7*(4), 220–226.

Jarrett, E. M., Yee, B. W. K., & Banks, M. E. (2007). Benefits of comprehensive health care for improving health outcomes in women. *Professional Psychology: Research and Practice, 38*(3), 305-313.

Kates, N., Crustolo, A., Farrar, S., & Nikolaou, L. (2001). Integrating mental health services into primary care: Lessons learnt. *Families, Systems & Health, 19*(1), 5–12.

Katon, W., Russo, J., Von Korff, M., Lin, E., Simon, G., Bush, T., Ludman, E., & Walker, E. (2002). Long-term effects of a collaborative care intervention in persistently depressed primary care patients. *Journal of General Internal Medicine, 17*(10), 741–748.

Kenkel, M. B., Deleon, P. H., Mantell, E. O., & Steep, A. E. (2005). Divided no more: Psychology's role in integrated health care. *Canadian Psychology/Psychologie canadienne, 46*(4), 189–202.

Kroenke K., Spitzer R. L., Williams J. B. (2001). The PHQ-9: Validity of a brief depression severity measure. *Journal of General Internal Medicine, 16*(9), 606–613.

Lubell, J., & Sloane, T. (2007, January 8). Time to act on medical coverage. *Modern Healthcare, 37*(2), 24–25. Retrieved from Academic Search Premier database.

Lurie, B. D., Bess, G., & Myers, J. (2007, November). Integrated behavioral health project. Paper presented at the annual meeting of the Collaborative Family Healthcare Association, Asheville, NC.

Mauer, B. J. (2009, April). *Behavioral health/primary care integration and the person-centered healthcare home.* Washington, DC: National Council for Community Behavioral Healthcare.

Mauer, B. J., & Druss, B. (2009, April). Designing a person-centered healthcare home for the population with serious mental illnesses. Webinar provided by NASMHPD Research Institute. Retrieved from http://www.thenationalcouncil.org/galleries/nc-live/MauerDruss%20NRI%20Final%204-21-09.pdf

Mauer, B. J., & Jarvis, D. (2010, June). The business case for bidirectional integrated care: Mental health and substance use services in primary care settings and primary care services in specialty mental health and substance use settings. California Integration Policy Initiative: A collaboration between the California Institute for Mental Health and the Integrated Behavioral Health Project. Retrieved from http://www.ibhp.org

Miller, C., Perry, C., & Wallace, F. (2007, November). Providing integrated care to persons with serious and persistent mental illness. Paper presented at the annual meeting of the Collaborative Family Healthcare Association, Asheville, NC.

Mims, S., & Vinson, N. (2007, November). Dollars and sense: One community's experience with integrated care services and costs data. Paper presented at the annual meeting of the Collaborative Family Healthcare Association, Asheville, NC.

Moran, M. (2007). Those with serious mental illness suffer from lack of integrated care. *Psychiatric News, 42*(1), 5. Retrieved from http://pn.psychiatryonline.org/cgi/content/full/42/1/5-a

O'Donohue, W. T., Byrd, M. R., Cummings, N. A., & Henderson, D. A. (Eds.). (2005). *Behavioral integrative care: Treatments that work in the primary care setting.* New York: Brunner-Routledge.

Pampel, F. C., & Rogers, R. G. (2004). Socioeconomic status, smoking, and health: A test of competing theories of cumulative advantage. *Journal of Health and Social Behavior, 45*(3), 306-321.

Patterson, J., Peek, C. J., Heinrich, R., Bischoff, R., & Scherger, J. (2002). *Mental health professionals in medical settings: A primer.* New York City: W. W. Norton & Company.

Peek, C. J. (2008). Planning care in the clinical, operational, and financial worlds. In R. Kessler & D. Stafford (Eds.), *Collaborative medicine case studies: Evidence in practice.* New York: Springer.

Peek, C. J. (2009, October). Collaborative care: Aids to navigation. White paper prepared for *Creating a Research Agenda for Collaborative Care*, a research agenda-setting conference of the Collaborative Care Research Network. Denver, CO.

Peek, C. J., & Heinrich, R. L. (1998). Integrating primary care and mental health in a health care organization. In A. Blount (Ed.), *Integrated primary care.* New York City: W. W. Norton & Company.

Pincus, H. A., & Petit, A. R. (2001). The societal costs of chronic major depression. *Journal of Clinical Psychiatry, 62*(Suppl. 6), 5–9.

Pincus, H. A., Tanielian, T. L., Marcus, S. C., Olfson, M., Zarin, D. A., Thompson, J., & Zito, J. M. (1998). Prescribing trends in psychotropic medications: Primary care, psychiatry, and other medical specialties. *JAMA, 279*(7), 526–531.

Rasmussen, N. H., Agerter, D. C., Colligan, R. C., Baird, M. A., Yunghans, C. E., & Cha, S. S. (2008). Somatisation and alexithymia in patients with high use of medical care and medically unexplained symptoms. *Mental Health Family Medicine, 5*(3), 139–148.

Rasmussen, N. H., Furst, J. W., Swenson-Dravis, D. M., Agerter, D. C., Smith, A. J., Baird, M. A., & Cha, S. S. (2006). Innovative reflecting interview: Effect on high-utilizing patients with medically unexplained symptoms. *Disease Management, 9*(6), 349–359.

Reynolds, K. M., Chesney, B. K., & Capobianco, J. (2006). A collaborative model for integrated care for the individual who is seriously and persistently mentally ill: The Washtenaw Community Health Organization. *Families, Systems, & Health, 24*(1), 19–27.

Robinson, P. J., & Reiter, J. T. (2007). *Behavioral consultation and primary care: A guide to integrating services.* New York: Springer.

Salovey, P., Rothman, A. J., Detweiler, J. B., & Steward, W. T. (2000). Emotional states and physical health. *American Psychologist, 55*(1), 110–121.

Schott, L., & Boardman, J. (2007, November). From the ground up: Behavioral health and primary care integration, Gloucester, MA. Paper presented at the annual meeting of the Collaborative Family Healthcare Association, Asheville, NC.

Schulberg, H., Raue, P., & Rollman, B. (2002). The effectiveness of psychotherapy in treating depressive disorders in primary care practice: Clinical and cost perspectives. *General Hospital Psychiatry, 24*, 203–212.

Seaburn, D., Lorenz, A., Gunn, W., Gawinski, B., & Mauksch, L. (1996). *Models of collaboration: A guide for mental health professionals working with health care practitioners.* New York: Basic Books.

Smith, R. C., Lein, C., Collins, C., Lyles, J. S., Given, B., Dwamena, F. C., Coffey, J., & Given, C. W. (2003). Treating patients with medically unexplained symptoms in primary care. *Journal of General Internal Medicine, 18*(6), 478–489. doi:10.1046/j.1525-1497.2003.20815.

Sotile, W. M. (2005). Biopsychosocial care of heart patients: Are we practicing what we preach? *Families, Systems & Health, 23*(4), 400–403.

Spitzer R. L., Kroenke K., & Williams J. B. (1999). Validation and utility of a self-report version of PRIME-MD: The PHQ primary care study. Primary Care Evaluation of Mental Disorders. Patient Health Questionnaire. *JAMA, 282*(18), 1737–1744.

Strohsal, K. (1998). Integrating behavioral health and primary care services: The primary mental health care model. In A. Blount (Ed.), *Integrated primary care.* New York City: W. W. Norton & Company.

Strosahl, K. (2007, November). Primary care behavioral health integration: Where do we go from here? Paper presented at the annual meeting of the Collaborative Family Healthcare Association, Asheville, NC.

U.S. Department of Health and Human Services, Agency for Healthcare Research and Quality. (2011). *Patient centered medical home resource center.* Retrieved from http://pcmh.ahrq.gov/portal/server.pt?open=514& objID=18011&parentname=CommunityPage&parentid=27&mode=2 &in_hi_userid=11787&cached=true

U.S. Department of Health, Education, and Welfare (HEW). (1979). *Healthy people: The surgeon general's report on health promotion and disease prevention.* DHEW Pub. No. (PHS) 79-55071. Washington, DC: U.S. Government Printing Office.

Wang, P. S., Simon, G. E., Avorn, J., Azocar, F., Ludman, E. J., McCulloch, J., Petukhova, M. Z., & Kessler, R. C. (2007). Telephone screening, outreach, and care management for depressed workers and impact on clinical and work productivity outcomes. *JAMA, 298*(12), 1401–1411.

Ware, J. Jr., Kosinski, M., & Keller, S. D. (1996). A 12-item short-form health survey: construction of scales and preliminary tests of reliability and validity. *Medical Care, 34*(3), 220–233.

Williams, D. R. (2003). The health of men: Structured inequalities and opportunities. *American Journal of Public Health, 93*(5), 724–731.

CHAPTER 2

Becoming the Behavioral Health Expert

MARYLYNN BARRETT and TONYA FRIBERG WARREN

Introduction

The placement of a mental health practitioner (MHP) in a medical practice does not inherently guarantee success for the practice of integrated care (IC). The onus of making the integrated care model successful lies primarily with behavioral health providers (BHPs) and is achieved through their ability to adapt to the medical setting and prove their skills to be of high value to the care of the primary care patient. The extent to which BHPs can become a practice's behavioral health expert will depend on how well they demonstrate usefulness to primary care providers (PCPs) and their patients, promote their skills in the practice, and show eagerness and effectuality during situations in which they are sought out for consultation by the PCP.

The medical setting varies greatly from the traditional mental health setting, and it may take some time for the experienced MHP to become accustomed to the medical culture. There are differences in language, the way information is shared, boundaries with staff and coworkers, and hierarchical structure. Some of the differences may initially make MHPs feel uncomfortable, since their professional training tends toward emphasis on a more egalitarian relationship with patients and coworkers, and emphasizes the conscious and considered use of language for naming, describing, and defining people and relationships.

In the mental health arena, the word *patient* was substituted years ago with either *client* or *consumer* in an attempt to put more responsibility for health care on the individual, as well as to use a term that might feel more "respectable" to those seeking services. Using the term *patient* may feel odd to the mental health clinician (Hinkle, 1978). In a medical setting, though, this terminology is still the norm, and since it is the accepted practice, the person receiving treatment will be referred to as the *patient* in this chapter.

A MHP working in a medical setting might be differently licensed or credentialed as a LCSW, LPC, LMFT, PhD, PsyD, or EdD, so a common terminology used in integrated care settings for MHPs is the BHP, and will be used throughout this chapter. The term MHP will be used to describe a provider in a traditional mental health setting. Depending on the level of integration of the medical practice, the role of the BHP can range from solely providing brief behavioral interventions and consults to functioning in the capacity of an MHP as well, with planned sessions that have a traditional psychotherapy format.

Cultural differences within the medical practice may be different from those in a more traditional mental health setting, specifically differences in the way patient information is shared between the BHP and PCP. There is ongoing debate between mental health practitioners and medical providers in IC settings about confidentiality and determining which information should be shared and is deemed important to the patient's health. Even seasoned IC BHPs will differ in their ideas about how much information to share with the PCP about a patient's mental health history. Inherent to the IC model is the idea that the mind and body are not separate and, as such, issues that may seem purely historical can in fact affect a patient's health care and are important for the medical provider to know.

In an IC setting, patients should be informed from the beginning of their care that the information related during their encounters will be shared with their PCP. They should be reminded of this as they enter into a relationship with a BHP and should be advised that if there is anything that they do not want shared, they should explicitly relate to the BHP what they want excluded. If a patient indicates they do not want something shared with their PCP, a conversation is warranted to be initiated by the BHP about the importance of including information that will affect their health care in the BHP's notes to the PCP. All things considered, it can be a delicate balance between sharing too much and sharing too little information. More in-depth information on the topic of ethics is found in Chapter 6.

Of utmost importance is to be sure that this information is protected in your clinic setting and will not be released to any other entity without the written and expressed permission of the patient. BHPs should be well versed in HIPPA laws and should take measures to protect the patient's personal information. If the practice uses electronic medical records, extra caution should be taken to ensure that the patient's notes are only included in the sharing of medical information if explicitly requested and approved by the patient.

Another norm of medical practices that can present challenges for the BHP is the acceptance and practice of dual relationships. It is commonplace in many medical practices for staff and their families to receive services at the practice. This is especially true in rural areas where accessible alternatives may not be available, but dual relationships are certainly not limited to rural practices. While the practice of dual relationships is not considered unethical in medicine, it is unacceptable in the behavioral health professions, as clearly written into the respective codes of ethics. Despite the ethical standards, it may be difficult for PCPs and the staff to understand why BHPs would refuse such a relationship. As such, it is important for BHPs to be able to explain the reasons, and to be aware of the mental health coverage and Employee Assistance Networks or Plans (EANs or EAPs, respectively) for their agency so that they can make appropriate referrals when necessary.

A final challenge to the traditionally trained MHP transitioning into an IC BHP is the hierarchical nature of the medical practice. Despite the desire to embrace IC as a "team approach," many times the PCP remains in the role of team leader, with other members of the team, such as the medical assistant or nurse, continuing in more subordinate roles. The initial treatment plan is usually for the PCP to meet with patients, with the BHP brought in as an ancillary provider. In order to develop more of an egalitarian role on the team and in the clinic, BHPs must prove how valuable their input and skills are in providing improved health care for patients. BHPs will need to place particular emphasis on building trustworthiness in their own expertise if the PCPs have never worked closely with BHPs.

As the PCP begins to seek out the BHP to assist with a patient's care, it is imperative that the BHP proves to have a valuable role on the team. Responding to a request for help with comments like "I don't treat that" or "That is not my specialty" will quickly disillusion providers. Just as the family practice physician is a "generalist" and is knowledgeable about a broad spectrum of issues, the BHP must also be a mental health and/or substance abuse generalist in the primary care setting. Certainly, it is not expected that BHPs should know how to handle and treat every situation or presenting problem, but they need to be confident to enter any situation, willing to assess them all, and to help determine the appropriate next step if they are to establish a meaningful role as a member of the IC team.

A general knowledge of community resources is necessary for BHPs entering into a medical practice, especially for accessing and identifying psychosocial issues. After an initial assessment, the BHP may decide that an MHP with a different skill set will provide the best treatment for the patient's presenting problems. It is crucial for BHPs to know when it is necessary and how to access resources with skill, efficiency, and expertise. Patients may require more extensive services that would not be appropriate to provide in the IC setting, such as long-term psychotherapy needs or enhanced wrap-around team-based services like Assertive Community Treatment Team (ACTT).

Although it is not within the BHP's scope of practice to prescribe medications, basic knowledge of medications used to treat the more common mental health diagnoses seen in primary care practices, including depression and anxiety, is important. BHPs should become familiar with both the generic and brand names of medications, which medications have a generic version as a less expensive equivalent, and ways to help patients get medications at a reduced rate. For example, one should be informed of local formularies and pharmacies that offer discounted medication programs such as superstore and grocery chain reduced-rate prescription lists, mail order, and pharmaceutical company prescription assistance. BHPs should also have a basic knowledge of which medications are best for which symptom sets, as well as potential side effects of medications (see Chapter 5, "Pharmacologic Competency," for more information on medications). Additionally, BHPs should have information at their disposal about evidence-based treatment protocols, such as the MacArthur Initiative on Depression in Primary Care (www.depression-primarycare. org) and the IMPACT model for treating depression (www.impact-uw. org), for the most common mental health disorders treated in primary care, as well as information about how to obtain proficiency in commonly used effective behavioral interventions.

While it is obvious that the BHP must be well versed in mental health diagnoses common to primary care, they must also have a basic knowledge of physical health as well. A principal tenant of the integrated care model is that the mind and body are not separate entities, and that in order to promote health with patients, both biomedical and psychosocial issues must be addressed simultaneously: This is considered the "biopsychosocial" approach to health care. As the BHP in a primary care practice, one should have basic knowledge of human anatomy and common medical conditions, and an understanding of the relationship between stress and illness. The BHP should also have knowledge of what mental health conditions commonly occur with certain medical conditions or treatments, such as symptoms of depression being caused by hypothyroidism or as a side effect of a medication like interferon, commonly taken to treat hepatitis C. In his book, *A Therapist's Guide to Understanding Common Medical Conditions*, Kolbasovsky (2008) encouraged BHPs to have some knowledge of chronic medical conditions (i.e., diabetes, heart disease), particularly when they are impacted by a patient's mental health. In addition to mental health factors, Kolbasovsky (2008) emphasized the important role of psychosocial

Table 2.1
Looking for a Change?

Our clinic offers behavioral health services to assist patients in making lifestyle changes. A behavioral health provider can help you make changes in a number of different areas of your life, including

- Sleep
- Smoking cessation
- Improved skills to cope with stress or depression
- Issues with attention or focus
- Changes in memory or thinking
- Chronic pain

Ask your provider about these services or schedule an appointment with a behavioral health provider at the clinic today.

factors in impacting a patient's health, and suggested that the "well-prepared" BHP be aware of such issues as those listed in Table 2.1.

Teaching

Teaching ability is another important skill necessary for BHPs in IC settings. In addition to teaching patients the skills they need to make positive changes in their health, the BHP must teach the PCPs, as well as the nursing and clerical staff, how to utilize the integrated care services. Often, providers have limited experience with mental health treatment; sometimes providers may even have a negative viewpoint of it based on the lack of feedback and communication previously experienced with MHPs. When teaching is done well, all clinic employees have an opportunity to fully understand and appreciate the benefits that a BHP and behavioral health programming can bring about for patients and the practice overall.

Primary Care Providers

Teaching PCPs about their skills, services, and the way these can be integrated to benefit a practice is especially key for BHPs. The integrated care model will thrive only if PCPs understand how to utilize BHPs and if they believe in the efficacy of collaboration. Just as it is important for the BHP to learn the medical culture, the PCP's practice can benefit from learning aspects of behavioral health. BHPs can find teaching opportunities by giving feedback to a provider about a patient who was referred, ensuring that medical providers are aware of the range of services that a BHP can offer, and shaping the experience for the patient and PCP; providing sample scripts to the PCP for use as a guide when talking with patients about behavioral health services is helpful (Robinson & Reiter, 2007). Following is an example of feedback given to a PCP about a patient's insomnia, when the PCP referred a patient for a behavioral health consult.

BHP: "I met with Mr. Smith about his insomnia. His afternoon caffeine intake was high so we discussed ways that he can begin to cut back. We also talked about options for relaxation before bedtime and he will try getting out of bed if he's still awake after 20 minutes. He will follow up with me in 3 weeks."

Feedback must be clear and concise; aim for 60 seconds or less (Hunter, Goodie, Oordt, & Dobmeyer, 2009). Wordy explanations are likely to be tuned out and run the risk of setting up a future pattern of avoidance by providers who are hurried.

If face-to-face feedback is not possible, BHPs can follow up in writing. A note can be put in the patient's chart, and with an electronic medical record, there should be a way to forward the note to the PCP. If this is method of communication is not available, a short form could be developed and used regularly to give feedback to the PCP. It should include information about the presenting problem, a brief synopsis of the intervention, and the plan for follow up. Whichever form it takes, giving feedback to the PCP is always an important step in effectively treating the whole person.

The BHP can also influence the PCP's communication and counseling skills with patients by example. During the following example consultation, the BHP assesses coping skills that a patient has utilized before, while the PCP is still in the room.

BHP: Have you ever experienced depression before?
Patient: Yes, about 5 years ago I went through a rough patch like this one.
BHP: Was there anything that helped back then?
Patient: Medication, oh and I started a walking program with my neighbor.
BHP: That's great. So even though you were feeling quite depressed you managed to start an exercise program. It sounds like you have determination.
Patient: I guess so. I remember it wasn't easy but once I got started I would look forward to the walks.
BHP: Could you try that again?

In this example, the PCP learns some of the healthy coping skills the patient has utilized in the past and how the BHP discovered that information through her conversation with the patient. In future sessions, the provider may remember to follow up on strengths and coping skills as well as the presenting medical issues.

Another component of teaching for the BHP is educating the PCP about how to offer behavioral health services to the patient. The way this referral is made is paramount, as it can have a major impact on whether the referral is accepted. It is good practice for the BHP to give the PCP some sample scripts to use. For example, the PCP can say that he or she needs the assistance of the BHP to best treat the presenting problem.

PCP: We have been addressing your issues with chronic pain for over 6 months now with only minimal progress. I would like you to see one of my colleagues who may be able to offer some further insight into the treatment plan. He will also be able to help you deal with the stress that your pain is causing you.

Nursing and Other Staff Members

PCPs are not the only members of the integrated care team who need to understand the value of the BHP. Nursing and clerical staff are often the team members who teach patients about the nature of the behavioral health services available in the practice. In the following scenario, a patient is discussing his chief complaint with a nurse. The patient came in to the clinic for a headache but also mentions some stress that he is experiencing.

Nurse: I understand that you're not feeling well today?
Patient: No, I have this terrible headache that won't go away. I think it started because I've been so run down. I have been completely stressed out and I haven't been sleeping well for a couple months now.
Nurse: That sounds rough. You know, we have a behavioral health provider in the clinic who might be helpful to you. She works with Dr. Martin and helps with things like stress and sleep trouble. I think you would like her. You could set up an appointment with her on your way out today.

Many times patients will give information to nursing staff that they don't later share with their provider, so nurses' encounters with patients present unique opportunities for education about behavioral health services. Primary care providers spend an average of only 20 minutes with a patient (Chen, Farwell, & Jha, 2009) and are typically focused on the chief complaint; there may not be adequate time for them to address new or secondary issues.

Finally, administrative staff members who schedule provider meetings should be made aware of which meetings the BHP should be included in. Also, as an additional method of referral, medical receptionists may direct a patient to behavioral health services based on the reason a patient gives when he or she calls to schedule an appointment.

Consultation

Ideally, an IC model will afford some level of consultation available to the medical providers and the BHP. This may range from the PCP's availability for a "warm handoff," which provides an introduction for the patient to the BHP and helps ensure the patient will follow up with the BHP (Collins, Hewson, Munger, & Wade, 2010), to a brief intervention while the patient is in the clinic. In order to make these consultations happen, BHPs must be creative in their scheduling and must be accessible and visible in the clinic.

The saying "Out of sight, out of mind" is a truism for BHPs working within the IC model. If BHPs rely on PCPs to seek them out, BHPs will fail to make countless potential contacts with patients. When imperceptible in the clinic, the most likely contacts for the BHP will be emergency related, and will not occur as often or allow BHPs to take advantage of the vast scope of ways in which they can be utilized. Visibility can prompt PCPs to utilize BHP's skills more often and for a broader range of issues. It also provides opportunity for case discussion and "curbside" consults, an informal characteristic of integrated primary care (IPC) models which provides opportunities for the impromptu sharing of important information among team members (Strosahl, 2001). Placing oneself in a central area where the providers go between patient visits is an ideal location in which to "perch," or perhaps frequenting a shared PCP office or the nurse's station. If at all possible, the BHP's office should be in the clinic and near the exam room for maximum accessibility and visibility.

In order to construct a successful IC model, scheduling may need to become somewhat of an art form for BHPs, with construction that promotes visibility and accessibility. With some creativity, BHPs can design a schedule that allows them to see scheduled patients for more reliable billable income, but also allows for gaps of time during which they can consult with PCPs on difficult cases, provide brief interventions or psycho education, or simply meet a patient to set up a future appointment. The central idea is that contact should try to be made while the patient is in the clinic in order to provide the service immediately, without needing to rely on a follow-up visit that is less likely to happen (Cummings, Dorken, Pallak, & Henke, 1990; Glenn, 1987).

"Gaps" or open slots in BHPs' schedules, times when it is known by providers that they will be available for consultation, can promote timely health care. The gaps should be at regular intervals so that patients do not have to wait too long before contact is made. They could also be set up as same-day appointment slots that can be filled by those patients PCPs would like to have seen by BHPs (of note, billing issues with same day appointments may exist, so it is important for BHPs to know who they can and cannot see in this schedule structure).

Another option for employing impromptu scheduling is through interruption of a patient visit, which may seem less palatable to providers but can be quite successful. This practice is used in many integrated settings in which the PCP interrupts the BHP, or vice versa, for urgent issues. In order to minimize discomfort, all providers should limit interruptions to urgent or time sensitive matters, and offer an apology to the patient whose session has been disrupted.

PCPs can communicate to BHPs that they have a patient for them to see using several different measures, depending on the technology available in the clinic and its ease of use. The method with the least use of technology would be leaving a note on the BHP's door or asking the front desk staff to alert the BHP that he or she is needed for a consult. Further up the technological scale would include the use of pagers, with a system of codes to alert the BHP of the level of urgency, walkie talkies, instant messaging on the computer, or even text messaging.

Advance knowledge about the patients who are scheduled in the clinic each day, and the times they are coming in, is useful for BHPs to plan ahead. It allows for some thought of predicting how potential behavioral health intervention could be utilized. It can be helpful to review the provider's schedules at the beginning of the day or half-day, paying particular attention to the reason for the visit. If the "reason for visit" reads, for example: "Follow-up for ADHD medications," then the BHP might ask the PCP if he or she anticipates involving behavioral health management in the appointment. This is a great opportunity to remind and demonstrate to providers the various ways that the BHP can be useful to their patients' care.

The example above is rather straightforward and obvious that a BHP might become involved, but if the reason for the visit read, "Acute Irritable Bowel Syndrome (IBS) flare," it would take a savvy BHP who understands the connection between stress and IBS to recognize that behavioral health management might be helpful. The BHP could approach the PCP prior to the appointment and suggest that if it is discovered that the patient's flare is related to a recent stressor, then the PCP could contact the BHP to help the patient with stress reduction techniques.

Programming

Streamlined access to the behavioral health program and a clear presence within the clinic are necessary for success for BHPs in IC settings. In a fast-paced primary care setting, if behavioral health services are hard to access, then they won't be utilized. While certain programmatic obstacles can be identified and problem solved after it is up and running, beginning with a smooth operation plan can help to ensure success.

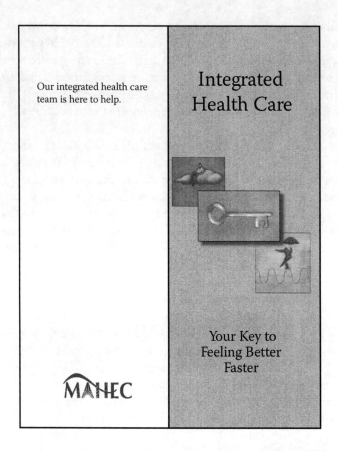

Our integrated health care team is here to help.

Integrated
Health Care

Your Key to
Feeling Better
Faster

MAHEC

Figure 2.1 Integrated Care brochure. With permission.

The BHP's office should be located within the patient care area, and, as stated earlier, when not with patients, BHPs should be visible. Their office door should be kept open unless a patient is in the room with them. Information on how the BHP should be contacted for urgent issues can be listed at nursing stations or other areas where providers can easily find it. There are several ways that the BHP's services can be marketed to the patients in the clinic, such as by placing brochures and displays in the exam and waiting rooms, which allows and encourages patients to self-refer to the BHP.

The sign shown in Figure 2.1 is an example of a brief and eye-catching way to inform patients about the behavioral health services available in the clinic. When creating such signs, avoid being too wordy and remember to use simple vocabulary. Adding color or a picture will help the sign to stand out. Notice that the majority of bullets focus on behavior change rather than typical mental health issues. Patients are most likely to be referred by PCPs for services when mental health issues are the presenting problem, so there is less need to "advertise" to these patients. Rather, the intent of these signs is to inform patients of behavioral topics they may be interested in exploring. Lengthier brochures can be displayed in the waiting or exam rooms as well, to provide more in-depth information about the BHP's services (Figure 2.1).

Brochures allows patients to read about common problems with which behavioral health providers can help, and offers relatable scenarios. Several of these brochures could be developed by BHPs, each focused on different presenting problems.

When there are television monitors in the exam room, information about the behavioral health program and providers can be displayed. Also, the clinic's website should feature the BHP(s) with information about how to access behavioral health services along with a list of example reasons for seeking those services.

To further inform patients, when a new patient enters the clinic, behavioral health services should be introduced in one of the pages of the new patient paperwork. Behavioral health screening tools can be also be included through the use of inventories or questionnaires to help providers learn more about their patients and determine whether they could benefit from the behavioral health services offered in the clinic. In IC settings, these inventories list questions not only about patients' current and historical health-related information, but also about the presence of behavioral health issues such as alcohol and drug use, depressive symptoms, and possibly domestic violence. Depending on the chosen screening tools, these criteria may be addressed in as few as four or five questions. The information gathered in screening tools can then be explored further with a more in-depth screening, discussion, and sometimes a BHP consultation. See Chapter 3, "A Screening and Assessment Primer," for further information on the use of screening tools.

Electronic medical records have the capacity to generate a reminder that behavioral health services should be offered when particular diagnostic codes are listed. A new diagnosis could be an early discovery tool and an opportunity for collaborative care. The following are examples of diagnoses that could generate a reminder to invite behavioral health services:

- Chronic pain
- Anxiety and panic
- Insomnia
- Attention deficit disorder
- Nicotine dependence
- Grief
- Depression
- Memory loss and/or cognitive impairment

Providers should introduce a referral as the routine way patient care is practiced in their clinic, rather than as if a particular patient is being distinguished because of their presenting issues. An example of the language a PCP might use to communicate behavioral health services to a patient follows:

PCP: We discussed your back pain today. As part of the treatment we offer in this clinic, I would like to refer you to see our behavioral health provider who has expertise in helping people deal with the emotional impact of having chronic pain. She could also help you figure out how to make some of the lifestyle changes we talked about. Can we set up that appointment today?

There should be an easy and routine channel for BHPs to get feedback about barriers to service or concerns from PCPs, that is, to find out about what is working well and what could be improved. Scheduling 5 or 10 minutes during regular provider meetings is an excellent way to do this. Also, being a part of most medical provider activities and meetings can help the BHP thrive in the IC setting.

Finally, as a BHP in an integrated setting, it is imperative to find a behavioral health champion in the clinic. This person is a primary care provider in the practice who values the services of the BHP and is vocal about the benefits of having one as an integral part of the treatment team. Including the "champion" in presentations or in service trainings promotes and educates the team about the way integration and BHPs add to superior patient care over all.

Conclusion

A successful IC practice is dependent on the BHP. The BHP must fill a variety of roles related to both patient care and to the operation of the practice. This person needs to be well versed in medical culture, medical diagnoses, and mental health issues. A willingness to provide assistance with any issue, as well as flexibility and creativity, are essential. The BHP must take on the roles of teacher and consultant, and work programmatically to ensure the success of this model. A person who chooses this career path can expect a challenging, fast-paced, and highly gratifying experience.

Discussion Questions

1. What skills would you need to strengthen to become an effective BHP in IC?
2. What is your opinion of pharmacotherapy, and how might it affect your work as a BHP?

3. How might you initially approach staff working in a non-integrated primary care practice about the benefits of IC?

Helpful Resources

www.depression-primarycare.org
www.impact-uw.org
www.ibhp.org

References

Chen, L., Farwell, W., & Jha, A. (2009). Primary care visit duration and quality. *Archives of Internal Medicine, 169*(20), 1866–1872.

Collins, C., Hewson, D.L., Munger, R., & Wade, T. (2010). *Evolving models of behavioral health: Integration in primary care.* New York: Milbank Memorial Fund.

Cummings, N.A., Dorken, H., Pallak, M.S., & Henke, C. (1990). *The impact of psychological intervention on healthcare utilization and costs: The Hawaii Medicaid project.* San Francisco, CA: Biodyne Institute.

Glenn, M.L. (1987). *Collaborative health care: A family oriented approach.* New York: Praeger.

Hinkle, A. (1978). Patient vs. client in community mental health. *Human Services in the Rural Environment, 3*, 3, 5, 26.

Hunter, C. L., Goodie, J. L., Oordt, M. S., & Dobmeyer, A.C. (2009). *Integrated behavioral health in primary care: Step by step guidance for assessment and intervention.* Washington, DC: American Psychological Association.

Kolbasovsky, A. (2008). *A therapist's guide to understanding common medical conditions.* New York: W. W. Norton & Company.

Robinson, P. J., & Reiter, J. T. (2007). *Behavioral consultation and primary care: A guide to integrating services.* New York: Springer.

Strosahl, K. (2001). The integration of primary care and behavioral health: Type II change in the era of managed care. In N. Cummings, W. O'Donohoe, S. Hayes, & V. Follette (Eds.), *Integrated behavioral healthcare: Positioning mental health practice with medical/surgical practice* (pp. 45–70). New York: Academic Press.

CHAPTER 3

A Screening and Assessment Primer

RUSS CURTIS and ERIC CHRISTIAN

The net effect is that diagnoses often are reached hastily using flawed data and then inappropriately bolstered and accepted.

—**Rabinowitz and Efron**

Consider the following scenario in a primary care practice:

Javier has unexplained stomach problems for which his doctor has ordered numerous tests in an effort to find a diagnosis, short of scoping his gastrointestinal tract. His lab results are normal, with no evident infection or parasite presence. The diagnostic tests have added up to about $1000 so far, and still his doctor can find no explanation for Javier's discomfort. After Javier waits 20 minutes in the waiting room and 10 minutes in the exam room, Dr. Jackson prepares to walk into the exam room. Just before her entry, Javier overheard her tell the nurse in the hall that she would be with her in just a minute, which was a clear sign to Javier that he would be given very little time with Dr. Jackson. Javier has made a list of questions he wants to ask his doctor. Upon entering, Dr. Jackson fails to make eye contact with Javier as she reviews his chart. Eventually she looks up and asks a few questions, then proceeds with a barrage of practical advice, most of which he's heard in previous visits. She stands to walk out, hands Javier a prescription, and asks him to call in a week if he doesn't feel better. Javier doesn't bother asking questions; he can tell she's too busy to answer them. He pays his $25 co-pay for his 7-minute visit with Dr. Jackson (he timed it), and goes to work and waits for the rest of his $75 bill to arrive in the mail. He'll need to pay the cost of the medication as well.

Unfortunately, this scenario is all too common in non-integrated primary health care. Physicians, nurses, and office staff are busy trying to meet the needs of their scheduled appointments in a timely manner, while also fitting in patients who show up unexpectedly. Unfortunately, the by-product of this practice is that patients may not always receive adequate care, especially when behavioral health issues are present (Robinson & Reiter, 2007). If, however, a behavioral health provider (BHP) were available to review the intake questionnaire and perform follow-up assessments with patients, the medical staff would have adequate time with patients and the quality of patient care would improve. A medical cost offset might be achieved for the practice if the BHP can identify behavioral health issues that may be causing the patient distress, before resorting to expensive and sometimes intensive medical tests and procedures (O'Donohue, Byrd, Cummings, & Henderson, 2005).

The purpose of this chapter, then, is to provide practical strategies that can be employed by BHPs to perform effective functional assessments that increase the likelihood of favorable treatment outcomes for patients. It is hoped that by incorporating some, if not all, of the subsequent recommendations, BHPs will enjoy increased confidence in assessing patients, regardless of their presenting issues. First, an assessment heuristic is presented and discussed to prompt BHPs to begin thinking systemically about the domains that commonly interact to affect patient well-being. Second, specific strategies for ensuring an assessment that is effective and thorough, yet time sensitive, will be introduced. Finally, the ways in which assessment results should be presented to patients, with considerations for ethical issues and treatment enhancement, will be presented.

After reading this chapter, BHPs may find that one of the following is true: only a few, several, or most of these assessment ideas could be incorporated into their IC practice. Incorporation will depend on the type and level of integration of the IC practice in which they work. If, for instance, the IC practice allows for a few 50-minute sessions per day, then the BHP may be able to progress at a slower pace and do a more thorough biopsychosocial history. However, if the practice is more fully integrated, the BHP may only be able to use pieces of the information described below. Ultimately, BHPs and primary care physicians (PCPs) have to determine what works best for their setting, with ongoing assessment of the practice protocol and its effectiveness in helping patients.

Before delving into assessment guidelines, it is important to note that BHPs need to become skilled with the following: (a) using the *Diagnostic and Statistical Manual of Mental Disorders* (currently the DSM-IV-TR; American Psychiatric Association, 2000), (b) conducting mental status exams (see Polanski & Hinkle, 2000), and (c) recognizing symptoms of some of the most common nonpsychiatric issues presented in primary care settings, including but not limited to chest pain, fatigue, dizziness, edema, back pain, dyspnea, insomnia, abdominal pain, numbness, impotence, weight loss, cough, and constipation (Kroenke & Mangelsdorff, 1989). Since most master's-level behavioral health programs (e.g., counseling, social work, psychology, and marriage and family therapy) require classes in assessment, the DSM-IV-TR, tests, and measurement, these topics will not be discussed at length in this chapter. Information about them can be found infused throughout this book.

Developing an Assessment Heuristic

Most people, even well-trained clinicians, lack ability as adept and astute diagnosticians. Research indicates that clinicians tend to base their decisions about assessment on first impressions and anecdotal information, and generally seek to support their initial impressions rather than systematically test alternative hypotheses (for a review, see Rabinowitz & Efron, 1996). These mistakes can lead to inaccurate diagnoses and, concomitantly, ineffective treatment. PCPs expect and rely on BHPs to make accurate diagnoses so that the appropriate treatment, often pharmacotherapy coupled with behavioral strategies, can be administered.

Knowledge of the nomenclature of the DSM-IV-TR (American Psychiatric Association, 2000) provides a common language by which health care professionals from various disciplines can logically converse about diagnoses. That said, it is important to bear in mind that the reliability and validity of the DSM are questionable at best (Craske & Waters, 2005; Watson, O'Hara, & Stuart, 2008). Moreover, research is clear that patients' personalities, their readiness to change, and the level of therapeutic alliance between patients and their health care providers are the most robust predictors of successful treatment outcome, regardless of diagnosis (Budd & Hughes, 2009; Kaplan, Greenfield, & Ware, 1989). Thus, although BHPs should continue to strive to improve their diagnostic acumen, they should also develop skills in assessing the subsequent variables that have been shown to have a profound impact on treatment outcome. Some of the variables affecting diagnosis are described below, along with examples of BHP dialogue that can enhance assessment.

Biological

PCPs are trained to answer questions like: Is it possible that the precursors to this patient's issues are genetic or metabolic in nature? Could it be hormones, blocked arteries, blood sugar, or some dysregulation of an internal organ or metabolic system that keeps this patient from sleeping? The BHP, however, is charged with thinking systemically. BHPs should consider all possible antecedents in order to assess issues quickly and efficiently. With biological and genetic issues in mind during assessment, a skilled BHP might say the following:

BHP: Belinda, it sounds like anxiety has been problematic for you for the last 3 months. I know Dr. Rodriguez is going to check your blood sugar and thyroid levels since abnormal results can sometimes explain symptoms of anxiety, but I was also wondering if anyone in your family has or has had diabetes, thyroid issues, or problems with regularly feeling nervous?

Biographical

Attend any mental health agency staff meeting and you will surely hear about the biographical issues that patients face. BHPs will discuss the context of patients' lives (often referred to as *clients* in specialty mental health), including their early and later childhood, family members, and experiences in school and at home. There is no doubt that these issues are important; the problem, however, is when these issues take precedence over and overshadow others that may be relevant to the assessment process. For instance, is it possible that an adolescent with undiagnosed ADHD, who exhibits disinhibition, is labeled defiant or conduct-disordered as a result? What impact will this misdiagnosis have on the patient's treatment? When BHPs assume that all behavioral problems are the result of patients' biographies, treatment options are limited and compromised, and consequently, the patient suffers.

BHP: Ms. McClarie, from what you're telling me, your son Gary has been having a lot of trouble succeeding in school and we can certainly work on a behavior plan. Before we start outlining a treatment plan, though, can you tell me if Gary has ever been tested for ADHD or other issues that could affect his ability to learn?

Environmental

Environmental considerations include determining whether there are toxins in patients' communities that could be contributing to their symptoms. PCPs have an ethical responsibility to report public health dangers when they are discovered (Solomon & Kirkhorn, 2009), and BHPs can assist by researching the community in which they work to determine if environmental hazards have ever been reported. If hazards do exist, it is usually unrealistic to expect that patients move from their neighborhoods, but IC professionals can use such information to alert, advocate, and educate local officials (e.g., department of public health, fire department, and medical community) about the possible harm being caused to residents.

BHP: Elena, we definitely want to look closely at what is causing frequent illness for you and your family. I'm wondering if anyone else in your neighborhood or community has experienced problems similar to what you've reported to me?

Existential

First, *never* use the term *existential* with team members in an IC setting. PCPs like succinct, timely, and cogent discussions (Hunter, et al 2009) which should be free of "psycho-jargon." That said, as a broad-minded BHP, it can be helpful to keep existential issues in mind when conducting assessments. An obvious existential issue presents when patients are given life-altering or life-threatening diagnoses, which can cause patients to consider a host of questions ranging from spiritual issues to guilt and anxiety. On a more subtle level, existential issues become significant when patients are faced with the following situations: relationship issues, divorce, unemployment, underemployment, lack of meaningful work, midlife crisis, and children leaving the home, to name just a few. Perhaps one or more of these life circumstances are contributing to "unexplained" pain, frequent illness, a feeling of panic, stomach and gastrointestinal distress, depression, anger, and sudden bouts of tearfulness or rage. Biological symptoms are interlinked with psychological processes, thereby affecting each other when the slightest change occurs in either. It is important to be mindful of how they might interact.

BHP: Javier, from what you're describing, it sounds like your stomach discomfort is causing you a lot of distress. We'll make sure that Dr. Jackson does a physical exam on you to find possible causes. To be sure we are looking at the whole picture, tell me how things are going with your family and at work.

Diagnoses Are Tentative

BHPs must be cognizant of the fact that diagnoses may change as different treatments are administered and new information emerges (Hood & Johnson, 2007). Therefore, when discussing the process of diagnosis with patients, it can be helpful to say something like the following:

BHP: In order to provide treatment, we need to decide upon a tentative diagnosis. But please keep in mind that only you can truly validate this diagnosis and our initial thoughts may change after treatment begins. In essence, this initial diagnosis is only valid at this point in time. In fact, it may change in the future, and we need your help and input to ensure that we are providing you with the most effective treatment possible.

Assessment Is Treatment

When assessments are conducted effectively, patients gain insight into their condition and can begin to develop coping strategies (Hood & Johnson, 2007). Thus, it is important for BHPs to understand that a good assessment should extend beyond merely diagnosing a patient. A good assessment should help the patient draw from his or her strengths and engender insight and self-understanding.

BHP: Jamal, be sure to stop me at any point while I go over your assessment results. Ultimately, you are the only one who can verify if these results are pertinent and meaningful to you, and I want to make sure we use this information to help you feel better, and live a more fulfilling life.

Continuous Assessment

BHPs should never settle on a diagnosis for the long term, or assume it will be permanent; all diagnoses are provisional. While providing treatment, whether pharmacotherapeutic, behavioral, or a combination of both, BHPs should continually consider the possibility of other factors that may be contributing to the issue (Rabinowitz & Efron, 1996). An example of the importance of regular reassessment follows:

A patient who has been taking an antidepressant medication and receiving cognitive behavioral therapy for depression begins to exhibit signs of mania. The BHP conducted further assessment, which revealed a history of bipolar disorder, thereby modifying the initial diagnosis.

Ultimately, the BHP's diligence in assessment efforts beyond the initial diagnosis prevents health care professionals from overlooking other pertinent factors.

Triangulation Helps Increase Assessment Validity

BHPs should gather patient data from other sources in an effort to achieve a more complete picture of the issue. At the very least (with signed consent from the patient), BHPs should attempt to obtain information from three different sources: (1) the patient, (2) a significant other (i.e., parent/child, partner, friend), and (3) the BHP and PCP.

Clinical Supervision Is Required

Lastly, since in general people are prone to error when diagnosing (Rabinowitz & Efron, 1996), it is important to regularly seek clinical supervision and consultation. Ideally a system will be established within the IC agency that allows for staff meetings for case review, but in lieu of this, accessing a network of BHPs who are available for consultation is also helpful. BHPs will not always have the luxury of meeting colleagues outside the IC setting, a hurdle that is especially true for those who work in a fast-paced IC setting. But seeking clinical supervision from a trained professional within an agency is a necessity for BHPs.

How to Conduct Effective Assessments in IC

All IC assessment should be functional. This means that the BHP should not initially look for underlying issues (they do not necessarily exist), but rather should seek to discover what the patient most wants and needs from the visit that day (Robinson & Reiter, 2007). Does the patient want better quality sleep? To feel a normal level of energy again? To feel less anxious or depressed? To experience less pain? These are often the reasons why patients schedule appointments with their PCPs, and BHPs will quickly lose credibility if they fail to acknowledge this reality (Robinson & Reiter, 2007). After the BHP asks the patient about his or her presenting issues, it can be helpful to explore the following areas, to provide a more thorough picture of the patient. Each is discussed in further detail after the list.

> See the instructional DVD *Integrated Care in Action*, vignettes 2–5, for demonstrations about how to conduct brief assessments in IC practices.

1. What methods have you tried to alleviate the issue or problem, and for how long did you try?
2. On a scale of 1 to 10 (with 1 indicating no problem and 10 being terrible), how would you rate the way this issue is affecting you today?
3. Tell me about a time recently, if possible, when the issue wasn't as problematic as it is now. What was different in your life at that time? What were you doing and/or thinking differently then?
4. We will work together for big changes, but what small changes could serve as an indication that treatment is beneficial for you?

1. What Methods Have You Tried to Alleviate Your Symptoms?

After asking the patient to state his or her presenting issue, ask, "How long has this persisted and what have you tried to improve it?" Anecdotal evidence suggests that most people try at least a few things to improve their condition before scheduling an appointment with their doctor; helping patients identify their internal coping mechanisms can be a crucial element for improving treatment outcome (DeShazer, 1991; Kaplan et al., 1989). Perhaps the patient tried something that made them feel worse, or maybe something that the doctor would have suggested. By asking patients about their attempts, not only will their answers help BHPs with diagnosing the issue but also the exchange demonstrates respect for patients and their desire to feel better. As respect is communicated, the likelihood that the patient will feel more motivated to adhere to treatment strategies is increased (Kaplan et al.). Below are two examples of dialogue intended to help determine the patient's most pressing concern. An ineffective response by a BHP is followed by an effective one.

Patient: I just want to get some sleep. I fall asleep fine but I wake up at 3:00 a.m. every morning, if I'm lucky, and then again around 5:30 a.m. Just when I start feeling sleepy again, I've got to get up and get my daughter ready for school, which means I have to drink caffeine all day to keep from sleeping at work, or worse, while I'm driving.

Ineffective Response for an IC Setting

BHP: It sounds like sleep is a big problem for you right now and I want to try to help, but I think we should spend some time getting to the underlying issues of your sleep problems, otherwise everything else we do here in the clinic will just be a Band-Aid® that won't work for long. So, I'd like to schedule you for a 50- minute session within the week so I can get to know you better. How does that sound?

Effective Response for an IC Setting

BHP: I can tell that sleep is a big issue for you and it appears that you are motivated to find solutions. We definitely want to address your sleep issue and it's possible that the doctor will want to run some tests to get a better picture of what may be going on. In the meantime, since we have about 10 minutes until you see the doctor, I'm wondering if you would be willing to tell me about when your sleep issues started and what you've done so far to try to alleviate the problem?

In the second response, the BHP affirms the patient's chief concern and demonstrates an understanding about how IC practices work. The second response also assures the patient that his or her time will be respected. This level of practicality and directness is needed when assessing in IC.

2. Scaling Question

The use of scaling questions can be a good way to help clients identify to what extent the problem is bothersome and can be a quick way to monitor success of treatment (De Shazer, 1991). By asking a patient to rate their issue on a numeric scale, the BHP invites the patient to think about the issue from a more objective standpoint. Scaling questions are also useful in helping patients to think in terms of small increments of change. For example, the BHP could ask, "You're saying your pain is an 8 out of 10. Between now and the next time we meet what do you think might bring your pain level down a point or two?"

3. Can You Think of a Time When Your Symptoms Were Not as Problematic?

The goal of this question is to encourage the patient to consider a time, if any, when he or she was experiencing less symptoms. The answer they offer can then lead to discussion about what the patient may have been doing differently at that time that could have been responsible for the improvement in his or her condition. For example, a patient might say that his symptoms were not as severe several months ago. After further questioning, the BHP finds out that the patient was walking everyday with his spouse, but stopped exercising since his divorce. Next, the BHP can assess the patient's motivation for change and then the BHP and patient could co-create a new exercise plan. Naturally, examples are a simplification, but with persistence and support, BHPs may help patients realize that they have more control over the symptoms they are experiencing than previously thought.

4. Small Changes

BHPs can encourage patients to consider positive outcomes during an initial assessment, giving credence to the idea of assessment as an integral component of treatment. Patients' answers give BHPs valuable information about their goals and motivations and can be used to help create a treatment plan with the patient. BHPs can then work collaboratively with the patient and his or her PCP to help the patient set small goals, such as taking medication as prescribed, eating two servings of vegetables per day, or walking for 20 minutes three times per week.

Assessment to Enhance Treatment Outcome

Imagine a BHP telling a patient, "OK Javier, based upon our assessment, it appears that your symptoms are the result of depression. Therefore, I am going to give you these handouts that list things you can do to alleviate your depression, and Dr. Jackson is going to write you a prescription for an antidepressant. I'll give you a phone call in a couple weeks to see how you are doing." Most BHPs recognize the futility of this type of "treatment." Does Javier understand the purpose and process of his treatment? Is he motivated to make behavioral changes or take medications? Does he feel able to make changes in his life? If questions like these are not processed with patients, then successful treatment outcome is dubious. Thus, once the initial diagnostic information has been gathered, the following research-based issues should be explored with patients to increase the likelihood of better patient outcome. Each is discussed in more detail after the list:

1. Clarifying patients' expectations about treatment
2. Assessing patients' readiness to change
3. Assessing patients' internal locus of control
4. Assessing patients' treatment experiences and outcomes

1. Clarifying Expectations

A patient's expectations for effective treatment comprise one of the most robust variables for determining his or her commitment to engaging in services and following through with treatment recommendations (Kakhnovets, 2011). When BHPs help patients to better understand the treatment process, the likelihood that they will set realistic goals for treatment increases. For instance, a patient may say that she expects to receive medicine that will make her anxiety go away. A BHP can help this patient by explaining that although some medicines are very effective in alleviating anxiety, they are rarely a long-term solution. The BHP can then describe how coping skills that reduce anxiety (e.g., relaxation, mindfulness, and assertiveness skills) can complement medication and improve symptoms. A typical patient–BHP discussion of expectations might proceed as follows:

Patient: I expect that you will ask a lot of questions and I'll do my best to answer them.

BHP: When you're talking about what happens in the exam room, you're absolutely right. The doctor is trying to figure out your symptoms so she can help you. But with me, I'd like you to do the talking because it's important for me to find out as much about you as possible. Then, we can create reasonable and realistic goals together, to help you feel better.

2. Assessing Readiness

Regardless of how efficient the IC system is in identifying patients who need behavioral health care, or how seamlessly BHPs work with PCPs, if the patient is not ready to make changes, little will be accomplished. Matching treatment with patients' levels of readiness is vitally important for a positive therapeutic outcome (Hettema & Hendricks, 2010). Patients commit to changes more quickly if BHPs tailor their interventions according the patient's stage of change (Prochaska & DiClemente, 1983). The following statement is one way to begin to explore stage of change issues with patients:

BHP: The next thing we need to address is your readiness to change. The way I like to describe this is that there are some areas of my life where I'm making changes and others where I'm not. For instance, I know I need to clean my garage but on the readiness scale of change, I'm only a 0. I have no desire to do so, yet. However, when it comes to sleeping well I'm a 10, in that I exercise every day because it helps me sleep better and I value good sleep. With that example in mind, where would you rate yourself on a change scale in terms of your sleep, anxiety, depression, diet, and so on?

3. Assessing Internal Locus of Control

One of the most powerful predictors of patients' abilities to make meaning of their experiences and increase the likelihood of positive treatment results is their belief in their ability to make changes, often termed *high internal locus of control* (Deniz, Tras, & Didem, 2009; Estrada, Dupoux, & Wolman, 2006). Research results are clear that people with a higher internal locus of control respond better to challenges and stress (Hahn, 2000; Twenge, Zhang, & Im, 2004). Skilled BHPs who are aware of this thought process can explore it with their patients to, hopefully, increase patients' internal locus of control.

Patient (Javier): Well that figures. Stuff like this is always happening to me. When it rains, it pours.

BHP: Javier, I can tell you're frustrated, and if you're willing to schedule a time with me this week I would like to talk with you more about your frustrations. Today, though, I'm wondering, (pause) considering your tentative diagnosis, what can you do to help yourself, even if it's just something little?

In the aforementioned scenario, the BHP is hoping to acknowledge Javier's concern. The BHP should not try to convince Javier to make changes at this point; the patient is upset and frustrated, and therefore is more likely to be resistant to suggestions for change. So, the BHP's goal is to validate Javier's resistance, then place the onus of self-care back on Javier. This lets Javier know that he has responsibility for improving his health and well-being, and also communicates the unspoken message that the BHP believes in Javier's ability to take positive action.

4. Session Evaluation

Since assessment is continuous, a simple step all BHPs can take to increase treatment outcome is to perform a type of quality assessment by asking patients about their experience with the visit at the end of it. Session evaluation only takes a few minutes to conduct and has been shown to increase treatment outcome and reduce malpractice claims (Cummings, O'Donohue, & Cummings, 2009; Miller, Duncan, Sorrell, & Brown, 2005). There is a formal instrument that can be used (visit http://www.talking-cure.com), but some relevant questions include the following: What was your experience in this session today? What was most and least helpful? What will you do differently as a result of your visit today? Sample dialogue to ensure quality assurance is presented below:

BHP: Felicia, I know you're busy but before you leave today I'm wondering if you'd be willing to answer a few questions about how you feel your visit went today?

Patient: Sure, I guess. Will it take long?

BHP: Thank you. It will probably only take about 5 minutes. I know that sometimes doctors' offices can seem very hectic and busy, and the purpose of these questions is to assess how you feel you're being treated so we can do whatever is reasonable to meet your needs.

To see an example of how to conduct a session evaluation, see the *Integrated Care in Action* DVD, vignette 6.

Screening and Assessment Instruments Appropriate for IC Settings

The screening and assessment instruments listed in Table 3.1 are valuable tools that can be used in IC settings to identify patients who have behavioral health needs, as well as to glean additional information that may otherwise be missed by providers during routine visits for other complaints. Some tools can also be used to monitor treatment efficacy over time.

Primary care approaches patient service from a population-based perspective in which the needs of patients are identified and providers are especially interested in early identification, illness prevention, a stepped-care approach, chronic disease management, and coordination with specialists (O'Donohue, et al., 2005). The entire practice population can be given short screens in the form of a brief questionnaire during their first visit to the clinic; the screens may also be repeated for patients during their annual visits. Practices often use these initial questionnaires to gather information about personal habits, family dynamics, and other

Table 3.1
Brief Assessments Appropriate For Use In Integrated Care Settings

Instrument	Purpose	Reference
Patient Health Questionnaire (PHQ-9)	A nine-item screening tool used to detect depressive symptoms	Kroenke, K., Spitzer, R. L., & Williams, J. B. (2001). The PHQ-9: Validity of a brief depression severity measure. *Journal of General Internal Medicine, 16*(9), 606–613. Retrieved from http://www. depression-primarycare.org/clinicians/ toolkits/materials/forms/phq9/
Patient Health Questionnaire-9 Adolescent (PHQ-A)	A nine-item screening instrument modified to detect adolescent depression	Johnson, J. G., Harris, E. S., Spitzer, R. L., & Williams, J. B. W. (2002). The patient health questionnaire for adolescents: Validation of an instrument for the assessment of mental disorders among adolescent primary care patients *Journal of Adolescent Health, 30*(3), 196–220. doi:10.1016/S1054-139X(01)00333-0
Generalized Anxiety Disorder (GAD-7)	A seven-item instrument used to screen for generalized anxiety disorder	Spitzer, R. L., Kroenke, K., Williams, J. B. W., & Löwe, B. (2006). A brief measure for assessing generalized anxiety disorder: The GAD-7. *Archives of Internal Medicine, 166*(10), 1092-1097. Retrieved from http://www.ncbi.nlm. nih.gov/pubmed/16717171
Beck Depression Inventory for Primary Care (BDI-PC)	A seven-item instrument to help screen for depression	Steer, R. A., Ball, R., Ranieri, W. F., & Beck, A. T. (1999). Dimensions of the Beck Depression Inventory–II in clinically depressed outpatients. *Journal of Clinical Psychology, 55,* 117–128.
Mood Disorders Questionnaire (MDQ)	A 13-item instrument used to detect bipolar disorder	Hirschfeld, R. M. A., Williams, J. B. W., Spitzer, R. L., Calabrese, J. R., Flynn, L., Keck Jr., P. E., Zajecka, J. (2000). Development and validation of a screening instrument for bipolar spectrum disorder: The Mood Disorder Questionnaire. *The American Journal of Psychiatry, 157,* 1873–1875.

(continued)

Table 3.1 (continued)
Brief Assessments Appropriate For Use In Integrated Care Settings

Instrument	Purpose	Reference
Pediatric Symptom Checklist (PSC)	A 35-question screen used with children to detect cognitive, emotional and behavior problems. The Y-PSC can be used with children ages 11 and older.	National Center for Education in Maternal and Child Health and Georgetown University. (2008). Bright futures. Retrieved from http://www.brightfutures.org/ A national health promotion initiative
Vanderbilt ADHD Diagnostic Teacher Rating Scale	A 43-question inventory used to collect attention-related information from a child's teacher. Parent scales are also available.	Wolraich, M. L., Feurer, I. D., Hannah, J. N., Pinnock, T. Y., & Baumgaertel, A. (1998). Obtaining systematic teacher reports of disruptive behavior disorders utilizing DSM-IV. *Journal of Abnormal Child Psychology 26*(2):141–152.
The Adverse Childhood Experiences (ACE) questionnaire	A questionnaire used to determine adverse childhood experiences	Felitti, V. J., Anda R. F., Nordenberg, D., Williamson, D. F., Spitz, A. M., Edwards, V., Marks, J. S. (1998). Relationship of childhood abuse and household dysfunction to many of the leading causes of death in adults: The Adverse Childhood Experiences (ACE) Study. *American Journal of Preventive Medicine, 14*(4), 245–258.
CAGE	A four-item instrument used to screen for problems with alcohol	Ewing, J. A. (1984). Detecting alcoholism: The CAGE questionnaire. *Journal of the American Medical Association, 252*(14), 1905–1907.
CAGE-AID	A four-item instrument used to screen for both alcohol and drug abuse	Brown, R. L., & Rounds, L. A. (1995). Conjoint screening questionnaires for alcohol and drug abuse. *Wisconsin Medical Journal, 94*, 135–140.

Table 3.1 (continued)
Brief Assessments Appropriate For Use In Integrated Care Settings

Instrument	Purpose	Reference
Alcohol Use Disorders Identification Test (AUDIT)	A 10 Item instrument used to screen for alcohol misuse	Saunders, J. B., Aasland, O. G., Babor, T. F., de la Fuente, J. R. & Grant, M. (1993). Development of the alcohol use disorders identification test (AUDIT): WHO collaborative project on early detection of persons with harmful alcohol consumption. II. *Addiction, 88,* 791–804.
Opioid Risk Tool (ORT)	A five-item instrument used to determine risk for developing aberrant behaviors when prescribed opioids for pain management	Webster, L.R., & Webster, R.M. (2005). Predicting aberrant behaviors in opioid-treated patients: Preliminary validation of the opioid risk tool. *Pain Medicine, 6*(6), 432–442.
Drug Abuse Screening Test (DAST)	A 28-item self-report scale used to screen for drug abuse other than alcohol	Gavin, D. R., Ross, H. E., and Skinner, H. A. (1989). Diagnostic validity of the DAST in the assessment of DSM-III drug disorders. *British Journal of Addiction, 84,* 301–307.
CRAFFT	A six-item screening tool used to detect adolescent substance abuse	Knight, J. R, Sherritt, L.,Shrier, L. A., Harris, S. K., Chang, G. (2002, June). Validity of the CRAFFT Substance Abuse Screening Test among adolescent clinic patients. *Archives of Pediatrics & Adolescent Medicine 156,* 607–614.
UNCOPE	A six-item screening tool used to indentify the risk for substance abuse	Hoffmann, N. G., Hunt, D. E., Rhodes, W. M., & Riley, K. J. (2003). UNCOPE: A brief screen for use with arrestees. *Journal of Drug Issues, 33*(1), 29–44.

(continued)

Table 3.1 (continued)
Brief Assessments Appropriate For Use In Integrated Care Settings

Instrument	Purpose	Reference
TWEAK	A five-question screening instrument used to detect at-risk drinking with pregnant women	Chan, A. K., Pristach, E. A., Welte, J. W., & Russell, M. (1993). The TWEAK test in screening for alcoholism/ heavy drinking in three populations. *Alcoholism: Clinical and Experimental Research 6,* 1188–1192.
T-ACE	A four-question instrument used to detect prenatal women who are at risk for alcohol use	Sokol, R. J., Martier, S. S., & Ager, J. W. (1989). The T-ACE questions: Practical prenatal detection of risk-drinking. *American Journal of Obstetrics and Gynecology, 160,* 863–871.
Substance Abuse in Vocational Rehabilitation Screener (SAVR-S)	A 43 item assessment used to identify medication-seeking patients needing professional assessment	Heinemann, A.W., Lazowski, L. E., Moore, D., Miller, F., & McAweeney, M. (2008). Validation of a substance use disorder screening instrument for use in vocational rehabilitation settings. *Rehabilitation Psychology, 53*(1), 63–72. doi: 10.1037/0090-5550.53.1.63
Rotter Locus of Control Scale (Rotter LOC)	A 29 item scale used to measure patients' internal versus external locus of control	Rotter. J. B. (1966). Generalized expectancies for internal versus external control of reinforcement. *Psyhological Monographs, 80* (Whole No. 609).
Sense of Coherence Scale – 13	A 13-item scale used to measure patients' internal resources	Antonovsky, A. (1987). *Unraveling the mystery of health—How people manage stress and stay well.* San Francisco: Jossey-Bass.
Symptom Checklist-90-R	A 90-item instrument that screens for mental health issues	Derogatis LR. (1977). SCL-90-R: Administration, scoring and procedures manual for the R (revised) version. Baltimore, MD: John Hopkins University, School of Medicine.

Table 3.1 (continued)
Brief Assessments Appropriate For Use In Integrated Care Settings

Instrument	Purpose	Reference
Substance abuse subtle screening inventory (SASSI)	A brief instrument used to detect substance dependence	Miller, G.A. (1985, 1999). The Substance Abuse Subtle Screening Inventory (SASSI) Manual (2nd ed). Springville, IN: The SASSI Institute.
Edinburgh Postpartum Depression Scale	A 10-item questionnaire aimed at detecting postpartum depression	Cox, J. L., Holden, J. M., & Sagovsky, R. (1987). Detection of postnatal depression development of the 10-item Edinburgh Postnatal Depression Scale. *British Journal of Psychiatry, 150,* 782–786.
Ecomap	Tool used to identify patient's family structure and sources of stress and strength	Hartman, A. (1995). Diagrammatic assessment of family relationships. *Families in Society, 76,* 111–122.
Short Form Health Survey (SF-36)	A 36-item instrument used to profile functional health and well being, as well as physical and behavioral health summary measures	Stewart A.L., Hays, R.D., Ware,Jr., J. E. (1988). The MOS short-form general health survey: Reliability and validity in a patient population. *Medical Care, 26*:724–735.

general and historical health factors. BHPs can work their programming areas into these questionnaires to seek out behavioral health concerns and attain referrals, but equally as important, it has the effect of demonstrating to patients and practice providers that behavioral health is part of usual and routine care at the clinic. When these initial screens reveal positive or suspect results, patients can be referred to the BHP, who can then conduct a more formal and thorough assessment involving the use of assessment tools when appropriate. Behavioral health subjects, such as substance abuse or domestic violence, might be addressed with one or two questions in the initial screening. An example of a brief probe for depression in an initial screening questionnaire would be the inclusion of a two-question depression screener called the PHQ-2 (Kroenke, Spitzer, & Williams, 2003), which may be asked verbally with a patient, or written in the questionnaire. The two questions that make up the PHQ-2 are the first two questions of the PHQ-9 screening tool, and focus on mood and ahedonia reported over the previous 2 weeks. Providers may follow-up with the PHQ-9 if the patient scores any points on either of the PHQ-2 questions. Though brief, the PHQ-2 screening tool is surprisingly sensitive; if patients have a combined score of three or more for these two questions, the Positive Predictive Value (PPV) of later diagnosis of a depressive disorder is 75%, and 38.4% for major depressive disorder (Kroenke et al., 2003). The SBIRT model (**S**creening, **B**rief **I**ntervention, and **R**eferral for **T**reatment) is proving to be feasible, clinically appropriate, and effective in identifying and addressing drug abuse when employed in various medical settings (Madras, Compton, Avula, Stegbauer, Stein, & Clark, 2009). This intervention model is often targeted at substance use and encourages the use of motivational interviewing during the brief intervention phase. The screening tool chosen for identifying substance use can vary depending on the target substance, clinician preference, time constraints, and the population to be screened.

When adding behavioral health screening tools into practice routines, BHPs should aim to align them with the processes and procedures already in place for physical health conditions, in order to establish a seamless integration of the two areas of health care. Behavioral health questions can be added to initial questionnaires, as described above, and follow-up screens can be conducted when appropriate. The clinical team (i.e., physician champion, lead nurse, office staff, and the BHP) may need to decide how the implementation can best function within the logistics of the practice routines (i.e., when and which patients will receive screens, by whom the screens will be scored, with whom patients will interact and at what point, and when the BHP will become involved in the patient encounter). Generally, all members of the practice team will have a role in screening; their collective input is critical to the success of the programming. New screening tools and associated routines should be piloted, evaluated, and adjusted when appropriate, prior to being implemented practice-wide. One way to ensure screenings take place when the treatment team becomes busy is by establishing flexibility within the team. That is, each team member should learn how to conduct the steps within screenings typically performed by other team members, as appropriate. For example, while a nurse may be the team member who regularly administers and scores a screener for the PCP to interpret, the PCP could step in to administer, score, and interpret findings with the patient if the nurse was unavailable.

Formal tests are essential tools for identifying patients who may be seeking medication for nontherapeutic purposes. Patients with this ill-intent are often called "medication seeking." It is an unfortunate fact in medical settings that some patients will over-report or feign symptoms to obtain desired medications. This most commonly occurs when patients are seeking opioids and/or benzodiazepines, but can also occur with stimulants. As such, PCPs may be reluctant to administer these types of medications, even when therapeutically warranted, as the patient could become addicted or sell the medication. Appropriately trained BHPs can be immensely helpful in detecting medication-seeking patients in an IC practice. Two instruments in particular that can aid in identifying these patients are the Substance Abuse in Vocational Rehabilitation Screener (SAVR-S; Heinemann, Lazowski, Moore, Miller, & McAweeney, 2008) and the Minnesota Multiphasic Personality Inventory-2-Restructured Form (MMPI-2-RF: Ben-Porath & Tellegen, 2008). While both instruments have been shown to detect overreporting of symptoms, the SAVR-S is more appropriate for IC settings for several reasons. First, it was created with the functional emphasis of detecting medication-seeking patients. Second, with only 43 questions, the SAVR-S can be completed and scored much quicker than the 338-item MMPI-2-RF. Third, the credentials needed to administer the SAVR-S, and the training requirements for it, are much less strenuous than those of the MMPI-2-RF. Instruments specific for the identification of patients at risk for developing aberrant behaviors when prescribed opioids for pain management, such as the Opioid Risk Tool (ORT), are presented in Table 3.1. In summary, the informed BHP can be an invaluable resource for ensuring, to the best extent possible, that medication-seeking patients are identified and treated appropriately.

Whether formal assessment instruments are used to monitor treatment efficacy or to identify medication-seeking patients, it is important for BHPs to follow a protocol to ensure that test results are communicated in an ethical and facilitative manner. Hood and Johnson (2007) outlined the following recommendations to be used when choosing, administering, and interpreting test results with patients:

- If there are more people present in the exam room or office than just the patient and BHP, make sure everyone is introduced and make their purpose for being in the meeting known.
- Prior to discussing test results, summarize the patient's chief concern and issues and provide reasons for why the tests were administered.
- Remember, test results are only a piece of the puzzle; other factors may be contributing to or exacerbating symptoms.
- Results should not be interpreted as infallible or incontrovertible.

- Encourage the patient and family members to ask questions throughout the process.
- The BHP may need to counsel parents and guardians after testing and when a child has been given a diagnosis.
- Understand the important test development characteristics (i.e., validity, reliability, and norming group), and be prepared to discuss these with patients so they know the purpose of the test and possible biases.
- Be prepared to tell the patient what the results mean, as well as what they do not mean.
- Discuss results in the context of other information that you have gathered from the patient. For example, "Your high score on this depression instrument makes sense considering what you told me about losing interest in things and your low energy level."
- To avoid overwhelming patients with information, check in with them periodically during the appointment by asking, "Can you tell me what you understand so far?"
- It is prudent for BHPs to have taken behavioral screening instruments or tests themselves to better understand possible problems (e.g., ambiguous questions and confusing results).
- At the end of the discussion, ask patients to summarize what they understand and what that means regarding their health and treatment.

Conclusion

After reading this chapter, it should be clear that simply learning the DSM-IV-TR (APA, 2000) is inadequate to ensure an effective assessment process. BHPs should appreciate that assessment is an ongoing process that is comprised of inextricably linked variables, and that when it is conducted well, it can significantly enhance treatment outcome. It is worth mentioning that there are several important items related to assessment that were not covered in this chapter, most notably documentation and communicating results to PCPs; these topics will be covered in Chapter 18. By following the steps defined in this chapter, BHPs will improve their assessment skills, thereby leading to more accurate diagnoses and, concomitantly, efficacious treatment plans.

Discussion Questions

1. What would be your opening statement to Javier to ensure the beginning of an effective assessment?

2. Consider the following dialogue in a case in which a 30-year-old male patient answered "positive" to questions on the CAGE-AID. What would your next response be, and why?

BHP: Thanks, Rowan, for completing the intake questionnaire. I want to spend a few minutes with you to discuss some of your answers in more detail.

Patient: OK.

BHP: You indicated that you have given thought to cutting down on the amount (of alcohol) you drink; I'm wondering if you would tell me more about that?

Patient: Yeah, I sometimes drink more than I'd like and feel terrible the next day.

BHP: (What would your response be?)

3. Using the case of Javier presented in the beginning of the chapter, role-play a brief 15-minute assessment using the principles discussed in this chapter.
4. Assume you are working with a patient who tested positive for "medication-seeking" behavior. How would you address this issue with the patient?
5. Consider a medical practice that is interested in identifying depression in patients who have not sought treatment for depression. How would you begin the inclusion process of adding brief behavioral health-screening tools to this medical practice's protocol?
6. With a partner, role-play the appropriate test interpretation procedures for one of the assessment instruments listed in Table 3.1.

References

American Psychiatric Association. (2000). *Diagnostic and statistical manual of mental disorders* (Rev. 4th ed.). Washington, DC: Author.

Ben-Porath, Y. S., & Tellegen, A. (2008). *MMPI-2-RF (Minnesota Multiphasic Personality Inventory-2 Restructured Form): Manual for administration, scoring, and interpretation*. Minneapolis: University of Minnesota Press.

Budd, R., & Hughes, I. (2009). The dodo bird verdict—controversial, inevitable and important: A commentary on 30 years of meta-analyses. *Clinical Psychology and Psychiatry, 16*, 510–522.

Craske, M. G., & Waters, A. M. (2005). Panic disorder, phobia and generalized anxiety disorder. *Annual Review of Clinical Psychology, 1*, 197–225.

Cummings, N. A., O'Donohue, W. T., & Cummings, J. L. (2009). The financial dimension of integrated behavioral/primary care. *Journal of Clinical Psychology in Medical Settings, 16*, 31–39. doi:10.1007/s10880-008-9139-2.

De Shazer, S. (1991). *Putting difference to work.* New York: Norton.

Deniz, M. E., Tras, Z., & Didem, A. (2009). An investigation of academic procrastination, locus of control, and emotional intelligence. *Educational Science: Theory & Practice, 9*(2), 623–632.

Estrada, L., Dupoux, E., & Wolman, C. (2006). The relationship between locus of control and personal-emotional adjustment to college life in students with and without learning disabilities. *College Student Journal, 40,* 43–54.

Hahn, S. E. (2000). The effects of locus of control on daily exposure, coping and reactivity to work interpersonal stressors: A diary study. *Personality and Individual Differences, 29*(4), 729–748. doi:10.1016/S0191-8869(99)00228-7

Hettema, J. E., & Hendricks, P. S. (2010). Motivational interviewing for smoking cessation: A meta-analytic review. *Journal of Consulting and Clinical Psychology, 78*(6), 868–884.

Hood, A. B., & Johnson, R. W. (2007). *Assessment in counseling: A guide to the use of psychological assessment procedures* (4th ed.). Alexandria, VA: American Counseling Association.

Heinemann, A. W., Lazowski, L. E., Moore, D., Miller, F., & McAweeney, M. (2008). Validation of a substance use disorder screening instrument for use in vocational rehabilitation settings. *Rehabilitation Psychology, 53*(1), 63–72. doi:10.1037/0090-5550.53.1.63

Hunter, C. L., Goodie, J. L., Oordt, M. S., & Dobmeyer, A. C. (2009). *Integrated behavioral health in primary care: Step-by-step guidance for assessment and intervention.* Washington, DC: American Psychological Association.

Kakhnovets, R. (2011). Relationships among personality, expectations about counseling, and help-seeking attitudes. *Journal of Counseling & Development, 89*(1), 11–19.

Kaplan, S. H., Greenfield, S., & Ware, J. E. (1989). Assessing the effects of physician-patient interaction on the outcomes of chronic disease. *Medical Care, 27*(3, Suppl.), 110–127.

Kroenke, K., & Mangelsdorff, A. D. (1989). Common symptoms in ambulatory care: Incidence, evaluation, therapy, and outcome. *The American Journal of Medicine, 86*(3), 262–266. doi:10.1016/0002-93439(89)90293-3

Kroenke, K., Spitzer, R. L., & Williams, J. B. W. (2003). The patient health questionnaire-2: Validity of a two-item depression screener. *Medical Care, 41*(11), 1284–1292.

Madras, B. K., Compton, W. M., Avula, D., Stegbauer, T., Stein, J. B., & Clark, H. W. (2009). Screening, brief interventions, referral to treatment (SBIRT) for illicit drug and alcohol use at multiple healthcare sites: Comparison at intake and six months. *Drug and Alcohol Dependence, 99*(1–3), 280–295. doi:10.1016/j.drugalcdep.2008.08.003

Miller, S. D., Duncan, B. L., Sorrell, R. and Brown, G. S. (2005). The partners for change outcome management system. *Journal of Clinical Psychology, 61,* 199–208. doi: 10.1002/jclp.20111

O'Donohue, W. T., Byrd, M. R., Cummings, N. A., & Henderson, D. A. (Eds.). (2005). *Behavioral integrative care: Treatments that work in the primary care setting.* New York: Brunner-Routledge.

Polanski, P. J., & Hinkle, J. S. (2000). The mental status examination: Its use by professional counselors. *Journal of Counseling & Development, 78,* 357–364.

Prochaska, J. O., & DiClemente, C. C. (1983). Stages and processes of self-change of smoking: Toward an integrated model of change. *Journal of Consulting and Clinical Psychology, 51*, 390–395.

Rabinowitz, J., & Efron, N. J. (1996). Diagnosis, dogmatism, and rationality. *Journal of Mental Health Counseling, 18*, 40–56.

Robinson, P. J., & Reiter, J. T. (2007). *Behavioral consultation and primary care: A guide to integrating services.* New York, NY: Springer.

Solomon, G. M., & Kirkhorn, S. R. (2009). Physician's duty to be aware of and report environment toxins. *Virtual Mentor, 11*(6), 434–442.

Twenge, J. M., Zhang, L., & Im, C. (2004). It's beyond my control: A cross-temporal meta-analysis of increasing external locus of control. *Personality and Social Psychology Review, 8*, 308–319.

Watson, D., O'Hara, M. W., & Stuart, S. (2008). Hierarchical structures of affect and psychopathology and their implications for the classification of emotional disorders. *Anxiety and Depression, 25*, 282–288.

CHAPTER 4

Brief Treatment

A Model for Clinical Guidelines in Integrated Care

RICHARD L. MUNGER and RUSS CURTIS

Behavioral health providers (BHPs) must be highly skilled and effective counselors in integrated care (IC) settings. The importance of their competency as counselors can be easily overshadowed when learning about integrated care because so much emphasis is placed on assessment, case management, consulting, systems of care, logistics, technology, medical records, management of at-risk populations, medications, and billing. BHPs are talented and educated professionals who can skillfully help patients with behavioral issues; otherwise their jobs could easily be given to paraprofessionals with little or no behavioral health training. The purpose of this chapter, then, is to discuss behavioral strategies that are efficient and effective to use within the fast-paced, time-limited IC environment, and to introduce a model of care for depression that can be used by BHPs as a guide to create similar protocols for other common symptoms presented within IC practices.

Stepped Care

Stepped care is the overarching treatment philosophy guiding IC. This concept harkens back to Hollister and Rae-Grant's (1972) concept of effective parsimony, meaning "begin with the simplest appropriate treatment." Except for acutely ill patients, BHPs and PCPs should attempt to meet the following criteria when providing treatment: (a) Cause the least disruption in a patient's life, (b) provide the least extensive treatment needed for positive results, (c) provide the least intensive treatment needed for positive results, (d) provide the least expensive treatment needed for positive results, and (e) utilize the least expensive method of training staff to provide effective treatment.

In stepped care, the intensity of treatment is customized according to the patient's response. The first step of care involves watchful waiting and minimal educational efforts, such as information sharing, referral to self-help groups, bibliotherapy (perhaps using an iPod), and other e-health (computer-based) technologies. In the second and more intensive step of care, BHPs provide psycho-educational interventions and engage in phone consultations with patients. The third level requires BHPs to provide treatment based upon illness-specific algorithms (O'Donohue & Draper, 2010). If a patient does not respond to stepped care, then the patient is referred to the specialty mental health system (Strosahl, 2005), in which the IC team works collaboratively with mental health specialists to ensure a seamless transition. Sometimes the patient's care can be transitioned back to primary care after an adequate dose of specialty mental health treatment, with ongoing collaboration between IC and specialty mental health professionals.

The stepped care approach is imperative in IC because the volume of behavioral health needs seen in IC settings can quickly outpace the capacity of a traditional mental health care model (Strosahl, 2001). Thus, BHPs must be skilled in providing "bite-sized" evidence-based care, usually in a psycho-educational format, with an emphasis on skill building and home-based practice (Strosahl, 2005). Moreover, based upon evidence from experienced BHPs working within IC practices, primary care patients will only tolerate about 3 hours of behavioral treatment over a 3-month period (Robinson, 2005). For example, a cognitive-behavioral approach to treat a patient with panic disorder can be done in three to four brief contacts with a BHP when supported with educational materials, home practice, and telephone follow-up.

Therapeutic Engagement

Before the appropriate level of care can be determined, the BHP must first engage patients in a way that demonstrates a genuine willingness to help. Although most BHPs are taught therapeutic engagement skills, the triage encounter in an IC setting presents unique challenges. Therapeutic engagement is a requisite to set the groundwork for effective treatment, and must be accomplished within the first few minutes of meeting the patient to be effectual. Personality traits of BHPs can either facilitate or impede engagement efforts (e.g., adaptable or timid), but successful engagement and rapport building are skills that can be mastered with practice by almost all

BHPs. Listed below are the goals of, and behaviors for, enhancing therapeutic engagement.

Goals of Therapeutic Engagement

- Maximize the effectiveness of the intervention.
- Enhance compliance.
- Reduce stigma. A major advantage of IC is the reduction of stigma, which many patients associate with mental health treatment.
- Enhance accurate communication, and thereby the ability to assess and treat the patient.
- Promote patient comfort with and willingness to access mental health treatment in the future.

Nonverbal Strategies

- Consult with the patient in the exam room.
- Position yourself physically, in relation to the patient, in a comfortable and open manner.
- Listen, listen, listen!

Verbal Strategies

- Avoid using traditional mental health titles. For example, a BHP can say, "I'm Sheila. I'm on Dr. Smith's healthcare team."
- Respect the patient's time. When you are talking to the patient after he or she has met with the PCP, the BHP can say, "I wanted to talk with you about the stress that you discussed with Dr. Smith; do you have a few minutes?"
- Ask the patient what he or she prefers to be called.
- Validate the patient's problem, for example, "I am sorry you've been feeling poorly. I'm glad you're here today; we'd like to help."
- Ask, "How long have you been feeling this way?"
- Ask, "What have your days been like; how have you been coping?"
- Empathize, "It must be scary knowing you'll be unemployed soon."
- Avoid using formal mental health terms and instead use phrases like "I hear you've been feeling down."
- Conceptualize the problem by using the patient's own language, as in "Tell me some more about how your bad nerves have been affecting you."
- Personal statements can be helpful when used to develop rapport and kept to a minimum. For example, "I have a daughter in elementary school too."
- Affirm positive steps taken. An example of such an exchange may be "Have you been taking your medication regularly? Great!"

- Have a solution focus; build on what the patient is doing right rather than spending all of the time focusing on what the patient is doing wrong, as in this phrasing: "While you've been drinking more than you want, you've been drinking less at each sitting. That's progress. Can you continue to do that?"
- Find something to compliment about the patient, such as "Your bright red purse looks perfect for holding a lot of stuff."
- Leave the patient with a plan and something to work on before the next session (homework); briefly summarize it at the end of the session.
- Conclude the session with a hopeful handshake (see "Engendering Hope" section).

Engendering Hope

An overriding goal of therapeutic engagement is to engender hope. Harpham (2009) stated that it only takes a few seconds to make a compassionate and supportive statement to a patient, and increasing evidence supports the treatment efficacy of addressing hope with patients (Cutcliffe, 2006; Hillbrand & Young, 2008). Each patient is unique; therefore, it is important for BHPs to tailor their approaches to meet each patient's specific needs and concerns. Examples of hopeful statements are listed below.

- "I know things haven't gotten any better for some time. But change is inevitable. It will change. It's just a question of when."
- "Getting better is like a healing curve; there are ups and downs, but in small steps things usually improve."
- "You may feel like you are falling apart, but it's a chance to be put back together in a new way; you can emerge a healthier person."
- "You've made the most important decision—not to give up. I will work with you to figure this out."
- "You've got lots of strengths to overcome this illness. It's making a difference."
- "You are working hard on your plan. I'm with you to help you feel better."

IC Appropriate Behavioral Therapies

Once therapeutic engagement and hope building are underway, the BHP can begin to use appropriate strategies from the theoretical approaches listed in Table 4.1. Research supports the use of cognitive-behavioral therapy (Tolin, 2010), solution-focused brief therapy (Kim, 2008), motivational interviewing (Hettema & Hendricks, 2010), and positive psychotherapy

Table 4.1
Counseling Strategies Used in Integrated Care Settings

Theory	Relevant Integrated Care Strategies
Motivational interviewing	• Assess patient's stage of change. • Use open-ended questions and reflective listening. • Avoid arguments and advice giving. • Tailor approach to fit patient's stage of change.
Solution-focused or brief therapy	• Help patients recognize times when their symptoms or issues are not as problematic. • Focus on patients' strengths. • Help co-create a treatment plan. • Help patient take small steps toward goals.
Cognitive behavioral therapy	• Help patients identify the thoughts, feelings, and behaviors associated with their symptoms. • Help patients identify more productive thoughts, feelings, and behaviors. • Help patients develop strategies to achieve goals.
Positive psychotherapy	• Help patients engage in activities that have been shown to increase well-being (i.e., mindfulness, acceptance, forgiveness, and service). • Co-create treatment plans with patients to help them take small steps toward their goals and to live according to their values.

(Seligman, Steen, Park, & Peterson, 2005). These four strategies are useful in IC settings because they are evidence-based and can be applied, as appropriate, in relatively brief formats. It is worth reiterating at this point, however, that BHPs will need to adapt their treatment strategies based on their patients' needs and the particular IC setting in which they work. It is important for some type of counseling to be made available to patients by BHPs, even in highly integrated IC practices, because evidence is clear that most patients are reluctant to accept referrals to "outside" mental health agencies (Cummings, 2002).

Motivational Interviewing (MI)

MI (Miller & Rollnick, 1991) is the therapeutic process through which BHPs match their interventions with patients' stage of change (Prochaska & DiClemente, 1983). If, for instance, a depressed patient indicates no willingness to follow through with behavioral strategies, a BHP skilled in MI would not barrage the patient with advice about the benefits of exercise or mindfulness. Instead, the BHP would acknowledge the patient's reluctance to make changes, listen empathically, and paraphrase the patient's comments in an attempt to build therapeutic alliance. The skilled BHP knows that a strong therapeutic alliance is one of the best indicators of positive patient outcome (Budd & Hughes, 2009). Alternately, if the patient is willing to make changes, then the BHP can begin to help the patient set appropriate goals (e.g., exercise and mindfulness strategies). Below is an example of a statement influenced by MI:

BHP: Rachel, you've talked about feeling depressed and the results of your PHQ-9 seem to confirm this. You've also mentioned some strategies you've used in the past that have helped to alleviate some of your depression. I'm wondering to what degree you are ready and willing to practice one or more of those strategies now?

Solution-Focused Brief Therapy (SFBT)

The primary purpose of SFBT is to help patients recognize and use their strengths to reduce or alleviate symptoms (DeShazer, 1991; O'Hanlon, 1999). The overriding belief of BHPs skilled in SFBT is that patients possess the necessary skills needed to improve their lives, but they may need help in remembering times when they effectively coped with problematic situations. Listed below are a couple of SFBT-informed statements that can be used to engage patients.

First example:

BHP: From what you're telling me, Trent, these intense feelings of anxiety you experience in social situations really bother you and are starting to degrade your quality of life. First of all, I want to acknowledge the courage it took to come here today and talk about this issue. Second, keeping in mind that your doctor and I will do everything we can to help you, I'm wondering if you could tell me about a time in your recent past when you experienced similar feelings but found ways cope with them, even if they worked just a little bit?

Second example:

BHP: Shelley, you've clearly been through a lot in your life and I want to schedule a time with you next week when we can talk more about your struggles. But I'm wondering if we could take a few minutes now to look at how you would like to see yourself in your life? In other words, what would you be doing differently if you were living a more fulfilling life now? (Metcalf, 1998)

Cognitive-Behavioral Therapy (CBT)

The purpose of CBT (Beck, 1976; Ellis, 1996; Meichenbaum, 1977) is two-fold: to help clients become aware of and then begin changing self-defeating thoughts and behaviors, and to help patients to begin taking steps that move them closer to their goals. BHPs can use CBT approaches within the IC environment by helping patients recognize how their thoughts, feelings, behavior, and physiology interact to affect their overall health. Below is an example dialogue between a patient and BHP demonstrating how CBT concepts can be introduced.

BHP: James, help me make sure I'm understanding your situation: First, you've said that you are feeling very nervous at times, especially at work. You feel your heart racing and you are sweating more frequently than usual. You have thoughts that something must be wrong with your heart and this is causing you to leave work more often and call in sick more than usual.

Patient: That's right. The doctor says there is nothing wrong with my heart, though. I know the pressure at work is probably causing all this, but nothing I do seems to help.

BHP: Yes, with all the layoffs within your company I bet it is very stressful. And I suspect you're not the only one feeling a lot of stress but I can tell that it bothers you a lot. So let's look at some strategies you have not tried yet and make a plan for the next week. I'd like to call you next Monday to see how things are going.

Positive Psychotherapy (PPT)

At its basic level, PPT (Csikszentmihalyi, 1990; Fredrickson, 2009; Seligman, 2002) is closely aligned with behavior therapy in that it is the process of helping patients take action. The difference between PPT and behavior therapy is that PPT treatment strategies have been shown to increase patients' well-being and sense of meaning in life (Seligman et al., 2005). When BHPs use PPT, they must be skilled in positioning the reason why such activities might be helpful, and in educating patients that they do not have to feel better to begin engaging in such activities. One such positioning statement is exemplified below.

BHP: Mrs. Johnson, Dr. Gibbons and I are going to do everything we can to help you feel better, and I know that right now it's hard to focus on anything but your symptoms. But I'm wondering, while you begin the medicine prescribed by Dr. Gibbons, do you think we could pick a treatment strategy or two that might complement your medical treatment?

See vignettes 3–5 on the *Integrated Care in Action* DVD for demonstrations on how to conduct brief treatment in IC practices.

To summarize, MI, SFBT, CBT, and PPT are important counseling approaches for BHPs to become proficient in practicing because they are supported by research and can be adapted to be used in IC settings by creative and skilled BHPs. Further, because of the unique challenges of working within an IC setting, specifically in a fast-paced environment, it is recommended that BHPs develop a structure (i.e., treatment checklists) to which they can refer when delivering treatment so that important elements of the aforementioned therapies are not overlooked.

The Need for Structure in IC Brief Treatment

The results of a recent study indicate the importance of using structured protocols in medical settings to reduce mistakes, which can ultimately decrease mortality rates (Haynes et al., 2009). Often, mistakes occur in medical settings because current treatment data have not been translated into simple, usable, and systematic protocols (Gawande, 2009). In fact, most physicians report that they simply forget to follow all the recommended steps of an assigned protocol (Kolata, 2004), an understandable oversight when considering that the volume and complexity of new treatment data have exceeded the health care professional's ability to deliver effective treatment correctly, safely, and reliably (Gawande, 2009).

Treatment protocols, then, should be created in accessible formats that can be carried in a notebook or digital device into the patient exam room, to ensure that all steps of reliable treatment strategies are used (Strosahl, 2005). For maximum effectiveness, each checklist should be concise and standardized, following a common format. Below is an example of a clinical checklist for working with patients who are experiencing depression-related symptoms. Treatment protocols for other commonly presented symptoms in IC settings are currently being developed.

Brief Treatment Clinical Model for Adult Depression

Assessment

- ✓ Screening form attached; score of 15+ on PHQ indicates significant depression
- ✓ Red flag questions:
    - ☐ During the past month, have you often been bothered by feeling down, depressed, or hopeless?
    - ☐ Have you often been bothered by little interest or pleasure in doing things?

Symptoms

- ☐ Feeling sad and hopeless, and having frequent crying spells

- ☐ Losing interest or pleasure in things you used to enjoy (including sex)
- ☐ Feeling guilty, helpless, or worthless
- ☐ Thinking about death or suicide
- ☐ Sleeping too much, or having problems sleeping
- ☐ Unintended weight loss or gain
- ☐ Feeling very tired all the time
- ☐ Having trouble paying attention and making decisions
- ☐ Having aches and pains that don't get better with treatment
- ☐ Feeling restless, irritated, and easily annoyed

Onset: _____ Duration: _____

Evaluation Issues

- ☐ Diurnal rhythms are disrupted: appetite, sleep.
- ☐ Assess current environmental stressors.
- ☐ Assess presence of suicidal ideation, including history of suicide attempts (see suicidal ideation guideline). "Sometimes when people feel really, really down, they feel like they would just rather be dead. Do you ever have any feelings like that?"
- ☐ Get thorough medication history, including medications that could be causing depressed mood.
- ☐ Assess abuse history.
- ☐ Assess crisis support resources available to patient.
- ☐ Rule out bipolar illness: Mood Disorders Questionnaire.
- ☐ Assess co-occurring disorder: substance abuse, or anxiety or panic.
- ☐ Cultural issues: "What are your thoughts about why you have been feeling this way?"

Diagnoses

- ☐ 309. 0   Adjustment Disorder With Depressed Mood
- ☐ 300. 4   Dysthymic Disorder
- ☐ 296. 2× Major Depressive Disorder, Single Episode
- ☐ 296. 3× Major Depressive Disorder, Recurrent
- ☐ V62. 82 Bereavement

Treatment Plan

Goal: Reduce depressed mood, and restore to previous level of functioning.

Objectives:

- ☐ Take prescribed medications.
- ☐ Identify and alter self-talk which supports depression.
- ☐ Use behavior modification strategies to mitigate depression.

- ☐ Identify supportive people in your life and describe how you could use specific relationships.
- ☐ Identify and talk about any unresolved grief issues.
- ☐ Use problem-solving skills to resolve interpersonal problems.
- ☐ Begin a regular exercise program, starting with small steps.
- ☐ Practice relapse prevention skills.
- ☐ Increase assertive communication.

Interventions

- ☐ Daily exercise.
- ☐ Daily activity; feelings follow behavior (e.g., important to just get out and do an activity, even if you don't feel like it; if you *do* it, it will help you feel better).
- ☐ Use personal support systems.
- ☐ Improve sleep (see insomnia guideline).
- ☐ Don't dwell on negative thoughts; OK to let them pass through your mind, but let them do just that—pass through; don't ruminate.

Medication

Antidepressants:

- ☐ Has anyone in your family taken an antidepressant that was helpful?
- ☐ The medication usually takes 2–4 weeks to work.
- ☐ Call if there are problems with side effects.
- ☐ Warn about possibility of increased suicidal thinking in rare instances, and to call you immediately if it occurs.
- ☐ If patient asks about how long he or she will have to take the medication: Don't stop when you start to feel better; usually doctors keep you on the medication for 9 months to a year, and then reevaluate.
- ☐ If, after a trial, the medication is not helping, we will try another. Sometimes it takes more than one trial to find the medication that will help you.
- ☐ Thyroid functioning should be checked if patient is not responsive to first trial of an antidepressant.
- ☐ Discuss chemical imbalance aspect of depression with patient.
- ☐ Discuss how stress can contribute to chemical imbalance.
- ☐ Discuss how physical symptoms can result from stress.

Handout: Adult Depression

What Is Depression?

When doctors talk about depression (which requires treatment), they are usually referring to *major depression*, as opposed to sadness, normal grief, or even mild depressive symptoms. People with major depression experience the symptoms listed below for a relatively long period of time—a few months or more.

People with major depression also frequently experience physical symptoms such as headache and digestive problems.

Typical Symptoms of Depression

Common symptoms of major depression are listed below; everyone does not experience all of them:

- Feelings of sadness and hopelessness
- Crying spells
- Loss of interest in pleasurable activities
- Feeling guilty or worthless
- Difficulty sleeping or sleeping too much
- Loss of appetite or excessive eating
- Lack of energy
- Difficulty concentrating
- Bodily aches and pains
- Feeling restless
- Easily irritated or annoyed
- Suicidal thinking

Do We Know the Cause of Depression?

Depression is often linked to stressful events in people's lives, for example the death of a loved one, divorce, job loss, or another traumatic event. Depression may be caused by a chemical imbalance in the brain, disrupting the ways that cells communicate to one another. Depression may run in family genes as well.

Some medications may have side effects which include depression. Abusing drugs or alcohol can lead to depression, and other mental illnesses may also have depression as part of their symptoms. Depression is never caused by lack of willpower or personal weakness.

How Is the Diagnosis of Depression Confirmed?

It's difficult to tell if someone is depressed by simply looking at him or her. Tell your doctor about all of your symptoms. The sooner treatment begins, the faster you will start feeling better.

What Are the Most Common Treatments for Depression?

Medication and counseling are both proven and effective treatments for depression.

How Can Medication Help?

Antidepressant medications are quite effective in treating depression. There are more than a dozen kinds that aim to correct the chemical imbalances in the brain.

Antidepressant medications affect each person differently; their side effects may or may not affect you. If one medication doesn't help, another one might, or a medication can be switched if a side effect bothers you. It usually takes several weeks for antidepressant medication to help you feel better, and sometimes as much as 2–3 months for you to get the full benefit. Some side effects also may disappear after a period of time, so physicians sometimes ask patients if they can tolerate the negative effect for a few weeks.

How Long Do You Take Antidepressant Medication?

Physicians usually recommend taking antidepressant medication for 9–12 months, in order to avoid a reoccurrence of the depression after you have shown improvement. But every case is different, so talk to your doctor about the best plan for you.

How Is Counseling Used for Depression?

Counseling may involve periodic visits to talk to your doctor, a professional counselor (such as a social worker or psychologist), or a psychiatrist. You'll talk about the many things that are going on in your life: your thoughts, your feelings, and your relationships. The goal is to identify things that you can do differently to help you feel better. Most counseling is fairly short term.

Does Depression Ever Require Hospitalization?

It is more common for depression to be treated by visiting your doctor or counselor. Treatment in the hospital may be necessary if a person has another high risk medical condition or in cases of high suicidal risk.

Suicide

Having suicidal thoughts is common in people with major depression. People usually don't want to die per se, but want to be dead so that they don't have the psychological pain.

Does Depression Last a Long Time?

The sooner you get treatment, the better. Depression, otherwise, can last many months or years. Untreated depression also raises the risk of suicide. Many people experience relief from depression after 2 to 3 months of treatment.

Changes in Lifestyle Which Help with Depression

- Don't try to keep your regular schedule. Slow down. Attend to the most important tasks.
- People with depression often have a lot of negative thoughts about themselves. Notice when this happens and change to other thoughts; don't dwell on negative thoughts.
- Stay involved in actives—even if you don't feel like it. Staying active will help treat the depression, so at least start with one activity per day and increase the number over time.
- It's not a good idea to make big life decisions when you are depressed (e.g., buying a new house or changing your job). If you must, let someone you trust help you with the decision.
- Avoid using drugs or alcohol when you are depressed. Both can make depression worse and less treatable, as well as interact negatively with antidepressant medications.
- Regular exercise is one of the best things that you can do to help your depression lift. If you are not physically active, start with 30 minutes of walking per day, and develop a plan with your doctor to increase.
- Be patient. Depression usually gets better. Give your treatment time to work.

Depression: Action Plan

1. Exercise Daily

Physical activity has been shown to improve mood and help to buffer stress. (For example, take a walk every day, beginning with a duration of time that is realistic for you.)

GOAL: Every day during the next week, I will spend at least _____ minutes doing _____.

2. Make Time for Pleasurable Activities

Even through you may not feel as motivated, or get the same amount of pleasure as you used to, schedule a pleasurable activity each day (for example, work on a hobby, listen to your favorite music, or watch a video).

GOAL: Every day during the next week, I will spend at least _____ minutes doing _____.

3. Spend Time With People Who Can Support You

It's common to avoid contact with people when you are depressed; however, the support of friends and loved ones can help you heal from depression.

Try to explain to them how you feel, but if you can't talk about it, just plan time to be with people who are supportive.

GOAL: During the next week, I will make contact for at least ____ minutes with _____ (name); doing or talking about _____ with _____ (name), doing or talking about _____

4. Don't Dwell on Negative Thoughts

When you are depressed, it is common to replay thoughts in your head about your stress. Having these negative thoughts is normal, but it's important not to dwell on those thoughts too long, because they will add to your stress. Use distracting thoughts or activities to stop dwelling on the negative thoughts.

GOAL: Every day during the next week, I will practice negative thought stopping _____ times.

5. Simple Goals and Small Steps

Depression can be so overwhelming that you feel immobilized. Even small tasks can seem impossible if you have little energy and aren't thinking clearly. Begin by breaking tasks into small steps. Give yourself credit for each step that you accomplish.

GOAL: This week, my goal is to _____ .

Note: Adapted from Community Care of Western North Carolina.

Conclusion

To summarize, integrating behavioral health care into the primary care system will not succeed if specialty mental health is simply merged within primary care practices. To best meet the needs of patients within the IC environment, it is necessary for BHPs to convert evidence-based knowledge into brief interventions that flow with the pace and treatment philosophy of the IC practice. Thus, the goal of creating protocols is to maximize the fidelity of the interventions offered in IC settings. The depression protocol presented in this chapter can serve as a model and guide for the creation of others to standardize care for the many common behavioral issues encountered in IC settings.

Discussion Questions

1. Do clinician's reliably deliver evidence-based interventions? Why do clinicians need checklists?
2. Give an example of a stepped care intervention for someone with panic disorder, from least to most intensive.

3. How much behavioral health treatment can a typical primary care patient tolerate?
4. What are some of the reasons that evidence-based clinical interventions developed for traditional counseling settings must be adapted for the IC setting?

References

Beck, A. T. (1976). *Cognitive therapy and emotional disorders.* New York: International Universities Press.

Budd, R., & Hughes, I. (2009). The dodo bird verdict—controversial, inevitable and important: A commentary on 30 years of meta-analyses. *Clinical Psychology and Psychiatry, 16,* 510–522.

Cummings, N. A. (2002). Are healthcare practitioners economic illiterates? *Families, Systems & Health, 20*(4), 383–393.

Cutcliffe, J. R. (2006). The principles and process of inspiring hope in bereavement counseling: A modified grounded theory study—part one. *Journal of Psychiatric and Mental Health Nursing, 13*(5), 598–603. DOI: 10.1111/j.1365-2850.2006.01019.

Csikszentmihalyi, M. (1990). *Flow: The psychology of optimal experience.* New York: Harper & Row.

De Shazer, S. (1991). *Putting difference to work.* New York: W.W. Norton.

Ellis, A. (1996). *Better, deeper, and more enduring brief therapy: The rational emotive behavior therapy approach.* New York: Brunner/Mazel.

Fredrickson, B. L. (2009). *Positivity: Groundbreaking research reveals how to embrace the hidden strength of positive emotions, overcome negativity, and thrive.* New York, NY: Crown.

Gawande, A. (2009). *The checklist manifesto: How to get things right.* New York: Metropolitan Books.

Harpham, W. (2009). *Only 10 seconds to care: Help and hope for busy clinicians.* Philadelphia: ACP Press.

Haynes, A. B., Weiser, T. G., Berry, W. R., Lipsitz, S. R., Breizat, A. H. S., Dellinger, E. P., Gawande, A. A. (2009). A surgical safety checklist to reduce morbidity and mortality in a global population. *New England Journal of Medicine, 360*(5), 491–499.

Hettema, J. E., & Hendricks, P. S. (2010). Motivational interviewing for smoking cessation: A meta-analytic review. *Journal of Consulting and Clinical Psychology, 78*(6), 868–884.

Hillbrand, M., & Young, J. L. (2008). Instilling hope into forensic treatment: The antidote to despair and desperation. *Journal of the American Academy of Psychiatry and the Law Online, 36*(1), 90–94. Retrieved from http://www.jaapl.org/cgi/content/abstract/36/1/90

Hollister, W., & Rae-Grant, Q. (1972). Principles of effective parsimony. *Canada's Mental Health, 20,* 18–24.

Kim, J. S. (2008). Examining the effectiveness of solution-focused brief therapy: A meta-analysis. *Research on Social Work Practice, 18*(2), 107–116.

Kolata, G. (2004, December 25). Program coaxes hospitals to see treatments under their noses. *New York Times.* Retrieved from http://www.nytimes.com/2004/12/25/health/25medicine.html

Meichenbaum, D. (1977). *Cognitive behavior modification: An integrative approach.* New York: Plenum Press.

Metcalf, L. (1998). *Solution focused brief therapy: Ideas for groups in private practice, schools, agencies and treatment programs.* New York: Free Press.

Miller, W. R. & Rollnick, S. (1991). *Motivational interviewing: Preparing people for change.* New York: Guilford Press.

O'Hanlon, W. H. (1999). *Do one thing different.* New York: Harper Collins.

Patterson, J., Peek, C., Heinrich, R., Bischoff, R., & Scherger, J. (2002). *Mental health professionals in medical settings: A primer.* New York: W. W. Norton.

Prochaska, J. O., & DiClemente, C. C. (1983). Stages and processes of self-change of smoking: Toward an integrated model of change. *Journal of Consulting and Clinical Psychology, 51,* 390–395.

Robinson, P. (2005). Adapting empirically supported treatments to the primary care setting: A template for success. In W. O'Donohue, M. Byrd, N. Cummings, & D. Henderson (Eds.), *Behavioral integrative care: Treatments that work in the primary care setting* (pp. 53–71). New York: Brunner-Routledge.

Seligman, M. (2002). *Authentic happiness: Using the new positive psychology to realize your potential for lasting fulfillment.* New York, NY: Free Press.

Seligman, M. E. P., Steen, T. A., Park, N., Peterson, C. (2005). Positive psychology progress: Empirical validation of interventions. *American Psychologist, 60,* 410–421.

Strosahl, K. (1999). Building primary care behavioral health systems that work: A compass and a horizon. In N. Cummings, J. Cummings, & J. Johnson (Eds.), *Behavioral Health in Primary Care: A Guide for Clinical Integration* (pp. 37–58). Madison, CT: Psychosocial Press.

Strosahl, K. (2001). The integration of primary care and behavioral health: Type II changes in the era of managed care. In N. Cummings, W. O'Donohue, S. Hayes, & V. Follette (Eds.), *Integrated behavioral healthcare: Positioning mental health practice with medical/surgical practice* (pp. 45–70). San Diego: Academic Press.

Strosahl, K. (2005). Training behavioral health and primary care providers for integrated care: A core competencies approach. In W. O'Donohue, M. Byrd, N. Cummings, & D. Henderson (Eds.), *Behavioral integrative care: Treatments that work in the primary care setting* (pp. 15–52). New York: Brunner-Routledge.

Tolin, D. F. (2010). Is cognitive-behavioral therapy more effective than other therapies? A meta-analytic review. *Clinical Psychology Review, 30,* 710–720.

CHAPTER 5

Pharmacologic Competency

CLAIRE DECRISTOFARO

Introduction

The 2003 Institute of Medicine Report, *Health Professions Education: A Bridge to Quality*, recommends that all health professionals achieve five core competencies, namely, the ability to deliver patient-centered care, work in interdisciplinary teams, perform evidence-based practice, apply quality improvement, and utilize informatics (Greiner & Elisa, 2003). The collaborative practice of clinicians across disciplines requires a shared language, appreciation of diagnostic and therapeutic paradigms, and acquisition of foundational knowledge. Individual providers may have an approach that is specific to their discipline, but achieving the goal of collaborative care in real-world practice settings will enhance patient care outcomes.

The educational strategies required for accomplishing this goal of collaborative care fall within many domains, including role issues, as well as the basic and clinical sciences. The author of this chapter is a medical doctor who has been involved in the education of nonphysician providers for many years, both in the academic and clinical setting. The success of an integrated care (IC) model of health care delivery requires an understanding of each profession's competencies and responsibilities. On a personal level, the author has seen IC fail when primary care providers (PCPs) were ignorant of the abilities and practice scope of behavioral health providers (BHPs). This lack of understanding resulted in insufficient utilization of BHPs on the team, and eventual dissolution of the IC model. Those BHPs finding themselves in a situation of underutilization can help educate

PCPs by providing information regarding BHP training, scope of practice, licensure, and certifications. For instance, PCPs can be directed to the National Board for Certified Counselors, which provides an online state board directory (National Board for Certified Counselors, 2009); even the varied professional acronyms used for licensure and certification may be a barrier to collaboration, and resources can be provided to improve understanding and acceptance of the various disciplines within a clinical team (see the appendix at the end of this chapter).

In the author's experience, consultation between the PCP and the BHP goes in two directions. Either the BHP contacts the PCP to discuss or request pharmacologic interventions, or the PCP contacts the BHP for input regarding patient response and/or progress to enhance pharmacotherapeutic decision making. For these consultations to be productive, the BHP needs a working knowledge of drug therapy in order to be an active partner in this type of discussion with the prescribing provider. Thus, a team approach to patient care is supported by a BHP who is able to demonstrate competency in pharmacotherapy. This collaborative environment is at the heart of the Institute of Medicine's vision for a health care system that utilizes the skills and expertise of all team members as they perform appropriate and extended roles (Greiner & Elisa, 2003).

Central Nervous System Neurotransmitters

The central nervous system (CNS) is by definition the combined brain and spinal cord. The peripheral nerves lead out from the spinal cord at different levels of the vertebral bones, and these spinal nerves are named by the level at which they enter or exit the spinal cord (except at the very tail of the spinal cord, which breaks into the *cauda equina*). Note that there is two-way traffic—motor nerves (originating from the CNS) leaving the spinal cord, and sensory nerves (originating from the body) entering it. They are enabled to pass through the vertebral bones due to the presence of *foramina* (holes) in the bones on both sides of the body. Thus, the neurologic system is bilaterally symmetrical, meaning that what happens on the right also happens on the left. Outside of the CNS is the peripheral nervous system (PNS), which is divided into the following: (a) enteric: controlling the gastrointestinal system; (b) somatic: voluntary control of skeletal muscles; and (c) autonomic: involuntary control of smooth muscle, cardiac muscle, and glands. In the PNS, the autonomic nervous system is further divided into opposing divisions called the *sympathetic* (fight or flight, and crisis–stressor response) and *parasympathetic* (rest and repair).

Neurons (nerve cells) are the functional cells that allow this system to work. They synthesize (manufacture) chemicals called *neurotransmitters* (NTs), which allow nerve cells to "transmit" information from one nerve cell to another, or from a nerve cell to another type of cell in the body. The synthesis of these NTs requires the nerve cells to take in chemicals (substrates) and then act on them with enzymes. Some drugs that are used in the management of psychiatric conditions, therefore, will affect the availability or intake of these substrates, or will affect the action of the synthetic enzymes.

After NTs are synthesized, they are released from the neuron into the space between cells, called the *synapse*. The "releasing" neuron is the presynaptic neuron. The NT travels across the synapse and then interacts with chemical receptors on the receiving cell, which can be another neuron, a muscle, or a gland. Thus, some drugs will affect this NT–receptor interaction—they can block or enhance the receptor effect. Other drugs may affect the actual density of receptors on the postsynaptic cell. In fact, the presynaptic neuron also may have receptors that respond to drugs, regulating the release of NT. Once the interaction between NT and the receptor occurs, the postsynaptic cell undergoes a physiologic change that explains the effect of the NT on the body.

Lastly, the NTs don't last forever. Their action is terminated by several methods. These include "reuptake," in which the presynaptic neuron takes the NT back into its cell and degrades it with a degrading enzyme, or the NT may be degraded by an enzyme in the synapse area itself. This gives us another potential pharmacologic target: NT action can be altered by affecting reuptake (increasing or decreasing) and/or by affecting the action of the degrading enzymes. If a degrading enzyme is inhibited, a common drug mechanism, then the chemical it degrades will stay around longer and have enhanced action.

In the CNS, different areas of the brain have varying concentrations of different NTs. It is thought that these different NTs are therefore involved in the distinct brain actions of those areas of the CNS. These actions could be, for example, learning, movement, memory, interpretation of sensory information, emotion, control of body temperature, and so on. Thus, if a behavioral condition is thought to arise from dysfunction of the CNS, it can be theorized that drugs that alter NT concentration (activity) in these brain regions would restore normal function. When reading further about the different types of drugs used in neuropsychiatric disorders, it is important to remember which NTs are targeted and why; different drugs will use different methods of altering the NT effects in the brain.

A lot is known about some CNS NTs, whereas others are still being studied. In general, they are discussed according to categories:

- *Amino acids*: inhibitory, such as glycine and gamma-amino butyric acid (GABA); excitatory, such as glutamate and aspartate (acting on N-methyl D-aspartate, or NMDA, receptors)

- *Acetylcholine*: may be abbreviated "ACh"
- *Monoamines*: serotonin (5-hydroxytryptamine or 5HT), epineph-rine, norepinephrine, and dopamine
- *Other*: peptides, substance P, histamine, thyroid-releasing hor-mone (TRH), and more

Each of these types of NTs interacts with specific receptors, and it is this interaction that is thought to be the basis of brain function. For instance, the interaction of ACh with brain receptors is implicated in learning and memory, and this is why dementia patients are given drugs designed to increase ACh activity in the brain.

Pharmacotherapeutics

What Are Drugs?

Drugs change the biologic functioning of a cell via specific chemical actions; sometimes, though, these actions are poorly understood. Generally, the "class" of a drug is defined by this physiologic action of the drug, and is usually called the *mechanism of action* (MOA) of the drug. In most cases, the reason a drug can exert this action is that the body is already produc-ing endogenous chemicals to exert similar effects. Thus, a drug is often referred to as an *exogenous* compound, because it is administered from the outside, rather than manufactured by the body "inside." Synonymous terminology includes the phrases *applied pharmacology* and *medical phar-macology* when referring to drug use in humans; the terms *pharmacother-apeutics* and *pharmacotherapy* are also used interchangeably. Drugs may be used either to treat or to prevent disease, and they are also used for rec-reational and religious or cultural purposes. The accepted understanding of why a drug's MOA would treat or prevent disease is based on the patho-physiologic etiology of that clinical condition. The term *toxicology* refers to undesirable effects of chemicals on living systems; poisons and toxins also fall into this category. The appendix (item 2) contains further basics of chemistry and chemical terms important to pharmacology.

Important Knowledge Domains in Pharmacology

The BHP will not require as comprehensive or in-depth knowledge of pharmacology as compared to the PCP or disciplines that dispense (i.e., the pharmacist) or administer (i.e., the nurse) drugs. However, pharmacol-ogy competency objectives for the BHP student should include knowledge of the following:

- Available medications on the market that will achieve the desired therapeutic effect

- Mechanism of action (MOA) to achieve therapeutic effects (the "class" of the drug)
- Basic pharmacologic profile for drugs in a particular class (drug–drug and drug–herb interactions, life span issues for pediatrics or geriatrics, and reproductive issues for pregnancy or nursing)
- Safety profile of the drug or drug class (special patient evaluations prior to using the drug, or laboratory or radiologic monitoring while taking the drug)
- Unique patient populations and use of the drug or drug class (age, sex, comorbid conditions, allergy history, cultural issues, and polypharmacy)

Having this knowledge will provide the BHP the necessary background when consulting with the PCP regarding a request to initiate, adjust, discontinue, or add drugs to the patient's regimen. Opportunities for continued collaboration and team interaction will be enhanced when the PCP realizes that the BHP possesses sufficient appreciation of patient selection and follow-up issues.

Additional benefits to collaboration arise when the BHP includes these competencies when providing patient education. In many cases, the BHP will have more regular and frequent interaction with the patient than the PCP, and reinforcement of safety and other considerations will mitigate adverse drug reactions. The BHP can use this knowledge for patient education regarding risks of sudden discontinuation, drug–drug interactions and drug–herb interactions, need for adherence to treatment regimens and monitoring requirements or follow-up, recognition of adverse drug reactions, and assessing if treatment goals have been met. For example, the BHP and/or the patient will be able to contact the PCP if signs and symptoms of toxicity occur, or if the current regimen is not efficacious. Attention to pharmacotherapeutics during every counseling session will enhance optimal outcomes.

Concepts in Pharmacology

Other than newer "engineered" (designer) drugs, the origin of most pharmaceuticals is in nature as botanicals; chemical research aims to modify the parent drug to preserve the drug effect and eliminate unwanted side effects. Thus, one hears of *generations* of drugs. This term means that an initial parent drug has been chemically modified several times to produce similar drugs that retain parent drug function and yet have gained desired improvements. Prescribing decisions are often made using the concept of the *drug of choice* (DOC), meaning that it is preferred, "first-line" (first choice) therapy for a particular clinical condition due to its efficacy and safety profile when used alone (monotherapy).

Drug chemistry has profound effects on drug action. Some drugs are *racemic*, meaning they have a "right" (dextro) or "left" (levo) orientation and are essentially mirror images; hold up your hands in the mirror thumb-to-thumb, and you will see that your hands are mirror images of each other but cannot be superimposed on each other. In fact, racemes are often referred to as *handedness*, and this may affect drug action on the body. Whether or not a drug is water soluble (hydrophilic), or lipid (fat) soluble (lipophilic), will determine the drug's distribution to various tissues and fluids in the body. A lipid-soluble drug will be better able to cross the *blood–brain barrier* (BBB), and thus have CNS effects.

Pharmaceuticals are typically organized by a "class" that either describes the drug effect (e.g., antidepressant), the MOA of the drug (e.g., beta-blocker drugs), or even the chemistry of the drug (e.g., tricyclic antidepressants). Typical MOAs for drugs include the following:

- Receptor agonist (turning on) or antagonist (blocking).
- Enzyme inhibitors (EIs):
  - Inhibiting a biosynthetic enzyme prevents synthesis of a chemical in the body, reducing its physiologic action.
  - Inhibiting a degrading enzyme means *more* of the enzyme's substrate will remain, increasing its physiologic action.
- Pump poisoners (pump inhibitors) prevent a cell membrane pump from moving a substance across the cell membrane.
- Pleiotropic ("many and varied") have multiple effects, not all explained by the presumed MOA.

Indications and Drug Categories

The Food and Drug Administration (FDA) controls the marketing of drugs in the United States. Conditions for which a drug should be used are the "indications," and many prescribers will prescribe only by indication. This information is contained in the drug's prescribing information (PI), also called the *package insert*, which is the printed material accompanying all drugs sold in the United States. Off-label (non-approved) prescribing is not malpractice, and in fact many conditions are routinely treated with drugs that are "nonlabeled" for that clinical condition. These indications also change over time, as pharmaceutical manufacturers provide data from randomized controlled trials (RCTs) that prove drug benefit for that diagnosis. However, if a drug is contraindicated, it means that it should not be used in that particular situation; usually, this involves patient characteristics such as comorbidities, life span subpopulations, or reproductive status. Even here, prescribers have some latitude for decision making. A "relative" contraindication means that there are some risks but the prescriber may determine that the risk–benefit analysis suggests the drug would be beneficial and thus still use the drug. On the other hand, an "absolute" contraindication means that the drug should never be used in this patient. Drug categories in the United States include legal (licit) drugs (as authorized by the FDA); these are legend (require a prescription), over the counter (OTC), or behind the counter (BTC). More than half of the drugs consumed in the United States are OTC; BTC simply means that the pharmacist must determine if the drug should be dispensed (a prescription is still not required). Last, some drugs are known to pose a high risk of substance abuse, and as such are further restricted as *controlled substances* (CS). Many drugs used in behavioral conditions are in fact CS drugs, and the prescriber will need to possess a special certification from the Drug Enforcement Administration (DEA) in order to prescribe these (see the appendix, item 3). Some states have additional certification requirements as well. State monitoring programs exist to provide a retrievable database regarding dispensation of CS drugs that is accessible to prescribers, nurses, and pharmacists. Herbals and nutritional supplements are not under FDA control and are sold as dietary supplements. These products are biologically active and thus have *drug effects*. Therefore they also potentially pose a risk for drug–herbal interactions as well as adverse effects.

Generics and Brand Names

The generic name of the drug may follow specific nomenclature (naming) rules, or it may not. The brand name is a proprietary trademarked name owned by the pharmaceutical company. Note that multinational drug companies may market different drugs under the same brand name in different countries! Usually, generic and brand name drugs are interchangeable in routine use and have bioequivalence per United States Pharmacopeia (USP) standards. However, some drugs used in behavioral management (e.g., amphetamines for attention deficit disorder and some seizure medications) may not be generic–branded interchangeable. The FDA may require a brand-name change if it is determined that the name is too similar to another drug, thus causing dispensing errors. Tall-man letters is a way to draw attention to look-alike drug names, for example metroNIDAZOLE and metFORMIN. The Institute for Safe Medication Practices publishes information on this topic as well as many others (e.g., safe drug disposal and avoiding medication errors) (see appendix, item 4).

Pharmacodynamics and Pharmacokinetics

To simplify, what a drug "does" to the body is pharmacodynamics; what the body "does" to the drug is pharmacokinetics. Pharmacodynamics is what most people think of when discussing a drug's therapeutic or adverse effects, including dose–response effects, efficacy, and toxicity. Pharmacokinetics includes information about absorption, distribution to body systems, metabolization (degradation or changing the drug in some way), and excretion (usually hepatic or renal). This information is important for drug selection if the patient has morbidities that cause reduced (subtherapeutic) or increased (potentially toxic) drug levels in the body. Many laboratory-monitoring requirements for drugs arise from these factors. Some drugs have a therapeutic window, meaning that the serum drug level must be maintained between a lower and an upper value to provide therapeutic effect without becoming toxic; laboratory monitoring is therefore essential.

Adverse Drug Reactions

Adverse drug reactions are dose related (i.e., as the dose increases, so does the chance for a toxic reaction), predictable (i.e., the MOA of the drug results in the toxic effect), or unpredictable. The unpredictable reactions are probably what most people think of when discussing adverse drug reactions (ADRs). These are either idiosyncratic (i.e., unrelated to drug action) or immunologic (i.e., some variant of allergic response). Some of these can be severe and life-threatening (e.g., anaphylaxis, or Stevens–Johnson syndrome).

Antidepressants

Antidepressant drugs are label-indicated for treatment of major depressive disorder (MDD), and many are also label-indicated for other mood disorders such as anxiety syndromes and other conditions with depressed mood. They have traditionally also been used off-label for other conditions (e.g., chronic pain and menopausal hot flashes), and some now have FDA label–indicated use for certain chronic pain syndromes (e.g., post-herpetic neuralgia, diabetic peripheral neuropathy, and fibromyalgia). The MOA of these drugs involves increasing availability of different neurotransmitters (NTs) at the neuron synapse, thus reversing the presumed etiology of the disorder (i.e., reduced NT amount and altered NT receptor density). In learning about classes of antidepressants, focus on which NTs are affected by the drug, whether or not the drug has anxiolytic benefits, and the side effect profile of each class. For depression, depletion of NT serotonin (5-hydroxytryptamine, or 5HT), norepinephrine (NE, a catecholamine formerly called *adrenalin*), and dopamine (DA) are implicated. Raising a type of NT allows us to describe the drug as (respectively) serotonergic, adrenergic, and dopaminergic. One method of increasing NT levels is to prevent its reuptake after it is released; a drug with this mechanism is called a *reuptake inhibitor* (RI). Anxiolysis is usually accomplished with serotonergic drugs. Currently, it is thought that antidepressants that affect more than one NT may be more efficacious and/or better at preventing relapse. Side effects seen with antidepressants may arise from an imbalance in the CNS due to the drug overly affecting one NT and not others (e.g., sexual dysfunction with serotonergic-only drugs).

Issues in Antidepressant Therapy

The goal of therapy is not to simply elicit a response from the antidepressant drug, but to achieve remission and recovery, defined as minimal or no symptoms for 6 or more months, in order to avoid relapse. Initial relief may be seen with somatic symptoms (i.e., headache, backache, chest pain, dyspepsia, limb pain, and insomnia); the dysphoria may take up to 6 weeks to respond. Reinforcing the somatic improvement with the patient may support his or her adherence to the treatment regimen. Patients with a diagnosis of MDD should be treated with drug therapy for at least 2 years to minimize relapse; some management guidelines currently recommend treating the first episode of MDD for 4 to 9 months and treating longer for recurrent episodes (see http://www.psych.org/guidelines/mdd2010). Protection against relapse may be achieved with maintenance therapy that is maintained for at least a year. Even with grief, medication may be of value in restoring normal cognition, assisting the grieving process toward healthy closure.

Any antidepressant can *worsen* depression symptoms and *raise* the risk of suicide. This is true of all ages and may be a higher risk for the pediatric population, including adolescents. Thus, in addition to assessing for efficacy, periodic follow-up is indicated in the initial phase of treatment. This is done usually every week for 4 weeks, then every other week for 4 weeks, and finally at 12 weeks, followed by periodic assessment every 3 to 4 months thereafter. Patients will receive a medication guide from the pharmacy outlining these risks, including information about the heightened concern for the adolescent age group.

Since many antidepressants raise serotonin levels, there is the risk of *serotonin syndrome*. This can develop when more than one serotonergic drug is used in treating the same patient. Examples of other serotonergic drugs are the herbal St. John's wort and some antimigraine drugs (some triptans). Serotonin syndrome can be severe, with hypertensive crisis and severe gastrointestinal and nervous system symptoms. Another negative issue to be considered with serotonergic drugs is the potential for the emergence of a "withdrawal syndrome" if the drug is suddenly discontinued. This is also called *serotonin withdrawal syndrome, serotonin discontinuation syndrome,* and *serotonin cessation syndrome.* Symptoms can be mild or severe, affecting the nervous system and causing gastrointestinal effects and nightmares. Symptoms are extinguished with reinstitution of the drug; to discontinue, a tapering dosage schedule is recommended. (See Table 5.1 for more information about antidepressants.)

Table 5.1
Selected Antidepressants by MOA Class

Class with MOA	CNS NT Effects	Examples of Available Drugs	Adverse Effects	Special Issues
Monoamine Oxidase Inhibitors (MAOIs): this enzyme inhibitor prevents the degradation of NTs, thus raising levels of serotonin and norepinephrine	Dual NT: • Adrenergic (NE) • Serotonergic (5HT)	phenelzine (Nardil), tranylcypromine (Parnate), isocarboxazid (Marplan), selegiline (Deprenyl, Eldepryl and the patch Emsam)	• Orthostatic hypotension, insomnia, sexual dysfunction. • Diet-induced hypertension (tyramine in foods stimulates NE release from neurons & may cause *fatal* hypertensive crisis (e.g., cheese, wine).	• Dietary restriction education to avoid hypertensive crisis • Potential severe (possibly fatal) drug-drug interaction with opiates and serotonergic drugs • Due to side effect profile, not commonly prescribed but may still be used in severe or refractory depression
Tricyclic Antidepressants (TCAs): SRI (serotonin reuptake inhibitor) – raises serotonin levels, NRI (NE reuptake inhibitor) – raises norepinephrine levels, other NT effects	Dual NT: • Adrenergic (NE) • Serotonergic (5HT)	clomipramine (Anafranil), imipramine (Tofranil), amitriptyline (Elavil), nortriptyline (Pamelor), protriptyline (Vivactil), maprotiline (Ludiomil), amoxapine (Asendin), doxepin (Sinequan), desipramine (Norpramin), trimipramine (Surmontil)	• Peripheral anti-cholinergic effects and anti-muscarinic effects cause side effects such as dry mouth, constipation, urinary outflow obstruction, worsening of glaucoma, blurred vision • Central alpha-1-antagonist effects include drowsiness, dizziness, hypotension	• Overdose is especially cardiotoxic to children • Amoxapine has neuroleptic qualities and may cause tardive dyskinesia • Avoided in geriatrics, those with prostate enlargement, glaucoma and suicidal patients (overdose toxicity) • May be needed in those with severe or refractory depression • Traditionally used in low doses for chronic pain

Selective serotonin reuptake inhibitors (SSRIs): only reduce reuptake of serotonin (5HT), thus raising levels of serotonin	Single NT: Serotonergic only (serotonin/5HT)	paroxetine (Paxil & Paxil-CR, Pexeva), sertraline (Zoloft), fluoxetine (Prozac, Sarafem), fluvoxamine (Luvox, Luvox-CR), citalopram (Celexa) and its related S-enantiomer escitalopram (Lexapro)	• Panicogenic (may precipitate panic attacks) • SSRI-induced sexual dysfunction common • Bruxism (teeth grinding, usually while asleep) • Akathisia (restless legs syndrome) • Risk of electrolyte imbalance (hyponatremia), especially important if taking diuretics • Risk of discontinuation syndrome • Risk of drug-drug serotonin syndrome	• This group is commonly first-line for initial therapy • Thought to have overall improved safety profile over MAOIs & TCAs • Anxiolysis an additional benefit • Associated with neonatal complications if given to pregnant woman, including teratogenicity • Many have additional label indications for anxiety disorders • Specific severe drug-drug interactions for individual drugs • Many off-label uses (urticaria, chronic pain)
Combined serotonin and norepinephrine reuptake inhibitors (SNRIs): supposed to raise levels of both serotonin and norepinephrine	Dual NT at low doses: • Adrenergic (NE) • Serotonergic (5HT) Possibly Triple NT at higher doses: • Adrenergic (NE) • Serotonergic (5HT) • Dopaminergic (DA)	venlafaxine-XR (Effexor, Effexor-XR) and its active metabolite desvenlafaxine (Pristiq), duloxetine (Cymbalta)	• All the side effects seen with SSRIs since these are highly serotonergic EXCEPT for sexual dysfunction • Hypertension • Duloxetine with specific Drug-drug interactions • Risk of hepatitis and jaundice	• Useful in prevention of relapse (possibly due to multiple NT effect) • May be useful in severe or refractory depression • Additional label indications for anxiety syndromes and chronic pain disorders

(continued)

Table 5.1 (continued)
Selected Antidepressants by MOA Class

Class with MOA	CNS NT Effects	Examples of Available Drugs	Adverse Effects	Special Issues
Noradrenergic and specific serotonergic antidepressants (NaSSAs): blocks α-2A receptors (does NOT block reuptake pumps), affecting activity of NTs	Dual NT effects: • Adrenergic (NE) • Serotonergic (5HT)	mirtazapine (Remeron)	• Antihistamine properties cause weight gain, sedation, and drowsiness, dizziness, dry mouth • Risk of elevated cholesterol & triglycerides • Risk of neutropenia (agranulocytosis)	• No gastrointestinal or sexual dysfunction side effects as seen with other serotonergic drugs • Cannot use in those with lipid disorders, seizure disorders, the elderly, those with blood dyscrasias, the immuno-compromised, or those with hypersomnia • Potentiates sedatives and specific severe drug-drug interactions
5HT blockers that are also reuptake inhibitors: 5HT receptor antagonist activity, some reuptake inhibition (raises serotonin levels), and α₁-adrenergic blockade (affects activity of norepinephrine)	Dual NT: • Adrenergic (NE) • Serotonergic (5HT) Effects are actually poorly understood.	trazodone (Desyrel), nefazodone (Serzone)	• Highly sedating • Priapism • Leukopenia • Seizure risk • Nefazodone has a BBW for liver failure	• Sedating side effects have been exploited as a hypnotic agent for insomnia • Trazodone is the safest of all antidepressants in terms of overdose

Norepinephrine & Dopamine reuptake inhibitor: Inhibits reuptake, thus raising norepinephrine and dopamine levels; this class has the most dopaminergic effects	buproprion (Wellbutrin & Wellbutrin-SR & Wellbutrin-XL, Zyban)	Dual NT: • Adrenergic (NE) • Dopaminergic (DA)	• Seizure risk • "Stimulating" (anxiety, nausea, insomnia)	• No anxiety benefit (no serotonin effects) • Not for those with renal impairment, seizure disorder or seizure risk, the elderly • Note that sold under another proprietary name is also marketed for smoking cessation
SSRI and serotonin agonist: both a serotonin agonist and reuptake inhibitor raising serotonin levels	Vilazodone (Viibryd)	Single NT: • Serotonergic (serotonin/5HT)	• May cause more GI side effects than other serotonergic agents	• Similar concerns as with all serotonergic drugs • Marketed as having fewer sexual side effects

Drugs for Attention Deficit and Attention Deficit/Hyperactivity Disorder

These conditions may be thought of as a collection of syndromes, and usually require a combination of clinical and psychological services to diagnose and manage them. The conditions can include a symptom profile that mainly affects educational ability, but also can include behavioral issues (e.g., oppositional behaviors). Up to 3–5% of school-age children are affected, usually boys more than girls; however, in recent years, medication for these conditions have been continued for use into the adult age group, and the initial diagnosis may not even be made until college-age or beyond. Due to the majority of patients being enrolled in traditional school settings, management of these conditions involves school services and often collaboration with a multidisciplinary team (clinician, psychologist, and social worker). Typically, the conditions are discussed under the umbrella term of attention deficit/hyperactivity disorder (ADHD).

The hallmark symptom profile includes impulsivity, distractibility, and organizational difficulties. Associated features are learning disabilities, emotional correlates (i.e., low self-esteem, impaired emotional controls, peer rejection, and social isolation), with concomitant development of depression. Substance abuse potential is high due to these latter concerns. The etiology is thought to be a neurochemical disturbance that involves a dysregulation of dopamine and/or norepinephrine in the reticular system, frontal cortex, and basal ganglia. Insufficient activity of catecholamines may result in poor focus and attention. This provides a rationale for drug therapy with both stimulants and nonstimulants, both of which are thought to increase availability of catecholamines in the brain. Other drug classes, such as antidepressants and mood stabilizers, are used for behavioral management.

Much of the controversy surrounding drug therapy for these conditions arises from disagreement as to whether these are actual clinical conditions or whether the symptom profile is a result of the traditional classroom environment. Arguments can be made that the cognitive findings in ADHD actually reflect a different means of learning and problem solving, resulting in more creative results. However, when making a decision regarding drug therapy, the same considerations for any clinical condition can be applied: (a) Is there functional disability that can be restored by drug therapy? (b) What nonpharmacologic approaches should be included in patient management? And (c) is the risk–benefit analysis for the drug(s) appropriate in terms of risk (safety issues) and functional improvement (benefit)?

A final issue to consider with ADHD is that most patients with this disorder will be minor children, and the decision to accept drug therapy is being made by the caregiver or parent. This poses ethical considerations, because these drugs are designed for chronic use and all have potential for harm. Depending on age and cognitive ability, it is worthwhile to involve the child in treatment decisions when appropriate.

Drugs used in management typically fall into categories of stimulant and nonstimulant. Some of these are controlled substances, requiring special prescriptions with limited refills. This may also limit the ability of some nonphysician prescribers to provide these drugs and may be a barrier to care. Many off-label therapies are used, some with specific risks and unproven benefit. The BHP can reinforce the need for accurate and valid information regarding unproven therapies, especially regarding the potential for risk to the patient. (See Table 5.2 for more information about ADHD medications.)

Drugs Used in Obesity Management

Overweight and obesity are considered epidemic in the United States; the Centers for Disease Control have published statistics related to recent trends (see the appendix, item 5). Statistics grouped by age show that people in their 50s tend to be the most overweight (73% of men, 64% of women), and that an estimated 17% of children and adolescents ages 2 to 19 years are obese. For this reason, there has been a recent emphasis on recognition of risk factors, prevention, and safe management. There are many methods used to measure these conditions, including "weight for height" (being 20–30% over ideal weight for height by sex and age tables), Body Mass Index (BMI) for both children and adults, waist-to-hip ratio (WHR), and weight and caliper measurements (triceps skinfold thickness). Waist measurement is also used to gain clues about whether a patient has metabolic syndrome, which has multiple clinical factors, including hyperglycemia, hyperlipidemia, hypertension, and low-HDL cholesterol. Clinical practice guidelines (CPGs) aim to define the condition, promote recognition and prevention strategies, and provide options for management (including nonpharmacologic, surgical, and drug therapies). The goal is for patients to reach and maintain a normal body weight. In recent years, the BMI has achieved prominence as a diagnostic tool with the following categories:

- *For adults*: underweight BMI <18.5, normal weight BMI 18.5–24.9, overweight BMI 25–29.9, obesity BMI 30–39.9, and morbid obesity BMI 40 or greater
- *For children*: percentiles by age and sex are used instead of absolute BMI values (underweight <5th percentile, healthy 5th to 85th percentile, at risk of overweight 85th to <95th percentile, overweight 95th percentile or higher)

Table 5.2
Selected Drugs Used in ADHD Management

Class	MOA	Examples of Available Drugs	Potential Adverse Effects	Special Issues
Stimulant amphetamines (adrenergic stimulants)	Raise levels of catecholamines in the brain	**Methyphenidate (MPH) (Ritalin, Methylin, Concerta, Metadate, Daytrana, Dexedrine)** in immediate- and extended-release as well as patch formulations, **dextroamphetamine** and related congeners (**Dexedrine, Dextrostat, Vyvanse**) in immediate- and extended-release formulations, **amphetamine mixed salts (Adderall)** in immediate- and extended-release formulations	Raise basal metabolic rate (BMR) and associated weight loss or poor weight gain	These are controlled substances with prescribing limitations
			Raise heart rate, blood pressure	Patches are taken off at night
			Cause CNS effects of sleeplessness, anxiety	Some of these require periodic blood tests for liver and renal functions and blood count
			FDA safety alert for ALL stimulants regarding clinical worsening, agitation, irritability, suicidal ideation, hypertension, cardiac arrythmias, chest pain; get initial EKG—ask about palpitations, chest pain and check BP at all visits	Black box warning regarding sudden death in those with cardiac structural problems
				Check height and weight at all visits to monitor pediatric growth
Nonstimulants				
Wakefulness-promoting agents	MOA unknown	**Modafinil (Sparlon)**	Many drug–drug interactions	Controlled substance due to euphoric effects in some people
			Potential for CNS side effects (hallucinations, anxiety, suicidal ideation)	
			Stevens–Johnson syndrome (severe cutaneous drug reaction)	

Selective norepinephrine reuptake inhibitor	Amoxetine (Strattera)	Raises levels of norepiphrine in the brain	Gastrointestinal, dizziness, mood swings, decreased appetite, slowed growth FDA warning regarding severe fatal hepatic injury–symptoms FDA warning regarding increased suicidality in teens	Look for evidence of liver injury (jaundice, itching, dark urine, upper abdominal tenderness, "flu") Observe for clinical worsening and suicidal ideation
Central α-2 agonists	Extended-release guanfacine (Intuniv), extended-release clonidine (Kapvay)	Stimulate presynaptic α-2 receptors in the brain	Bradycardia and heart block, orthostatic hypotension, galactorrhea, sexual dysfunction, worsening of heart failure Abrupt discontinuance may cause acute withdrawal syndrome (hypertension, tachycardia, diaphoresis)	Monitor blood pressure, cardiac function, heart rate Patient education to NOT suddenly stop this drug
Selected OFF-label medications				
Central alpha-2 agonist	Clonidine patch (Catapress TTS Patch)	See above for same class of agent	See above for same class of agents	See above for same class of agents
Central dopaminergic	Amantadine (Symmetrel)	Raises dopamine levels in the brain, NMDA-antagonist	Normally used in Parkinson management	Cannot be used if seizure diagnosis or psychiatric history
Minerals and supplements	Zinc	Various MOA	No evidence of benefit—may cause copper deficiency and anemia	Do not recommend

(continued)

Table 5.2 (continued)
Selected Drugs Used in ADHD Management

Class	MOA	Examples of Available Drugs	Potential Adverse Effects	Special Issues
		St. Johns wort	No evidence of benefit and many potential adverse effects and drug–drug interactions	Do not recommend
Selected behavioral management drugs				
Antidepressant	Multiple MOA	Tricyclics, bupropion extended release, venlafaxine extended release	See information on antidepressants	See information on antidepressants
Mood stabilizers (antipsychotics and anti-epileptics)	Multiple MOA	Anti-epileptics (valproate, carbamazepine)	Each anti-epileptic has multiple considerations for use in terms of safety, monitoring, and patient selection	Check each anti-epileptic for adverse effects, monitoring, life span issues, and patient selection
		Antipsychotics (neuroleptics) both typical and atypical	See information on antipsychotics	See information on antipsychotics

Note that for children, even the terminology is different: The terms for children are *at risk for overweight* (AROW) and *overweight*, rather than *obesity* or *morbid obesity* as used with adults.

Other than addressing cosmetic or psychological issues, the clinical concerns that arise in overweight and obesity are numerous. These include increased risk of cardiovascular disease, non-alcoholic fatty liver diseases (NAFLD), development of type 2 diabetes mellitus (T2DM), neural tube defects in infants of obese women, and dementia in the elderly. For the elderly, the situation is complex—mild to moderate obesity in this age group is not as prognostic of medical complications; in fact, a drop in BMI in the elderly is associated with dementia. Overall "all-cause" mortality in adults increases with BMI at any level above normal. However, if cardiovascular risk factors such as hyperglycemia, hypertension, and hyperlipidemia are managed, the risk to the overweight individual is not as great, buts functional disability levels remain high.

The mainstay for obesity management is proper diet and physical activity. Those areas of the United States with the most sedentary activity (i.e., Appalachia and the South) are known to have the highest incidence of obesity and overweight. Group therapy has proven effective as an adjunct to weight management, and in children, family involvement in the therapeutic regimen is beneficial. For adults, anti-obesity drug therapy is usually considered only when the BMI is >30, or when the BMI is between 27.0 and 29.9 with additional comorbidities. Additional criteria apply for bariatric surgery.

Management of childhood obesity is complex. One concern is that calorie deprivation may result in nutritional deficiencies. Many expert guidelines exist, mainly developed by pediatric professional societies (see the appendix, item 5). For children without comorbidities, the approach is to increase physical activity while maintaining a healthy diet, and allowing the child to "grow into his or her weight."

Drug therapy for obesity includes the use of "fat blockers" (lipase inhibitors that prevent absorption of fats from the gut) and appetite suppressants (essentially, adrenergic stimulants) (see Table 5.3). Both categories of drugs carry specific risks and benefits, although in recent years, reported adverse drug effects have resulted in the withdrawal of many products from the U.S. market. In other countries, another category of drug (the endocannabinoid receptor antagonists, CB-1 receptor blockers) is approved, but these have been denied approval in the United States due to drug side effects. Another approach is to combine drugs that block food-related reward-based behavior (the naltrexone + bupropion SR combination); this has recently been denied approval by the FDA. Lastly, off-label use of some diabetes drugs is seen in the medical community; these include metformin (Glucophage), exenatide (Byetta), and pramlintide (Symlin).

Table 5.3
Selected Label-indicated Anti-Obesity Agents

Class	MOA	Examples of Available Drugs	Potential Adverse Effects	Special Issues
Lipase Inhibitors	Prevent digestion and absorption of fats from the gut ("fat blockers")	Orlistat (Xenical) and the OTC orlistat (Alli – this is half the dose)	• Causes "anal soilage" if a fatty meal is eaten (uncontrolled leakage of fatty feces) • Reduces absorption of fat-soluble vitamins • Risk of liver damage	• Not for those with IBS or Crohn's disease (or other inflammatory GI conditions) • Must take a good multivitamin supplement to replace fat-soluble vitamins (taken several hours away from the drug) • Not for those with nutritional deficiencies (e.g., cystic fibrosis, elderly) • Stop drug if signs of liver injury such as itching, yellow eyes or skin, dark urine, light-colored stools, or loss of appetite
Appetite Suppressants	Adrenergic stimulants raise levels of catecholamines in the CNS	Phentermine (Ionamin, Adipex), mazindol (Sanorex)	• Primary Pulmonary Hypertension (PPH) (fatal and irreversible) • Waxy degeneration of the heart valves • Many now off the market due to adverse drug effects	• Should be used cautiously, if at all (research has shown that weight loss achieved with suppressants will return in 6–24 months, with the person reaching a greater weight than at the start of therapy) • Patients must be told to watch for shortness of breath, edema, chest pain, and syncope as possible herald symptoms of PPH and cardiac valvular damage • These are stimulants, and thus controlled substances

Drugs Used in the Management of Eating Disorders

Management of bulimia (i.e., purging and binge-eating) and anorexia (i.e., starvation) is difficult and requires a multidisciplinary approach. Individuals with these conditions have an abnormal body view and some psychiatric components of obsessive-compulsive disorder. Effective non-pharmacologic approaches include group psychotherapy; in the child, family involvement is key to normalize eating patterns and encourage the social aspects of family mealtimes. These conditions are now recognized as potentially persistent psychological and medical problems, probably persisting for life. Therefore, clinical management includes life-long attention to periodic height and weight measurements, with evaluation for essential nutritional intake.

Pathologic weight loss can be caused by many clinical conditions such as endocrine disorders (e.g., thyroid and Addison's disease, and hypogonadism), gastrointestinal ailments (e.g., celiac disease), and other debilitating conditions (e.g., burns, and HIV/AIDS). Anorexia nervosa patients tend to be predominantly female (20:1 ratio). A huge clinical concern is the 5% mortality statistic (mainly contributed to by suicide). Females may become amenorrheic due to loss of body fat. Hospitalization criteria include the need for force feeding if weight loss exceeds 25% below ideal body weight for height and age/sex. Drug therapy has been disappointing, with antidepressants such as the TCAs and SSRIs used to prevent a "too-full feeling," but these drugs do not prevent relapse, so behavioral and psychological interventions must be provided over the life span.

Bulimia nervosa includes binge-eating episodes and overeating with purging. Patients may use cathartics that cause diarrhea, or emetics that induce vomiting. Medical consequences of recurrent vomiting can be severe, including esophagitis, drug toxicities, dental erosion, and esophageal tears and bleeding. Although various antidepressants have been used as adjuncts, this condition also requires lifelong attention with behavioral and psychological management.

Drugs for Anxiety and Insomnia

Many conditions fall under the general classification of anxiety, and drugs that are used to relieve anxiety are called *anxiolytics*. With some exceptions, these drugs enhance the naturally occurring neurotransmitter gamma-aminobutyric acid (GABA), which is an agonist for the GABA receptor. This type of effect causes sedation, and so really, all anxiolytics are actually also sedatives (see Table 5.4).

In the past, these drugs were called *minor tranquilizers* (the common term was *tranquilizer*), and they are used to control anxiety, for sedation, and also to induce sleep, known as the *hypnagogic effect*. Potential problems are related to the actual action of the drug, including disinhibition (release of punishment-suppressed behavior), euphoria (increases abuse potential), impaired judgment, impulsivity, anterograde amnesia, and anesthesia. The effects are usually dose dependent, and different drugs have different levels of sedation. Use for different clinical settings therefore depends on the drug and the dose, and can range from relief of anxiety and treatment of insomnia to use in the anesthesia setting (e.g., for procedural sedation or general anesthesia). Drug classes by chemical include benzodiazepines, nonbenzodiazepines, barbiturates, and others. The barbiturates are rarely used today, other than for induction of general anesthesia. Note that combination with any other sedatives (e.g., alcohol) will create a synergistic situation, enhancing the sedative effect of both agents. Due to the abuse potential of these drugs, most are classified as controlled substances. Some of these drugs are used to treat insomnia in the short term, but long-term use (e.g., for insomnia) may cause problems with dependence, tolerance, and abnormal sleep. Long-term use resulting in dependence, or the development of substance use disorder, may require using another drug in the same class to wean the patient from the substance and avoid withdrawal; drugs with a slower onset of action may have less potential for abuse and these are often used in detoxification regimens.

Why is one drug considered an anxiolytic and another a sedative? This is related to the chemical properties of the drug, which determine how fast the drug enters the brain and has its effect (onset). These drugs can pass through the placenta, and may cause respiratory depression in the newborn, so they are therefore not recommended for use by pregnant women. If these drugs have been taken over the long term, they cannot be suddenly discontinued, but rather need to be tapered down in order to avoid withdrawal syndrome.

There are drugs that can be used in the clinical setting of anxiety and insomnia that are not controlled substances. These include the nonsedating anxiolytics (e.g., buspirone, whose MOA is as a serotonin receptor agonist) and melatonin-receptor agonists (e.g., ramelteon). There are also many OTC sleep aids available to the general public, most of which are antihistamines that have sedating side effects. These should also not be taken long term (no OTC products are designed to be taken long term); the goal is to restore normal sleep patterns and sleep quality, and these drugs interfere with normal sleep patterns. Long-term use may result in a withdrawal effect called *rebound*, with disturbed sleep and nightmares. Discontinuation will require a taper and may take a long time.

Prescription sleep aids may be benzodiazepines, nonbenzodiazepines, melatonin agonists, or antihistamines. Some of these products have sophisticated drug delivery systems so that medication is released immediately for initial sedation, and then released later during the sleep period to keep the person from waking up. Others are designed to have a shorter length of action. The FDA has mandated that all sleep aids have a warning for possible anaphylaxis (i.e., severe swelling and edema of the face and airway) as well as *complex sleep-related behaviors* which may include sleep driving, making phone calls, and preparing and eating food—*all while asleep*—with no memory of having done so.

Because of the potential for long-term problems with sleep quality, dependence, and tolerance, chronic anxiety syndromes and chronic insomnia are usually managed with other types of drugs, such as the serotonergic antidepressants or antidepressants with sedating side effects. Evaluation of the insomnia will also be a clue to treatment, as insomnia may accompany other disorders (anxiety syndromes and depression) and will respond to treatment of the underlying condition. Anxiety syndromes include general anxiety disorder (GAD), posttraumatic stress disorder (PTSD), panic attack and panic disorder, social phobia (social anxiety disorder), and obsessive-compulsive disorder (OCD). Depending on the particular anxiety syndrome, most practitioners now rely on drugs that are serotonergic antidepressants, nonsedating anxiolytics, and even beta-blockers for symptom relief.

Last, note that some of these agents have other uses. Benzodiazepines (especially clonazepam and diazepam) are used for seizure disorders as anti-epileptics. Benzodiazepines can also be used to reduce symptoms of Meniere's disease as they lessen tinnitus and allow the patient to fall asleep. Others may be found in prescription headache medications, in combination with analgesics.

Antipsychotic Drugs

The name of this class of drugs can be misleading. Originally, psychiatric conditions were grouped as *neuroses* (less severe) or *psychoses* (more severe). Thus, the drug names followed these designations: *minor tranquilizers* for neuroses (e.g., anxiety syndromes) and *major tranquilizers* for psychoses (e.g., schizophrenia, mania). Sometimes these drugs are called *neuroleptics* since they produce a state of apathy, lack of initiative, and limited range of emotion; when used to treat psychotic symptoms, there is a reduction in confusion and agitation with a normalization of psychomotor activity (from the Greek *lepsis*, meaning "to take hold"). The MOA of these drugs is to act in the CNS as a dopamine antagonist.

The terms for psychiatric diagnosis have changed to Axis-I disorders, with specific criteria for diagnosis, but the idea of psychotic behavior still exists, mainly to emphasize loss of reality testing (i.e., presence of hallucinations and/or delusions), often with severe agitation, and a suggestion of

Table 5.4
Selected Prescription Drugs Used for Anxiety and Insomnia

Class	MOA	Examples of Available Drugs	Potential Adverse Effects	Special Issues
Benzodiazepines	Agonist for the brain GABA receptor creates sedating and hypnogogic effects	diazepam (Valium), triazolam (Halcion), alprazolam (Xanax, Xanax-XR, orally disintegrating Niravam), chlordiazepoxide (Librium), lorazepam (Ativan), clonazepam (Klonopin), oxazepam (Serax), temazepam (Restoril)	Dependence, tolerance, abuse potential; Drug–drug interactions; Sleep quality disturbance (interference with stages of sleep); FDA warning regarding anaphylaxis; FDA warning regarding complex sleep-related behaviors	These are controlled substances due to abuse potential; Nontherapeutic use associated with impaired judgment; Even therapeutic use may cause amnesia and abnormal behaviors
Nonbenzodiazepine sleep aids	Agonist for the brain GABA receptor creates sedating and hypnogogic effects	zolpidem (Ambien, Ambien-CR), zaleplon (Sonata), eszopiclone (Lunesta)	No effect on the stages of sleep; Little tolerance; Next-day drowsiness, dizziness, "drugged feeling"; Rebound insomnia, sleepwalking, and cognitive reactions (hallucinations, amnesia, confusion); FDA warning regarding anaphylaxis; FDA warning regarding complex sleep-related behaviors	These are controlled substances eszopiclone (Lunesta) has FDA indication for long-term use
Melatonin agonists	Agonist on melatonin receptor in brain	ramelteon (Rozerem)	Increased prolactin; Decreased testosterone; Potential thyroid function issues	Some drug–drug interaction issues; No rebound on discontinuation

Category	Drug	Mechanism	Adverse effects / cautions	Notes
Prescribed alcohols	choral hydrate (Noctec)	Affects multiple systems in the brain ("global" effect)	Long-term use leads to tolerance, dependence, and withdrawal nightmares on discontinuation; Can be fatal in *overdose* as low as 4 g (which is four of the 500 mg capsules)	Very inexpensive; Often used in institutional settings; May be used prior to procedures in pediatrics
Nonsedating anxiolytics	buspirone (Buspar)	Agonist for serotonin receptor in brain	May take several weeks to work	Used in benzodiazepine addiction; Used in smoking cessation
Antihistamines	hydroxyzine (Vistaril, Atarax)	CNS sedation from disruption of neurocortical transmission via blockade of ion channels	Anticholinergic side effects such as dry mouth, urinary outflow obstruction, blurred vision, worsening of glaucoma, confusion (may be more important in the elderly); Overdose can cause respiratory depression and hypotension	Has been used off-label for many conditions; Also an anti-emetic with skeletal muscle relaxant and analgesic properties; Not a controlled substance
Beta-blockers	propranolol (Inderal)	Antagonist of beta-receptors in sympathetic nervous system	Potential adverse effects on serum glucose and lipids; May cause hypotension and bradycardia	Doses used for anxiety are very low; Typically used prior to anxiety-provoking activity (e.g., stage fright)
Antidepressants	TCA antidepressants, for example doxepin (Silenor)	The sedating antidepressants may be used at bedtime for their sedating quality to enhance sleep onset	Anticholinergic side effects such as dry mouth, urinary outflow obstruction, blurred vision, worsening of glaucoma; Confusion (may be more important in the elderly); Overdose especially cardiotoxic to children	See section on antidepressants
	SSRI and SNRI antidepressants	The serotonergic antidepressants are used to normalize sleep patterns and sleep quality		See section on antidepressants

familial or genetic predisposition with a triggering event. The more common conditions in this group are schizophrenia and bipolar affective disorder (manic-depressive illness); sometimes, you may hear autism referred to as *childhood schizophrenia* because of some similarities in the symptom profile. In addition, some nonpsychiatric conditions may be associated with psychotic behaviors or symptoms, and may be treated with these drugs. Examples include dementia (with agitation), head injury, and other delirium states.

Schizophrenia should not be confused with the very rare multiple personality disorder called *schizoid disorder*. The condition may have "positive" symptoms (i.e., agitation, delusions, and hallucinations; this includes brief psychotic reaction) or "negative" symptoms (i.e., flat affect, anhedonia, and social withdrawal). When a diagnosis of schizophrenia is considered, a clinical evaluation is mandatory:

- Many medical conditions can mimic this severe psychiatric illness (e.g., CNS infections, various hormone imbalances, vitamin deficiencies, lupus, and porphyria), and so a complete medical evaluation is needed that includes a physical exam, and laboratory and possibly imaging studies.
- Some drugs can cause schizophrenic behaviors or symptoms (e.g., cocaine, corticosteroids and anabolic steroids, anti-Parkinson drugs, and hallucinogens), and so a review of medications is also indicated as part of the clinical evaluation.

One important consideration in the use of antipsychotic drugs is that they are typically used in the long term. With long-term administration, there is the potential for many significant adverse drug effects, some of which are permanent and even life-threatening. For this reason, many experts recommend that prior to committing a patient to long-term therapy with these drugs, an *informed consent* should be signed, outlining these potential risks. Common side effects include drop in blood pressure (hypotension), anticholinergic or antimuscarinic side effects (such as dry mouth, constipation, urinary outflow obstruction, worsening of glaucoma, and blurred vision), seizures, hypothermia, cardiac arrhythmias, respiratory depression, restlessness (an "urge to move" called *akathisia*), and hormone imbalances that may result in nipple discharge (galactorrhea). Although the above-mentioned side effects are potentially serious, the more important issues are as follows:

- Development of a movement disorder called *extrapyramidal syndrome* (EPS), and *tardive dyskinesia*. EPS includes a variety of drug-induced dystonias (acute muscular spasms such as torticollis), an appearance similar to Parkinsonism (slow movements or bradykinesia, shuffling gait, muscular rigidity, and tremor), and motor restlessness (akathisia). Tardive dyskinesia may be considered a subset of EPS, with abnormal movements of the hand and face, characterized by involuntary repetitive movement of the lips and tongue (buccolingual dysplasia), limbs (choreoathetosis), and eyes (rapid blinking movements). After 7 years of continuous treatment, tardive dyskinesia can occur in up to 25% of patients. Although there are some drug treatments available, for the most part these will not fully remedy the condition. These conditions can even develop in babies born to mothers who take antipsychotics during pregnancy (see appendix, item 6).

- Development of neuroleptic malignant syndrome (NMS) is actually a severe form of EPS, and is similar to malignant hyperthermia syndrome, which can occur during surgery as a result of anesthetic drugs. It includes hyperthermia, muscular rigidity, elevations in white blood cell count (leukocytosis), and evidence of muscle damage (laboratory testing with creatine kinase levels). This can be life-threatening and requires emergent hospital-level care.
- Metabolic consequences include weight gain, hyperglycemia that appears similar to type-2 diabetes mellitus, and elevated lipids (cholesterol). These metabolic changes are thought by many to cause the known increased risk of cardiovascular events in the elderly (including stroke in the elderly demented), and increased risk of death in the elderly.
- Foundational knowledge concerning neuroleptics involves recognizing that they are often referred to as either "traditional" (first-generation) antipsychotics (FGAs) or "atypical" (second-generation) antipsychotics (SGAs). The FGAs are characterized as *low potency* or *high potency*; the high potency may have an increased risk of EPS or tardive dyskinesia. These may also be fatal to patients with a diagnosis of a specific type of dementia (i.e., Lewy body dementia). The SGAs were initially thought to have a lower risk of EPS or tardive dyskinesia; over time, it has been discovered that they also carry a risk of this side effect, with additional concerns of metabolic side effects including significant weight gain, stroke in the elderly demented, and increased death rates in the elderly (see above). Other than long-term use, many of these drugs are available in injectable formulations that may be used for acute management (one-time dosing) of agitation or delirium, usually in the hospital setting. (See Table 5.5 for more information about antipsychotic medications.)

Table 5.5
Selected Antipsychotic (Neuroleptic) Medications

Class	MOA	Examples of Available Drugs	Potential Adverse Effects	Special Issues
First-generation antipsychotics ("traditional" FGAs)	Dopamine antagonist in the CNS	*Selected high potency:* molinedone (Moban), perphenazine (Trilafon), loxapine (Loxitane), trifluoroperaxine (Stelazine), flupehanzine (Prolixin), thiothixene (Navane), haloperidol (Haldol), pimozide (Orap) *Selected low potency:* chlorpromazine (Thorazine), thioridazine (Mellaril), clozapine (Clozaril, FazaClo ODT), mesoridazine (Serentil)	*High potency:* Low sedation Low anticholinergic side effects Higher occurrence of EPS and tardive dyskinesia *Low potency:* High levels of sedation High levels of anticholinergic side effects Lower occurrence of EPS and tardive dyskinesia	See notes regarding issues such as EPS and tardive dyskinesia, deaths in the elderly demented, and metabolic issues Typically, these agents are second-line for long-term use (only used long-term after failure with the SGAs below)
Second-generation antipsychotics ("traditional" SGAs)	Dopamine antagonist in the CNS	risperidone (Risperdal), olanzapine (Zyprexa), quetiapine (Seroquel, Seroquel XR), ziprasidone (Geodon), aripiprazole (Abilify), paliperidone (Invega, Invega Sustenna), iloperidone (Fanapt), asenapine (Saphris), lurasidone (Latuda)	Sedation (but less than the FGAs) Anticholinergic side effects (but less than the FGAs) Potential for EPS or tardive dyskinesia after very long-term use or use at higher doses More concerns regarding metabolic issues such as hyperglycemia & hyperlipidemia than in the FGAs	See notes regarding issues such as EPS and tardive dyskinesia, deaths in the elderly demented, and metabolic issues Typically, these agents are first-line for long-term use, due to their lower risk of EPS or tardive dyskinesia

Mood-Stabilizing Drugs

These medications are used to provide an "antimanic" benefit, preventing mood swings. Typically, the conditions in which they are used include bipolar affective disorder (BPAD, formerly known as *manic-depressive illness*) and refractory depression. These individuals usually require both an antidepressant and a mood stabilizer to prevent mania.

There are many categories of drugs that can provide this mood-stabilizing effect, including some antipsychotics (mainly the SGA neuroleptics), lithium, and various anti-epileptic drugs (AEDs) (see Table 5.6). For refractory depression and bipolar illness, there are label-indicated fixed-dose proprietary combination products (e.g., olanzapine + fluoxetine). Sometimes patients on lithium therapy may need additional mood stabilizers for acute management, because the onset of lithium therapy is slow.

Lithium therapy is probably the drug of choice for antimanic control in bipolar illness, unless contraindicated. Monitoring is required to ensure a proper therapeutic level to avoid subtherapeutic effect and toxicity, as well as for specific potential clinical toxicities such as development of hypothyroidism. There are many drug–drug interactions, including with anesthesia drugs. In addition to use in bipolar illness, sometimes this drug is used to manage agitation in schizophrenia.

Drugs Used in Autism Spectrum Disorders

Autism (pervasive developmental disorder) manifests with stereotypic behaviors, lack of normal social interactions, communication abnormalities, and associated developmental delay. "High-level" (high IQ) autistic persons may gain ability to function in society, but all will retain deficits for life. Many of the antipsychotic drugs are used mainly to control behavioral manifestations. Most drugs used in behavioral management, or for alleviation and control of symptoms, are used off-label. There are multiple therapeutic approaches, based on different models of etiology. A good resource is the National Institute of Mental Health website (appendix, item 8).

Nonpharmacologic approaches include hearing and speech pathology services. One model of the illness suggests an improper sensory nerve function so that normal sounds are heard by the autistic child as excruciatingly loud. Intensive speech and language pathology with sound recognition and tolerance training helps both communicative skills and other deficits. Many interventions that include behavioral and educational modification typically are intensive therapy for targeted skills as opposed to global improvement, such as reward–punishment models as

Table 5.6
Selected Mood Stabilizers

Drug Class	MOA	Available Drugs	Issues and Adverse Effects
Second-generation antipsychotics (SGA neuroleptics)	See Table 5.5.	Typically for this purpose, olanzapine (Zyprexa), ziprasidone (Geodon), aripiprazole (Abilify), risperidone (Risperdal), quetiapine (Seroquel)	See Table 5.5.
Anti-epileptic drugs (AEDs)	See Table 5.7.	Typically for this purpose, carbamazepine XR (Equetro), valproate (Depakote), lamotrigine (Lamictal)	See Table 5.7.
Lithium	May affect sodium channels in the CNS	Lithium (Eskalith), lithium CR (Eskalith CR)	Hypothyroidism Elevated white blood cell count (leukocytosis) Acne, psoriasis Teratogenesis (not for pregnancy or nursing mothers) Nephrogenic Diabetes Renal damage Pseudotumor cerebri (increased intracranial pressure) Unmasking of Brugada syndrome (sudden cardiac death in young adults)

well as intensive educational strategies. Dietary exclusion trials may also be employed, such as a gluten-free diet.

Pharmacologic management may be used to reduce or control symptoms, assist with educational support, or treat associated morbidity. These drugs may include medications from many of the prior categories of drugs that have already been discussed. Examples include the following:

- *Neuroleptics*: Label-indicated medication does include the SGA risperidone (Risperdal) to control irritability in ages 5 to 16 years old. Other neuroleptics may be used off-label to manage agitation and aggression.
- *Antidepressants*: Other (off-label) examples include the SSRI–SNRI and tricyclic antidepressants. They may improve mood and behavior, and possibly reduce repetitive behaviors. However, these may worsen agitation or induce mania.
- *Anti-epileptic drugs*: These may be used to manage seizure disorder (one in four autistic children develops epilepsy), or as mood stabilizers to prevent mania or reduce aggression.
- *Stimulants*: These may be prescribed off-label to improve attentiveness and support educational interventions.
- *Experimental drugs*: These are chosen for use based on varying neurotransmitter theories, so that drugs that are seemingly not psychiatric or behavioral medications, may be used. Examples are the gastrointestinal anti-acid H2-blockers, such as famotidine (Pepcid) and intravenous oxytocin (a pituitary hormone) for repetitive behaviors in Asperger's syndrome.

Dementia Drugs

Dementia is considered a progressively worsening cognitive disorder, with loss of memory and executive (decision-making) capacity. Most dementia syndromes affect the elderly. Associated findings include changes in personality that actually may be more upsetting to loved ones than the cognitive deficits. In the United States and northern Europe, Alzheimer's dementia is the most common, followed by vascular dementia (associated with the same risk factors as for cardiovascular disease, such as hypertension and dyslipidemia), then the "mixed" dementias (combinations of Alzheimer's and vascular), and lastly other dementias (such as Lewy body dementia) (see http://www.ninds.nih.gov/disorders/dementiawithlewy-bodies/dementiawithlewybodies.htm). The etiologic theory underlying dementia development is a loss (by death) of cholinergic neurons in the CNS as well as increased glutamate neurotransmission that overstimulates NMDA receptors, again resulting in death of brain neurons. Different dementia syndromes may have additional pathologic characteristics (e.g., beta-amyloid plaque in Alzheimer's, and Lewy bodies in LBD).

Typically, the symptoms can be described as "ABC": activity (functional ability to perform tasks of daily life), behavior (depression, agitation, outbursts, and resistance to care), and cognition (memory, language, attention, and orientation). Cognitive deficits are considered the hallmark of dementia. Goals of therapy include slowing the progression of the disease, improving the symptom profile for better quality of life for both the patient and caregiver, and reducing the need for institutionalization and antipsychotic therapy. In addition to nonpharmacologic approaches, such as providing a regulated schedule of daily activities and a calm environment, drug therapy is available that meets some of these goals. Currently, though, no drug therapy can stop progression of the illness. Eventually, despite all available therapies, the condition progresses toward final deterioration and death.

Primary dementia drugs are thought to address the underlying neurochemical pathology of the condition (see Table 5.7). Loss of cholinergic neurons, and neurons involved in the glutamate pathway (NMDA receptors) are thought to be involved in learning and memory. Thus, cholinesterase inhibitors (i.e., AChEIs and ChEIs) are "cholinergic" because they inhibit the enzyme that degrades acetylcholine, thus keeping more of this NT available at the synapse and helping to maintain the health of cholinergic neurons. Other drugs, the NMDA antagonists, are thought to prevent the overstimulation of NMDA receptors, again preserving the health and life span of neurons.

Adjunctive (secondary) drugs used in dementia management include antioxidants and adrenergic agents active in the CNS. Due to associated behavioral and psychiatric conditions that may accompany dementia, other drug categories are often required. These include treatment of agitation and psychosis with antipsychotics (neuroleptics) either acutely or long term (with specific known toxicities in this population of stroke and increased death rate in the elderly). Depression may be managed with antidepressants, but those with anticholinergic side effects (e.g., the TCAs) should be avoided. Treatment of sleep disturbances may be managed with sedating antidepressants (e.g., trazodone) and nonbenzodiazepine sedatives (e.g., zolpidem and zaleplon); again, avoidance of those with anticholinergic side effects is important (e.g., the OTC sleep aids such as diphenhydramine). Bright light therapy may be of benefit here as well.

Complementary and alternative therapies are often sought out by family members of patients afflicted with dementia. These have included supplements such as gingko biloba (Egb), hyperzine-A (club moss), and melatonin. To date, no large-scale randomized clinical trial has shown any of these to be of benefit. Of even greater importance is that these supplements can cause potential toxicities (e.g., gingko can cause bleeding, cardiac palpitations, and seizures).

Family members of dementia patients are often afraid of developing the illness themselves, and may ask about prevention strategies. Prevention with drug therapy has been disappointing, although an investigational vaccine against beta-amyloid has been successful in the mouse model of Alzheimer's disease. Other preventive strategies that may hold benefit for prevention include regular exercise, attaining a higher level of education, moderate alcohol intake, and maintaining robust social networks and interaction.

Drug Therapy for Chronic Pain

Pain is an unpleasant sensory and emotional experience associated with actual or potential tissue damage or described in terms of such damage. Acute pain is the normal, predicted physiological response to a noxious chemical, thermal, or mechanical stimulus and typically is associated with invasive procedures, trauma, and disease; it is generally time-limited. Chronic pain is a state in which pain persists beyond the usual course of an acute disease or healing of an injury, or that may or may not be associated with an acute or chronic pathologic process that causes continuous or intermittent pain over months or years. Perception of and reaction to pain are influenced by social and environmental cues, as well as by cultural norms and personal experience. Both cortical and limbic systems are involved in conscious awareness and perception of pain. Recognition of location, intensity, and quality of pain is mediated by the processing of signals from the spinothalamic tract, to the thalamus, and then on to the somatosensory cortex. Pain information processing in the brainstem, midbrain, and limbic system appears to mediate affective, motivational, and behavioral responses to painful stimuli. We are capable of modulating pain through antinociceptive pathways using NTs such as NE, serotonin, GABA, and cannabinoids, all of which modifies our awareness of the sensation. However, other NTs may facilitate pain transmission (e.g., substance P and glutamate).

Clinically, it may be important to think of different types of pain to better understand the individual's pain response and also to develop approaches to pain management that will be more effective. Some different "types" of pain include the following:

- *Somatic*: originating from bone, ligaments, tendons, muscle, or fascia. This is dull, poorly localized pain.
- *Visceral*: originating from the body's internal organs. This is aching, difficult-to-localize, "referred" pain (localized to another area of the body) that, involving smooth muscle (e.g., ureter or gut), may be colicky.

Table 5.7
Selected Primary Dementia Drugs

Class of Drug	MOA	Selected Available Drugs	Issues and Concerns
Cholinesterase inhibitors	Inhibit acetylcholinesterase and butylcholinesterase in the CNS, thus preserving acetylcholine (ACh) levels and protecting cholinergic neurons from death	*First generation:* tacrine (Cognex) *Second generation:* donepezil (Aricept), rivastigmine (Exelon), galamantamine (Razadyne)	First generation no longer used due to side effects Some of the second generation are available in multiple formulations (e.g. patch delivery systems) May exacerbate pulmonary disease (asthma, chronic bronchitis) May cause "Pisa" syndrome (severe lower back spasm) May exacerbate peptic ulcer Some interactions with anesthesia drugs
NMDA-receptor antagonists	Prevent overstimulation of NMDA receptors in the glutamate pathway, protecting neurons from death	memantine (Namenda, Namenda-XR)	Headache, confusion, fatigue, somnolence, dizziness Dyspnea, cough Constipation

- *Cutaneous*: originating from injury to skin and skin structures; a high concentration of nerve endings allows for good localization (lacerations or burns).
- *Neuropathic*: originating from nerves, spinal cord, or brain. This is burning, tingling, and hypersensitivity to touch or cold, or *lancinating*.
- *Inflammatory*: The result of an inflammatory response. Inflammatory cytokines (chemical mediators) like PGE2 produced by the COX2 enzyme, bradykinins, and others bind to neuron receptors and increase their excitability (increasing pain sensation). This is perceived as burning or itching.
- *Psychogenic*: This is entirely or mostly related to psychological disorder (rare).

Although acute pain alerts us to a physical problem and is limited in duration, it also causes a physiological response in the autonomic nervous system of increased heart rate, sweating, and elevated blood pressure and respiratory rate. However, chronic pain no longer causes these responses. This may make it difficult for providers and others to believe the patient's report of pain because more "objective" signs may not be present. You will therefore hear chronic pain discussed as the *disease of pain*, where the pain has outlasted any underlying disorder or healed injury. Pain management requires clinicians to treat chronic pain as separate from any causative factor. Both nonpharmacologic and pharmacologic interventions are available as interventions for the management of chronic pain. The choice of therapy usually depends on the type and level of severity of the chronic pain.

When thinking of pain control, the layperson assumes that analgesics will be used (see Table 5.8). All analgesics raise the threshold for pain perception, and also reduce the subjective response to pain (thus, even continued pain may be better tolerated). However, in addition to typical analgesic drug classes, a wide variety of drug classes may be employed to manage special pain syndromes (e.g., neuropathic pain). One consideration regarding analgesics is that many are controlled substances (CS) due to their risk of substance abuse and drug diversion. These analgesics may also cause euphoria, tolerance, and dependence. The CS analgesics may be opioids, or may be analgesics of a different drug class. Other organ system side effects can include sedation, respiratory depression, cough suppression, and constipation, among others. Many other analgesics are non-CS drugs; this does not mean, however, that they have no potential for adverse drug effects. The non-CS analgesics are used to manage mild to moderate pain, and can be added to opioids as adjunctive drugs. Because an adjunctive drug helps the primary drug to work better, this means that a lower dose of opioid will be required.

Table 5.8
Selected Noncontrolled Substance Analgesics

Class	MOA	Examples	Comments
Salicylates (aspirin, ASA)	Both anti-inflammatory and analgesic via multiple MOA, including blockade of cyclo-oxygenase enzyme from synthesizing prostaglandins and thromboxanes; some action against inflammatory cells; also reduces fever	*Acetylated:* aspirin extended release (Zorprin), aspirin enteric coated (Ecotrin, Bayer), diflusinal (Dolobid), olsalazine (Dipentum), mesalamine (Pentasa) *Nonacetylated:* magnesium salicylate (Magan), choline salicylate (Arthropan), choline magnesium salicylate (Trilisate), salsalate (Disalcid, Mono-Gesic)	Acetylated salicylates have side effects of potentially serious gastrointestinal bleeding, especially if combined with alcohol or anticoagulant drugs May also confer cardiovascular protection Nonaceylated salicylates cause less gastrointestinal side effects but do not confer cardiovascular protection Low doses unlikely to cause kidney damage (but high doses in the long term may) Unsafe in pregnancy
Nonsteroidal anti-inflammatory drugs (NSAIDs)	Both anti-inflammatory and analgesic via MOA of inhibition of cyclo-oxygenase enzyme (prevents synthesis of prostaglandins); also reduces fever	*Nonselective NSAIDs:* fenoprofen (Nalfon), flurbiprofen (Ansaid), ibuprofen (Advil, Motrin, Rufen), ketoprofen (Orudis, Oruvail), naproxen (Aleve, Anaprox, Naprosyn), oxaprozin (Daypro), indomethacin (Indocin), sulindac (Clinoril), tolmetin (Tolectin), nabumetone (Relafen), piroxicam (Feldene), diclofenac (Cataflam, Voltaren (Feldene), diclofenac (Cataflam, Voltaren (TOPICAL Flector Patch, and Voltaren gel), etodolac (Lodine), ketorolac (Toradol), meclofenamate (Meclomen) *Selective NSAIDs:* celecoxib (Celebrex)	Potentially serious gastrointestinal bleeding, especially if combined with alcohol or anticoagulant drugs (selective have less of this risk) Long-term use may cause kidney damage (selective have less of this risk) Potential for liver damage (especially if combined with alcohol) May raise blood pressure (hypertension) and may increase cardiovascular risk Many are over-the-counter (OTC) Unsafe in third trimester of pregnancy May block aspirin's cardiovascular protection Selective NSAIDs may cause cardiovascular risk (several removed from market due to this side effect) May interact with some blood pressure drugs

Acetaminophen	Acetaminophen (multiple brand names, OTC)	Some minor cyclo-oxygenase inhibition (like the aspirins and NSAIDs); also effects on the CNS to reduce fever and pain	Long-term use may cause kidney damage (selective have less of this risk) Half of the cases of acute liver failure are due to acetaminophen toxicity; do not take > 4 grams/day; do not drink alcohol > 3 drinks per day May raise blood pressure and may increase cardiovascular risk
Tramadol	tramadol (Ultram, Ultracet [37.5 mg tramadol + 325 mg acetaminophen]), Tramadol ER (once daily), Tramadol ODT ([orally disintegrating tablets])	Analog of codeine, has agonist effects on CNS opiate receptors	Highly controversial Some categorize as a synthetic opiate because its chemical structure is similar to codeine Other countries and some states *do* categorize this as a controlled substance Many drug–drug interactions Should not be mixed with serotonergic drugs due to risk of serotonin syndrome (SSRI, TCA, MAOI, etc.) May increase seizure risk
Ziconotide	ziconotide (Prialt)	Blocks ion channels in the brain to prevent release of nociceptive NTs	Intrathecal drug for severe chronic pain unresponsive to other therapies Programmable implanted microinfusion device is used to deliver the drug to the brain ventricles
Antidepressants	milnacipran (Savella)	SNRIs approved for management of chronic pain syndromes, including neuropathic pain	See information relating to serotonergic antidepressant drugs
	duloxetine (Cymbalta)		See information relating to antidepressant SNRI drugs

On the other hand, drugs used for moderate to severe pain tend to be controlled substance analgesics such as the opioids. In our brain, there are opiate-type chemicals that are naturally occurring; these are called opiopeptics (e.g., enkephalins and endorphins). They are released during pain and stress and work by acting as agonists on opioid receptors (e.g., *mu, kappa,* and *delta*). Note that these opioid receptors occur outside of the brain as well, explaining some of the side effects of opioids. Drugs that are opioids have agonist action on these same opiate receptors.

Considerations in Opioid Use

Opioids are sometimes referred to by the layperson as *narcotics*. Narcosis is actually the sleepiness and mental depression that occurs with opioid use. Morphine is the prototype drug, named for Morpheus, the Greek god of dreams. These drugs are reserved for moderate to severe pain that may be either acute or chronic (long-acting formulations should be used in chronic pain management) (see Table 5.9).

Long-term use of opioids presents other issues. Drug tolerance is expected to develop, meaning that over time a higher dose may be needed to achieve the same clinical benefit. In addition, dependence is expected to occur, meaning that abrupt discontinuation of the drug will result in a specific withdrawal (abstinence) syndrome. The development of tolerance and dependence does *not* equate with substance abuse, substance use disorder, or addiction. These pharmacologic syndromes are the expected result of long-term, chronic use. Other clinical concerns include organ system effects such as bradycardia (slowed heart rate), respiratory depression, constipation, and nausea. Some patients can even develop an uncommon syndrome called *opioid hyperalgesia*, in which the pain intensity actually worsens with administration of opioids. Last, an obvious concern is the potential for substance abuse and drug diversion.

For this last concern, prior to committing a patient to long-term opioids, most experts recommend pre-screening to stratify for risk behaviors that predict substance abuse and drug diversion. Serious and dangerous behaviors suggestive of the high-risk individual are illegal or criminal behaviors; active diversion (selling drugs or providing drugs to others); prescription forgery; stealing, "borrowing," or buying drugs from others; and dangerous behaviors (e.g., motor vehicle crash and/or arrest related to opioid or illicit drug or alcohol intoxication or effects, intentional or unintentional overdose or suicide attempt, assault, and aggressive or threatening behavior in the clinic).

Many psychometric tools are available for gauging this risk, and these should be used in an empathetic manner, reassuring the patient that his or her answers are confidential and will not adversely affect pain management. If an individual is identified as high risk, care would be optimized by referral to pain management specialists. Many tools are available for such pre-screening use in the primary care setting, such as the Screener and Opioid Assessment for Patients With Pain (SOAPP); the SOAPP-Revised (SOAPP-R); the Opioid Risk Tool (ORT); the Pain Medication Questionnaire (PMQ); the Screening Tool for Addiction Risk (STAR); the Drug Abuse Problem Assessment for Primary Care (DAPA-PC); the Cut Down, Annoyed, Guilt, Eye-Opener—Adapted to Include Drugs (CAGE-AID); the Screening Instrument for Substance Abuse Potential (SISAP); and the Diagnosis, Intractability, Risk, Efficacy (DIRE) evaluation. Attributes that are desirable in such tools include being quantifiable, having diagnostic predictive value, being capable of being self-administered, being brief, having a patient deception safeguard, and public domain availability. These attributes are all found in the SOAPP-R (see appendix, item 9 9).

In addition to pre-screening to determine risk status prior to initiating long-term opioid therapy, patients are usually asked to become partners in an opioid patient care agreement (OPCA). This outlines the rights and responsibilities of both the provider team and the patient. Components of the written, signed agreement (that becomes part of the legal patient chart) include: goals and expectations, tolerance, physical dependency, withdrawal symptoms, prescriptions, adherence to the treatment plan, obtaining medications from a single prescriber (or clinic) and pharmacy, keeping a pain diary, dosing and timing of drugs, and other recommendations (e.g., participation in physical therapy or occupational therapy). Without such an OPCA, many providers will not prescribe opioids long-term. Ongoing care will involve periodic evaluations for efficacy of treatment, continued need for treatment, functional ability, and laboratory testing such as urine drug screens (UDS).

> See vignette 7 in the *Integrated Care in Action* video for a role-play demonstrating how to approach patients about the need to screen for substance abuse before being prescribed pain medication.

In the management of pain, it is imperative to recognize that the reporting of pain is the gold standard in assessment. In the past, placebos were frequently used, administering inert substances and telling the patient that the pills contained active drug. *Placebo* is Latin for "I shall please," and use of placebos is currently not considered a part of recommended care. In addition to ethical considerations, continuous nociceptive stimuli can actually alter brain microanatomy and induce opioid tolerance, similar to what happens in a special pain syndrome called *wind-up pain*. Lack of appropriate pain control can result in the development of a condition called *pseudo-addiction* in which the patient exhibits drug-seeking behaviors simply because of inadequate pain management. This false labeling will further exacerbate inappropriate care.

Table 5.9
Selected Opioids and Related Drugs

Drug	Examples	Comments
Morphine	Liquid (Roxanol), extended release (MS Contin, Avinza, Kadian), Embeda (XR morphine plus naltrexone)	• CS-II controlled substance • Potential morphine histamine reaction (urticaria, airway edema) • With Avinza and Kadian, drinking alcohol can cause fatal morphine dose • Combination with naltrexone as a substance abuse deterrent
Oxycodone	Immediate and controlled release (OxyContin, Roxicodone); combination with ibuprofen (Combunox), aspirin (Percodan), acetaminophen (Percocet, Roxicet)	• CS-II controlled substance • Many drug-drug interactions (FDA Black Box Warning)
Hydromorphone	Dilaudid, Exalgo	• CS-II controlled substance • Potential morphine histamine reaction (urticaria, airway edema) • Available as tablets & suppositories & intravenous • May cause less nausea
Hydrocodone	Alone or in combination with non-narcotic analgesic (Lorcet, Vicodin, Bancap HC), with guaifenisin as cough remedy (Tussionex, Codichlear DH, Kwelcof), in combination with pseudoepehdrine (Histussin D)	• CS-III in combination with non-narcotic analgesic such as Lorcet, Vicodin, Bancap HC • CS-III in combination with guaifenasin as Tussionex, Codichlear DH, Kwelcof • CS-III in combination with pseudoephedrine (Histussin D)
Levomethadyl	Orlaam	• Only for opiate addicted enrolled in SAMHSA program • May cause cardiac arrhythmias
Methadone	Methadone	• To treat narcotic addiction • Also for chronic pain management

Drug	Notes
Oxymorphone	Open injectable, Numorphan suppository, Opana and Opana-ER	• CS-II controlled substance • Potential morphine histamine reaction (urticaria, airway edema)
Fentanyl	Dissolving lozenge (Actiq) for cancer breakthrough pain; Fentora buccal tablet (for opioid tolerant patients with cancer); Abstral transmucosal tablet; IV Sublimaze (mostly used for anesthesia); Ionysys iontophoretic transdermal system (Alza); Duragesic Transdermal Patch	• 100 times more potent than morphine • Duragesic Transdermal Patch ONLY for people who have ALREADY been on around-the-clock narcotics for at least a week and NOT for children
Codeine and dihydrocodeine	Fiorinal with codeine, acetaminophen with codeine (Tylenol with codeine), cough remedies with codeine (Pediacof, Robitussin-AC)	• A prodrug – 10% converted to morphine • Mostly prescribed in combinations with non-narcotics and CS-III or CS-V • Infants of nursing mothers given codeine can have *FATAL* reactions (some people are "rapid metabolizers" and cause a very rapid increase in morphine levels that can be transmitted to the breast milk)—monitor for excessive sleepiness in the infant
Mixed agonist-antagonists	Pentazocine (Talwin; CS-IV), nalbuphine (Nubain) (often for preanesthesia), dezocine (Dalgan), buprenorphine (Buprenex, Subutex, Butrans Transdermal) (CS-III), butorphanol (Stadol, both parenteral and intranasal preparations; CS-IV)	• Act as both an agonist and antagonist on opiate receptors • Some only used for pain management • Others (e.g. buprenorphine) also used for substance use disorder treatment • May cause withdrawal syndrome in those dependent on opioids

In order to avoid such a scenario, multiple clinical assessment tools are available to assist with both initial evaluation for pain as well as ongoing evaluation for treatment efficacy. These pain scales may be of a visual analog scale (VAS) type, or numeric rating scales. They may be developed for various cohorts (neonatal, pediatric, and geriatric) and clinical settings (intensive care, and perioperative) or comorbid conditions (abstinence syndrome, dementia, and cancer). See appendix, item 10, for resources relating to pain scales. Use of pain scales for initial evaluation as well as ongoing care provides objective criteria for use of opioids, and also helps patient and provider remain aware of fluctuations in pain syndromes and causative clinical conditions.

Currently, in many municipalities, there is an extreme concern over the increased incidence of overdose from prescription drugs. These may have found their way to the street via drug diversion. Part of education includes proper disposal of these drugs to avoid diversion (see FDA guidance, http://www.fda.gov/drugs/resourcesforyou/consumers/buyingusingmedicinesafely/ensuringsafeuseofmedicine/safedisposalofmedicines/ucm186187.htm). However, many drug overdoses are actually from valid prescriptions given to the individual from a bona fide clinical encounter. It is hoped that education of both the provider and the patient, and adherence to appropriate management policies will reduce the incidence of overdose in the community.

Conclusion

It is apparent from the brief discussion of selected psychiatric and other morbidities that pharmacologic competency is an important aspect of the professional counselor's knowledge base. Whether the goal is relief of suffering or normalization of function, a wide variety of pathology is managed with psychotropic and other pharmacologic agents. Awareness of available medications and current treatment approaches will enable the counselor to provide patient education, help optimize clinical interventions, suggest modifications in therapy, support the patient's adherence to therapeutic regimens, recognize adverse drug effects and reactions, and reduce risk. The clinical partnership that results will help the healthcare team achieve therapeutic goals in individual patients, as well as increase professional satisfaction by enriching the professional resources of the multidisciplinary team. The enhanced confidence obtained by expanding the counselor's clinical knowledge base will empower true professional relationships, creating a strong collaborative paradigm for the practice. Fostering such interactions and utilizing the specialized training of all members of the team will result in positive outcomes for patients and providers alike.

Discussion Questions and Answers

1. What behavioral management drugs should not be suddenly discontinued?

   Answer: Serotonergic drugs (e.g., SSRI, SNRI, TCA), opioids, benzodiazepines, and anti-epileptics all have the potential for withdrawal syndromes if suddenly discontinued after long-term use.

2. A patient has taken an opioid daily for chronic pain for many years. He now complains that the drug seems to "not be working anymore." Is this an indication of drug-seeking behavior or substance use disorder?

   Answer: Long-term use of opioids results in tolerance, meaning an increased dose over time may be needed to provide the same drug effect. When tolerance has developed, this usually means that dependence is also present, and the drug should not suddenly be discontinued or a withdrawal (abstinence) syndrome may occur. The BHP can discuss the possibility of tolerance and dependence, providing appropriate counseling to not suddenly discontinue such drugs in order to avoid developing such a withdrawal syndrome (these include, for example, in addition to opioids, the SSRI, SNRI, epilepsy, blood pressure, and other categories or classes of drugs). Another rare cause of pain with opioids is hyperalgesia syndrome; this individual must actually be weaned off opioids and receive another class of drugs. The BHP can encourage the patient to bring up this concern with the prescriber, who can work with the patient to determine a course of action. This may include increasing the opioid dose, switching to a different opioid or delivery system, adjusting the opioid (e.g., from short-acting to extended-release), adding an adjunctive drug, or using alternative drugs rather than opioids.

3. Why is it usually recommended to take an antidepressant for 6 weeks before determining if it is effective?

   Answer: Although initial benefit may be seen in some symptoms (such as somatization), this is a result of the immediate increase in neurotransmitters, augmenting a deficiency state of the neurotransmitter. However, the dysphoria and other symptoms of depression (including suicidal ideation) may take weeks to show resolution, because it takes this long to restore normal receptor density in the brain neurons (this receptor dysregulation occurs as a consequence of the reduced neurotransmitters).

4. An individual is diagnosed with anxiety syndrome that has frequent symptoms (more than three times weekly), and is prescribed an SNRI antidepressant to take daily. The patient complains that they want a "nerve pill" that will immediately relieve their anxiety, and which they want to only take when needed. What patient education is indicated?

   Answer: Patients with very infrequent anxiety symptoms can be given anxiolytics of the benzodiazepine class to use PRN (as needed). However, these drugs cause sedation and interfere with normal sleep, as well as pose concerns for drug diversion and substance abuse. For someone with symptoms occurring this frequently, concerns arise regarding long-term use of benzodiazepines due to tolerance and dependence. Antidepressants with serotonergic activity are also anxiolytic, and will help normalize sleep and prevent anxiety and panic if taken on a regular basis. Substance abuse, substance use disorder, and drug diversion are not a concern, although these drugs should also not be suddenly discontinued due to possibility of a withdrawal syndrome (this does *not* mean the patient is "addicted" to antidepressants).

5. You are meeting with the family of an elderly individual who has been diagnosed with Alzheimer's dementia. They would like to know what to expect.

   Answer: Do not "oversell" the available drugs. Explain that the currently available drugs only slow the progression of the illness; at some point, a conversion to serious symptomatology and death will occur. Discuss the possibility of personality changes, lack of recognition of family members, and need for alternate care arrangements. Family members often feel very guilty about nursing home placement or day care, and support for these decisions is crucial. Younger family members may have a concern regarding their own eventual development of this condition—recommend maintaining robust social interactions, hobbies, and regular exercise.

6. A middle-aged woman is diagnosed with severe osteoarthritis and requires opioids to manage her pain. She has been asked to sign an opioid patient care agreement (OPCA) and submit to urine drug screening. The patient is very upset, feeling that these

requirements are labeling her as a "drug addict" and she cannot understand why these approaches are necessary. What counseling approach would help the patient and the care team?

Answer: Advise the patient that this approach is now routine and asked of all patients who are committing to long-term opioid therapy. Educate regarding the fact that this approach provides safeguards for the patient, creates the necessary chart paperwork required by law, and also helps to assess if ongoing care is effective, thus optimizing her management.

References

Chou, R. (2009). 2009 Clinical guidelines from the American Pain Society and the American Academy of Pain Medicine on the use of chronic opioid therapy in chronic noncancer pain: What are the key messages for clinical practice? *Polskie Archiwum MedycynyWewnętrznej, 119*(7–8), 469–477.

Greiner, A. C., & Elisa, E. (Eds.). (2003). *Health professions education: A bridge to quality.* Institute of Medicine of the National Academies. Washington, DC: National Academies Press. Retrieved from http://books.nap.edu/openbook.php?record_id=10681&page=4

National Board for Certified Counselors. (2009). *State board directory.* Retrieved from http://www.nbcc.org/directory/Default.aspx

Appendix

1. Understanding acronyms for professional licensure and certifications. See: Morris, Don H. (2007). Guide to acronyms in the helping professions. Encouragement Plus Coaching. Retrieved from http://www.encouragementplus.com/acronyms.html
2. Basics of chemistry pertaining to pharmacology.
   - An *atom* is the smallest part of matter, *elements* are made up of only one type of atom (e.g., oxygen), *molecules* (compounds) are composed of more than one type of atom (e.g., H_2O). *Molecular weight* (MW) is the total atomic weight of all the atoms in a molecule.
   - Matter exists in three *physical states* of solid, liquid, or gas; these characteristics are determined by ambient (environmental) pressure and temperature.
   - *Organic compounds*:
     - Based on carbon (C), hydrogen (H), oxygen (O), nitrogen (N), and some sulfur (S) (often written as "CHONS."
   - *Inorganic compounds* are elements other than CHONS.
     - May be BULK inorganics (e.g., calcium and sodium)

- May be TRACE inorganics (e.g., selenium and boron)
- Chemistry of solutions (fluids):
  - *Solute*: the solid substance that is dissolved in the liquid
  - *Solvent*: the liquid (which is always *water* in living systems)
- *Ions*: are electrically charged particles in solution.
  - *Cations* (positive) and *anions* (negative).
  - *Electrolytes* are ions in living systems.
  - *Neutral* means no electrical charge.
- Acids and bases:
  - *pH* measures how acidic the solution is—the concentration of positively charged hydrogen ions (H+) (also called *protons* or hydronium ions, H3O+)
  - *Acids*: reversibly dissociate (break up) into a "conjugate base" and a hydronium ion (H+, hyodrogen ion) in water—thus, they are said to "give up" hydrogen ions
  - *Bases*: chemicals that can accept a hydronium ion (H+) in solution

3. *Controlled substances*: These are drugs considered to have abuse potential and are under control of the DEA; usually written as **C-I**, **C-II**, **C-III**, **C-IV**, and **C-V** for the different "scheduled" drugs. Basic information by schedule number:
   - Codes and numbers:
     - The DEA assigns each CS a schedule number (Roman numerals I through V) according to its medicinal value, harmfulness, and potential for abuse or addiction. A higher schedule number indicates the substance has more medicinal value and less potential for abuse or addiction.
     - There is a LETTER after the Roman numeral. The letter *N* can also accompany the schedule number, signifying the substance is a non-narcotic. The absence of the "N" (e.g., II) means it is a narcotic.
     - The DEA also assigns a 4-digit number assigned to each CS called the DEA code number.
     - *Example*: diazepam, IVN, 2765.
   - *C-I*: High potential for abuse, no accepted medical use in treatment in the United States, lack of accepted safety for use in treatment. *Nobody* may prescribe these drugs. *Example*: LSD, mescaline, PCP, heroin, and marijuana; mostly fall into the classes of opium derivatives, hallucinogens, depressants, stimulants. *Usage is illicit* (use subject to legal penalties). *Exceptions*: use for religious purposes (e.g., Native Americans and peyote) with DEA approval case by case. Some states (e.g., California) have enabling legislation for marijuana as an

anti-emetic and pain control in the terminally ill, but this is not officially sanctioned by the DEA.

- *C-II*: Drugs with a high potential for abuse, have currently accepted medical use in treatment in the United States, or currently accepted medical use with severe restrictions; abuse may lead to severe psychic or physical dependence. *Narcotic examples*: **methadone, meperidine, hydromorphone (Dilaudid), oxycodone (Tylox), uncombined codeine (combining with nonnarcotic analgesics reduces their abuse potential), Percodan, Percocet.** *Nonnarcotic examples*: **amphetamines (methylphenidate—Ritalin), barbiturates (amobartibal, etc.).** Both the prescriber *and* the pharmacist must keep a record of the prescription and/or dispensing. Some states have even more stringent requirements for usage and prescribing than others (triplicate pads, etc.). **No telephone prescriptions or refills allowed by any provider.**
- *C-III*: Potential for abuse, but less than Schedule II. *Narcotic examples*: combined codeines (**hydrocodone such as Vicodin, Lortab), Tussionex, Fionrinal with codeine, others.** *Nonnarcotic examples*: different forms of barbiturates and anabolic steroids. **Refills and telephone prescription rules vary by state.**
- *C-IV*: Drugs with less potential for abuse than Schedules II and III. *Examples*: depressants (e.g., **Xanax, Valium, phenobarbital**), stimulants (**Fenfluramine**). Telephone prescriptions are usually permitted.
- *C-V*: Drug with a low potential for abuse relative to the above. *Examples*: **Tylenol III with codeine elixir, Novahistine DH, Lomotil** (generally, codeine combinations with 200 mg/200 mL or less) Some states allow dispensing without a prescription, such as **low-dose codeine** combinations in cough suppressant formulas, but most require prescriptions, telephone or written.

4. *Institute for Safe Medication Practices (ISMP).* Institute for Safe Medicine Practices. (2008). *Tall man letters.* Retrieved from http://www.ismp.org/tools/tallmanletters.pdf
5. *Obesity and overweight.*
- Printable table of Body Mass Index (BMI): http://www.nhlbi.nih.gov/guidelines/obesity/bmi_tbl.pdf
- BMI calculator from the NIH: http://www.nhlbisupport.com/bmi/

- CDC information on BMI-for-age in children: http://www.cdc.gov/nccdphp/dnpa/bmi/childrens_BMI/about_childrens_BMI.htm
- CDC 2009 statistics on state-specific obesity in adults: http://www.cdc.gov/mmwr/preview/mmwrhtml/mm59e0803a1.htm
- NHLBI, *Practical Guide to Obesity and Overweight in Adults*: http://www.nhlbi.nih.gov/guidelines/obesity/prctgd_c.pdf
- American Academy of Pediatrics, *Expert Committee Recommendations Regarding the Prevention, Assessment, and Treatment of Child and Adolescent Overweight and Obesity*: http://pediatrics.aappublications.org/cgi/reprint/120/Supplement_4/S164

6. *FDA links regarding antipsychotic drugs*:
   http://www.fda.gov/Drugs/DrugSafety/ucm243903.htm
   http://www.fda.gov/Drugs/DrugSafety/PostmarketDrugSafetyInformationforPatientsandProviders/ucm124830.htm
   http://www.fda.gov/Drugs/DrugSafety/PostmarketDrugSafetyInformationforPatientsandProviders/DrugSafetyInformationforHeathcareProfessionals/PublicHealthAdvisories/ucm053171.htm

7. *Clinical Practice Guidelines (CPGs) repository.* http://www.guideline.gov (simply type into the search box for the condition to see current CPGs)

8. National Institute of Mental Health website on autism spectrum disorders (Pervasive Developmental Disorders): http://www.nimh.nih.gov/health/topics/autism-spectrum-disorders-pervasive-developmental-disorders/index.shtml

9. *Long-term opioid use resources.* Psychometric screening tools for pre-screening prior to long-term opioid use:
   - Screener and Opioid Assessment for Patients with Pain (SOAPP): http://www.algosresearch.org/PracticeTools/DxTestForms/SOAPPTest.pdf
   - Revised Screener and Opioid Assessment for Patients with Pain (SOAPP-R): http://home.fammed.org/Various/SOAPP-R.pdf
   - Opioid Risk Tool (ORT): http://www.painknowledge.org/physiciantools/ORT/ORT%20Patient%20Form.pdf
   - Pain Medication Questionnaire (PMQ) : http://download.journals.elsevierhealth.com/pdfs/journals/0885-3924/PIIS0885392404001010.pdf
   - Drug Abuse Problem Assessment for Primary Care (DAPA-PC): http://www.dapaonline.com

- Cut Down, Annoyed, Guilt, Eye-Opener, Adapted to Include Drugs (CAGE-AID) questionnaire http://www.partnersagainstpain.com/printouts/A7012DA4.pdf
- Screening Instrument for Substance Abuse Potential (SISAP): http://www.pulsus.com/journals/abstract.jsp?jnlKy=7&atlKy=2908&isuKy=520&isArt=t&HCtype=Consumer
- Diagnosis, Intractability, Risk, Efficacy (DIRE) evaluation: http://www.icsi.org/pain__chronic__assessment_and_management_of_14399/pain__chronic__assessment_and_management_of__guideline_summary_.html

Pain Management Resources

http://www.painedu.org
http://www.partnersagainstpain.com
http://painconsortium.nih.gov

CHAPTER 6

Ethics in Integrated Care

DARREN S. BOICE

Professional ethical standards exist to protect both consumers of care and practitioners who provide care. Those who have chosen careers as behavioral health providers (BHPs) are committed to the service and betterment of the human condition, and should be reassured by the ethical framework that exists for each of their professions. The integrated health care (IC) field provides opportunities for BHPs to impact the people they serve in new and exciting ways. Novelty encourages practices to operate in ways that are ahead of the curve, bringing forth issues that are not specifically addressed in the professional code of ethics. Fortunately, BHPs can manage these issues, because the ethical codes have been written to guide and inform practice rather than to restrict and prescribe it.

Attempts to bridge the gaps among the different disciplines of the behavioral health profession are rarely made in the professional literature. In IC settings, though, BHPs from varied professions find more commonality than is generally acknowledged. This chapter will describe how BHPs in different disciplines are united in common ethical codes, and demonstrate how BHPs bring positive ethical standards of care to the IC setting. It will also examine some of the similarities and differences among ethical standards of the medical and behavioral health professions. Indeed, many of the codes of ethics for behavioral health professions seem to be written as enhancements of the distinguished and historical ethical practices of the medical profession.

Professional pride is often a positive sentiment, and the various BHP professional codes of ethics are both inspiring and challenging when the implications of each are considered. As a point of caution for BHPs, professional pride runs the risk of compelling BHPs to view the practice of patient care only through the lens of their own particular code of ethics. In the spirit of true collaboration, each profession needs to be able to recognize that all disciplines have ethical codes that hold value and practicality. Although IC advances the level of patient care with effective and efficient treatment, it does present some challenges in the areas of integrating the many different professional codes of ethics into cohesive and respectful patient-centered care.

The remainder of this chapter will highlight several ethical issues (listed here) that are of particular import in the integration of the medical and behavioral worlds of patient care into one IC practice.

- Informed consent
- Confidentiality
- Relationships with patients
- Relationships with colleagues
- Scope of practice

Each section will begin with relevant excerpts from the following five professional codes of ethics: medicine, represented by the American Medical Association's (AMA) *Code of Medical Ethics* (AMA, 2008); psychology, represented by the American Psychological Association's (APA) *Ethical Principles of Psychologists and Code of Conduct* (APA, 2010a); clinical social work, represented by the National Association of Social Workers' (NASW) *Code of Ethics* (Workers, 2008); marriage and family therapy, represented by the American Association for Marriage and Family Therapy's (AAMFT) *Code of Ethics* (AAMFT, 2001); and counseling, represented by the American Counseling Association's (ACA) *Code of Ethics and Standards of Practice* (ACA, 2005), followed by discussion and suggestions for how to address ethical issues within IC practices.

Informed Consent

American Medical Association[1]

Code of Medical Ethics, Opinion 8.08 The patient's right of self-decision can be effectively exercised only if the patient possesses enough information to enable an informed choice. The patient should make his or her own determination about treatment. The physician's obligation is to present the medical facts accurately to the patient or to the individual responsible for the patient's care and to make recommendations for management in accordance with good medical practice. The physician has an ethical obligation to help the patient make choices from among the therapeutic alternatives consistent with good medical practice. Informed consent is a basic policy in both ethics and law that physicians must honor, unless the patient is unconscious or otherwise incapable of consenting and harm from failure to treat is imminent.

American Psychological Association[2]

Ethical Principles of Psychologists and Code of Conduct (2002), 3.10 (a) When psychologists conduct research or provide assessment, therapy, counseling, or consulting services in person or via electronic transmission or other forms of communication, they obtain the informed consent of the individual or individuals using language that is reasonably understandable to that person or persons except when conducting such activities without consent is mandated by law or governmental regulation or as otherwise provided in this Ethics Code.

National Association of Social Workers[3]

Code of Ethics (2008) 1.03(a) Social workers should provide services to clients only in the context of a professional relationship based, when appropriate, on valid informed consent. Social workers should use clear and understandable language to inform clients of the purpose of the services, risks related to the services, limits to services because of the requirements of a thirdparty payer, relevant costs, reasonable alternatives, clients' right to refuse or withdraw consent, and the time frame covered by the consent. Social workers should provide clients with an opportunity to ask questions.

American Association for Marriage and Family Therapy[4]

Code of Ethics (2001), 1.2 Marriage and family therapists obtain appropriate informed consent to therapy or related procedures as early as feasible in the therapeutic relationship, and use language that is reasonably understandable to clients. The content of informed consent may vary depending upon the client and treatment plan.

American Counseling Association[5]

Code of Ethics and Standards of Practice (2005), A.2.a Clients have the freedom to choose whether to enter into or remain in a counseling relationship and need adequate information about the counseling process and the counselor. Counselors have an obligation to review in writing and verbally with clients the rights and responsibilities of both the counselor and the client. Informed consent is an ongoing part of the counseling process, and counselors appropriately document discussions of informed consent throughout the counseling relationship.

* * *

It is universally understood by BHPs and medical professionals that informed consent must be obtained from patients prior to the provision of health care treatment. Fortunately, each of the disciplines referenced above values the patient's right to understand treatment options and to freely choose whether to participate in treatment.

That said, BHPs may find the informed consent process inadequate in an IC practice because of the way it has been streamlined by the medical profession. In our society, it has become necessary for medical providers to avoid litigation by preventing liability, bolstered with the creation of mechanisms that guarantee that every patient consents to the treatment they receive. Prior to meeting the provider of care, clinical settings often ask patients to sign a consent form that covers every conceivable and potential treatment that may be provided. In doing so, the clinic meets the letter of the informed consent standard, although the spirit of the ethics that require it is diminished. The AMA's code indicates that patients require adequate information to make an informed choice regarding their medical treatment. But, clearly, most patients do not have this information during their first encounter with a provider. Medical practices and hospitals have become so efficient at obtaining consents that the PCP is often left out of the process, as the office staff secures consent from the patient.

The BHP's primary concern is the manner in which consent is secured in the medical practice. The four behavioral health codes listed here describe informed consent as part of the therapeutic relationship, placing the responsibility to inform on the BHP. The goal of this ethic is to ensure that patients have ultimate control of their own treatment. BHPs also benefit from this ethic as they value the reciprocal nature surrounding informed consent. Considerations for whether the patient understands the identified condition and the treatment options available, and whether the patient wants to begin or continue treatment, promote the ethical process of securing informed consent.

Whereas signing a consent form is a single act, securing informed consent is a process that is dependent on a therapeutic relationship that places an inherent value on a patient's right to self-determination. BHPs practicing in IC should not rely solely on a signed consent for treatment as part of the registration protocol because, although this form may cover BHPs legally, it will not cover their professional ethical responsibility to protect their patients in the treatment process. Upon meeting with patients, BHPs should become accustomed to explaining their role within the IC clinic and confirming patients' understanding and agreement to participate in behavioral treatment (Robinson & Reiter, 2007). BHPs are encouraged to include language in the forms for standard consent for treatment that highlights the IC model. In some large health systems, though, the forms are highly standardized and changing them is nearly impossible. In any case, it would be wise for BHPs to document the process by which they obtained informed consent, in addition to the standard form. The following is sample dialogue of a BHP obtaining consent within an IC practice:

> Hello Mrs. Rodriguez, I'm Donna Greene and, as Dr. Shah explained, I am a licensed professional counselor and I have been working with this clinic as the behavioral health provider to ensure that patients get comprehensive care. This care can include assessment, consultation, counseling, and case management. Information related to my education, areas of competency, confidentiality, and who to contact if you have a grievance with the services I provide is listed in this brochure, which is yours to take. Dr. Shah asked me to meet with you so that together we can find some strategies that may help alleviate some of the symptoms you mentioned. I know I just gave you a lot of information, so please let me know what you understand and what questions you have for me.

Confidentiality

American Medical Association

Code of Medical Ethics, Opinion 5.05   The information disclosed to a physician by a patient should be held in confidence. The patient should feel free to make a full disclosure of information to the physician in order that the physician may most effectively provide needed services. The patient should be able to make this disclosure with the knowledge that the physician will respect the confidential nature of the communication. The physician should not reveal confidential information without the express consent of the patient, subject to certain exceptions which are ethically justified because of overriding considerations.

Opinion 5.059   Privacy is not absolute, and must be balanced with the need for the efficient provision of medical care and the availability of resources. Physicians should be aware of and respect the special concerns of their patients regarding privacy....

American Psychological Association

Ethical Principles of Psychologists and Code of Conduct (2002)   4.01 Psychologists have a primary obligation and take reasonable precautions to protect confidential information obtained through or stored in any medium, recognizing that the extent and limits of confidentiality may be regulated by law or established by institutional rules or professional or scientific relationship.

4.02 (a) Psychologists discuss with persons (including, to the extent feasible, persons who are legally incapable of giving informed consent and their legal representatives) and organizations with whom they establish a scientific or professional relationship (1) the relevant limits of confidentiality and (2) the foreseeable uses of the information generated through their psychological activities.

4.02 (c) Psychologists who offer services, products, or information via electronic transmission inform clients/patients of the risks to privacy and limits of confidentiality.

4.04 (a) Psychologists include in written and oral reports and consultations, only information germane to the purpose for which the communication is made.

4.04 (b) Psychologists discuss confidential information obtained in their work only for appropriate scientific or professional purposes and only with persons clearly concerned with such matters. Copyright © 2010 by the American Psychological Association. Reproduced with permission (APA, 2010a).

National Association of Social Workers

Code of Ethics (2008) 1.07 (b) Social workers may disclose confidential information when appropriate with valid consent from a client or a person legally authorized to consent on behalf of a client.

2.02 Social workers should respect confidential information shared by colleagues in the course of their professional relationships and transactions. Social workers should ensure that such colleagues understand social workers' obligation to respect confidentiality and any exceptions related to it.

3.04 (c) Social workers' documentation should protect clients' privacy to the extent that is possible and appropriate and should include only information that is directly relevant to the delivery of services.

American Association for Marriage and Family Therapy

Code of Ethics (2001), 2.1 Marriage and family therapists disclose to clients and other interested parties, as early as feasible in their professional contacts, the nature of confidentiality and possible limitations of the clients' right to confidentiality. Therapists review with clients the circumstances where confidential information may be requested and where disclosure of confidential information may be legally required. Circumstances may necessitate repeated disclosures.

American Counseling Association

Code of Ethics and Standards of Practice (2005) Counselors do not share confidential information without client consent or without sound legal or ethical justification. *B.1.d.* At initiation and throughout the counseling process, counselors inform clients of the limitations of confidentiality and seek to identify foreseeable situations in which confidentiality must be breached.

* * *

The similarities between the ethical standards of the medical and behavioral health professions are evident in the area of confidentiality. The AMA's *Code of Medical Ethics* has meaningful language guiding the physician to respect the confidential nature of communication with the patient. The distinctions in the characterization of confidentiality for medical versus behavioral health professions are not in the essential nature of patient confidentiality, but rather on how much information and what kind of information should be shared between the BHP and PCP. The methods of communicating shared knowledge must also be carefully considered.

The move toward IC in this country is steadily closing the gap that still exists in terms of treating the whole person in health care. The federal government has passed laws regulating the exchange of personal health information and requiring parity in health care coverage. All levels of health care now readily acknowledge the interplay of the mind and body, though different values may be placed on the importance of each. One of the benefits of IC is for both BHPs and PCPs to better understand and respect the information each has gathered from patients.

In IC settings with high levels of integration, BHPs should be sharing the same patient record with PCPs, thereby requiring robust ethical practices regarding confidentiality. Additionally, it is important to communicate clearly and verify that the patient understands the relationship between the BHP and the PCP. BHPs should explain the level of collaboration in the clinic and the ways in which confidential information may be shared among providers (e.g., shared record, team meetings, rounds, consults, and/or joint treatment), as well as the reasons why patient information may be shared.

Varied levels of confidentiality exist in IC. Health systems have rules restricting access to patient records with a "need to know" designation, and all staff is trained to avoid HIPPA violations. For example, a support staff person may have access to insurance information for verification purposes, but is not permitted to read clinical notes. Primary care providers, including BHPs, routinely enter brief progress notes into the shared electronic health record (EHR). As a safeguard for patient confidentiality, most EHRs also allow providers to create different levels of privacy; they are capable of keeping behavioral health notes separate from the rest of the record, for exclusive BHP and PCP access. This practice not only prevents nonprovider staff from accessing behavioral health notes but also prevents confidential behavioral health information from being divulged during the release of general medical records. Especially sensitive information can even be communicated verbally to the PCP rather than detailing it in the EHR (O'Donohue, Byrd, Cummings, & Henderson, 2005). BHPs may choose to educate members of their IC group to recognize the sensitivity of the patient's behavioral health notes and the need to treat such information with particular respect. Progress notes in the IC setting should document treatment as well as communicate the progress of the behavioral health intervention to the PCP. One way to introduce confidentiality to patients in IC practices is as follows:

> Mrs. Rodriguez, it is important for you to know that Dr. Shah and I consult with each other about patients to help determine the best possible treatment plans. I also make brief notes of my meetings with patients that are stored in our electronic health record, which we call the EHR. I want to make you aware that Dr. Shah and I are the only two people in this practice who have access to the notes that I write in your record, and that all other staff members only have access to Dr. Shah's notes. Also, if you ever share something with me that you do not wish to share with Dr. Shah, please tell me and I will keep that information confidential, between you and me only. There are, however, a few times when I am required to notify others, including Dr. Shah. This would include if you shared thoughts of a suicidal nature, which are thoughts of hurting yourself, or of a homicidal nature, which are thoughts of hurting others. I would also be required to notify others if you mentioned the abuse of a minor or elderly person, or if I was court ordered to release my notes. I can assure you that in all of these incidents, I would disclose the least amount of relevant information as necessary, to ensure your safety. I know that may have been a lot to take in at once, tell me what questions you have about your confidentiality.

See vignette 1 on the *Integrated Care in Action* DVD demonstrating how a discussion about confidentiality can be initiated with patients in IC practices.

Relationships With Patients

American Medical Association

Code of Medical Ethics, Opinion 10.015 The relationship between patient and physician is based on trust and gives rise to physicians' ethical obligations to place patients' welfare above their own self-interest and above obligations to other groups, and to advocate for their patients' welfare.

Within the patient-physician relationship, a physician is ethically required to use sound medical judgment, holding the best interests of the patient as paramount.

American Psychological Association

Ethical Principles of Psychologists and Code of Conduct (2002). 3.05 (a) A multiple relationship occurs when a psychologist is in a professional role with a person and (1) at the same time is in another role with the same person, (2) at the same time is in a relationship with a person closely associated with or related to the person with whom the psychologist has the professional relationship, or (3) promises to enter into another relationship in the future with the person or a person closely associated with or related to the person. © 2010 by the American Psychological Association. Reproduced with permission (APA, 2010a).

National Association of Social Workers

Code of Ethics (2008), 1.06 (c) Social workers should not engage in dual or multiple relationships with clients or former clients in which there is a risk of exploitation or potential harm to the client. In instances when dual or multiple relationships are unavoidable, social workers should take steps to protect clients and are responsible for setting clear, appropriate, and culturally sensitive boundaries. (Dual or multiple relationships occur when social workers relate to clients in more than one relationship, whether professional, social, or business. Dual or multiple relationships can occur simultaneously or consecutively.)

American Association for Marriage and Family Therapy

Code of Ethics (2001), 1.3 Marriage and family therapists are aware of their influential positions with respect to clients, and they avoid exploiting the trust and dependency of such persons. Therapists, therefore, make every effort to avoid conditions and multiple relationships with clients that could impair professional judgment or increase the risk of exploitation. Such relationships include, but are not limited to, business or close personal relationships with a client or the client's immediate family. When the risk of impairment or exploitation exists due to conditions or multiple roles, therapists take appropriate precautions.

American Counseling Association

Code of Ethics and Standards of Practice (2005), A.5.c Counselor–client nonprofessional relationships with clients, former clients, their romantic partners, or their family members should be avoided, except when the interaction is potentially beneficial to the client.

* * *

The provider bears the responsibility of properly managing the professional relationship with the patient. The therapeutic relationship is built on trust, respect, and protection of the patient. BHPs need to be particularly aware of the inequities present in a professional relationship and must be careful not to use their influence for personal gain of any sort. All providers are guided by their codes to put the needs of patients before their own and to avoid any risk of exploitation or harm to the patient. Although an ethical basis for protecting the relationship between patient and provider is consistent in both medical and behavioral health care, a difference exists between the two disciplines with regard to the presence of multiple relationships between patient and provider. BHPs who are new to an IC setting might be surprised to witness their PCP colleagues medically treating patients who are relatives of coworkers, or even coworkers themselves. Historically, medical professionals have treated patients with whom they have personal relationships. This practice might seem unethical to a BHP, but a closer look at the AMA code reveals that multiple relationships are not prohibited like they are in all of the behavioral health ethical codes. BHPs need to spend time getting to know the culture of the health care world before making judgments about ethical violations in relationships with patients, and should remember that their medical colleagues may not have been aware of any concern in regard to dual relationships with patients prior to integration. BHPs have a unique opportunity to influence the culture in IC by modeling a different way of thinking about and behaving within the patient–provider relationship. This issue may even give rise to enlightening discussions among providers that can actually strengthen the BHP's role in the clinic. The myriad of permutations in which these codes can impact PCPs and BHPs are seemingly infinite, but a way to handle one common aspect of this code is demonstrated in the subsequent statement.

> Mrs. Rodriguez, I'd like to talk to you about an occurrence that sometimes comes up and can be confusing or even disconcerting to some patients. If I were to see you in public, for example in the supermarket or mall, out of respect for your privacy, I typically wouldn't speak to you unless you initiate the conversation. This may seem like rude behavior, but it is so that I don't put you in an awkward position in having to explain who I am to your friends, family members, or colleagues if you wish to keep our relationship confidential. There is no pressure to do so, but please feel free to approach me if you feel comfortable. Dr. Shah follows a different code of ethics, though,

which is not as strict about "outside-the-office" communication with patients. Dr. Shah and I discuss this issue often so we can be as consistent as possible, but I just wanted to let you know in advance so that if this situation arises you won't feel offended.

Relationship With Colleagues

American Medical Association

Code of Medical Ethics, Opinion 3.03   It is ethical for a physician to work in consultation with or employ allied health professionals, as long as they are appropriately trained and duly licensed to perform the activities being requested.

American Psychological Association

Ethical Principles of Psychologists and Code of Conduct (2002), 3.09   When indicated and professionally appropriate, psychologists cooperate with other professionals in order to serve their clients/patients effectively and appropriately. © 2010 by the American Psychological Association. Reproduced with permission (APA, 2010a).

National Association of Social Workers

Code of Ethics (2008)   2.01 (a) (a) Social workers should treat colleagues with respect and should represent accurately and fairly the qualifications, views, and obligations of colleagues. (b) Social workers should avoid unwarranted negative criticism of colleagues in communications with clients or with other professionals. Unwarranted negative criticism may include demeaning comments that refer to colleagues' level of competence or to individuals' attributes such as race, ethnicity, national origin, color, sex, sexual orientation, gender identity or expression, age, marital status, political belief, religion, immigration status, and mental or physical disability. (c) Social workers should cooperate with social work colleagues and with colleagues of other professions when such cooperation serves the wellbeing of clients.

2.03 (a) (a) Social workers who are members of an interdisciplinary team should participate in and contribute to decisions that affect the wellbeing of clients by drawing on the perspectives, values, and experiences of the social work profession. Professional and ethical obligations of the interdisciplinary team as a whole and of its individual members should be clearly established.

American Counseling Association

Code of Ethics and Standards of Practice (2005) D.1.a. Counselors are respectful of approaches to counseling services that differ from their own. Counselors are respectful of traditions and practices of other professional groups with which they work.

D.1.b. Counselors work to develop and strengthen interdisciplinary relations with colleagues from other disciplines to best serve clients.

D.1.c. Counselors who are members of interdisciplinary teams delivering multifaceted services to clients keep the focus on how to best serve the clients. They participate in and contribute to decisions that affect the well-being of clients by drawing on the perspectives, values, and experiences of the counseling profession and those of colleagues from other disciplines.

B.3.b. When client treatment involves a continued review or participation by a treatment team, the client will be informed of the team's existence and composition, information being shared, and the purposes of sharing such information.

* * *

In this section, the ethical concept of professional relationships, and some of the significant differences in the medical and behavioral health care codes, will be discussed. The medical profession is traditionally structured as a hierarchy. PCPs are trained to be leaders and decision makers; in contrast, BHPs are trained to be facilitators and consensus builders. Prior to the IC movement, physicians generally shared their practice with partners, who were equal colleagues, or with extenders, who worked on their behalf. The IC model encourages PCPs and BHPs to collaborate as colleagues. This particular AMA ethical code refers to physicians employing nonphysician providers or requesting consultation from other professionals. The behavioral codes speak to the goal of cooperation and respect in professional relationships.

The merging of medical and behavioral health cultures is one of the greatest challenges of IC, but it is a critical one to master, as the relationship that develops between the PCP and the BHP is the key to successful integration. BHPs should refer to their codes of ethics to help guide relationship building. The well-being of the patient should always be primary and can be achieved through mutual respect, which leads to better provider relationships, then improved collaboration, and, ultimately, enhanced patient care. BHPs who are new to an IC setting might feel offended at times by the cultural norms of the medical office or feel distanced from the PCPs, but they should resist the temptation to abandon their ethical standards in these moments. Instead, BHPs should work diligently at building collaborative relationships while being careful to respect and avoid criticizing the culture.

A BHP can advance his or her role as a true team member by developing relationships with the nursing staff. Nurses have a unique understanding of the dynamics of a practice, and are familiar with the distinct styles and personalities of the PCPs. Moreover, nurses coordinate and manage much of the patient care and often have great insights into patients' needs. BHPs should also strive to build relationships with their office staff (e.g., those charged with scheduling, billing, and insurance filing), a group that is a valuable resource to BHPs working toward truly integrated care, as they have critical knowledge of the inner workings of the practice (Robinson & Reiter, 2007).

Once BHPs have taken the time to learn the culture of a particular IC practice, they will begin to develop relationships with the PCPs in the practice. There is no timetable for forming "good" relationships; it is an ever-evolving process. BHPs can solidify their status and promote themselves as valuable assets to the team and the PCP by helping the PCP with particularly difficult patients or by taking on a project that improves the general practice. As rapport and trust are gained (remember that BHPs also represent a different culture to PCPs), so too will BHPs' contributions to collaborative patient care. IC functions similarly to an interdisciplinary team. As a member of the team, the BHP should bring his or her own ethics and experience regarding patient care into the discourse. Providers will almost certainly disagree at times, but with mutual investment in integration, these differences can promote the natural progression of a clinically dynamic relationship as the parties learn about one another's strengths and perspectives. If BHPs remain true to their ethics and keep the lines of communication open, successful integration can be the reward.

Finally, in IC settings, BHPs may find they have an opportunity to work with BHPs from other disciplines. In fact, IC systems sometimes purposely recruit a variety of masters and doctoral level BHPs to work in the same setting. There is the potential for "turf" issues to arise over which professional should treat a given condition. It can also reveal discipline specific loyalties that make collaboration more difficult. But open, respectful communication focused on the patient's best interest will head off most conflicts. All parties should remember that they share very similar ethics about how to interact with one another and how to care for patients.

Dynamic relationship building is a critical part of working in an IC practice and there are varied incidents that may cause friction among IC staff members. But, as described above, disagreements among colleagues, when handled well, can be opportunities for further clarification of practice ideals and, ultimately, increased patient care. Consider a situation in which a PCP wants the BHP to do a task for the patient (e.g., make phone calls to locate transportation), one that the patient is quite capable of completing on her own. The BHP may believe strongly that doing things for patients that they can do for themselves sends the message to patients that they are incapable, and that encouraging patients to take more responsibility for their care ultimately increases the well-being of the patient. Discussing such ideological differences in patient care should be approached professionally and respectfully. Below is one way to begin such dialogue:

> Dr. Shah, I'm concerned that if I arrange transportation for Mrs. Rodriguez to come to her follow-up visit, we'll fail to encourage self-reliance. Unlike some of our patients who may need a lot of support, Mrs. Rodriguez would benefit from some initial support to assist with her first appointment. I can then encourage her to make the follow-up appointments on her own while monitoring and supporting her efforts to ultimately promote a higher level of self-management.

Scope of Practice

American Medical Association

Code of Medical Ethics, Opinion 9.12   The creation of the patient–physician relationship is contractual in nature. Generally, both the physician and the patient are free to enter into or decline the relationship. A physician may decline to undertake the care of a patient whose medical condition is not within the physician's current competence….

American Psychological Association

Ethical Principles of Psychologists and Code of Conduct (2002) 2.01   (d) When psychologists are asked to provide services to individuals for whom appropriate mental health services are not available and for which psychologists have not obtained the competence necessary, psychologists with closely related prior training or experience may provide such services in order to ensure that services are not denied if they make a reasonable effort to obtain the competence required by using relevant research, training, consultation, or study.

(e) In those emerging areas in which generally recognized standards for preparatory training do not yet exist, psychologists nevertheless take reasonable steps to ensure the competence of their work and to protect clients/patients, students, supervisees, research participants, organizational clients, and others from harm. Copyright © 2010 by the American Psychological Association. Reproduced with permission (APA, 2010a).

National Association of Social Workers

Code of Ethics (2008) 1.04 (a)   (a) Social workers should provide services and represent themselves as competent only within the boundaries of their education, training, license, certification, consultation received, supervised experience, or other relevant professional experience.

4.01 (a)   (a) Social workers should accept responsibility or employment only on the basis of existing competence or the intention to acquire the necessary competence.

4.01   (b) Social workers should strive to become and remain proficient in professional practice and the performance of professional functions. Social workers should critically examine and keep current with emerging knowledge relevant to social work. Social workers should routinely review the professional literature and participate in continuing education relevant to social work practice and social work ethics.

American Association for Marriage and Family Therapy

Code of Ethics (2001) 3.7   While developing new skills in specialty areas, marriage and family therapists take steps to ensure the competence of their work and to protect clients from possible harm. Marriage and family therapists practice in specialty areas new to them only after appropriate education, training, or supervised experience.

3.11   Marriage and family therapists do not diagnose, treat, or advise on problems outside the recognized boundaries of their competencies.

American Counseling Association

Code of Ethics and Standards of Practice (2005), C.2.b   Counselors practice in specialty areas new to them only after appropriate education, training, and supervised experience. While developing skills in new specialty areas, counselors take steps to ensure the competence of their work and to protect others from possible harm.

* * *

IC is emerging as a viable alternative to the aging models of segregated physical and behavioral health care. As IC gains momentum, it attracts BHPs who want to serve patients in this more efficient and effective manner. Statistics found in Chapter 1 of Salovey, Rothman, Detweiler, and Steward (2000) stated that 50–70% of people who present to primary care have mental or behavioral health issues, and that 50–90% of these patients do not follow through with mental health referrals (Escobar, Interian, Diaz-Martinez, & Gara, 2006). As exciting as the prospect of reaching patients who would otherwise miss out on behavioral services may be, BHPs must remain mindful that specific ethical codes for this innovative care model have not yet been developed. More professional guidance is needed for the appropriate application of traditional ethics in the IC setting. Because IC would be considered by behavioral health codes of ethics as an "emerging" or "new" area of practice, BHPs have an ethical duty to continually improve their competence in order to protect patients from harm.

BHPs who are transitioning from a traditional mental health setting to an IC setting need to be oriented and educated, and take advantage of the many opportunities available for improving one's competency in the new practice model. There is a growing body of IC literature to help inform and guide practice. Further, national and regional conferences and workshops provide educational opportunities to learn more about IC. More formal training is also available through select graduate schools and post-graduate training programs devoted to the behavioral aspect of IC. Finally, becoming a member of a professional association focused on IC is another good way to gain practical understanding.

Keeping in regular contact with other BHPs is a practical way of maintaining ethical practices in IC. The behavioral health ethical codes recommend peer consultation and supervision as safeguards to ethical practice. Finding a clinical supervisor with IC experience can be extremely helpful and prevent a sense of isolation by the BHP if he or she is the only mental health provider in a practice. If a supervisor is not available on-site, BHPs can seek supervision outside the clinic, through phone or email contact with another BHP. Some supervisors may ask for compensation for their service, though many will donate their time as they appreciate the difficulty of securing supervision outside of an integrated care practice (Robinson & Reiter, 2007). BHPs who are full employees of the practice, rather than contractual providers to it, may be more likely to obtain support from their practice if payment for supervision is needed. If BHPs practice in an area where there are multiple IC sites, a peer group for consultation and support could be organized. Alternately, if local support is difficult to find, attending IC conferences and networking with other BHPs in order to develop relationships may be solutions. Also, joining professional associations like the Collaborative Family Healthcare Association provides access to a national community of integrated care providers and resources. Taking these steps will ensure that competency will grow in tandem with the demands of the IC scope of practice.

BHPs might have ethical concerns about being asked to perform patient care duties outside of their professional scope of practice, such as medication management or physical symptom monitoring. It is important to remember that BHPs in IC are not transitioning into medical providers when they perform these duties, but rather, they are professionally integrating into a medical practice. A BHP's role is to add to the care profile offered at the clinic without duplicating services. A BHP should be expected to learn about the medical care of the patients they are treating just as the PCP would be expected to learn about behavioral care. In this way, providers can support one another and better serve the patient. A BHP who has an affinity for the medical setting will become adept at helping the PCP with treatment options based on the information gained from behavioral treatment.

Another scope of practice concern relates to the level of psychiatric care provided in an integrated primary care clinic. A well-integrated practice should be able to appropriately serve more mental health issues than a traditional health care clinic. Clinic professionals need to be aware of the risk of treating patients whose mental health issues may be beyond the scope of the collaborating team. In these cases, communication between the BHP and the PCP is critical for treating the patient effectively and responsibly. There must be agreement on the diagnosis and treatment plan, as well as a safety plan if a patient cannot be adequately cared for in the setting. Clinical supervision for BHPs is a valuable resource in these special cases; the practice should seek to develop a relationship with a local psychiatrist for consultation or even co-treatment. In some remote IC settings where none of these resources are available, IC is the best and only care available to the patient. In this scenario, the ethical mandate would be to provide the best care possible and protect the patient from possible harm. Additionally, careful documentation of the situation is an essential ethical requirement. The following statement is an example of how to convey "scope of practice" issues with clients:

> Mrs. Rodriguez, as I mentioned earlier, Dr. Shah and I work together as a team to ensure you get the best care possible. Even though I will ask you about the medicines you are taking and any side effects that you are experiencing, Dr. Shah is ultimately in charge of the medical aspects of your care, with your input, of course. And, if we find that your concerns or symptoms are beyond our capabilities, we will do everything possible to make sure you get referred to a specialist who can better treat your symptoms while communicating with us. That said, your feedback about whether you feel your needs are being met is very important to us, so please feel free to share any concerns with us at any time.

Conclusion

The integration of different ethical standards into one clinic has the potential of strengthening patient-centered care. The merging of ethical codes in an integrated setting can be quite challenging, but when providers learn to appreciate the complexities of the human condition and work in careful collaboration, quality of patient care and provider satisfaction are enhanced. When providers rise to the highest ethical standards in IC settings, all aspects of treatment and the caring relationship are advanced.

Discussion Questions

1. In terms of informed consent, how might you approach this with patients in a way that is thorough yet brief enough to work within the fast-paced IC environment?
2. What if Mrs. Rodriguez mentioned to you, the BHP, that she drinks to excess 5–6 nights per week but does not want you to share this with Dr. Shah?
3. How would you handle it if a patient gave you a gift (i.e., candles or a picture frame) while you were walking through the waiting room?
4. What steps would you take to get to know the culture of an IC practice, and how long would you wait before addressing practice processes that seem to conflict with your ideology of good patient care?
5. How would you handle the following situation? A patient presents with an issue that you are not qualified to treat, but the patient either has no other options for treatment (i.e., lives in a rural area without specialists) or refuses to accept a referral.

Endnotes

1. All excerpts from the American Medical Association's *Code of Medical Ethics* are © 1995–2012 by the American Medical Association. Reprinted with permission. All rights reserved.
2. All excerpts from the American Psychological Association's *Ethical Principles of Psychologists and Code of Conduct* is © 2010 by the American Psychological Association. Reprinted with permission.
3. All excerpts from the National Association of Social Workers' *Code of Ethics* are © 2008 by the National Association of Social Workers. Reprinted with permission.
4. All excerpts from the American Association for Marriage and Family Therapy's *AAMFT Code of Ethics* are © 2001 by the American Association for Marriage and Family Therapy. Reprinted with permission.
5. All excerpts from the American Counseling Association's *Code of Ethics and Standards of Practice* are © 2005 by the American Counseling Association. Reprinted with permission.

References

American Association for Marriage and Family Therapy (AAMFT). (2001, July 1). *AAMFT code of ethics.* Retrieved from http://www.aamft.org/resources/lrm_plan/ethics/ethicscode2001.asp

American Counseling Association (ACA). (2005). *ACA code of ethics.* Alexandria, VA: Author.

American Medical Association (AMA). (2008). *AMA code of medical ethics.* Chicago, IL: Author. Retrieved from http://www.ama-assn.org/ama/pub/physician-resources/medical-ethics/code-medical-ethics/opinion808.shtml

American Psychological Association (APA). (2010a, June 1). *Ethical principles of psychologists and code of conduct* (amended). Retrieved from http://www.apa.org/ethics/code/index.aspx

Escobar, J. I., Interian, A., Diaz-Martinez, A., & Gara, M. (2006). Idiopathic physical symptoms: A common manifestation of psychiatric disorders in primary care. *CNS Spectrum, 11*(3), 201–210.

National Association of Social Workers (2008). *NASW code of ethics (guide to the everyday professional conduct of social workers).* Washington, DC: Author.

O'Donohue, W. T., Byrd, M. R., Cummings N. A., & Henderson, D. A. (2005). *Behavioral integrative care: Treatments that work in the primary care setting.* New York: Brunner-Routledge.

Robinson, P. J., & Reiter, J. T. (2007). *Behavioral consultation and primary care: A guide to integrating services.* New York: Springer.

Salovey, P., Rothman, A. J., Detweiler, J. B., & Steward, W. T. (2000). Emotional states and physical health. *American Psychologist, 55*(1), 110–121.

Bibliography

Frank, R. G., McDaniel, S. H., Bray, J. H., & Heldring, M. (2004). *Primary care psychology.* Washington, DC: American Psychological Association.

Haynes, R., Corey, G., & Moulton, P. (2003). *Clinical supervision in the helping professions: A practical guide.* Pacific Grove, CA: Brooks/Cole – Thompson Learning.

Hunter, C. L., Goodie, J. L., Oordt, M. S., & Dobmeyer, A. C. (2009). *Integrated behavioral health in primary care: Step-by-step guidance for assessment and intervention.* Washington, DC: American Psychological Association.

Veatch, R. M. (1997). *Medical Ethics.* Sudbury, MA: Jones and Bartlett.

CHAPTER 7

Cross-Cultural Issues in Integrated Care

PHYLLIS ROBERTSON and DOUG ZEH

The changing face of the United States requires behavioral health providers (BHPs) to become knowledgeable of the different cultural perspectives of their patients in order to provide culturally sensitive services. The United States is a country with a population that is living longer and becoming more racially and ethnically diverse, composed of a wide variety of cultural groups. A cultural group is broadly defined as a collection of individuals who share a common heritage or set of beliefs, norms, and values (U.S. Department of Health and Human Services [DHHS], 2003). For many generations, the dominant culture for much of U.S. history has focused on the beliefs, norms, and values of European Americans. As our understanding and appreciation of culture has begun to expand beyond a Eurocentric worldview, we embrace new ways of defining cultural groups that go beyond race and ethnicity to include factors such as gender, religion, geographic region, age, sexual orientation, ability, and class. With these new characteristics of diversity, many people consider themselves as having multiple cultural identities (U.S. DHHS, 2005). We will briefly explore the need for considering integrated care from a culturally sensitive point of view by drawing attention to four population trends within the United States: the influence of immigration and interracial parenting, language differences, the aging and feminization of the workforce, and the attention being drawn to sexual minorities.

Browning of America

Rodriguez (1998), an American essayist, coined the phrase "browning of America" to reflect the influence of immigration and birth of biracial children on the racial landscape of the United States. In 2006, almost 30% of adults and 40% of children were members of racial or ethnic minority populations (U.S. Census Bureau, 2006). The percentage of people identifying as Hispanic or Asian has doubled in recent decades, with 33% of the U.S. population identifying as part of a group other than single-race non-Hispanic White (U.S. Census Bureau, 2006, 2009). Explanations for this trend point to the continued immigration of people from Asia and Latin America and the increasing birthrates for Hispanic women (O'Neil, 2008). It is anticipated that the number of U.S. citizens reporting to be multiracial will increase, as the 2010 U.S. census report allows for 57 possible combinations of the six racial groups: White, Black or African American, Asian, American Indian or Alaskan Native, Hawaiian or other Pacific Islander, and some other race (U.S. Census Bureau, 2010). The number of children being raised in biracial or multiracial households is also likely to increase proportionately as racial minority group population numbers increase.

Language Diversity

The diagnosis and treatment of mental disorders greatly depend on verbal communication and trust between patient and clinician. Almost 20% of the U.S. population can speak a language other than English, with 44% speaking English less than well (U.S. Census Bureau, 2009). Among these bilingual people, 92.4% identify themselves as native or naturalized U.S. citizens. Many people experience difficulty in accessing health care because of their immigration status and the scarcity of providers who speak their language (Ku & Matani, 2001). Furthermore, interventions provided in a limited- or non-English-speaking patient's native language have been found to be twice as effective as those that are employed in English only (Griner & Smith, 2006). It is becoming imperative that BHPs either develop into bilingual speakers or have access to translators for work with their limited- or non-English-speaking patients.

Aging and Feminization of Workforce

It is projected that the United States will see an increase in the population of people over 75 years of age, with the group doubling between 2005 and 2050 (U.S. Department of Health and Human Services: Center for Disease Control, 2007). Many in this older generation, who enjoy greater life expectancies, will remain in the workforce beyond the age of retirement and will continue to need services for both physical and mental health concerns well into their later years.

"It is still women who are doing the lion's share of family care and giving up substantial working time and earnings to do so, with seriously negative effects on their current income, as well as their retirement security" (Hartmann, Lovell, & Werschkul, 2004, p. 5). Furthermore, women continue to earn less than men regardless of employment position, education, or years of experience. As women continue to make up a high proportion of the U.S. workforce, they have begun to experience the same health concerns related to work stress as men, such as heart disease (Wilkins, 2010). Generally, women and adults over the age of 50 years were more likely than men and younger adults to use mental health services for the treatment of depression (National Institute of Mental Health, 2008). Therefore, services for these minority groups need to incorporate gender- and age-based interventions with sensitivity to issues unique to these populations. Such issues for women may include conflicts between work and child rearing and/or parental caretaking responsibilities, and for older women, issues include coping with the fear of declining physical and cognitive health and end-of-life decisions.

Growing Awareness of Sexual Minorities

Recent efforts to have same-sex marriage or unions recognized as lawful and constitutional have focused on the discriminatory practices and policies affecting sexual minority groups. The recognition of oppression and acceptance of sexual minorities by the mental health professions is reflected by the inclusion of ethical treatment guidelines for working with gay, lesbian, bisexual, transgender, and questioning (GLBTQ) patients (Remley & Herlihy, 2010). Homosexuality was declassified as a mental disorder in the early 1970s, and today, requests have been made for the American Psychiatric Association to remove the gender identity disorder classification from the *Diagnostic and Statistical Manual of Mental Disorders*, 4th edition (*DSM-IV*; American Psychiatric Association, 2000), so that gender and gender nonconforming people can have easier access to the medical treatment they need (National Coalition for LGBT Health, 2010). With growing numbers of individuals expressing their sexual identity as other than heterosexual, it is paramount that BHPs examine their own biases and attitudes reflective of homophobia, homonegativity, and heterosexism that have led to harmful practices with GLBTQ clients. Furthermore, it is recommended that providers acquire specialized knowledge to adequately employ best practices for work with GLBTQ patients (Atkinson & Hackett, 2004).

Utilization of Services by Minority Groups

Research has shown that minority clients tend to underutilize or terminate treatment early from mental health services (Barnes, 1994; Kearney, Draper, & Baron, 2005; Teh Wei, Snowden, Jerrell, & Nguyen, 1991; S. Sue, Fujino, Hu, Takeuchi, & Zane, 1991). Reasons for underutilization stem from lack of knowledge about services (Atkinson, Morton, & Sue, 1998), mistrust of services and providers (Whaley, 2001), cultural value systems that oppose use of services (Altarriba & Bauer, 1998; McMiller & Weisz, 1996; Root, 1998), and provider insensitivity to minority client needs, values, and beliefs (Atkinson, Jennings, & Liongson, 1990; Atkinson et al., 1998; Cokley, 2005). Furthermore, traditional therapy through a nondirective individualistic approach to helping may be seen as culturally insensitive by some racial and lower socioeconomic groups. Research has shown that many minority patients prefer a more active influencing approach and the inclusion of family members in therapy (D. W. Sue & Sue, 2008). It is the perception of many minority clients that mental health providers are not knowledgeable about their circumstances or capable of communicating effectively within cultural frameworks. This perception has helped to fuel the need for BHPs to value and incorporate cross-cultural counseling competencies into their approaches to patient services.

Cross-Cultural Counseling Competencies

The American Psychological Association (APA) and the American Counseling Association (ACA) have incorporated cross-cultural counseling competencies within their ethical guidelines for cultural sensitivity in the delivery of counseling services (ACA, 2005; APA, 2002). These guidelines call for the need for awareness of self and others as cultural beings, knowledge of diverse cultural worldviews, and skills for working with diverse individuals who identify differently from the majority (D. W. Sue & Sue, 2008). Traditionally, mental health services have focused on issues related to a Eurocentric view of mental health with limited understanding and exploration of perspectives beyond those of the majority. Researchers, educators, and practitioners are now asked to examine the limitations that are imposed by holding this perspective and the injustices invoked on people of color, women, sexual minorities, lower socioeconomic income groups, people with disabilities, and others who represent minority groups within the United States. BHPs are encouraged to explore their values and beliefs, including biases and prejudices about different cultural groups, in order to become more culturally sensitive. This process often proves challenging for students in mental health training programs, as it requires them to examine topics that evoke strong emotions and a desire to retreat to the belief that treating all people with respect means treating everyone the same. This approach of color blindness or sameness, though, tends to deny the experiences of people who live with oppression and discrimination solely because of their minority status (Atkinson & Hackett, 2004). In addition, the perception of sameness can lead some providers to inadvertently communicate discriminatory actions and statements toward their minority patients that can lead, at a minimum, to confusion by the patient and, at the most, to early termination of services.

Inadvertent discriminatory behaviors and words, whether intended or not, are called microaggressions, and they can damage the trust in a therapeutic relationship, communicate biases, and be injurious to the patient's spiritual self (D. W. Sue et al., 2007). Microaggressions are different from what is traditionally recognized as racism, sexism, heterosexism, classism, and ageism, as oftentimes the perpetrators are unaware they are communicating them and because they are very subtle in nature. The cumulative effect of experiencing these discriminations can leave a person feeling disenfranchised and reluctant to trust individuals from majority groups. One example of a microaggression is the communication of the assumption that a patient is heterosexual through the act of referring to the patient's partner as the opposite gender. This form of heterosexism conveys the idea to the nonheterosexual patient that opposite-sex relationships are more valued than other types of relationships. Another common microaggression is to imply that an Asian American's or Mexican American's use of English is very good, which asserts that the person is assumed to be foreign born. For more examples of microaggressions, we suggest you consult D. W. Sue et al. (2007). Microaggressions sometimes originate from lack of understanding about majority group privilege and stereotypes of minority people, which later become biases that are communicated by staff and BHPs. It is the responsibility of providers to examine their own thoughts, values, and behaviors toward minority clients, as well as to raise awareness in others to create a culturally sensitive environment for all patients. Furthermore, it is necessary for health providers to be aware of their own cultural group identities and how these might be perceived by patients who are seeking reassurance through understanding and the absence of judgment in their treatment.

Barriers to mental health services exist for all Americans: cost, fragmentation of services, lack of availability of services, and societal stigma toward mental illness (U.S. DHHS, 1999). Additional barriers exist that deter minorities, including mistrust and fear of treatment, institutional racism and discrimination, differences in language and communication patterns, and limited access to health providers from the same racial, ethnic, and sexual orientation groups. Racial and ethnic minorities collectively experience a greater disability burden from mental illness than do Whites. "This higher level of burden stems from minorities receiving less care and poorer quality of care, rather than from their illnesses being inherently more severe or prevalent in the community" (U.S. DHHS, 2005). The 2005 surgeon general report indicates that the mental health profession is disproportionately represented by White therapists and that the staff is not representative of the patients they serve (U.S. DHHS, 2005). Minority patients experience language barriers that can limit their understanding of services rendered and expectations on their part in the process. Indeed, language barriers contribute significantly to lack of access to services and early termination by non-English- or limited-English-speaking clients (Sentell, Shemwany, & Snowden, 2007). Fear of being "outed" or facing familial and religious condemnation are concerns expressed by people in sexual minority groups when seeking treatment (Bond, Hefner, & Drogos, 2009; Vaughan & Waehler, 2010). Barriers to mental health services exist for members of lower social economic classes; adults without transportation are 10 times more likely to delay accessing medical care, with poor women ages 45 to 64 years reporting the highest rates of delay (U.S. DHHS: Center for Disease Control, 2007). Lack of insurance because of poverty and unemployment also limits access to preventive care. These delays for services often result in the occurrence of minority patients presenting with mental health concerns in emergency rooms and crisis care clinics (Teh Wei, Snowden, Jerrell, & Nguyen, 1991; Snowden, 2001). In an effort to reduce these barriers, agencies and clinics need to be more conscious of the effort made by individuals in various cultural groups to seek services and of the messages that BHPs send the potential patient upon first entering their offices. The following case demonstrates how a BHP and agency can work through barriers to create a welcoming environment and culturally sensitive treatment plan for the patient.

Treatment Approach with Stacy

Flexibility in therapeutic roles and treatment approaches must be adopted by the BHP to address patient needs and wants within a cultural context. As a general suggestion, a provider should adopt a style that is both concrete and directive but one that also allows a connection with the patient's value and belief system. One such strategy, motivational interviewing, appears to have some efficacy in working across cultural difference (Venner, Feldstein, & Tafoya, 2007).

The following case represents the work provided with a patient who identifies with multiple minority groups: race, gender, sexual orientation, socioeconomic status, and ability.

Case Study

Stacy is a 38-year-old bisexual, African American female with a long history of substance abuse and mental health problems. She comes from a background of significant poverty and limited education (her highest level of education was the seventh grade). In the past she has had a strong connection to her Christian faith. Stacy has been in and out of treatment for the past several years, but she recently returned to care after several months during which she was on a binge of alcohol and crack cocaine. During this time Stacy was homeless and had been cut off from family members, including her children, who have been permanently placed in kinship care, with Stacy's parental rights terminated. Stacy lacks healthy support systems and presents to treatment again primarily because of concerns over her physical health and housing issues. Her primary diagnoses include bipolar disorder I, PTSD, polysubstance dependence, and multiple chronic health issues including hypertension, diabetes, chronic back pain, and multiple STDs (both chronic and acute). In the process of interviewing Stacy, the therapist identified the following goals:

Patient goals and motivating factors:

- reconnection with her children
- improved relationship with her family of origin
- stable housing
- consistent income
- treatment for chronic pain issues

Treatment team goals:

- medication adherence
- safe sex practices
- disease management (diet, exercise, sleep, checking blood sugar, etc.)
- recovery from active addiction

Outcomes: Interventions were initially focused on dealing with barriers by helping Stacy obtain income and insurance so that treatment could be delivered effectively. She was assisted with obtaining housing and transportation to establish a reliable environment for treatment adherence and change. The focus during sessions was on helping the patient identify and commit to small steps that could be achieved on a weekly basis to help build confidence. After these steps were made and Stacy was reasonably compliant with care, additional supports were added, including recovery support groups, exercise and disease management programs, and reconnection with church and her spirituality. During this time, conversation with Stacy's family members had been initiated, as they had always indicated a desire to have her connected with the family. Core members of the patient's family system were identified and asked to participate in treatment sessions so that trust and rapport could be rebuilt.

One year after treatment began, Stacy had maintained stable housing, was compliant with all medications with no requirement for crisis or legal services, and had significantly reduced her use of substances with only minor relapse present instead of chronic abuse. In addition, the patient had regular contact with family, including her children, and had an increase in her global assessment of functioning of over 30 points.

Stacy's case demonstrates the multiple barriers to service this patient had to face in accessing services and managing her treatment plan. Trust with the treatment agency and the therapist had to be reestablished, as she had had multiple dealings with agencies in the past, including having custody of her children removed. Furthermore, lack of access to housing and transportation, inability to afford medications, and lack of a support system outside of the agency setting presented as barriers to the successful implementation of her treatment. At the agency level, provider fatigue was also a deterrent that had to be overcome, as Stacy had overutilized some services in the past without full adherence to a more detailed plan toward recovery and maintenance of a stable lifestyle.

It is important to note that the role of the BHP became quite diverse in helping this patient manage her health care needs. As we continue a shift toward integrated care within our field, the ever-growing need of BHPs to serve in multiple roles is becoming more and more evident. Gone are the days of traditional one-on-one therapy, as ultimately time and availability dictate this shift, and there is a growing recognition that this mode of treatment is not effective for many different populations (Kreiger, Collier, Song, & Martin, 1999; D. W. Sue & Sue, 2008; S. Sue et al., 1991). This shift has challenged BHPs to focus on expanding their roles and developing a wide range of interventions and styles to assist a diverse group of patients on their path to wellness. D. W. Sue and Sue (2008) explained that therapists must assume multiple roles in delivery of services to minority patients because of varying developmental needs, preferences in helping styles, desires for inclusion of family members, language barriers, varying communication styles, and variations in interpretations of mental health diagnoses and treatment practices. Table 7.1 represents the multiple roles to which BHPs within integrated care may find themselves ascribed in order to provide effective and comprehensive care to patients.

In the case of Stacy, the therapist not only provided weekly individual therapy but also served in the roles of an educator; an access person for disability income, entitlements, and housing; a provider of connections with other supportive services; a support person for reconnection with

Table 7.1
Roles of the Culturally Sensitive Behavioral Health Provider

- *Case manager:* Make referrals to community-based resources such as support organizations, medication assistance programs, and shelters.
- *Patient advocate:* Address legal issues, provide access to social services, and help with writing letters, communicating with landlords, accessing employment services, and accessing necessary forms for social security and unemployment benefits.
- *Health coach:* Encourage medication adherence for both mental and physical health. Requires that the BHP has a general knowledge of issues such as diabetes, HIV, hypertension, COPD/asthma, and other chronic health issues.
- *Therapist:* Provide individual, family, and group therapy.
- *Crisis interventionist:* Provide triage/brief/solution-focused work.
- *Job coach:* Provide education and access to career and employment services.
- *Collaborator/consultant:* Communicate with medical and psychiatric care providers.
- *Marketer/educator:* Provide outreach programs that educate community members on services.
- *Change agent:* Educate others about cultural issues within the agency, advocate for flexible hours (evenings and weekends), and provide services in the home or in the community.
- *Community consultant:* Collaborate with indigenous health workers or community lay helpers in provision of services.

the patient's family; and a provider of weekly group therapy sessions. This diversification of roles is further demonstrated in the case of Antonio.

Treatment Approach With Antonio

As noted previously, minority patients may be reluctant to seek services for a wide array of reasons. The case that follows presents evidence that these barriers to treatment may result in a patient presenting in a state of crisis. This crisis can sometimes be precipitated directly by cultural issues such as language barriers, fear of immigration policies, lack of trust and understanding of services, and limited financial resources.

Case Study

Antonio is a 20-year-old heterosexual, Mexican male with a recent onset of severe psychotic symptoms and mood instability. Antonio is also an immigrant to the United States on a church-sponsored visa, which is reflective of his strong faith. However, upon his entering treatment, it was discovered that his visa had expired, and he was now living in the United States illegally. Antonio has a high school education with hopes of attending college, comes from a lower-middle-class background, and currently lives with a large family including multiple generations. Antonio presented to care as directed by his family because of his increasingly bizarre behavior including hyperreligiosity, prolonged lack of sleep, outbursts of anger, mood instability, delusional thinking, ideas of reference, and paranoia. These symptoms, which had presented over the past several months, have led to loss of work, which has significantly impacted the family's ability to meets its needs, as well as the patient's ability to effectively care for himself.

Although Antonio's life was highly disregulated, he presented as a kind and engaging individual who appeared motivated for treatment with a strong desire to resolve issues in order to return to work. His language of origin was Spanish with the ability to speak and understand English on a very informal basis. Therefore, interpreter services were arranged to provide accurate translation. The treatment team requested that his family members, as well as his church pastor, be present during sessions, as many of them were bilingual and were able to provide collateral information regarding presenting issues. Importantly, Antonio expressed greater comfort having them present. Another primary reason for including family was the presence of a belief by family members that the patient's symptoms were only temporary and would resolve with time and medication. Antonio was diagnosed with schizoaffective disorder, hypertension, and type 2 diabetes, due to a poor diet, lack of exercise, and morbid obesity.

Patient goals and motivating factors:

- ability to return to work and support his family
- education
- being a valuable and active member of his church community

Treatment team goals:

- education for patient and family regarding the chronic nature of his issues
- medication adherence
- disease management
- safety for the patient and his family

Outcomes: Crisis services were immediately provided to Antonio so that he could begin taking medication. In concurrence with this, several sessions were spent with the patient and his family so that education could be provided in terms of his diagnosis and need for consistency with the medication. Initially, Antonio stabilized quite well and began to see a remission of some of his presenting issues. This, however, led to the patient's initial discontinuation of treatment, which was due primarily to the belief by both the patient and his family that he had been cured. After the first occurrence of termination of treatment, future treatment focused heavily on education for the patient and his family about the need for ongoing treatment of a severe and persistent mental illness.

This lack of understanding of mental disorders and treatment protocol, however, proved to be very difficult to change, and the patient experienced several more episodes of rapid decompensation. It was then determined that Antonio required a higher level of care. A referral was made to a local agency that provided outreach and case management services so that Antonio could be followed more closely outside of the clinical setting. Therapeutic work was still continued with Antonio in order to facilitate the transition to the new agency and to continue to address his physical health issues. After approximately 6 months in a higher level of care, Antonio was able to resume care at the integrated level. At this time Antonio was able to return to part-time work, connect with an immigration attorney to address citizenship issues, and volunteer regularly at his church.

Antonio's case exemplifies several cultural factors of which the BHP must be aware in order to provide culturally sensitive services. While working with Antonio, particularly in the early stages of treatment, the provider gave attention to the Latino concepts of *personalismo* (a preference for developing a relationship with the BHP instead of the clinic as a whole), *familismo* (a strong sense of unity and interdependence with family), and *machismo* (a strong sense of masculine pride and responsibility) (Anez, Silva, Paris, & Bedregal, 2008; Santiago-Rivera, Arredondo, & Gallardo-Cooper, 2002). The provider's awareness of these concepts, and ability to address them early in treatment, greatly increases the chances of compliance with care and successful outcomes. Antonio's value system is reflective of the importance placed on family and religious community. The incorporation of cultural values of familismo into the initial sessions helped to establish rapport and credibility with this patient. However, commitment toward receiving help beyond medication was limited because of the patient's and family members' lack of understanding about mental illness. It is important for the BHP to recognize that this behavior should not be treated as resistance, but rather the BHP should employ tact and patience to educate the patient and family members. His immigration status also complicated his ability to afford treatment, as well as brought about the potential for mistrust of the agency in fear of being reported to immigration authorities. Antonio's limited use of English and lack of education about Western medicine practices is challenging, as issues and concepts are not always communicated effectively across languages. Utilization of a translator is necessary, and the BHP should solicit regular feedback from patients and provide ample opportunity for them to ask questions. It can also be helpful to have patients explain in their own words their understanding of topics discussed, as this will increase the likelihood of appropriate follow-through.

Group Identity and Within-Group Differences

The two cases presented in this chapter draw into light the importance of group identity and within-group differences for patients. A thorough discussion of these differences is beyond the scope of this chapter; however, it is important to recognize that within-group differences have actually been found to be greater than those between racial groups (Atkinson & Hackett, 2004). For instance, immigration status and generational differences affect levels of acculturation within racial and ethnic groups and can impact a family's receptivity to services (Santiago-Rivera et al., 2002). Socioeconomic status and gender can also contribute to within-group differences, as both of these affect accessibility to services and present variability in support systems. Religious affiliation, educational level, employment status, ability, and military membership also separate individuals into groups of people who may have unique worldviews and thus require sensitivity in the delivery of services. The continuing inequality of income and economic resource access for people of color, women, people with disabilities, and individuals in rural communities draws our attention to the disparity that exists within cultural groups. This further supports the idea that adhering to any particular treatment model will likely result in alienation of more patients than it will serve; no single approach is best for working with any specific minority group because of these within-group differences (D. W. Sue & Sue, 2008). Flexibility in practicing and knowledge of multiple treatment modalities are inherent assets for the BHP in integrated care settings and are particularly helpful when treating patients with multicultural backgrounds.

Conclusion

Professional ethical standards call for BHPs to become culturally competent in the delivery of services to people from diverse backgrounds. The process for becoming competent is ongoing and requires the provider to remain diligent in attaining knowledge, awareness, and skills across multiple dimensions when serving minority patients. Some questions to ask yourself as a BHP follow.

- How prepared are you to work with patients from a variety of cultural backgrounds?

- How have you explored your own prejudices, biases, and stereotypes of people with cultural backgrounds that are different from yours?
- How knowledgeable are you about the belief and value systems of a diverse group of people? How could you learn about these systems?
- What can you do to increase your awareness, knowledge, and skills for working with sexual minority clients? People with disabilities? People with nonmainstream religious beliefs?
- How have you explored your own identity, and how might others perceive you based on race, ethnicity, age, gender, sexual orientation, ability, religion, and socioeconomic status?

Furthermore, there are questions to ask of your integrated care facility.

- How do you train your staff to be culturally sensitive?
- How is feedback from minority patients generated at the agency level?
- How receptive is your facility to non-English-speaking patients, and how do you utilize translators?
- What type of outreach programs do you have in place to educate the public about services?
- How are community leaders engaged in the planning and delivery of services?
- What opportunities exist for low-income patients to have affordable transportation, medication, and fees of payment?

Cultural diversity is the norm in the United States, and it is our responsibility to assure our patients that we are educated and prepared to address issues that arise from these differences. This chapter provides an introduction to these issues, but it is our hope that this will be the first of many experiences for current and future BHPs to gain awareness of the impact of cross-cultural competency. Cultural competency should be viewed as an ongoing developmental process rather than a state of awareness that can be achieved. As we move ahead in our understanding, a frequent and open examination of these issues will ensure that we are able to address the ever-changing landscape of the integrated health care field.

Discussion Questions

1. What types of microaggressions have you witnessed committed against others? For example, GLBTQ youth indicate that they hear insults on a daily basis in their schools. "That's so gay" is a phrase that is used to imply something is stupid. Locate online

the suicide prevention campaign at The Trevor Project (www.thetrevorproject.org/organization) and the It Gets Better Project (www.itgetsbetter.org/) to learn of the support that exists for these youth. After accessing the sites, talk with at least one other person about what you have learned.

2. If Stacy were your patient, how would you approach the issues related to her desire to reunify with her children? Examine in particular the nature of the patient's treatment goals as compared with the goals of the treatment team.

3. As individuals, we are all products of our social and cultural contexts. We have accordingly adopted certain values and worldviews. The examination and awareness of our own cultural biases is an important part of providing effective care and sometimes requires us to *un*learn some things. As you consider the case of Antonio, what potential issues do you think could impact your ability to work effectively with this patient? Would it be possible to have these biases and still provide effective care? Please explain.

4. What cultural groups do you identify with? What cultural groups do you think your clients will attribute to you? How do you think your cross-cultural differences might affect the counseling relationship?

5. The website Understanding Prejudice (www.understandingprejudice.org/), created by the Social Psychology Network, contains a variety of interactive exercises for you to examine perspectives on prejudice, stereotyping, and discrimination. Go to the website and take several of the assessments to examine your knowledge about the history of oppression in the United States and increase your awareness of your own biases.

References

Altarriba, J., & Bauer, L. M. (1998). Counseling Cuban Americans. In D. R. Atkinson, G. Morton, & D. W. Sue (Eds.). *Counseling American minorities* (pp. 280–300). Boston: McGraw-Hill.

American Counseling Association. (2005). *ACA code of ethics*. Retrieved from http://www.counseling.org/Resources/CodeOfEthics/TP/Home/CT2.aspx

American Psychiatric Association. (2000). *Diagnostic and statistical manual of mental disorders* (Rev. 4th ed.). Washington, DC: Author.

American Psychological Association. (2002). Ethical principles of psychologists and code of conduct. *American Psychologist, 57*(12), 1060.

Anez, L. M., Silva, M. A., Paris, M., Jr., & Bedregal, L. E. (2008). Engaging Latinos through the integration of cultural values and motivational interviewing principles. *Professional Psychology: Research and Practice, 39*, 153–159. doi:10.1037/0735-7028.39.2.153

Atkinson, D., & Hackett, G. (2004). *Counseling diverse populations* (3rd ed.). New York: McGraw-Hill.

Atkinson, D., Jennings, R., & Liongson, L. (1990). Minority students reasoning for not seeking counseling and suggestions for improving services. *Journal of College Student Development, 31*(4), 342–350.

Atkinson, D. R., Morton, G., & Sue, D. W. (1998). *Counseling American minorities* (5th ed.). Boston: McGraw-Hill.

Barnes, M. (1994). Clinical treatment issues regarding Black African-Americans. In J. L. Ronch, W. Van Ornum, & N. C. Stilwell (Eds.), *The counseling sourcebook: A practical reference on contemporary issues* (pp. 157–164). New York: Crossroad.

Bond, B., Hefner, V., & Drogos, K. (2009). Information-seeking practices during the sexual development of lesbian, gay, and bisexual individuals: The influence and effects of coming out in a mediated environment. *Sexuality and Culture, 13*, 32–50. doi:10.1007/s12119-008-9041-y

Cokley, K. (2005). The use of race and ethnicity in psychological practice: A review. In R. T. Carter (Ed.). *Handbook of racial-cultural psychology and counseling: Training and practice* (Vol. 2, pp. 249–261). Hoboken, NJ: John Wiley.

Griner, D., & Smith, T. (2006). Culturally adapted mental health interventions: A meta-analytic review. *Psychotherapy: Theory, Research, Practice, Training, 43*, 531–548. doi:10.1037/0033-3204.43.4.531

Hartmann, H., Lovell, V., & Werschkul, M. (2004). *Women and the economy: Recent trends in job loss, labor force participation, and wages* (Pub. No. B245). Retrieved from http://www.iwpr.org/publications/pubs/women-and-the-economy-recent-trends-in-job-loss-labor-force-participation-and-wages-b245

Kearney, L. K., Draper, M., & Baron, A. (2005). Counseling utilization by ethnic minority college students. *Cultural Diversity and Ethnic Minority Psychology, 11*(3), 272–285. doi:10.1037/1099-9809.11.3.272

Kreiger, J., Collier, C., Song, L., & Martin, D. (1999). Linking community-based blood pressure measurement to clinical care: A randomized controlled trial of outreach and tracking by community health workers. *American Journal of Public Health, 89*, 856–861.

Ku, L., & Matani, S. (2001). Left out: Immigrants access to health care and insurance. *Health Affairs, 20*(1), 247–256.

McMiller, W. P., & Weisz, J. R. (1996). Help-seeking preceding mental health clinic intake among African American, Latino, and Caucasian youths. *Journal of the American Academy of Child and Adolescent Psychiatry, 35*, 1086–1094.

National Coalition for LGBT Health. (2010). *Statement on gender identity in the diagnostic and statistical manual.* Retrieved from http://lgbthealth.webolutionary.com/content/statement-gender-identity-diagnostic-and-statistical-manual

National Institute of Mental Health. (2008). *Use of mental health services and treatment by adults.* Retrieved from http://www.nimh.nih.gov/statistics/3USE_MT_ADULT.shtml

O'Neil, D. (2008). *Ethnicity and race: American diversity patterns.* Retrieved from http://anthro.palomar.edu/ethnicity/ethnic_6.htm

Remley, T. P., Jr., & Herlihy, B. (2010). *Ethical, legal and professional issues in counseling* (3rd ed.). Upper Saddle River, NJ: Merrill.

Rodriguez, R. (1998). *The browning of America*. Retrieved from http://www.pbs. org/newshour/essays/february98/rodriguez_2-18.html

Root, M. P. P. (1998). Facilitating psychotherapy with Asian American clients. In D. R. Atkinson, G. Morton, & D. W. Sue (Eds.). *Counseling American minorities* (pp. 214–234). Boston: McGraw-Hill.

Santiago-Rivera, A. L., Arredondo, P., & Gallardo-Cooper, M. (2002). *Counseling Latinos and la familia: A practical guide*. Thousand Oaks, CA: Sage.

Sentell, T., Shemwany, M., & Snowden, L. (2007). Access to mental health treatment by English language proficiency and race/ethnicity. *Journal of General Internal Medicine, 22*(Suppl. 2), 289–293. doi:10.1007/s11606-007-0345-7

Snowden, L. R. (2001). Social embeddedness and mental health among African Americans and Whites. *American Journal of Community Psychologist, 45*(3), 347–355.

Sue, D. W., Capodilupo, C., Torino, G., Bucceri, J., Holder, A., Nadal, K., & Esquilin, M. (2007). Racial microaggressions in everyday life: Implications for clinical practice. *American Psychologist, 62*, 271–286.

Sue, D. W., & Sue, D. (2008). *Counseling the culturally diverse: Theory and practice* (5th ed.). Hoboken, NY: John Wiley.

Sue, S., Fujino, D., Hu, L., Takeuchi, D., & Zane, N. (1991). Community mental health services for ethnic minority populations: A test of the cultural responsiveness hypothesis. *Consulting and Clinical Psychology, 59*, 533–540.

Teh-Wei, H., Snowden, L. K., Jerrell, J. M., & Nguyen, T. D. (1991). Ethnic Populations in Public Mental Health: Services Choice and Level of Use. *American Journal of Public Health, 81*(11), 1429–1434.

U.S. Census Bureau. (2006). *Overview of race and Hispanic origin 2000*. Retrieved from http://www.census.gov/prod/2001pubs/c2kbr01-1.pdf

U.S. Census Bureau. (2009). *American community survey: CS demographic and housing estimates: 2005–2009*. Retrieved from http://factfinder.census.gov/servlet/DatasetMainPageServlet?_program=ACS&_submenuId=&_lang=en&_ts=

U.S. Census Bureau. (2010). *U.S. Census Bureau delivers Idaho's 2010 census population totals, including first look at race and Hispanic origin data for legislative redistricting*. Retrieved from http://2010.census.gov/news/releases/operations/cb11-cn78.html

U.S. Department of Health and Human Services. (1999). *Mental health: A report of the surgeon general*. Rockville, MD: Author.

U.S. Department of Health and Human Services. (2003). *Developing cultural competence in disaster mental health programs: Guiding principles and recommendations* (DHHS Pub. No. SMA 3828). Rockville, MD: Center for Mental Health Services, Substance Abuse and Mental Health Services Administration.

U.S. Department of Health and Human Services. (2005). *Mental health: Culture, race, and ethnicity. A supplement to mental health: A report of the surgeon general*. Retrieved from http://www.surgeongeneral.gov/library/mentalhealth/cre/execsummary-1.html

U.S. Department of Health and Human Services: Center for Disease Control. (2007). *Health, United States 2007*. Retrieved from http://www.cdc.gov/nchs/data/hus/hus07.pdf

ment, 17*, 94–109. doi:10.1007/s10804-009-9084-9

Venner, K. L., Feldstein, S. W., & Tafoya, N. (2007). Helping clients feel welcome: Principles of adapting treatment cross-culturally. *Alcoholism Treatment Quarterly, 25*, 11–30. doi:10.1300/J020v25n04_02

Whaley, A. L. (2001). Cultural mistrust: An important psychological construct for diagnosis and treatment of African Americans. *Professional Psychology: Research and Practice, 32*(6), 555–562. doi:10.1037//0735-7028.32.6.555

Wilkins, R. (2010). Stress raises risk of heart disease among women under 50. *British Medical Journal, 340*(7755), 1052. doi:10.1136/bmj.c2508

PART II

Speciality Areas Within Integrated Care

CHAPTER 8

Psychiatric Consultation in Integrated Care and Telepsychiatry

STEPHEN E. BUIE

The integration of psychiatry into primary care settings improves patient care in numerous ways, as has been previously described. The behavioral health provider (BHP) plays a pivotal role in the integrated practice through direct patient care, as well as by acting as a liaison between primary care physicians and the consulting psychiatrist. This chapter will focus on the BHP's collaboration with the psychiatrist.

BHPs in a primary care setting may be asked to serve as a liaison between the primary care providers (PCPs) and the consulting psychiatrist. This role may involve several different forms of action, such as evaluating a patient and deciding whether a psychiatric consultation is indicated, conveying information between the PCP and the psychiatrist, and working with the psychiatrist to implement psychotherapeutic or behavioral interventions.

In an integrated setting, once the PCP identifies contributing psychosocial problems, a referral to the BHP should occur. The BHP can then obtain a more comprehensive history to achieve a more complete understanding of the patient's overall condition and the factors that may be contributing to the current difficulty.

Scenario

Mary, a 55-year-old woman with type 2 diabetes, presented to her PCP with symptoms suggesting that her diabetic control was worsening. She had gained weight and reported increased thirst and increased frequency of urination. Her hemoglobin A1C, a measure of blood glucose that reflects blood sugar levels over the previous 3 months, was elevated at 7.2%. She reported feeling depressed over the past several months. With the downturn in the economy, her home-based business was failing, and the bank was threatening foreclosure on her house after several missed mortgage payments. She was referred for evaluation by the BHP who began seeing her for cognitive behavioral therapy (CBT) and also referred her to the psychiatrist for medication consultation. Her depression was severe enough that she endured several months of medication trials before success in remission was found with a final treatment plan that combined the use of antidepressants and augmentation with aripriprazole, an atypical antipsychotic medication.

Mary's case demonstrates the importance of going beyond the primary health concern to address all aspects of the patient's problem. If the PCP had focused only on Mary's diabetes, then the stress contributing to her poor disease control would not have been addressed. Furthermore, if the BHP were not immediately available, the patient might not have followed through with the appointment. In Mary's case, when her depression was treated, she was able to rally to get another job and to apply for a mortgage adjustment, which allowed her to keep her house. Although depressed, she felt hopeless that there was no way to keep her home and had not been able to look for work or to apply for the mortgage modification.

Pan et al. (2010) analyzed data from 65,000 participants in the Nurses' Health Study, indicating a bidirectional relationship between diabetes and depression. That is, if one has depression, then one is at higher risk for developing type 2 diabetes; if one is diabetic, then one is at higher risk for developing depression. In Mary's case, we were able to vigorously treat her depression and diabetes simultaneously and in close coordination, thereby resulting in improvement in her depression and in her diabetes control, with her hemoglobin A1C and weight both declining.

Psychosocial Stressors

Psychosocial stressors, such as the significant ones with which Mary was faced, may lead to a variety of physical symptoms. Some other examples follow: (a) a patient who is experiencing marital strife develops chronic headaches and other stress-related symptoms, (b) an adolescent whose parents are going through divorce presents with abdominal pain of unclear etiology that occurs after every visit to her father, and (c) an older woman who has recently become estranged from her only daughter is experiencing loss of appetite and weight loss. There are infinite ways that psychosocial stressors can influence health and present in the medical setting. The value of an integrated setting is that these problems, along with the medical implications, can be addressed and resolved in the setting of the patient's primary care home.

Noncompliance

Integrated care (IC) is a more successful treatment environment for noncompliance of treatment recommendations compared to traditional medical care. Frequently, and for a variety of reasons, patients do not take medications as prescribed by their physicians. Patients may not take a new medication because it implies a dependence on something and threatens their self-image of being strong and independent. Or patients may be fearful of side effects or medication interactions. Still others may experience medication as a marker of illness, and abstaining supports their denial. In adolescent patients, noncompliance can be a form of rebellion. In many cases, the PCP can address these issues directly with the patient, but in situations where there has been recurrent noncompliance, a referral to the BHP may be warranted. A BHP can work with patients to identify the reasons for resistance and help them resolve those issues to increase adherence to a prescribed regimen. The opposite situation, when patients take more medication than prescribed, will be addressed later in this chapter.

Severe Psychiatric Illnesses

The BHP will also encounter patients who present with more severe psychiatric illnesses. Most PCPs are comfortable treating depression and most anxiety disorders but are likely to seek psychiatric consultation if their first efforts at treating the depression or anxiety symptoms are unsuccessful. PCPs typically ask for psychiatric consultation when treating patients with bipolar disorder, adults with attention-deficit/hyperactivity disorder, and patients with substance abuse issues or psychotic illnesses. The following scenarios are presented to further demonstrate the importance of collaboration between BHPs and psychiatrists in IC settings.

Scenarios

Susan, a 27-year-old woman, gave birth to her first child 4 months ago and presented to her PCP with postpartum depression within a few weeks of delivery. She was prescribed an antidepressant medication and referred for therapy. She has had difficulty bonding with the infant and has begun having fears that her depression is bad for her baby. This week she began having auditory hallucinations.

Jacob, a 42-year-old man, presents to his PCP for an initial evaluation. He completely disrobes for his physical and talks nonstop throughout the entire exam, focusing on ideas for turning his real estate investments into a real estate investment trust.

Bill, a 19-year-old college student, reports to his PCP that he suspects that his suite mates are really working for the CIA and that he hears voices murmuring to him that he needs to be careful because his cell phone is bugged.

These three scenarios are examples of primary care situations that warrant a psychiatrist's involvement. They represent, respectively, a woman with postpartum psychosis, a man in an acute manic state, and a young college student with a first episode of psychotic illness.

Importance of Biopsychosocial Formulations

BHPs may need to modify the way they present their patient's history to most effectively interface with the psychiatrist for a referral. BHPs will be most effective if their assessment develops a diagnostic formulation, including a list of biological contributors to the problem, so that a *bio*psychosocial formulation can be presented to the consulting psychiatrist. This may differ from the training received by many BHPs, which typically focuses on the *psycho*social aspects of the client's condition, sometimes even to the exclusion of a diagnosis.

Psychiatrists are trained to determine a diagnosis or diagnoses based on established diagnostic criteria and to then plan treatment accordingly. Communication between the psychiatrist and the BHP will be facilitated by the presentation of patient histories that include diagnostic criteria from the *Diagnostic and Statistical Manual of Mental Disorders* (American Psychiatric Association, 2000). An extensive discussion of psychiatric diagnoses is beyond the scope of this chapter, but as an example, a common issue that arises in the primary care setting is differentiating between depression and bipolar disorder. A BHP who evaluates a client with treatment-resistant depression should be familiar with the signs and symptoms of mania and hypomania, as they help determine if the client has undiagnosed bipolar disorder, thereby explaining a poor response to previous treatments with antidepressants. Although the BHP does not have to make a final diagnostic determination, exploring biopsychosocial issues and documenting them in the record will facilitate the psychiatrist's evaluation. This is particularly true if the BHP is asking the psychiatrist to make a recommendation based on chart review; the BHP should not expect the psychiatrist to make treatment recommendations without a thorough diagnostic evaluation documented in the chart.

Another example of the importance of taking a biopsychosocial history follows for a patient who is incorrectly diagnosed with bipolar disorder and is having difficulty with anger management. Interestingly, based on anecdotal evidence, this type of misdiagnosis seems more prevalent for female patients than male; it may be because women with anger outbursts trigger a mood disorder diagnosis by physicians more often than when presented by male patients. In a typical case, the episodes of anger outbursts are seen as "mood swings," and the patient is diagnosed as having bipolar disorder. Further examination of the history is crucial. In this example, it is revealed that she grew up in a household where anger was prevalent. Her anger outbursts are precipitated by something that upset her and are not accompanied by other signs of mood disturbance such as a decreased need for sleep, pressured speech, racing thoughts, and so on. The anger also comes and goes quickly, whereas mood cycles in bipolar disorder are typically of longer duration. Although bipolar disorder can present with a history of angry outbursts, one needs to closely attend to the presence or absence of signs and symptoms of mood disturbance to differentiate between an anger management problem and a mood disorder.

Another component of the biopsychosocial formulation is the detailed documentation of past medication trials. The BHP should elicit a history of the medications previously tried, noting doses, duration of trial, and both positive and negative responses to the medications. For an accurate record, the BHP will need to become familiar with the general psychotropic medication classes, the medications within those classes, and the most common side effects of those medications.

Finally, a family history describing relationships and family dynamics and the presence of psychiatric illness in family members is important to document. Many mental illnesses are highly heritable, and the presence of particular illnesses in family members may give some indication of the patient's diagnosis.

Scenario

Jane, a 20-year-old woman, had been treated at the clinic for depressive symptoms that started at age 14 years. She was first treated with citalopram 20mg at age 16 years and had a favorable response, with resolution of her depression. Jane continued the citalopram for about 6 months, and because she was feeling better, she stopped taking it. She felt free of depressive symptoms for about 2 years until just after her boyfriend broke up with her, when she again became depressed. Her symptoms included a persistently depressed mood, high levels of anxiety, and difficulty sleeping. At this time, Jane was again treated with citalopram but did not enjoy relief of symptoms from the 20mg dose as she had previously. So after 6 weeks, the dose was increased to 40mg. Over the next 2 months, her symptoms gradually improved, but after taking the medication for about 6 months, she again tapered herself off of it. Jane then moved away to attend college, and in the less-structured setting, her lifestyle became more erratic. She was staying up late and then sleeping in the next day. When assignments were nearly due, she would pull all-nighters to get her paper written or her project completed. On occasion, she would have trouble getting to sleep even when, as she described, "my body was tired but my brain would not shut off." To calm herself and to help herself sleep, Jane started smoking marijuana at night. Her dress and makeup became more flamboyant, and when she presented to the student health center, her face was garishly made up with three colors of eyeliner, she had dyed bright red and blue hair, and she wore wildly mismatched clothes. Over the past year she has had several different sexual relationships, some lasting only a few weeks. Jane described sometimes leaving at night to drive 5 hours to the coast so that she could watch the sun rise. She felt that college has been a wonderful experience for her so far and that her creative powers were the highest they have ever been. She feels that she often has to slow herself down, as others can't keep up with her thought processes, and friends have complained to her that she sometimes talks too much and is "irritating."

This patient's history illustrates a common pathway to the emergence of bipolar disorder II, with early onset of depressive symptoms, treatment with antidepressant medications, and later emergence of hypomanic symptoms. The differentiating characteristic of hypomanic symptoms versus manic symptoms is one of functionality: If the person is able to maintain functioning in the presence of elevated mood and energy, then he or she has hypomania rather than mania. In a patient like Jane, one also has to consider whether her disorder is substance induced. Although she denied using other substances, she reported smoking marijuana. A urine toxicology screen should be obtained, however, to evaluate for stimulant or cocaine use, which can mimic hypomanic episodes.

Communication

Communication in a bustling primary care practice can be challenging; everyone is busy, and demand for services is high. Therefore, communication among providers needs to be efficient. The BHP can serve as a conduit for communicating information between the PCP and the psychiatrist, with the electronic health record (EHR) providing the platform for much of that communication, using internal messaging, work lists, and progress notes that are accessible to all providers. In some systems the "mental health" notes are kept separate from other providers, though this practice seems to defeat the purpose of integration. Instead, only sensitive information that requires confidentiality should be kept separate from the EHR. HIPAA guidelines label such notes as "psychotherapy" notes and are given extra protection under that law, so they are not discoverable in the event of lawsuits. Notes by the psychiatrist and BHP should be consistent with other notes in the medical record, whereas issues of an extremely sensitive nature that are not pertinent to the medical record should be omitted from the EHR note; if necessary, psychotherapy notes can be kept separately in a psychotherapy note file.

The BHP will often be asked to convey questions from the PCP to the psychiatrist. One area where particular care must be taken is in the communication of medication recommendations. The psychiatrist should not give the BHP verbal recommendations for medication changes because of the potential for errors with serious consequences, as the BHP may not be familiar with all medications. Medication recommendations should therefore be communicated directly from the psychiatrist to the PCP or through notes in the EHR.

The BHP's Role in Shaping Integration in a Primary Care Practice

BHPs should take broad views of their role in the IC setting. If they see their role as setting up a psychotherapy practice in a primary care setting, they will miss an opportunity to have a much broader impact on patients' health. In many ways, primary care at its best is about prevention of illness rather than treatment of illness. The prevention model that is painted with a behavioral brush yields the greatest potential for positive impact on patients' lives.

Whether the BHP is the first to integrate a primary care setting or is joining a practice with an established integration model, he or she has an opportunity to help shape the model of integration. Some IC practices follow the Oxman, Dietrich, and Schulberg (2005) pyramid model as a way of structuring the integration of their services. This pyramid model is composed of four levels beginning at the base with community-based care and self-care, then moving to primary care, then behavioral health care, and finally psychiatry.

The base of the pyramid represents the provision of support and preventative services for members of the community. Often, illness results from, or is exacerbated by, patients becoming disconnected from their network of support. Social support ameliorates the severity of many disease states, and conversely, the lack of social support complicates the management of many illnesses. The base of the pyramid represents the provision of a variety of services that are preventative in nature and in which patients should be encouraged to participate.

Exercise is an area in which BHPs may provide support and preventative services to their patients, as it is vital to the prevention and management of so many illnesses. Unfortunately most people do not exercise enough to maintain optimum health. A body mass index (BMI) of 30 or greater is considered obese. The BHP can encourage patients to start an exercise program to improve their health and can assist in setting up the program. If adult patients and their children are encouraged to engage in regular exercise and a healthy diet, obesity can be prevented. It is much more effective to teach the skills to prevent obesity than to try to get the obese adult to lose weight. Of course, the younger one is, the easier it is to start and maintain an exercise regimen, so patients should be encouraged to include exercise as part of their daily activity beginning in childhood. Low-cost health clubs have been established in many cities across the country that provide exercise equipment and personal instruction in setting up an exercise plan. Providers can encourage patients to develop a regular exercise plan, even one as simple as walking just 20 minutes each day.

Scenario

Saul, a 72-year-old male patient, was referred to the primary care clinic for severe depression after hospitalization for hip replacement. He was wheelchair bound and appeared to be on death's doorstep. His depression was so profound that the psychiatrist thought he was in an early stage of dementia. The psychiatrist prescribed an antidepressant medication, and the patient moved from his residence in a retirement community, where he felt isolated and alone, to living with his son. Three years have passed, and Saul now walks 3 to 4 miles a day, 6 or 7 days a week. His recovery to vigorous health is due in part to his commitment to regular exercise, coupled with a more stimulating living environment in his son's home; his son encouraged him in his exercise program and made him an actively participating member of the household. Furthermore, Saul enjoys social interaction and support in his community, as he participates in a weekly "coffee klatch" at his synagogue and weekly bridge games.

As exemplified by Saul's story, exercise can have a tremendously positive impact on the physical and mental health of individuals. Some of the many benefits include improved mood and sense of well-being, decreased risk from cardiovascular death, improved lipid metabolism, improved weight management, prevention of chronic illnesses such as diabetes and hypertension, improved sexual functioning, better sleep, and increased energy (Fletcher et al., 1996). It is an unfortunate reality, however, that fewer than 50% of people who start an exercise program will continue with it. BHPs have an opportunity to use their expertise in behavioral management to help patients maintain a program of exercise that will improve their overall health. The BHP can assess patients' level of motivation for change and support patients in choosing realistic exercise goals. Many who have not exercised since childhood find it uncomfortable and stop exercising because of soreness, stiffness, aches, and pains. The BHP can explain the body's response to change and encourage patients to continue with their exercise plan with the expectation that these feelings of discomfort will wane with time. Patients should also be instructed in the benefits of a program that combines weight-bearing and aerobic exercise. BHPs can employ the maxim "start low and go slow" in helping patients establish exercise programs that begin at the level of the patient's current capability and then build gradually for better maintenance outcomes.

Stress management, another opportunity for support and prevention of illness for patients, can be encouraged by the BHP. Community resources are available that focus on stress management, such as yoga classes, meditation groups, prayer groups, hiking groups, and so on. Some examples of medical conditions that are improved by stress management are chronic pain, hypertension, cardiovascular conditions, and irritable bowel syndrome, among others.

Kabat-Zinn (1990) developed a mindfulness-based stress management (MBSM) program at the University of Massachusetts School of Medicine with the intent of assisting in the management of chronic pain. It has since been shown to be helpful in managing a variety of other health conditions as well. Speca, Carlson, Goodey, and Angen (2000) studied the effects of MBSM on depression, anxiety, and stress-related symptoms in patients diagnosed with cancer. They found significant reduction in symptoms after the MBSM training. It is worthwhile for BHPs to develop a relationship with leaders of community MBSM programs to be able to easily refer patients. If local programs are not available, the BHP might consider obtaining training so that he or she can teach patients about mindfulness in the primary care clinic. The University of Massachusetts and Duke University both offer MBSM training programs.

Finally, patients who are socially isolated should be encouraged to engage in their community. This can be achieved through participation in activities like volunteer work, involvement in a religious group, or attendance at a supportive day program for older people.

At the next level of the pyramid, the PCP evaluates patients for the presence of biopsychosocial contributors to their states of disease. Because PCPs are usually the first to treat depression and anxiety disorders, they typically prescribe more antidepressants than do psychiatrists.

CBT is generally a structured and time-limited treatment intervention that lends itself to the time constraints inherent in a primary care setting. BHPs interested in working in an integrated setting should develop competency in CBT during their training to prepare to work with patients who are prescribed medication by their PCP or the consulting psychiatrist. A third wave of CBT, called acceptance and commitment therapy (ACT; Hayes, Strosahl, & Wilson, 1999), is also a useful tool. ACT is a well-studied, evidence-based treatment that would enhance the BHP's skill set.

Patient flow will need to be considered as practices develop their IC models. It is unrealistic to enter into ongoing psychotherapeutic relationships with all of the patients referred, as the practice would soon exceed its ability to offer in-depth psychotherapeutic services. To identify those clients who would benefit most from mental health services, the BHP should employ behavioral triage: evaluate patients, treat the patients for whom short-term intervention seems to have the potential for beneficial outcomes, assess the need for psychiatric intervention, and then refer patients who need longer term and more intensive psychotherapy or community support services. The BHP and PCP will need to establish criteria for determining which patients to refer for individual psychotherapy or psychiatric evaluation. These referrals should be accompanied by a document giving permission to release patient information so that information between the community therapist and the primary care home can be exchanged.

The IC model also involves consideration of case management services. Some IC practices have found that the combination of therapy and case management leads to the best outcomes for patients. Case management involves calling patients to see if they are taking and tolerating their medication and its side effects and to address any questions they may have about their medications. BHPs will need to become familiar with common side effects, most of which are short-lived, so that they can discuss them with patients. Case management enhances patient care by increasing medication compliance, decreasing overall medical resource utilization, and providing patient support and education between clinic visits. The practice's nursing staff can assist in case management as well, as it relates to their knowledge of medication compliance, management of medication side effects, and monitoring patient response to medications.

In addition to providing psychotherapy and case management, the BHP will need to interface with providers outside the primary care setting and can serve as a valuable liaison who coordinates the primary and specialty care. Some patients in the primary care setting will already be involved in specialty psychiatric care, especially those with chronic mental illnesses such as schizophrenia and bipolar disorder, who, incidentally, often have concurrent medical conditions. Patients with severe mental illness have elevated rates of respiratory illness (even when controlled for smoking), diabetes (even when controlled for weight), and liver disease (Sokal et al., 2004). Nearly 50% of patients with schizophrenia have a comorbid medical illness, though these conditions are often underdiagnosed and untreated. Patients with schizophrenia, for instance, have a life expectancy that is 15 years shorter than that of the general population (Hennekens, Hennekens, Hollar, & Casey, 2005); patients with schizophrenia are also 10 times more likely to commit suicide than the general population (10% vs. 1%), and about 66% of people diagnosed with schizophrenia will die of cardiovascular illness (Goldman, 1999). IC is most effectual for those with severe psychiatric illness when it improves patient access to psychiatric services and medical care.

The psychiatrist, representing the top of the pyramid, receives referrals for patients from the PCP when he or she does not feel comfortable managing their treatment or when patients do not respond to initial treatment approaches. The following list of conditions will generally be referred to the psychiatrist for management, though this may vary somewhat by site depending on the comfort level of the PCP in managing various psychiatric disorders: bipolar disorder, schizophrenia and other disorders of the psychotic spectrum, substance use disorders, and adult attention deficit disorder.

PCPs who treat patients with bipolar disorder often request diagnostic clarification from a psychiatrist, particularly for bipolar disorder II. Bipolar disorder frequently goes undiagnosed or misdiagnosed, with studies showing an average of 8 to 9 years from the first attempt to seek treatment to receiving a diagnosis (Ghaemi, Boiman, & Goodwin, 2000). An accurate and timelier diagnosis may be achieved if PCPs and psychiatrists are able to work together to treat patients with bipolar disorder. An emphasis in my work has been to correctly identify patients with bipolar disorder and to put them on a mood stabilizing medication. Oftentimes, they have been treated with a combination of an antidepressant and antipsychotic medication, which leaves them with continued mood instability and exposes them to the risk of metabolic syndrome and tardive dyskinesia, a side effect of the antipsychotic medication. These patients respond better to mood stabilizing medications (lithium, divalproex, carbamazepine, and lamotrigine).

Patients with depression and anxiety disorders are likely to be referred when they are treatment resistant. It is common for PCPs to treat depression with one or two medication trials, but if unsuccessful, they will likely refer the patient to a psychiatrist.

Often, after the psychiatrist has seen the patient and stabilized him or her with medication, the PCP will then feel comfortable resuming management of the patient's psychiatric condition.

Patients often fail to act on referrals to psychiatrists and therapists because of the psychological, and sometimes logistical, hurdles of an unfamiliar office and provider. The perceived stigma associated with receiving psychiatric care presents yet another roadblock to patient follow-through with referrals. An on-site psychiatrist in a primary care practice allows patients to attend sessions in their familiar medical home and to interact with known office staff for appointments and check-in and checkout proceedings. In this way, patients do not have to take the initiative of calling the psychiatrist's office, finding the new location, and going through the process of enlisting as a patient at a new and unfamiliar office.

The primary care setting demands a high degree of flexibility from all who work within it. Patients who present with a wide range of conditions are likely to push providers repeatedly out of their comfort zones. Success in this environment requires a willingness to apply varying approaches that best suit the situation, to learn how and when to make referrals, and to provide an atmosphere of cooperation and collaboration among providers.

Substance Use Evaluation and Management

Substance abuse presents a vexing challenge in the primary care setting. Medical complications secondary to alcohol abuse and dependence account for a high number of hospitalizations. The economic impact of alcohol abuse and dependence in this country is staggering, estimated at $184.6 billion in 1998, the last year for which figures are available (Grant et al., 2004). In the outpatient setting, substance abuse can present in great variation, such that it often goes undetected, unless health care workers maintain vigilance about the possibility that substance use may be culpable for health problems.

Scenario

A 20-year-old college student presented to the campus student health center with low energy, lack of motivation, difficulty concentrating, excessive sleep, and a problem with missing classes. A medical evaluation ruled out hypothyroidism, vitamin deficiency, anemia, and mononucleosis. The student was referred for psychiatric evaluation where he denied depressed mood, anhedonia, and substance use. When the psychiatrist recommended urine toxicology, the student then admitted to daily marijuana use. The consequences of daily marijuana use were subsequently discussed with the student, including impaired concentration, low energy, and an amotivational syndrome. The student was not willing to completely abstain, but he did moderate his use, and his symptoms lessened.

All patients should initially be screened for substance use, and the screening should be repeated at yearly intervals or at any sign of emergence of a substance use disorder. This was a lesson I learned during my medical internship when I evaluated a 50-year-old woman who came into the emergency room because of a fall. In reviewing her past history, I noted that she had a number of ER visits for injuries related to falls. She had plausible explanations for each fall, and in my naïveté I accepted those at face value. When I presented the case to my attending physician, he asked how much alcohol the patient drank, and I admitted I had not asked her. When I returned to her bedside, I obtained a history of extensive alcohol abuse that had never been diagnosed or treated. Unfortunately, she refused referral for treatment until a later date, after a fall caused a broken hip resulting in hospitalization, including detoxification.

It has been shown that brief interventions for alcohol use disorders are effective in decreasing the level of alcohol consumption (Bien, Miller, & Tonigan, 1993). Miller and Sanchez (1994) described six elements of brief intervention that have proved effective, included under the acronym FRAMES: feedback, responsibility, advice, menu, empathy, and self-efficacy. Although the reader should refer to the article for a more detailed discussion, in brief, the interventions involve conducting an evaluation that demonstrates the patient is engaging in problem drinking, providing feedback regarding the potential negative consequences of the problem drinking, advising the patient to decrease or stop drinking, and providing a variety of approaches to promote the decrease or cease of intake. The therapist interacts in a supportive and understanding way, rather than confrontational and antagonistic way, and emphasizes the patient's ability to affect change and exert self-control. Perhaps surprisingly, such brief intervention is as effective as a referral to specialized substance abuse treatment services. This may be because so few patients follow through on referral to specialized addiction treatment services, another strong argument for the effectiveness and value of integrated primary care.

It is important to monitor the patient's response to the brief intervention in follow-up visits. If a decision is made to refer to specialized treatment, the appointment should be made by the BHP during the follow-up visit, with the patient present. The BHP should later call the patient to confirm that the patient plans to follow through with his or her appointment. These approaches have been shown to significantly increase the chances of patient compliance (Bien et al., 1993).

In an integrated setting, the BHP can collaborate with the psychiatrist by identifying patients who are having difficulty decreasing their alcohol intake and asking the psychiatrist to provide pharmacological support. Naltrexone (ReVia), acamprosate (Campral), and disulfiram (Antabuse) have all been approved for use in maintaining abstinence in alcoholics.

The BHP should be alert to the signs that a patient needs medical detoxification, such as if the patient reports withdrawal symptoms upon cessation. The severity of the withdrawal symptoms will help determine whether a patient needs to undergo inpatient or outpatient detoxification.

Patients who report difficulty in tolerating cravings for alcohol may respond well to acamprosate, which decreases cravings. The drug naltrexone, either the oral or the time-released injectable form, has been found to increase abstention from alcohol. Patients with a genetic predisposition to alcohol abuse often report feeling stimulated rather than sedated by alcohol and exhibit a high tolerance level. Naltrexone may be particularly effective for these patients, as it reduces the positive reinforcement they receive from drinking.

Kalivas and Volkow (2005) conducted a series of studies elucidating the neural effects of addiction. The studies show that addiction leads to a decrease in positive goal-motivated behavior focused on providing food, shelter, and companionship for the individual and an increase in response to cues related to the addicting substance. It is important to understand that there is a spectrum of problem drinking when evaluating alcohol use. As indicated previously, for many patients brief intervention with feedback and advice regarding their drinking will be effective. For others, moderate drinking is unrealistic, and complete abstention is the goal. This group of patients has the best chance of recovery with referral to specialty substance abuse treatment, participation in a 12-step program, and pharmacological support.

Nicotine dependence is so ubiquitous that we hardly notice it anymore. In decades past and for a long time, it was the norm to smoke, and in some parts of the country it remains commonplace. Nevertheless, nicotine use poses a tremendous health hazard and should be addressed as part of the patient's overall health program. Unfortunately, smoking cessation programs have not been particularly successful in helping smokers quit. About the same percentage of smokers quit on their own as those who use smoking cessation programs (Fiore et al., 1990). Nicotine replacement therapies (i.e., nicotine gum, transdermal nicotine patches, nasal spray, and inhaled nicotine) have all been shown to be effective, with inhaled nicotine demonstrating the highest level of effectiveness when evaluated in a meta-analysis (Silagy, 1994).

Sustainability of an IC Practice

Initially, we developed our consultation model in a teaching clinic with grants from various sources to provide support. Later, we worked to develop a model that could continue after these grants had terminated. The challenges we faced stemmed from the fact that a primary care setting is often not prepared to bill for behavioral health codes. The psychiatrist's time spent in consultation with residents or attending physicians, although instrumental in helping his primary care colleagues manage many psychiatric problems in the primary care setting, was not an activity that could be billed. This may be changing for treatment of the Medicaid population in North Carolina, though, as there is discussion of providing billing codes for consultation without patient contact.

In our center, PCPs have found psychiatric consultation to be helpful enough in their practice to warrant payment for consultation from their general revenue. Our current model utilizes a half day of psychiatric time per week. Half of that time is spent in direct patient care, for which the psychiatrist bills through his own office, and the other half is spent doing chart consultations or being available for what we term "curbside" consultations.

A development in our clinic has been a testament to the effectiveness and shared learning in IC; over the few years that on-site psychiatric consultation has been occurring, the PCPs have developed a higher level of expertise in managing psychiatric disorders and are now willing to manage more psychiatrically complex patients. They also have an increased willingness to treat these patients because they feel secure that they have readily available psychotherapeutic and psychiatric support.

Telepsychiatry

There are many situations in which a psychiatrist is not available for colocation in a primary care clinic. Many rural communities even lack a psychiatrist who practices in the community. A valuable option that is being developed for these offices is telepsychiatric consultation. For example, through grant funding from the Western Highlands Network, consultation is being provided to two rural clinics in western North Carolina. North Carolina has a statewide medical education network called Area Health Education Centers (AHEC), which has developed a videoconferencing network that is being used to link psychiatric offices with rural primary care offices. Point-to-point T1 connections are used to make secure links to protect confidential patient encounters. Wide-screen televisions are used as monitors to transmit images from high-resolution cameras that can be remotely controlled. Thus, the psychiatrist can zoom in on the patient if close examination is needed, such as in the evaluation of a movement disorder. Our system allows for the BHP to be in the room with the patient during the consultation to provide access to the primary care chart. The BHP is also able to support the patient in answering questions about lab results, consultation questions, and medications.

The telepsychiatry system is a powerful tool. We have been able to do an involuntary commitment evaluation on a patient who was overusing his prescription narcotics and was putting himself in danger with impaired judgment. His impairment was apparent even by video, and a physician petition for commitment was filed.

We have employed telepsychiatry consultation for over a year now, and patients report that they appreciate that they do not have to drive over an hour each way for a psychiatric consultation. The physicians are also grateful for more readily available access to psychiatric consultation than they have ever maintained. With telepsychiatry, we are now successfully managing patients with depression, bipolar disorder, schizophrenia, autism, and anxiety disorders, and we recently enhanced this service by adding access to a child psychiatrist for about an hour a week.

Conclusion

As discussed, a consulting psychiatrist can serve as an invaluable resource to professionals working in IC practices. Psychiatrists' expertise in psychotropic medication coupled with their experience working with patients who have severe and often persistent mental illnesses make them an excellent resource for ensuring optimal patient care, and serves to train PCPs and BHPs in how to best treat patients who present with complex psychological issues. It is hoped that this chapter enlightens IC professionals in the various ways all health care professionals can work as a team to provide enhanced patient care.

Discussion Questions

1. With what type of patient issues might you find psychiatric consultation essential?
2. Which patient mental health issues could be handled without psychiatric consultation?
3. What might be the ethical concerns associated with telepsychiatry?
4. What steps could you take to reduce the risk of ethical violations in telepsychiatry?

References

American Psychiatric Association. (2000). *Diagnostic and statistical manual of mental disorders* (Rev. 4th ed.). Washington, DC: Author.

Bien, T., Miller, W., & Tonigan, J. (1993). Brief interventions for alcohol problems: A review. *Addiction, 88*, 315–335.

Fiore, M., Novotny, T., Pierce, J., Giovino, G. A., Hatziandreu, E. J., Newcomb, P. A., Davis, R. M. (1990). Methods used to quit smoking in the United States: Do cessation programs help? *JAMA, 263*, 2760–2765.

Fletcher, G. F., Balady, G., Blair, S. N., Blumenthal, J., Caspersen, C., Chaitman, B., Pollock, M. L. (1996). Statement on exercise: Benefits and recommendations for physical activity programs for all Americans. *Circulation, 94*, 857–862.

Ghaemi, S., Boiman, B., & Goodwin, F. (2000). Diagnosing bipolar disorder and the effect of antidepressants: A naturalistic study. *Journal of Clinical Psychiatry, 61*, 804–808.

Goldman, L. (1999). Increasing global burden of cardiovascular disease in general populations and patients with schizophrenia. *Journal of Clinical Psychiatry, 60*(Suppl. 21), 1–5.

Grant, B., Dawson, D., Stinson, F., Chou, S., Dufour, M., & Pickering, R. (2004). The 12-month prevalence and trends in DSM-IV alcohol abuse and dependence: United States, 1991–1992 and 2001–2002. *Drug and Alcohol Dependence, 74*, 223–234.

Hayes, S. C., Strosahl, K. D., & Wilson, K. G. (1999). *Acceptance and commitment therapy: An experimental approach to behavior change*. New York: Guilford Press.

Hennekens, C., Hennekens, A., Hollar, D., & Casey, D. (2005). Schizophrenia and increased risks of cardiovascular disease. *American Heart Journal, 150*(6), 1115–1121.

Kabat-Zinn, J. (1990). *Full catastrophe living: Using the wisdom of your body and mind to face stress, pain, and illness*. New York: Delta.

Kalivas, P. W., & Volkow, N. D. (2005). The neural basis of addiction: A pathology of motivation and choice. *American Journal of Psychiatry, 162*, 1403–1413.

Miller, W. R., & Sanchez, V. C. (1994). Motivating young adults for treatment and lifestyle change. In G. S. Howard & P. E. Nathan (Eds.), *Alcohol use and misuse by young adults* (pp. 55–81). Notre Dame, IN: University of Notre Dame Press.

Oxman, T. E., Dietrich, A. J., & Schulberg, H. C. (2005). Evidence-based models of integrated management of depression in primary care. *Psychiatric Clinics of North America, 28*, 1061–1077.

Pan, A., Lucas, M., Sun, Q., van Dam, R., Franco, O., Manson, J., Hu, F. (2010). Bidirectional association between depression and type II diabetes in women. *Archives of Internal Medicine, 170*(21), 1884–1891.

Silagy, C. (1994). Meta-analysis on efficacy of nicotine replacement therapies in smoking cessation. *The Lancet, 343*(8890), 139–142.

Sokal, J., Erick, M., Dickerson, F., Kreyenbuhl, J., Brown, C., Goldberg, R., & Dixon, L. (2004). Comorbidity of medical illnesses among adults with serious mental illness who are receiving community psychiatric services. *Journal of Nervous and Mental Disease, 192*(6), 421–427.

Speca, M., Carlson, L., Goodey, E., & Angen, M. (2000). A randomized, wait-list controlled clinical trial: The effect of a mindfulness meditation-based stress reduction program on mood and symptoms of stress in cancer outpatients. *Psychosomatic Medicine, 62*, 613–622.

CHAPTER 9

Treating Patients with Substance Abuse Issues in Integrated Care

DON TEATER and MARTHA TEATER

Introduction

Kim began using pain pills after having dental surgery 7 years ago. Her pain was legitimate, and she was prescribed Percocet. The pills worked well, and she pressed her dentist for another prescription. She then went to her family doctor, various emergency rooms, dentists, and urgent care centers complaining of other painful conditions, obtaining prescriptions for Vicodin and Oxycontin as well. Soon she was buying pills off the street and using pills just to feel normal. Eventually her situation spiraled downward to the point where she decided to get help. That's when she presented to our practice to enter our outpatient Suboxone opiate addiction program.

The integrated care (IC) model is effective and practical in managing patients who abuse substances. The accounts of our experiences in an integrated primary care clinic will demonstrate the value of using IC to bring about successful patient outcomes. This chapter will focus on what we have learned through our shared involvement in a buprenorphine (Suboxone) treatment program for patients with opioid dependence.

Background

We are fully integrated, both professionally and personally, as Don is a family physician, and Martha is a licensed clinical addictions specialist and licensed marriage and family therapist. We have been married since 1981 and have worked together in family practice settings since 1990.

In the early years of our colocation, we practiced IC through consulting about our shared patients. At that time there was no specific term for the way we were practicing, but it seemed our commonsense approach impacted our patients' lives for the better. Our shared patients were informed that we worked together and seemed glad for us to share information concerning their care. Many of them were pleased with this level of collaboration and seemed to feel cared for because of it.

Our early attempts at integration would place us at a level three, according to Peek's (2007) chart titled "A Range of Goals for Collaborative Practice: Levels or Bands of Collaboration" (see Table 1.1 in Chapter 1 of this text). We had separate systems, shared facilities, regular communication, and some face-to-face consults. We appreciated each other's role, but because we were housed in a family practice, the medical side did have more influence.

Our Buprenorphine Experience

Don became licensed to prescribe buprenorphine in 2004. At that time he was the only buprenorphine provider in our practice's small rural county with a population of only 55,000. To become licensed to prescribe buprenorphine, a primary care physician (PCP) must complete a daylong training course and register with the state. There are a number of restrictions and laws that apply to those licensed to prescribe buprenorphine for treatment. As a protection for patients' health, part of the treatment protocol involves having all patients complete a substance abuse evaluation with a licensed counselor and to participate in counseling. Our patients can choose any behavioral health provider (BHP) in the community to complement their buprenorphine treatment, and many of them come to our BHP since she is integrated into the same practice as their PCP and the setting is familiar to them.

Expanding Integration

In 2008, we were awarded a $25,000 grant from a local nonprofit foundation committed to bettering regional health care, among other community causes, to expand our practice's level of integration. The focus of our grant proposal for treating specific groups of patients in an integrated setting was threefold: diabetes, depression, and an opioid treatment program. We have developed initiatives in these three areas to improve patient care through deliberate collaborative efforts.

Don, hereafter referred to as the PCP, treats patients who have been prescribed buprenorphine one half day each week, and with 100 people in the program needing to be seen monthly, his caseload includes about 25 people presenting for treatment during each of the half days. In response to this schedule, Martha, hereafter referred to as the BHP, began dedicating her own schedule to treating patients taking buprenorphine to match the clinic hours. This allowed her to be available for a "warm handoff," that is, joining the PCP and patient in the exam room to be introduced by the PCP as a member of the team. This approach was chosen because when patients have been briefly introduced to the BHP by their trusted PCP, then follow-up is improved. Sharing a visit in this way may take longer than a standard referral, and the extended visit time can be captured when billing insurance providers.

The BHP created an information sheet to give to patients, who have been prescribed buprenorphine, during their first session. The sheet serves as a tangible reminder of some key points related to buprenorphine, available local resources, and information about the counseling process. A paper resource promotes the likelihood that patients will make an effort to follow-through with counseling appointments.

All new patients in this practice are given the Patient Health Questionnaire (PHQ-9; Kroenke, Spitzer, & Williams, 2001) to screen for depressive symptoms during their initial visit and again in subsequent visits as deemed appropriate for tracking progress throughout treatment. The scores are recorded in the patient's record for use by both the PCP and the BHP to address and track this common comorbidity.

One of the benefits of the grant funding is that it allowed the PCP and BHP to create an outcome survey to gauge patient satisfaction with the counseling they receive. Specific to patients' appraisals of the practice's success in integration, one of the survey items asks patient to rate the following statement on a scale of 1 to 5, with 5 indicating strong agreement: "I am satisfied with the communication between my counselor and my health care provider." This practice's survey results demonstrate that most patients rate this statement at a 4.5, which is a strong endorsement for the success of its integration efforts.

During the grant period, a psychiatrist came to the practice to consult with staff twice monthly. These meetings were beneficial for our practice as they afforded us the opportunity for regular psychiatric consultation about how to best manage patient care. The local psychiatry clinic benefited as well: As this practice's providers learned greater skills in consultation, more of the psychiatric needs of patients could be met within the practice, without the need for referrals to a specialty mental health clinic, thus reducing the load on the overcrowded and understaffed local psychiatric clinic. The changes that were implemented during the grant period helped this practice move from a level three to a level five of integration, with close collaboration in a fully integrated system. Patient compliance and follow-up were improved, as well as patient satisfaction and successful outcomes. BHPs and PCPs now share facilities, staff, and electronic medical records (EMRs), which allows progress notes from both medical and counseling visits to be reviewed. Included in the shared EMRs are medical records received from referral notes from other providers, PHQ-9 scores, medications, and drug test results. Patients expect the members of this practice to work as a team, and in response collaborative routines have become routine and smooth. The PCP and BHP deliberately influence each other based on each one's expertise and the presenting situation.

Opioid Replacement Therapy

The results of a study published in the *British Medical Journal* (Cornish, Macleod, Strang, Vickerman, & Hickman, 2010) showed that if people who are opiate dependent are treated with replacement therapy (methadone or buprenorphine) for 1 year, their risk of death decreases by 85%. Replacement therapy greatly increases the chance of successful recovery, prevents the challenging withdrawal syndrome, and minimizes the cravings that can continue long after withdrawal symptoms have resolved.

Studies have shown that without replacement therapy, 90% of those who are opioid dependent will use opioids again within 1 year of detox (Sees et al., 2000). Relapse occurs because of the cravings that persist for years beyond the cessation of physical withdrawal symptoms, which are secondary to an endorphin imbalance in the brain caused by previous chronic exposure to opioid substances. Replacement therapy compensates for the endorphin imbalance and prevents the cravings, thereby resulting in a much higher success rate of remaining opioid free.

Two medications are prescribed for opioid replacement therapy: methadone and buprenorphine. Methadone, utilized since the 1970s, is the classic drug prescribed to help with opioid addiction recovery because it is very effective in preventing cravings and reducing the risk of relapse. Its benefit and effectiveness come from its long half-life and the way it can be administered once a day in the controlled environment of a methadone clinic, under the supervision of a physician and trained staff. A concern, however, is that methadone is a full opioid agonist, meaning that it has all of the same risks and side effects of other opioid medications.

Long-term abstinence from narcotics is extremely difficult for those who are addicted to them. Even after an intensive 180-day detox program with counseling, 90% of people start using pain pills within several months of completing the program (Sees et al., 2000). The outcome is quite different for patients managed through a continued methadone maintenance program, though, with a stronger rate of 40% abstinence. Moreover, of the 60% in the methadone program who use narcotics, the rate of use is only 5 days per month. Added to this improvement gained from a methadone maintenance program is a decrease in AIDS-risk behavior (injecting drugs) and a 66% reduction in death rate.

Buprenorphine is a relatively new medication used for replacement therapy for opioid addiction. It is a partial agonist, rather than full like methadone, has only some of the effects of the opioid drugs, and has a long half-life. Buprenorphine prevents withdrawal symptoms and cravings very effectively and has some mild pain-relieving properties. Its side effects do not include respiratory depression or significant drowsiness, and response time and mood are not affected significantly. Unlike with other opioid medications, buprenorphine does not give patients a "buzz" or high feeling. Because of these properties, buprenorphine has a low potential for abuse. Although there is some street value for it, our experience is that most people take this when they cannot get other opioids. They use this to prevent the withdrawal symptoms until they can attain their opioid of choice.

Buprenorphine is safer than methadone because of its property of preferentially binding to the opioid receptors in the brain, thereby preventing other opioids from binding to these sites. This means that if a person is taking buprenorphine and then takes another opioid (e.g., Percocet, Vicodin, Oxycontin, or others), the narcotic they take to get high will have little to no euphoric effect. Although buprenorphine is safer than a full agonist such as methadone, it can be dangerous when large doses are combined with benzodiazepines or alcohol.

Buprenorphine can be administered by PCPs and specialists who have received brief training and earned licensure to prescribe it. Patient management can be conducted in the office setting, with patients presenting for follow-up visits approximately every 1 to 2 months when they are deemed stable.

Prescribing Practices

Although this practice runs an opioid addiction treatment program, it also functions as a primary care family medical practice. In the family medical practice, we do treat patients who have legitimate problems with pain or anxiety and occasionally prescribe controlled and addictive substances. Rigorous policies and procedures, with key points highlighted next, are followed in this practice when prescribing benzodiazepine and opioid medications:

- Clonazepam (Klonopin) or lorazepam (Ativan) may be used for up to 3 months while starting patients on other, nonaddicting, medication treatment. These resources are reserved for a small subset of patients who have had numerous failed attempts at recovery. The use of these powerful medications must be monitored closely.
- Alprazolam (Xanax) is not prescribed because it is the benzodiazepine that is most frequently abused (Roache & Meisch, 1995).
- Long-term or chronic opioid medications are not prescribed. However, short-term opioids for acute injuries or illness are prescribed.
- Patients must be engaged in counseling during pharmacologic therapies.
- Before prescribing, this practice accesses the NC Controlled Substance Reporting System (NCRS) to see if the patient has active prescriptions for benzodiazepines or narcotics from other providers. The NCRS is a reporting system that provides an account of all prescriptions for controlled substances that patients have received from all doctors, pharmacies, and facilities in the state of North Carolina, regardless of insurance or method of payment.
- This practice also checks the NC Department of Corrections website to see if the patient has a history of substance-abuse-related offenses.
- There are no early refills for lost or stolen prescriptions. In this event, the medication will usually be discontinued.

Kim relates, "I was able to get pain medications from doctors for a long time; it wasn't hard to do. I would complain that I had a toothache, a migraine, or a back injury that was still causing me problems. The doctors just took my word for it, and I could get pain pills pretty easily. If I said I was anxious and had panic attacks, I got Xanax or some other benzo. If I said I was in pain, I got opiates."

Medications for Other Substance Use Disorders

Table 9.1 is a list of substances that are commonly abused, along with the respective medications that can be prescribed to help people recover from addiction to them. More detailed information about the medications' relevance to the associated addiction follows the table. These medications should seldom be prescribed and taken without concomitant counseling, as the combination produces the most effective results (National Institutes of Health, National Institute on Drug Abuse, 2005).

The mechanisms of and purposes for prescribing methadone and buprenorphine to treat opioid addictions were described earlier. Prescribing

Table 9.1
Medications Used to Treat Substance Abuse/Dependence

Commonly Abused Substances	Medications to Aid Recovery From Addiction
Opioids	Methadone, buprenorphine, clonidine, naltrexone
Alcohol	Disulfiram (Antabuse), acamprosate (Campral), naltrexone (ReVia, Vivitrol)
Tobacco	Nicotine replacement, bupropion (Zyban, Wellbutrin), varenicline (Chantix)

clonidine is an additional option that is available for treating opioid addiction. Clonidine is a medication that reduces blood pressure by blocking alpha-adrenergic receptors in the brain, which are the same receptors that are activated during withdrawal from opioids. Therefore, clonidine can be an effective, if somewhat limited, catalyst to reducing troublesome withdrawal symptoms. Naltrexone is an opioid antagonist, which blocks the sought-after effects of opiods by blocking the binding of the opioid medication to the opioid receptors in the brain. It is expensive compared to the other medication options and is available in pill form that is taken daily or as a long-acting intramuscular injection that lasts for 4 weeks. Naltrexone does not prevent cravings, which may limit it to treatment for highly motivated people who can withstand the continued cravings. For this reason its success rate is considerably lower than methadone or buprenorphine for opioid addiction treatment, although it has been shown to lessen the effects of comorbid depression when compared to methadone (Dean et al., 2006).

The mainstay of treatment for alcohol dependency is a combination of counseling and a 12-step program, but there are also several medications that may be helpful, including disulfiram (Antabuse), acamprosate (Campral), and naltrexone (ReVia, Vivitrol). Acute alcohol withdrawal can be life threatening; if a person develops delirium tremens (DTs) during withdrawal, he or she faces a 15% chance of dying (Feuerlein, Kufner, & Flohrschutz, 1995). Evidence of DTs or severe physical manifestations of withdrawal in people with alcohol withdrawal require an immediate visit to an emergency room where they will be treated with a benzodiazepine and may be discharged home on a tapering dose of the same.

Disulfiram (Antabuse) blocks one of the enzymes that helps to metabolize alcohol, causing the buildup of one of the metabolites that has a toxic effect of nausea and vomiting. People who take disulfiram on a regular basis will get violently ill after drinking even a small amount of alcohol. Disulfiram is usually given only to people who have a family member or significant other who can administer the medication each morning.

Although disulfiram does seem to help some people and is not cost prohibitive, a significant study that has proven its effectiveness is not available to date.

Acamprosate (Campral) is used to decrease the cravings and desire to drink, though it is not scientifically clear exactly how it works. Used to help people maintain abstinence, it has been shown to be slightly effective, but unfortunately it is expensive and must be taken frequently at three times a day.

Naltrexone, described earlier as a treatment for opioid dependency, is also used to treat alcohol dependency. Some of the effect of alcohol results from its impact on the opioid receptors in the brain. The mechanism by which naltrexone blocks these opioid receptors reduces the effects of alcohol on the brain and also seems to decrease cravings for it.

Smoking cessation treatment for tobacco abuse includes the use of medication such as bupropion (Zyban, Wellbutrin) and varenicline (Chantix). Nicotine replacements are available in the form of chewing gum, a patch, a lozenge, or an inhaler. These will slightly increase one's chance of success, with none having been shown to be significantly more effective than the others. However, bupropion (Zyban, Wellbutrin) has been shown to have a slight advantage in effectiveness for smoking cessation when compared to nicotine replacement options (Wittchen, Hoch, Klotsche, & Muehlig, 2011).

Varenicline (Chantix) is the most effective treatment for nicotine dependence that is currently available. A 2006 study (Jorenby et al., 2006) showed that 20% of people can be expected to remain abstinent after 1 year when treated with a combination of varenicline and brief counseling. Although modest, its effectiveness is considerably better than the success rate of other treatments. Varenicline is considered a partial agonist, and it is believed to act by binding to the nicotine receptors in the brain, thereby reducing the pleasurable effects of nicotine (antagonist) and reducing the level of craving or response from nicotine withdrawal (agonist) (Steensland, Simms, Holgate, Richards, & Bartlett, 2007).

Brief Screening Tools

Patients sometimes present to primary care and self-identify to their PCP as having a problem with overusing drugs and alcohol. More often, though, this is not the case, so it is especially important for PCPs to listen for subtle hints that patients may be experiencing problems with substance dependency and/or use. Some indicators include when a patient

- asks for prescriptions for pain pills or "nerve pills";
- asks for a specific medication, like Percocet or Xanax;

- claims to be "allergic" to ibuprofen and all anti-inflammatory medications;
- uses street slang, like stating, "I ate a Perc 10 and felt better";
- says that he or she has tried "everything else" and the only thing that works is a specific controlled substance;
- complains of continued pain after a remote injury in which a bone was broken, because bones do not usually hurt after they have healed;
- refuses other types of therapy such as counseling or physical therapy; and
- has multiple pain complaints without concurrent objective findings (consider pain syndrome).

See Vignette 7 in the *Integrated Care in Action* video for how to approach patients about the need to screen for the risk of substance abuse.

Because patients who are taking buprenorphine in this clinic are self-referred, they present with having self-identified a problem with pain pills, which certainly eliminates some barriers in assessing for a substance abuse problem. Despite this awareness, many patients in this clinic are minimally committed to treatment, often coming to please a concerned family member. PCPs and BHPs in our clinic therefore use a couple of brief but effective screening methods to support our suggestion that they do in fact have a problem with pain pills and would benefit from the clinic's help.

The CAGE-AID is a four-question, well-accepted screening tool that gives PCPs, BHPs, and the patient some initial feedback about areas of concern (Brown & Rounds, 1995). Another screening tool option is to use a very brief one-question screen to see if the patient has continued to use substances in spite of the negative consequences, potentially including but not limited to arrests, family discord, tardiness or absenteeism at work, over-spending on the substance, and underemployment. Many patients describe the "chase" to get substances and the amount of stress it brings them. Living in a state of perpetual pursuit, making sure there is a supply on hand, and worrying about getting caught can be draining. Added to these stresses are money-related problems when money is spent on substances rather than other needs, the risk of legal problems, and the strain of maintaining a state of secrecy in an effort to keep the extent of substance use from family. For all of these reasons and more, struggling with feelings of guilt, shame, and spiritual distress are common for people who abuse substances.

Substance Use Assessment

Many BHPs provide screening and assessment for substance abuse despite some having only little training in the area of addictions. This section describes some ways that assessing for substance abuse differs from performing a general mental health assessment.

First, it is important for BHPs to take a thorough history of the patient's drug and alcohol use, asking for as much specificity from the patient as possible. Each substance should be inquired about separately, including the age at first use for each, duration, and amount used. BHPs should also ask patients about whether they were involved in prior treatment programs, including outpatient, inpatient, and intensive outpatient types, as well as how long the program(s) lasted and the level of success achieved. Family history of substance use issues should be taken, as substance use disorders have a high rate of inheritability. A family history of substance abuse can also be important from a social standpoint, with learned behaviors from unhealthy environments possibly playing a role in the patient's own struggle with substance use.

Next, ask questions to gain information about how patients use substances and to describe their attempts to cut back or stop using if they have tried to stop. Also ask if they felt the need to take more of the substance over time. If the BHP is assessing pain pill use, patients should be questioned about how it feels if they have to do without the pills for a couple of days. For the regular user, abrupt cessation can be a miserable experience.

The next part of the substance use assessment is given to determine the consequences of drug and alcohol use in patients' lives. BHPs should ask specifically about arrests (including DUIs), amount of money spent on the substance, the implications of substance use on job performance and ability to maintain a job, family concerns, health issues, behavior changes while using (e.g., increased arguing, aggressiveness), and impact on education (e.g., dropping out or poor academic performance). Finally, BHPs should ask if patients have encountered legal problems or experiences with children's protective services as a result of their substance use.

Motivational interviewing skills are extremely helpful when working with patients who abuse substances. It is important to discover why patients desire a change in their substance use and not to make assumptions about motivation for them.

The BHP's Role in Supporting the PCP

The IC model enables both disciplines to benefit from the expertise and training opportunities afforded by working together closely. In support of the PCP's treatment, BHPs should take on the role of educating patients regarding the chronic nature of addiction and the risk of relapse and helping them to develop other support systems and healthy activities.

The following list includes the information BHPs should share with PCPs when treating patients with substance use in an IC setting:

- other mental health diagnoses that may complicate care;
- information about the patient's support systems (i.e., on whom does the patient depend and respect for support?);
- an assessment of the patient's level of commitment to recovery;
- communication if the patient is struggling with recovery because of a change in his or her environment, mood, or altered life circumstances;
- recommendations on medication management (e.g., does the BHP think the patient can benefit from a change in his or her antidepressant prescription or a change in the dose?); and
- discharge planning (e.g., should the patient get involved in a 12-step program?).

It is often difficult to determine when a patient should be removed from the program; addiction is a chronic disease associated with setbacks from repeated or novel difficulties that patients face over time. When patients are motivated and committed, our practice allows for second and third chances at recovery programs after patients experience challenges with sobriety. For those with repeated failures in the community-based treatment setting, though, decisions need to be made jointly by BHPs and PCPs about continuing to extend services.

The PCP's Role in Supporting the BHP

The PCP's medical expertise and consultation are invaluable assets to BHPs who are working to develop diagnoses for patients. PCPs who see patients who return to the clinic with some frequency are able to collect more extensive histories. This opportunity gives PCPs greater insight for making treatment decisions in tandem with BHPs, based on information about possible comorbidities and social stressors affecting substance use, as well as allows for the formation of an impression of the patient's strengths that may have positive treatment outcome implications. PCPs can also shed light on patients' medical conditions for BHPs and share their thoughts on how specific physical challenges may impact patients' treatment plans.

Another advantage for BHPs who work closely with PCPs is evident in physicians' knowledge of medications and how they may effect a patient's overall health. PCPs can articulate the medications intended effect, list potential side effects, and predict and/or prevent possible interactions among multiple medications. Both providers can monitor the impact of medication changes so the dosage and prescriptions may be altered by PCPs as needed.

Reimbursement

In this practice, coding is adjusted for IC visits based on time and complexity through North Carolina Medicaid. Medicaid covers expenses for screenings for tobacco and other substance use disorders, and this practice bills Medicaid for the administration of the PHQ-9 depression screening as well. All counseling visits that are completed as recommended by the PCP and documented in his notes are billed "incident to" the physician, yielding a higher reimbursement rate.

Medicaid Billing Opportunities

- *Substance abuse screening*: Using a structured screening assessment like the CAGE-AID allows the provider to charge $30.73 for a 15- to 30-minute intervention.
- *PHQ-9*: NC Medicaid reimburses $8.14 to administer the PHQ-9.
- *Smoking cessation*: Talking about tobacco cessation for 3 to 10 minutes is reimbursed at $11.93.
- *"Incident to" billing*: When the PCP diagnosis the patient and documents the need for the BHP to treat the patient, the BHPs who work for the practice are able to be reimbursed at a higher rate than without the PCP's indication for treatment. For an initial session, reimbursement is $141, and for subsequent sessions of 45 to 50 minutes, the reimbursement is $95.

Ethical Issues

Because both providers are employed by the same practice and work from the PCP's treatment plan in this practice, a signed release for the BHP and PCP to communicate with each other is not required. Patients learn about the team-based model when completing initial paperwork and consent for treatment at the clinic and expect that we will communicate about their care.

This protocol would differ for providers from separate practices who treat the same patient; a signed release from the patient should be obtained for the providers to share information with one another about the patient's care. For example, when this practice has a patient on buprenorphine treatment who sees a BHP in another practice for counseling, a release permitting communication with that BHP is signed by the patient. In this way, we can discuss the patient's care and follow up with his or her BHP as needed.

Kim expressed relief knowing that her PCP and her BHP were communicating about her care: "I like knowing that they are both talking about my treatment. It is so much easier than trying to get providers in different practices to talk to each other. It makes me feel like they are paying attention to me and working together for me."

Benefits of IC in Buprenorphine Treatment

As a BHP and PCP who work together in an IC setting for a buprenorphine clinic, we appreciate our ability to make decisions as a team, without the obstacle of delayed communication. Both providers' observations and opinions are valued and utilized in treatment plans, and diagnostic impressions are honed via shared expertise stemming from medical and behavioral backgrounds.

Sharing information about a patient's social circumstances benefits both the BHP's and the PCP's work with the patient, and either can share valuable insights with the other about topics with the potential to increase a patient's risk of using again, such as an unhealthy relationship, family history of drug use, or stressful changes in his or her life. Unimpeded and sometimes immediate information exchange benefits the patient's care, as it allows us to respond quickly, as a team, to relapse. The PCP is able to interact in the moment and may provide a prescription while the patient is in the office with the BHP. In turn, the BHP can provide the PCP with feedback about medication side effects and the patient's challenges and successes during a medical exam. In short, treatment of urgent buprenorphine treatment needs, when provided in an IC setting, gets an immediate response, and patients feel their health is being well managed when both their medical and their behavioral concerns are being addressed simultaneously.

What Factors Predict Success?

In our experience over the past several years, it is still challenging to accurately predict which patients will do well and which will have difficulty with their recovery. There are certain factors, however, that do appear to increase a patient's chances of successful recovery:

- Continued involvement in therapy is a strong predictor of the patient's willingness to work on making lasting changes.
- Family involvement and support of the patient's recovery have a strong influence on successful long-term recovery.
- Active involvement in any kind of community support group for addiction recovery boosts chances of success (Atkins & Hawdon, 2007). Examples include but are not limited to Alcoholics Anonymous, Al-Anon, Narcotics Anonymous, and Celebrate Recovery.
- Involvement in purposeful activities such as returning to school, finding employment, going to religious services, volunteering, or becoming more active and involved in the community all help to maintain recovery.

Kim is now clean and thrilled with the changes in her life. Her daughter came with her to a visit with Don. When he complimented her daughter on her new light-up tennis shoes, Kim began to cry. "This is the first time I've had the money to buy my daughter something special like that. When I was using, if I had $20, I'd spend it on pain pills. I can't believe how much money I wasted. Getting into treatment has saved my life. I am getting counseling, going to Narcotics Anonymous meetings, my husband is supporting my treatment, and I've gotten a job."

It is important to assess patients' stage of change. Many of the patients who present to our clinic are not yet even in the precontemplative stage but come in perhaps because of pressure from family or the legal system. People can certainly achieve wellness from a starting point of some outside pressure, but it is important to use motivational interviewing to help patients move to the next level of change, which is called contemplation, to encourage self-motivation and improve chances of successful and lasting recovery. Most of the patients who present to our clinic enter at the contemplation level. They realize that they have a problem with narcotics in some way and feel ready to make some initial changes or to at least find out what options are available to them.

Recovery looks different for each person. For most, recovery means a freedom from the anxiety and worry of chasing the next high. In fact, many of our patients tell us about their experiences of the program working when they feel relief upon waking up in the morning and not having to think about where they will get the next pill. Recovery brings about positive changes like having more money to spend on other things, having peaceful family relationships, and getting better sleep. People are better able to get and keep a job, function in the community, get involved in religion, and stay clear of legal problems. The comment we hear most frequently from those who thrive in treatment is simple: "I feel normal." Many will also say that they feel like they are starting over with a new life and what a significant relief that is for them after being addicted to pain pills for years.

Conclusion

IC is a dynamic way of helping those who suffer with addictions. Addressing the physical and mental health issues of patients in one place at one time is a simple and effective approach. BHPs and PCPs benefit from each other's expertise, patients are comforted that their concerns can be addressed in one place, and the affirming result is one of more efficient and comprehensive patient care.

Discussion Questions

1. How does the PCP benefit from using the IC model in treating substance abuse?
2. In what ways does the BHP professional use the expertise of the PCP in substance abuse treatment?
3. How does the patient benefit from an IC approach to substance abuse treatment?
4. What are some brief screening tools for substance abuse?
5. What skills are beneficial for the BHP to have in treating substance abuse?

Acknowledgments

The authors are grateful to Rachel Kepes for editorial assistance with this chapter.

Resources

www.buprenorphine.samhsa.gov
www.icarenc.org
www.sa4docs.org
www.suboxone.com

References

Atkins, R. G., Jr., & Hawdon, J. E. (2007). Religiosity and participation in mutual-aid support groups for addiction. *Journal of Substance Abuse Treatment*, *33*(3), 321–331. doi:10.1016/j.jsat.2007.07.001

Brown, R. L., & Rounds, L. A. (1995). Conjoint screening questionnaires for alcohol and other drug abuse: Criterion validity in a primary care practice. *Wisconsin Medical Journal*, *94*(3), 135–140.

Cornish, R., Macleod, J., Strang, J., Vickerman, P., & Hickman, M. (2010, October 26). Risk of death during and after opiate substitution treatment in primary care: Prospective observational study in UK General Practice Research Database. *BMJ*, *341*. doi:10.1136/bmj.c5475

Dean, A. J., Saunders, J. B., Jones, R. T., Young, R. M., Connor, J. P., & Lawford, B. R. (2006). Does naltrexone treatment lead to depression? Findings from a randomized controlled trial in subjects with opioid dependence. *Journal of Psychiatry Neuroscience*, *31*(1), 38–45.

Feuerlein, W., Kufner, H., & Flohrschutz, T. (1995). The mortality rate of alcoholic patients 4 years after inpatient treatment. *Versicherungsmedizin*, *47*(1), 10–14.

Jorenby, D., Hays, T., Rigotti, N., Azoulay, S., Watsky, E., Williams, K., Reeves, K. (2006). Varenicline, an α4β2 nicotinic acetylcholine receptor partial agonist, vs. sustained-release bupropion and placebo for smoking cessation. *JAMA*, *296*(1), 47–55. doi:10.1001/jama.296.1.47

Kroenke, K., Spitzer, R. L., & Williams, J. B. (2001). The PHQ-9: Validity of a brief depression severity measure. *Journal of General Internal Medicine, 16*(9), 606–613.

National Institutes of Health, National Institute on Drug Abuse. (2005). *Prescription drugs: Abuse and addiction; Treating prescription drug addiction* (NIH Publication No. 05-4881). Retrieved from http://www.drugabuse.gov/ResearchReports/Prescription/prescription7.html#Treating

Peek, C. J. (2007, October). *Integrated care: Aids to navigation.* Study packet for the Pennsylvania, Eastern Ohio, and West Virginia Summit: Integrating Mental Health and Primary Care, Pittsburgh, PA.

Roache, J. D., & Meisch, R. A. (1995). Findings from self-administration research on the addiction potential of benzodiazepines. *Psychiatric Annals, 25*(3), 153–157.

Sees, K., Delucchi, K., Masson, C., Rosen, A., Clark, H., Robillard, H., Hall, S. (2000). Methadone maintenance vs. 180-day psychosocially enriched detoxification for treatment of opioid dependence: A randomized controlled trial. *JAMA, 283*, 1303–1310.

Steensland, P., Simms, J. A., Holgate, J., Richards, J. K., & Bartlett, S. E. (2007). Varenicline, an $\alpha4\beta2$ nicotinic acetylcholine receptor partial agonist, selectively decreases ethanol consumption and seeking. *Proceedings of the National Academy of Sciences of the United States of America, 104*(30), 12518–12523. doi:10.1073/pnas.0705368104

Wittchen, H. U., Hoch, E., Klotsche, J., & Muehlig, S. (2011). Smoking cessation in primary care: A randomized controlled trial of bupropione, nicotine replacements, CBT and a minimal intervention. *International Journal of Methods of Psychiatric Research, 20*(1), 28–39. doi:10.1002/mpr.328

CHAPTER 10

Pediatric Integrated Care

VALERIE KRALL

Providing behavioral health services to children in an integrated care (IC) setting is an especially rewarding and unique way to work with this population. As described earlier in this text, there are several models for providing IC, with the level of integration occurring on a continuum that ranges from little collaboration between separate systems to the complete integration and merging of systems (Doherty, McDaniel, & Baird, 1996). Children commonly receive primary medical care in general family medicine practices and "specialty" pediatric practices; both settings support the integration of a behavioral health provider (BHP). A pediatric practice may integrate a BHP to address the behavioral health issues that occur in the context of the family during the childhood years. Parents often initially seek mental health services in the primary care setting and view their family's primary care provider (PCP) as the person to whom they turn for all of their families' health-related concerns (Kelleher, Campo, & Gardner, 2006). It is estimated that approximately 75% of children with psychiatric issues are seen by PCPs before other professionals (Miller, 2007). Moreover, PCPs are often the primary prescribers of psychiatric medications for children (Campo, Shafer, Strohm, & Lucas, 2005). Unique to pediatric settings, the BHP will provide treatment to patients within the context of the family. Therefore, a BHP needs to feel comfortable with and be proficient in treating patients across the life span.

IC models have varying guidelines for serving patients, each with differing types of behavioral health services: Colocation models mainly provide traditional psychotherapy sessions, whereas fully integrated models allow for the provision of more immediate consultation services. In this chapter, there will be some discussion about how traditional therapy occurs in the medical setting; however, the primary objective will be to describe how real-time consultation between the medical provider and the BHP can serve the pediatric patient. This treatment model is unique to IC settings and is one that is novel and unfamiliar to many students and providers of traditional behavioral health care.

Preparing to Work as a BHP in a Pediatric IC Setting

Students who are interested in becoming a BHP in a pediatric IC setting will find some useful guidelines for preparation in the following section.

Understanding Child and Adolescent Development

It is important for BHPs to be well versed in the developmental stages of children and adolescents. BHPs-in-training interested in working within IC pediatric agencies should take as many courses as possible in areas such as developmental theories, counseling children and adolescents, special education, and play therapy. Related information can be found in textbooks written on the topic of child development or in websites for the American Academy of Pediatrics, American Academy of Child and Adolescent Psychiatry, and Zero to Three: National Center for Infants, Toddlers, and Families (see the section titled "Helpful Websites for Pediatric IC" at the end of this chapter).

Knowledge of Childhood Disorders

BHPs should become well acquainted with the child and adolescent section of the *Diagnostic and Statistical Manual of Mental Disorders (DSM-IV-TR*; American Psychiatric Association, 2000) so they can provide initial diagnoses, consult with PCPs, provide effective treatment, and bill for their services. Families often seek help in the primary care setting for the following common diagnoses: attention-deficit/hyperactivity disorder, oppositional defiant disorder, elimination disorders, separation anxiety disorder, and adjustment disorders. Other disorders that PCPs and BHPs may encounter include autistic disorder, Asperger's disorder, and learning disorders. BHPs should be familiar with the criteria for these disorders in order to make appropriate referrals for in-depth evaluations by developmental pediatricians or psychologists.

When PCPs or BHPs encounter children and teens with conduct disorder, for instance, BHPs will determine whether to treat the patient in the medical setting and/or to make additional referrals to community mental health providers and programs. Pediatric BHPs will need to become fluent in the language used in the *DSM-IV-TR* (American Psychiatric Association, 2000), as it will prepare them to communicate with physicians and other providers. Furthermore, pediatric BHPs should become familiar with psychoeducational and problem-solving approaches for addressing common pediatric problems. These approaches, in addition to cognitive behavioral therapy strategies, are well suited for primary care as they are designed to be brief and solution-focused therapies as opposed to insight-oriented therapies (James & Folen, 2005).

Resources That Serve Children, Adolescents, and Families

Pediatric BHPs should maintain current information about local resources and agencies that serve children, adolescents, and families in order to comprehensively help their patients and families. Examples of agencies include, but are not limited to, departments of social services, public and private school systems, other community mental health providers, child psychiatrists for in-depth analysis and treatment, hospitals or emergency rooms for emergency psychiatric evaluations, child development centers (agencies that perform developmental evaluations for children ages 0 to 3 years), and agencies that manage the coordination and allocation of mental health, substance abuse, and developmental disability services to counties in their catchment area.

Initial Pediatric Consultations in IC

Consultation visits are usually brief encounters (5 to 15 minutes) with patients during which their presenting problem is assessed and an initial plan of action is developed. Following are descriptions of the varying levels of intervention and examples of how behavioral health consultations at each level influence treatment outcomes.

Introduction Only

An introduction-only interaction aims to inform the patient and family about the behavioral health services that are offered at the practice, as well as to associate a "friendly face" with the service. Physician availability will dictate whether physicians can introduce patients to BHPs or whether BHPs will need to introduce themselves to patients. The BHP describes himself or herself to patients and families using terms such as *team member* or *coworker* of the physician and emphasizes that both parties are available to help. If the patient and family are amenable, formal follow-up services can be scheduled during the consultation. Alternately, should the patient and family need time to consider options, the BHP would provide information about how to arrange services at a later date. BHPs can help patients feel at ease about accessing services by employing strategies such as inviting families to call them directly or requesting that the office verify the patient's behavioral health benefits prior to making an appointment.

Brief Intervention or Psychoeducation

In many cases, the physician has already addressed the patient's concerns during the exam and wants the BHP to support the child and family by providing additional strategies to promote overall health. An example of brief intervention follows:

> *Scenario:* Accompanied by her grandmother, a 17-year-old girl presents at the family medical center with concerns that she is not sleeping well. They wonder if there is a medicine the girl should take, as they fear her performance at school will suffer. The physician listens to their description of some poor sleep habits and asks if the family would talk further with the BHP to review sleep hygiene. In agreement, the girl and her grandmother talk with the BHP for 15 minutes while the PCP moves on to his next patient.
>
> During their discussion, the BHP learns that the patient takes a 2-hour nap each day after school and then drinks soda or tea upon waking to help her focus to do her homework. Most nights she does her homework on her bed and then watches TV in bed until she falls asleep. After discussing several aspects of sleep hygiene and stimulus control strategies for sleep, the family agrees with the plan for the patient to relax for a while after school but avoid taking a nap, drink only caffeine-free beverages after school, do her homework while sitting at the desk in her room, and turn off the TV before getting into bed. Although the patient is not sure if she is ready to give up taking naps on weekends, she expresses understanding of the rationale for the changes that are suggested during the school week and is glad that she has alternatives to taking a medication. Her grandmother comments that she might change a few things in her own bedtime routine in order to improve her sleep as well. She notes that the patient's doctor is her doctor as well and that he had encouraged her to work to improve her sleep in order to better manage her chronic pain issues. She jokes that she looks forward to being able to tell her PCP how much she has improved her own sleep hygiene by the time they have their next appointment.

This scenario typifies IC in a family practice with brief intervention occurring in the context of a team approach, benefitting the patient and the family.

Obtaining Information to Help With Decision Making

Circumstances in which the BHP might help the PCP with decision making include helping with diagnostic issues that can aid in decisions regarding medication choices, assisting with obtaining a more detailed psychosocial history to determine if symptoms are chronic or situational, and gathering information about what treatment strategies have been used in the past. The BHP can also inquire about factors that may affect treatment choices such as history of substance use or safety issues.

> *Scenario:* The physician is running behind because of an emergency earlier in the day. She notices that a new adolescent patient on her schedule for later that day is listed with the presenting concern of "feeling depressed and agitated." The doctor knows that she won't have ample time to meet with her, so she asks the BHP to meet with the patient to assess her condition, which may include determining if the patient is at risk for harm to herself or others. The doctor feels she will be able to focus on helping the patient medically if she has additional assessment information and recommendations from the BHP before she sees the patient.

This teamwork approach to obtaining assessment information helps the patient feel supported and ensures that the physician is able to carefully treat the patient despite a busy day. The PCP is also able to preserve adequate time for other scheduled patients.

Scheduling Traditional Evaluations With the BHP

Sometimes the PCP may request that the BHP comprehensively assess a patient's behavioral health before any further medical treatment is prescribed. In light of the challenges inherent in outside referrals (i.e., lack of follow-through, scheduling, location, etc.), a BHP who is integrated into a primary care practice can be quite effective. The following scenario describes an interaction that warrants a more complete assessment by the BHP:

> *Scenario:* An 8-year-old boy and his parents present to the boy's well-child visit. The parents report that the boy is getting into trouble at school and that teachers have sent home notes stating that the boy is falling behind academically, is not completing his class work or following the teacher's directives, and is talking in class and disturbing others. The parents request advice from the physician about how to help their son. The PCP introduces the BHP to the family, and after a brief consult in the exam room, the BHP learns that the family has encountered several stressors in recent months. The mother notes, however, that the child has been having similar problems since he started school. The BHP offers the family more information about the IC services available at the clinic and then arranges for the family to return for a more complete assessment. In the meantime, the BHP

provides the parents with a child behavior questionnaire for them and his teachers to complete.

Referral to Other Community Support Agencies

The BHP can help make referrals during a brief consult by providing the family with contact information for social service support resources in the community, such as economic aid and child care vouchers, services in the school system including accessing psychoeducational testing and accommodations for special needs, in-home behavioral health or psychiatry services, programs for victims of domestic violence, programs for pregnant teens, transportation assistance, developmental evaluations for young children, and programs for families with children with disabilities, among others. The BHP can make the initial phone call from the exam room with the family present to facilitate the first interaction with the agency.

Coordinating With Outside BHPs

In circumstances where children and adolescents receive behavioral health services from another local provider, the BHP can assist a busy PCP by identifying and locating the provider, requesting the medical records, helping to review the records to promote coordination of care, and, if necessary, directly contacting the provider to discuss a child's behavioral health needs.

Rewards, Challenges, and Unique Aspects of IC in a Pediatric Setting

Parents are often pleased to learn that behavioral health services are available for their children in their medical office, a familiar place that offers convenience. They report a feeling of comfort due to their doctor's trust in the BHP who works in the office. BHPs also find rewards in IC as they provide immediate, as well as long-term, service that is effective and efficient. Interactions between families and BHPs create streamlined medical services to enhance care. For example, if a caregiver and/or patient has a question about a medication prescribed by the PCP, the BHP can facilitate a timely answer while the patient is in the office for counseling sessions rather than having to wait for the next scheduled medical appointment. In an IC setting, the BHP often serves as a case manager of sorts, providing an additional access point for patients and promoting accurate and effective treatment. In the following scenario, the BHP helps with behavioral and emotional issues, as well overall health care:

> *Scenario:* The mother of a teenage patient has been attending counseling sessions with her daughter and the BHP in the PCP's office.

The mother has been overwhelmed by family stressors and financial difficulties while caring for her daughter, and because it is difficult for her to attend appointments because of transportation challenges, she contacts the BHP by phone. During the call, she expresses her frustration that the fax for her daughter's prescription for asthma medication did not arrive at the pharmacy. She is concerned that without her medication, her daughter will likely miss a day or two of school because of an asthma flare-up. While on the phone, the BHP is able to review the patient's electronic medical record, determine that the prescription was in fact sent but to the old pharmacy on record, and take action to request that the doctor send the prescription to the new pharmacy that is on the bus route.

Although there are ample rewards, challenges also exist in IC settings. One example is in the use of ethical codes, which are slightly different for the similar but not identical medical International Statistical Classification of Diseases and Health Related Problems (ICD-9) and mental health systems (*DSM-IV-TR*). Though *DSM-IV-TR* (American Psychiatric Association, 2000) codes are designed to coincide with the ICD-9, confusion may arise because not all codes, criteria, and diagnostic labels are identical. Another challenge exists concerning the sharing of patient information. In medical settings, discussion with other medical providers occurs under the umbrella of "coordination of care," with less formal consent measures. In mental health settings, patient information is shared only when formal written consent is obtained. Medical health providers and BHPs may not be fully aware of the ethical codes to which the other is bound, and finding the balance between upholding all professional ethical codes while also doing what is needed to work effectively within the IC setting can be challenging. In addition, confidentiality and boundary issues may differ for PCPs and BHPs. For example, although family practice physicians often treat members of the same family for continuity, some mental health professionals have been taught that treating individual members of the same family could present a conflict of interest. For all of these challenges, ongoing discussion among coworkers is essential to increase communication and understanding of the differences in philosophies and practices.

The medical setting is a unique environment for the provision of behavioral health, unlike that of the traditional treatment room. In an IC setting, BHPs will at times interact with patients in medical exam rooms, in various states of dress, and perhaps while involved in a medical procedure. In this environment, BHPs will be privy to patients' personal medical information and will have access to medical records. Patients may also ask the BHP medical questions given the setting. Initially BHPs will need to adjust from a traditional mental health setting to an IC setting, where the medical culture is prominent. Over time, BHPs may enjoy learning to work within a medical environment and discovering new ways to care for patients who are offered access to behavioral health care.

Conclusion

As discussed in this chapter, the provision of pediatric behavioral health services in an IC setting offers many unique experiences. In this author's experience, an IC setting offers the BHP a rewarding way of interacting with patients, families, and medical colleagues. IC also provides physicians with much-needed support and access to services that can otherwise be difficult. Most important, IC allows children and families to receive a more complete range of services at the time that the service is needed, and by doing so, enhance the overall quality of their health care.

Discussion Questions

1. If you were the parent of a child needing behavioral health services, what might you see as the pros and cons of seeking services in an IC setting?
2. What are some common childhood problems that you think would be ideal to be addressed in an IC setting?
3. If you were to take a position as a BHP in an IC setting, what strengths do you think you would bring to that role? What areas would you want to improve upon?
4. When comparing the medical field with that of specialty mental health, what similarities and differences do you believe exist?

Helpful Websites for Pediatric IC

American Academy of Child and Adolescent Psychiatry: www.aacap.org/
American Academy of Pediatrics: www.aap.org/
Bright Futures at Georgetown University: www.brightfutures.org/mentalhealth/pdf/tools.html
The Merck Manuals: Online Medical Library: http://merckmanuals.com
National Initiative for Children's Healthcare Quality: www.nichq.org/index.html
National Institute of Mental Health: Child and Adolescent Mental Health: www.nimh.nih.gov/health/topics/child-and-adolescent-mental-health/
Zero to Three: National Center for Infants, Toddlers, and Families: www.zerotothree.org/child-development/

Recommended Reading for Pediatric IC

Augustyn, M., Zuckerman, B., & Caronna, E. B. (Eds.). (2010). The *Zuckerman Parker handbook of developmental and behavioral pediatrics for primary care.* Philadelphia: Wolters Kluwer/Lippincott Williams & Wilkins.

Barkley, R. A. (2005). *Taking charge of ADHD: The complete, authoritative guide for parents.* New York: Guilford Press.

Bergman, A. B. (Ed.). (2001). *20 common problems in pediatrics.* New York: McGraw-Hill.

Friedberg, R., & McClure, J. (2002). *Clinical practice of cognitive therapy with children and adolescent: The nuts and bolts.* New York: Guilford Press.

Weisz, J., & Kazdin, A. (2010). *Evidence-based psychotherapies for children and adolescents* (2nd ed.). New York: Guilford Press.

References

American Psychiatric Association. (2000). *Diagnostic and statistical manual of mental disorders* (Rev. 4th ed.). Washington, DC: Author.

Doherty, W. J., McDaniel, S. H., & Baird, M. A. (1996). Five levels of primary care/behavioral healthcare collaboration. *Behavioral Healthcare Tomorrow, 5*(5), 25–28.

Campo, J., Shafer, S., Strohm, J., & Lucas, A. (2005). Pediatric behavioral health in primary care: A collaborative approach. *Journal of American Psychiatric Nurses Association, 11*(5), 276–282.

James, L., & Folen, R. (2005). *The primary care consultant: The next frontier for psychologists in hospitals and clinics.* Washington, DC: American Psychological Association.

Kelleher, K., Campo, J., & Gardner, W. (2006). Management of pediatric mental disorders in primary care: Where are we now and where are we going? *Current Opinion in Pediatrics, 18,* 649–653.

Miller, J. (2007). Screening children for developmental behavioral problems: Principles for the practitioner. *Primary Care Clinics in Office Practice, 34,* 177–201.

CHAPTER 11

Suicide Screening, Assessment, and Intervention with Adult Patients in Integrated Care

HEATHER THOMPSON

Suicide is a serious public health concern that ranks among one of the leading causes of death in many countries worldwide (World Health Organization, 2006). Nearly 1 million people commit suicide each year, yet the number of attempts is believed to be more than 10 times greater than the number of actual deaths caused by suicide (Beautrais, Soubrier, Vijayakumar, & Wasserman, 2006). Notably, most of those who commit suicide struggle with treatable mental health concerns (Feldman et al., 2007; E. C. Harris & Barraclough, 1997), but pervasive stigma about mental illness may prevent suicidal patients from seeking mental health treatment. Rather, they will see their primary care provider (PCP) for physical health concerns. In fact, many of those who attempt suicide share their intent with their PCP. On average, 77% of individuals who die by suicide contact their PCP within the year before their death (Luoma, Martin, & Pearson, 2002). Forty-five percent of those intending to commit suicide contact their PCP within the month before their suicide (Luoma et al., 2002), and nearly 20% contact their PCP within 1 day of their death (Pirkis & Burgess, 1998). Integrated care (IC) bridges the gap in mental and physical health treatment, thereby enhancing the likelihood of detection and intervention with suicidal patients. The primary purpose of this chapter is to describe how screening, assessment, and intervention of complicated and sometimes deadly suicidality can be addressed by behavioral health providers (BHPs) in IC.

PCPs appear uniquely positioned to provide assessment and intervention for patients with suicidal thoughts and behaviors (Milton, Ferguson, & Mills 1999; Posner, Melvin, Stanley, Oquendo, & Gould, 2007). Yet, research indicates that PCPs do not believe they are adequately prepared to work with suicidal patients (Hawgood, Krysinska, Ide, & De Leo, 2008; Palmieri et al., 2008). Research further reveals that PCPs often fail to assess for patient suicide risk (Bartels et al., 2002; Feldman et al., 2007; Schulberg et al., 2004), and they lack risk management skills (Goldman, Nielsen, & Champion, 1999; Milton et al., 1999).

Practice Recommendations

Screening

BHPs in IC can improve suicide screening, assessment, and interventions. Risk factors are included in Table 11.1.

A higher risk of suicide is associated with the presence of multiple risk factors (Schwartz & Rogers, 2004); however, it should not be assumed that a patient is not suicidal based on the lack of multiple risk factors (Laux, 2002). As such, all patients who appear even minimally at risk for suicide should be screened (Bryan, Corso, Neal-Walden, & Rudd, 2009).

Most patients who are thinking about killing themselves will not spontaneously share their distress (Matthews, Milne, & Ashcroft, 1994). Research indicates that 44% of people who have attempted suicide in the past answered "no" to a general suicide screening question such as "Have you ever felt suicidal?" (Barber, Marzuk, Leon, & Portera, 1998). Therefore,

Table 11.1
Suicide Risk Factors

Anxiety	Lack of social support
Between the ages 15–24 years	Living alone
Bipolar disorder	Male
Borderline personality disorder	Medical illnesses and/or chronic pain
Depression	Older than 60 years old
Eating disorders	Preoccupation with loss or trauma
Family history	Previous attempts
Family history of abuse	Recent loss
Helplessness	Schizophrenia
Hopelessness	Substance abuse
Ideas of persecution	Trauma
Impulsivity	Unemployment

screening should include a combination of questions about suicidal thoughts and feelings (Fiedorowicz, Weldon, & Bergus, 2010; Granello, 2010a). Asking about suicidal thoughts and behaviors does not increase the likelihood of suicide (Gould et al., 2005; Schwartz & Rogers, 2004). A screening may include a series of questions on a continuum of directness:

- Have you lost hope?
- Do you think about running away from your problems?
- People who feel depressed sometimes think about hurting themselves. Have you considered hurting yourself?
- Do things ever get so bad that you think about ending your life?
- Have you *ever* felt suicidal?
- Do you feel suicidal now?

When screening for suicide, BHPs should use a nonjudgmental and direct approach to communicate to the patient that it is safe and acceptable to have an honest conversation about suicidal thoughts and feelings.

Assessment

A positive screening must be followed by a more thorough assessment of suicidal behaviors and ideation. Suicide assessment mnemonics include but are not limited to PIMP (Plan, Intent, Means, and Prior Attempts), SAD PERSONS (Sex, Age, Depression, Previous attempt, Ethanol use, Rational thinking loss, Social supports lacking, Organized plan, No spouse, and Sickness) (Patterson, Dohn, Bird, & Patterson, 1983), IS PATH WARM (Ideation, Substance abuse, Purposelessness, Anger, Trapped, Hopelessness, Withdrawing, Anxiety, Recklessness, and Mood Change) (Juhnke, Granello, & Lebrón-Striker, 2007), and SIMPLE STEPS (Suicidal, Ideation, Means, Perturbation, Loss, Earlier Attemps, Substance use, Trouble shooting, Emotional factors, Parental or family history, and Stress) (McGlothlin, 2010). Numerous standardized measures of suicidal ideation and personality characteristics common to people with suicidal tendencies are available to help BHPs in their clinical decision making. They include the Patient Health Questionnaire (PHQ-9; Kroenke, Spitzer, & Williams, 2001), the Behavioral Health Measure (BHM-20; Kopta & Lowry, 2002), the Columbia-Suicide Severity Rating Scale (C-SSRS; Posner et al., 2008), the Minnesota Multiphasic Personality Inventory: 2 (MMPI-2; Hathaway & McKinley, 1989), the Beck Depression Inventory (Beck & Steer, 1987), and the Psychological Pain Assessment Scale (Shneidman, 1999). According to most BHPs' ethical codes and standards, appropriate training and supervision are necessary before administering and interpreting such assessments.

A suicide assessment should be facilitated in a way that is culturally sensitive and therapeutic instead of prescriptive and diagnostic. In fact, a strong therapeutic alliance is a protective factor for suicidal patients, whereas a poor therapeutic relationship is considered a risk factor for suicide (American Psychiatric Association [APA], 2003). Culturally sensitive suicide assessment entails an understanding of particular cultural and religious messages about suicide and mental illness that may have been internalized by the patient (Granello, 2010a). These messages may serve as either protective factors or barriers to treatment.

A thorough suicide assessment should include the following: an inquiry into the patient's thoughts and intentions about suicide, plan and means to carry out suicide, harm to others, previous attempts, family history of suicide, degree of emotional pain, experiences of loss, traumatic experiences, substance abuse, medication use and compliance, and protective factors (Bryan et al., 2009; James, 2008; Juhnke et al., 2007; McGlothin, 2010; Patterson et al., 1983; Posner et al., 2007). A suicide assessment serves as the initial step in a crisis intervention plan. The core components of a suicide assessment are depicted in Figure 11.1.

Thoughts, Intent, Plan, and Means

For a positive suicide screening, one in which the patient indicated suicidal thoughts, assess intent by gathering information about the extent to which the patient wants to die and if he or she has created a suicide plan (APA, 2003; Bryan et al., 2009). Suicidal planning is one of the strongest predictors of suicidal behavior (Beck, Brown, & Steer, 1997). As such, it is important to assess the level of detail, feasibility, and lethality of the plan (Sobczak, 2009) and probe for access to the potentially lethal means of suicide (Fiedorowicz et al., 2010). For example, does the patient own a firearm and have ammunition or posses the quantity of pills needed to overdose? McGlothlin (2010) warned that BHPs may not have an accurate understanding of the potential lethality of their patient's plan, so it is wise to assume that the patient's intention (e.g., to take 10 aspirin) is in fact deadly. Probes may include the following:

- What led to your thoughts that you want to die?
- How often do you have thoughts of wanting to die?
- How long do the thoughts last? (fleeting or ruminating)
- Have you come close to attempting suicide but stopped yourself? What stopped you?
- What do you think would happen if you actually killed yourself?
- Do you have a plan?
- What is your plan?
- Do you have access to the (gun, pills, rope, etc.)?
- What other preparations have you made?

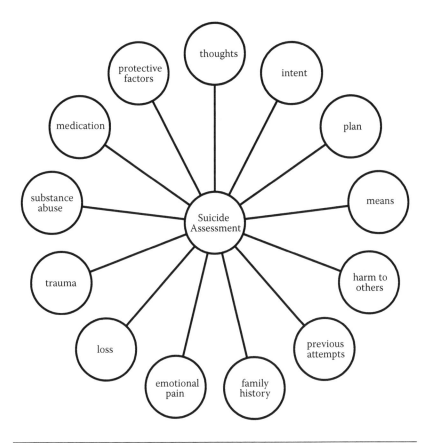

Figure 11.1 Factors to be addressed in suicide assessments of adult patients.

Harm to Others

Suicidal patients may believe that others are responsible for their suicidal thoughts and feelings and seek retribution for perceived wrongdoing. This is particularly evident in cases of domestic homicide–suicide in which the perpetrator murders the victim and then takes her or his own life. BHPs have an ethical responsibility to assess the risk of lethality if direct or indirect threats of violence are made toward another. General risk factors for homicide include previous violent behavior, social stressors, substance abuse, and certain personality traits such as low frustration tolerance, poor problem-solving skills, impulsivity, and a glamorized perception of violence (Cavaiola & Colford, 2011). Intermittent explosive disorder, paranoid schizophrenia, and antisocial personality disorder are often associated with elevated risk for violent behavior (Cavaiola & Colford, 2011).

The purpose of the assessment should be to decipher between expressions of anger and genuine homicidal intent. Risk assessments should combine clinical judgment, which takes into consideration the risk factors that may be unique to the individual or the situation, and structured assessments (Haggard-Grann, 2007). Questions to ask a suicidal patient when assessing for intent to harm others include the following:

- Are there other people who you think are responsible for your feelings right now?
- Are you thinking about harming them?
- Are you thinking about killing them? If yes, then how? When? Where?

There are several well-established assessments that can be used to measure the degree of the threat of intention to harm others. Assessments of general violent behavior include the Violence Risk Appraisal Guide (VRAG; G. T. Harris, Rice, & Quinsey, 1993) and the Historical, Clinical, and Risk Management Violence Risk Assessment Scheme (HCR-20; Webster, Douglas, Eaves, & Hart, 1997). The potential risk for sexual violence may be assessed by the Static-99 (Hanson & Thornton, 1999) or the Sexual Violence Risk-20 (SVR-20; Boer, Hart, Kropp, & Webster, 1997). Structured assessments for intimate partner violence include the Danger Assessment Scale (DAS; Campbell, 1986) and Spousal Assault Risk Assessment (SARA; Kropp, Hart, Webster, & Eaves, 1995).

Previous Attempts and Family History

The BHP should obtain an understanding of patients' previous suicidal behaviors and attempt to better understand the potential risk involved with a current suicidal episode (Bryan et al., 2009); a history of previous suicide attempts is strongly associated with an increased risk of suicide (APA, 2003). In the case of previous attempts, ask the patient about his or her suicidal attempt and desired outcome. Patients who regret having survived a previous attempt may be at a greater risk of suicide than those who are happy to have survived (Brown, Steer, Henriques, & Beck, 2005). Appropriate questions include the following:

- Have you attempted to commit suicide before?
- If yes, how many times?
- When was the most recent time?
- What was the most serious attempt?
- What happened before the attempt?
- What thoughts did you have before the attempt?
- What did you hope would happen?
- How did you feel afterward?
- What type of help did you get afterward?
- Who supported you after the attempt?

Further assess suicide potential by determining if the patient has a parental or family history of suicide (McGlothlin, 2006) or hospitalization for mental health disorders (APA, 2003).

Emotional Pain

The degree of emotional distress, also known as perturbation, influences suicidal risk. McGlothin (2006) recommended using a series of scaling questions to assess lethality and the emotional pain of suicidal patients. The following question may serve as a basic assessment of lethality:

> On a scale of 1 to 10, with 1 indicating not likely at all and 10 indicating that it will happen within 72 hours if someone does not intervene, how likely are you to attempt to kill yourself? (McGlothin, 2006, p. 130)

McGlothin (2006) recommended that an assessment of lethality should be followed by a scaling question about the degree of emotional pain:

> On a scale of 1 to 10, with 1 indicating no pain and 10 indicating unbearable pain, how much pain are you in? (McGlothin, 2006, p. 130)

An appraisal of the relationship between lethality and perturbation may be assessed by asking the following:

> On a scale of 1 to 10, how likely would it be that you would attempt to kill yourself if your pain was an unbearable 10? (McGlothin, 2006, p. 130)

This should be followed by a question about what it would take to move the patient from the present number indicating emotional pain to a 10 (McGlothin, 2010). Additional probes about emotional distress and likelihood of lethality include the following:

- How likely are you to act on your plan?
- What kinds of things would make you more likely to act on your plan?

Loss, Trauma, and Substance Use

When assessing for risk of suicide, ask the patient if he or she has recently experienced a loss or if there is an upcoming anniversary of a loss (James, 2008; McGlothin, 2010). Perceived losses may be the result of many different types of events that include but are not limited to death, divorce, separation, job loss, housing loss, health problems, and educational failure (APA, 2003; James, 2008). Suicide risk may also be elevated for those who experienced childhood abuse (Cavaiola & Colford, 2006; Plunkett et al., 2001). When assessing for traumatic childhood experiences, ask about physical, emotional, and/or sexual abuse (James, 2008). Assess if the patient has a history of substance abuse (James, 2008). Substance abuse and dependence is a significant risk factor for suicide and suicidal attempts (Henriksson et al., 1993). Suicide is more likely to occur during a depressive episode for those struggling with substance abuse and dependence (Lonnqvist et al., 1995). Moreover, depression may be intensified by the use of mood-altering substances. The disinhibiting effects of drugs and alcohol may place the patient at a greater risk of acting on suicidal thoughts and feelings (APA, 2003; Cavaiola & Colford, 2011).

Medications

Assess if the patient is medication compliant or if his or her medications have recently changed. A change in some medications may result in disequilibrium. With such cases, consult with the PCP about typical side effects and the possible need for a medication evaluation.

Protective Factors

Assess for protective factors that can be helpful in crafting an intervention for the patient. Protective factors include coping skills, social support, a patient's degree of resilience, emotional tolerance, capacity for reality testing, good health, religious activity, pregnancy, and having children in the home. Appropriate questions include the following:

- What might make you feel more hopeful about your future?
- What might make you less likely to attempt suicide?
- What things or people in life are worth living for?
- When else have you dealt with this type of emotional distress?
- How did you manage that distressing experience?

Consultation and Documentation

Although there are numerous suicide screenings and models available, none completely diminish the uncertainty associated with suicide assessment (Simon, 2006). Uncertainty is a trademark of lethality assessment (Granello, 2010a; James, 2008). The presence of risk factors cannot predict the likelihood of lethal behavior. Therefore, consultation and supervision are best practice (McGlothin, 2006), the results of which must be documented (Granello, 2010a).

Suicide Risk Levels

Patients are considered low risk when ideation is present but a specific plan is not evident (Granello & Granello, 2011). A moderate risk level, which may require hospitalization, is associated with suicidal ideation and a general plan but reasonable self-control. Patients with a high level of risk have clearly articulated plans, the means to carry out the plans, and feelings of hopelessness, in addition to other risk factors such as previous suicide attempts (World Health Organization, 2006). In the case of a high-level suicidal risk, stay with the patient until the hospital is contacted and transportation arrives. It is advised that the BHP be present if possible, or calls the hospital when the patient is admitted so important information can be relayed to the hospital staff (Granello, 2010b). Hospitalization serves to enhance the safety of the patient, but it should not be the final step in treatment. Follow-up intervention is essential for reducing the risk of future suicide attempts (Asarnow, Berk, & Baraff, 2009). Examples of high-level suicidal emergencies include the following:

- A widowed male cancer patient in late adulthood with a prognosis of only a few more months to live has a gun, and he maintains that he is going to go home tonight to load his gun and kill himself.
- A male patient in early adulthood with substance dependence reports command hallucinations that are directing him to kill himself and others.
- A female adolescent with depression, frequent anxiety attacks, and a previous suicidal attempt reports that she is going to take 30 Xanax pills. The bottle is in her purse. She does not think things will ever get better.
- A woman in early adulthood, who lacks social support and has a history of substance dependence and impulsivity, reports dramatic mood changes and daily ruminating thoughts about ways to commit suicide. Her distressing thoughts last from the time she wakes up until the time she goes to bed at night. She maintains that she sees no reason to continue living, and she does not see any other way than death to deal with her emotional pain.

Crisis Intervention With Suicidal Patients

The majority of patients assessed for suicide in the primary care setting will not need to be hospitalized (Bryan et al., 2009), and multidisciplinary care may be the optimal form of suicide intervention for these individuals (APA, 2003). An IC practice provides an ideal forum for collaborative intervention that may combine psychotherapy and pharmacology (APA, 2003). The patient should be considered an active member of the treatment team and should be aware of each team member's role (APA, 2003).

After a careful risk assessment, a crisis intervention response plan is essential to returning patients to equilibrium (Granello, 2010b;

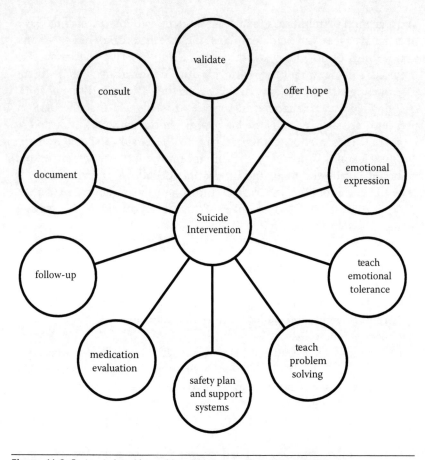

Figure 11.2 Factors to be addressed in suicide interventions with adult patients.

James, 2008). Suicide interventions should be approached with the same therapeutic foundation as other mental-health-related concerns (Granello, 2010a). As such, the BHP must build a therapeutic relationship by demonstrating genuine acceptance, empathy, and validation of the patient's life story (Bongar, 2002; Granello, 2010a; Westefeld et al., 2000). To work effectively with suicidal patients, the BHP must be skilled in the following: listening, normalizing, validating, communicating hope, facilitating emotional expression, teaching emotional tolerance, reframing, teaching problem solving, addressing isolation, making a safety plan, evaluating medication, and following up (APA, 2003; Asarnow et al., 2009; Cavaiola & Colford, 2006; Granello, 2010b; James, 2008; Laux, 2002). A visual representation of these factors can be found in Figure 11.2.

Validate and Communicate Hope

Patients should be given the opportunity to tell their story and be heard by someone who accepts them unconditionally (Granello, 2010b). It is likely that patients who are struggling with suicidal thoughts and feelings have expressed their concerns to someone who may have minimized their suffering, discounted their pain, or judged their suicidal thoughts as a moral deficit (Granello, 2010a). BHPs should make a concerted effort to communicate to the patient that it is acceptable to talk about suicidal thoughts and feelings and to validate his or her experience because patients who feel invalidated by the BHP may be less inclined to learn how to develop emotional tolerance and regulation, problem-solving skills, and safety planning (Asarnow et al., 2009; Cavaiola & Colford, 2006; Granello, 2010b; James, 2008).

Emotional Ventilation and Tolerance

The purpose of emotional ventilation, not escalation, is to help patients learn that emotional pain ebbs and flows, and painful feelings can be tolerated and worked through (Granello, 2010b; James, 2008). BHPs can help patients learn to identify the thoughts, feelings, and behaviors that trigger their suicidal ideation (Asarnow et al., 2009). Ideally this awareness helps patients learn how to regulate maladaptive emotional, cognitive, and behavioral interactions that lead to suicidal behaviors (Asarnow et al., 2009).

Problem Solving

Reframing suicidal tendencies as maladaptive attempts at problem solving sets the tone for a collaborative effort aimed at identifying new ways of dealing with problems that are risk factors for suicide (Granello, 2010b). Problem solving is an essential skill to daily living, yet it is rarely taught. BHPs can teach patients how to identify their concerns, discover potential strategies or solutions to problems, evaluate outcomes related to identified strategies and solutions, select problem-solving strategies, implement strategies, and evaluate their effectiveness. BHPs can also teach patients how to categorize and prioritize concerns in terms of which ones can be more easily addressed. Giving patients an opportunity to experience success through the resolution of modifiable problems can enhance their self-efficacy and sense of hope (Granello, 2010b), which bolsters their commitment to therapy. The identification and modification of risk factors should be augmented with the strengthening of protective factors (Jacobs & Brewer, 2006).

Safety Planning and Support Systems

Safety planning is an essential aspect of suicide interventions. Because the safety of the patient is the most essential goal of the crisis intervention, potentially lethal methods of suicide should be removed to reduce the risk of an impulsive attempt to commit suicide (APA, 2003). In an effort to further enhance patient safety, written safety plans should include collaboratively generated coping strategies that are personally appropriate to the patient. Coping strategies may include cognitive restructuring, thought stopping, relaxation practices, distraction exercises, seeking support (Asarnow et al., 2009; Granello, 2010b), practicing affirmations, and exercise. Included in the safety plan should be the names and phone numbers of support people, social support services, and emergency contact information (Granello, 2010b). BHPs should help patients brainstorm potential complications that may serve as obstructions to the utilization of the safety plan. The generation and rehearsal of strategies for overcoming those complications are also advised (Chiles & Strosahl, 2005). Family involvement, if appropriate and potentially helpful to the patient, should be encouraged. Family and loved ones also may benefit from counseling and psychoeducation about suicide and the possible mental health concerns related to the suicidal individual (Laux, 2002). Safety planning should be thoroughly documented in the patient's record, and the documentation should be easily accessible to the BHP in the event that the patient is in crisis and attempts or commits suicide.

Medication Evaluation

If the patient is depressed, the BHP and the patient should work in collaboration with the PCP to find an appropriate medication. Hirschfeld and Russell (1997) suggested that fluoxetine, sertraline, paroxetine, nefazodone, venlafaxine, and mirtazapine may be appropriate options for depressed patients who are suicidal, but the PCP, after his or her evaluation, will determine what would work best for the patient. Patients with alcohol or substance abuse should be referred to a substance abuse/dependence treatment program.

Follow-up and Referral

Suicidal thoughts, feelings, and behaviors are likely to vary in intensity over the course of treatment (APA, 2003). Continued assessment is needed, and follow-up should be exercised. Once the patient is stabilized, ongoing counseling may be helpful to address the underlying stressors and core issues related to the suicidality (Granello, 2010a). A referral for more specialized or intensified behavioral health services (mental health and substance abuse services) should be considered, especially when the medical practice and BHP feel the level of monitoring and need for service intervention are beyond the reach of the IC model. Patients at this level of risk may require agency-based outpatient psychiatry and therapy services, inpatient psychiatric care, or intensive wraparound services such as Assertive Community Treatment Teams (ACTT).

Crisis Intervention With Homicidal Patients

If a suicidal patient reveals significant risk for violent behavior toward another person, the patient should be admitted to a hospital so an emergency psychiatric evaluation can be obtained. In accordance with *Tarasoff v. Regents of the University of California* (1976), the police should be notified, and the potential victims of violence should be warned. It should be noted that some states are not "duty to warn" states, and BHPs are not required to notify the authorities or the intended victim.

Depending on the unique nature of the presenting problem and the patient's motivation to change, patients who report hostile feelings but do not express intent to act on them may benefit from discussing coping mechanisms, support systems, anger management strategies, and referral to support groups or mental health professionals who can work with the patient about the presenting concern that triggers volatile feelings and thoughts, as well as the underlying issues.

It may be appropriate to use directive methods such as motivational interviewing to assess the stage of change, explore motivation, and resolve ambivalence toward change. Interventions should be tailored to the perpetrator's level of motivation and simultaneously work to advance the perpetrator to the next stage of change (Kistenmacher & Weiss, 2008). In the context of unconditional positive regard and a genuine desire to understand the perpetrator's perspective, the BHP encourages the perpetrator to prepare for change by exploring the need, desire, reasons, and ability to change. Change plans are negotiated based on the perpetrator's readiness and commitment to change.

Conclusion

Significant mental health issues are associated with an elevated risk of suicide. More than 90% of individuals who commit suicide experience mental health issues (Henriksson et al., 1993) such as depression, anxiety, bipolar disorder, eating disorders, schizophrenia, substance abuse (E. C. Harris & Barraclough, 1997), and traumatic experiences (James, 2008). Unfortunately, many who struggle with mental health concerns do not utilize the services of mental health professionals (Pirkis & Burgess, 1998). In fact, approximately 1 in 4 people in the United States struggle with a diagnosable mental illness (National Institute for Mental

Health, n.d.), yet in 2008, less than 14% of the population received mental health care (Substance Abuse and Mental Health Services Administration, 2008). Limited access, financial constraints, and perceived stigma (Sobczak, 2009) impede help-seeking for mental health concerns that if left untreated may have deleterious effects on individuals, families, communities, and society. Fortunately, a therapeutic window of opportunity exists in IC because 45% of those who commit suicide contact their PCP within a month prior to their death (Luoma et al., 2002). Collaborative care models in which BHPs are embedded in primary care present a most important venue for identifying potentially suicidal patients. Well-informed BHPs may significantly enhance assessment and crisis intervention for suicidal patients (Schulberg et al., 2004), which may ultimately lead to the prevention of numerous suicide attempts and deaths.

Discussion Questions

1. Choosing from one of the brief scenarios in the "Suicide Risk Levels" section, describe what steps you would take to ensure the patient's safety.
2. Assume your day is busy with consultations and a few 30-minute counseling sessions are scheduled, when based on a PCP's request, you meet with a patient who is suicidal and going to need hospitalization. What steps can you take to make sure the patient gets the services he or she needs while also juggling the rest of your schedule?
3. Create a scenario about a patient who expresses suicidal thoughts but no plan, and describe what steps you would take to create a safety contract with this person.

References

American Psychiatric Association. (2003). *Practice guideline for the assessment and treatment of patients with suicidal behaviors.* Retrieved February 2, 2011, from http://psychiatryonline.com/content.aspx?aID=56135

Asarnow, J. R., Berk, M. S., & Baraff, L. J. (2009). Family intervention for suicide prevention: A specialized emergency department intervention for suicidal youth. *Professional Psychology: Research and Practice, 40*(2), 118–125. doi:10.1037/a0012599

Barber, M. E., Marzuk, P. M., Leon, A. C., & Portera, L. (1998). Aborted suicide attempts: A new classification of suicidal behavior. *American Journal of Psychiatry, 155,* 385–389.

Bartels, S. J., Coakley, E., Oxman, T. E., Giessupe, C., Oslin, D., Chen, H., Sanchez, H. (2002). Suicidal and death ideation in older primary care patients with depression, anxiety and at-risk alcohol use. *American Journal of Geriatric Psychiatry, 10*, 417–427.

Beautrais, A., Soubrier, J. P., Vijayakumar, L., & Wasserman, D. (2006). *Preventing suicide: A resource guide for counsellors.* Retrieved from http://www.who.int/mental_health/resources/suicide/en/index.html

Beck, A. T., Brown, G. K., & Steer, R. A. (1997). Psychometric characteristics of the Scale for Suicidal Ideation with psychiatric outpatients. *Behaviour Research and Therapy, 35*, 1039–1046.

Beck, A. T., & Steer, R. A. (1987). *Beck Depression Inventory manual.* San Antonio, TX: Psychological Corporation.

Boer, D., Hart, S., Kropp, P., & Webster, C. (1997). *Manual for the Sexual Violence Risk-20.* Burnaby, British Columbia, Canada: The British Columbia Institute Against Family Violence, copublished with the Mental Health, Law, and Policy Institute at Simon Fraser University.

Bongar, B. (2002). *The suicidal patient: Clinical and legal standards of care* (2nd ed.). Washington, DC: American Psychological Association.

Brown, G. K., Steer, R. A., Henriques, G. R., & Beck, A. T. (2005). The internal struggle between the wish to die and the wish to live: A risk factor for suicide. *American Journal of Psychiatry, 162*, 1977–1979. doi:10.1176/appi.ajp.162.10.1977

Bryan, C. J., Corso, K. A., Neal-Walden, T. A., & Rudd, D. M. (2009). Managing suicide risk in primary care: Practice recommendations for behavioral health consultants. *Professional Psychology: Research and Practice, 40*(2), 148–155. doi:10.1037/a0011141

Campbell, J. (1986). Nursing assessment for risk of homicide with battered women. *Advances in Nursing Science, 8*, 36–51.

Cavaiola, A., & Colford, J. (2006). *A practical guide to crisis intervention.* Boston: Houghton Mifflin.

Cavaiola, A., & Colford, J. E. (2011). *Crisis intervention case book.* Belmont, CA: Brooks/Cole.

Chiles, J. A., & Strosahl, K. D. (2005). *Clinical manual for assessment and treatment of suicidal patients.* Washington, DC: American Psychiatric Press.

Feldman, M. D., Franks, P., Duberstein, P. R., Vannoy, S., Epstein, R., & Kravitz, R. L. (2007). *Annuals of Family Medicine, 5*(5), 412–418.

Fiedorowicz, J. G., Weldon, K., & Bergus, G. (2010). Determining suicide risk (hint: a screen is not enough). *Journal of Family Practice, 59*(5), 256–260.

Goldman, L. S., Nielsen, N. H., & Champion, H. C. (1999). Awareness, diagnosis, and treatment of depression. *Journal of Internal Medicine, 14*, 569–580. doi:10.1046/j.1525-1497.1999.03478.x

Gould, M. S., Marrocco, F. A., Kleinman, M., Thomas, J. G., Mostkoff, K., Cote, J., & Davies, M. (2005). Evaluating iatrogenic risk of youth suicide screening programs: A randomized controlled trial. *Journal of the American Medical Association, 293*(13), 1635–1643.

Granello, D. H. (2010a). The process of suicide risk assessment: Twelve core principals. *Journal of Counseling and Development, 88*, 363–371.

Granello, D. H. (2010b). A suicide crisis intervention model with 25 practical strategies for implementation. *Journal of Mental Health Counseling, 32*(3), 218–235.

Granello, D. H., & Granello, P. F. (2011, March). *Clinical techniques for managing suicidal patients.* Paper presented at Association for Counselor Education and Supervision, New Orleans, LA.

Haggard-Grann, U. (2007). Assessing violence risk: A review and clinical recommendations. *Journal of Counseling and Development, 85*(3), 294–303.

Hanson, R. K., & Thornton, D. (1999). *Static 99: Improving actuarial risk assessments for sex offenders* (User Report 99-02). Ottawa: Department of the Solicitor General of Canada.

Harris, E. C., & Barraclough, B. (1997). Suicide as an outcome for mental disorders: A meta-analysis. *British Journal of Psychiatry, 170*, 205–228.

Harris, G. T., Rice, M. E., & Quinsey, V. L. (1993). Violent recidivism of mentally disordered offenders: The development of a statistical prediction instrument. *Criminal Justice and Behavior, 20*, 315–335.

Hathaway, S. R., & McKinley, J. C. (1989). *Minnesota Multiphasic Personality Inventory-2 (MMPI-2): Manual for administration and scoring.* Minneapolis: University of Minnesota Press.

Hawgood, J. L., Krysinska, K. E., Ide, N., & De Leo, D. (2008). Is suicide prevention properly taught in medical schools? *Medical Teacher, 30*, 287–295. doi:10.1080/01421590701753542

Henriksson, M. M., Aro, H. M., Marttunen, M. J., Heikkinen, M. E., Isometsa, E. T., Kuoppasalmi, K. I., & Lonnqvist, J. K. (1993). Mental disorders and comorbidity in suicide. *American Journal of Psychiatry, 150*, 935–940.

Hirschfeld, R. M., & Russell, J. M. (1997). Assessment and treatment of suicidal patients. *The New England Journal of Medicine, 337*(13), 910–915.

Jacobs, D. G., & Brewer, M. L. (2006). Application of the APA practice guidelines on suicide to clinical practice. *CNS Spectrums, 11*, 447–454.

James, R. (2008). *Crisis intervention strategies* (6th ed.). Belmont, CA: Brooks/ Cole Thompson.

Juhnke, G. A., Granello, P. F., & Lebrón-Striker, M. (2007). IS PATH WARM? A suicide assessment mnemonic for counselors. *ACA Professional Counseling Digest.* Retrieved from http://counselingoutfitters.com/vistas/ACAPCD/ACAPCD-03.pdf

Kistenmacher, B. R., & Weiss, R. L. (2008). Motivational interviewing as a mechanism for change in men who batter: A randomized controlled trial. *Violence and Victims, 23*, 558–570.

Kopta, S. M., & Lowry, J. L. (2002). Psychometric evaluation of the Behavioral Health Questionnaire-20: A brief instrument for assessing global mental health and the three phases of psychotherapy outcome. *Psychotherapy Research, 12*, 413–426.

Kroenke, K., Spitzer, R. L., & Williams, J. B. (2001). The PHQ-9: Validity of a brief depression severity measure. *Journal of General Internal Medicine, 16*(9), 606–613.

Kropp, P. R., Hart, S. D., Webster, C. W., & Eaves, D. (1995). *Manual for the Spousal Assault Risk Assessment Guide* (2nd ed.). Vancouver: British Columbia Institute on Family Violence.

Laux, J. M. (2002). A primer on suicidology: Implications for counselors. *Journal of Counseling and Development, 80*, 380–383.

Lonnqvist, J. K., Henriksson, M. M., Isometsa, E. T., Marttunen, M. J., Heikkinen, M. E., Aro, H. M., & Kuoppasalmi, K. I. (1995). Mental disorders and suicide prevention. *Psychiatry and Clinical Neurosciences, 49*, S111–S116.

Luoma, J. B., Martin, C. E., & Pearson, J. L. (2002). Contact with mental health and primary care providers before suicide: A review of the evidence. *American Journal of Psychiatry, 159*, 909–916.

Matthews, K., Milne, S., & Ashcroft, G. W. (1994). Role of doctors in the prevention of suicide: The final consultation. *British Journal of General Practice, 44*, 345–348.

McGlothlin, J. M. (2006). Assessing perturbation and suicide in families. *The Family Journal: Counseling and Therapy for Couples and Families, 14*(2), 129–134. doi:10.1177/1066480705285740

McGlothlin, J. (2010). *Sharpen your clinical skills* [audio podcast]. Retrieved from http://www.counseling.org/Counselors/TP/PodcastsHome/CT2.aspx

Milton, J., Ferguson, B., & Mills, T. (1999). Risk assessment and suicide prevention in primary care. *Crisis, 20*, 171–177.

National Institute for Mental Health. (n.d.). *The numbers count: Mental disorders in America.* Retrieved from http://www.nimh.nih.gov/statistics/index.shtml

Palmieri, G., Forghieri, M., Ferrara, S., Pinggani, L., Coppola, P., & Colombini, N. (2008). Suicide intervention skills in health professionals: A multidisciplinary approach. *Archives of Suicide Research, 12*, 232–237.

Patterson, W., Dohn, H., Bird, J., & Patterson, G. (1983). Evaluation of suicidal patients: The SAD PERSONS scale. *Psychosomatics, 24*, 343–349.

Pirkis, J., & Burgess, P. (1998). Suicide and recency of health care contacts: A systematic review. *The British Journal of Psychiatry, 173*, 462–474.

Plunkett, A., O'Toole, B., Swanston, H., Oates, R. K., Shrimpton, S., & Parkinson, P. (2001). Suicide risk following child sexual abuse. *Ambulatory Pediatrics, 1*, 262–266.

Posner, K., Brent, D., Lucas, C., Gould, M., Stanley, B., Brown, G., Mann, J. (2008). *Columbia suicide severity rating scale.* New York: Research Foundation for Mental Hygiene. Retrieved from http://www.cssrs.columbia.edu/docs/C-SSRS_1_14_09_Baseline.pdf

Posner, K., Melvin, G. A., Stanley, B., Oquendo, M. A., & Gould, M. (2007). Factors in the assessment of suicidality in youth. *CNS Spectrums, 12*, 156–162.

Schulberg, H. C., Hyg, M. S., Bruce, M. L., Lee, P. W., Williams, J. W., & Dietrich, A. J. (2004). Preventing suicide in primary care patients: The primary care physician's role. *General Hospital Psychiatry, 26*, 337–345.

Schwartz, R. C., & Rogers, J. R. (2004). Suicide assessment and evaluation strategies: A primer for counseling psychologists. *Counseling Psychology Quarterly, 17*(1), 89–97. doi:10.1080/09515070410001665712

Shneidman, E. (1999). The Psychological Pain Assessment Scale. *Suicide and Life-Threatening Behavior, 29*, 287–294.

Simon, R. (2006). Imminent suicide: The illusion of short-term prediction. *Suicide and Life-Threatening Behavior, 36*(3), 296–302.

Sobczak, J. A. (2009). Managing high-acuity-depressed adults in primary care. *Journal of the American Academy of Nurse Practitioners, 21*, 362–370.

Substance Abuse and Mental Health Services Administration. (2008). *National Survey on Drug and Health*. Retrieved from http://www.nimh.nih.gov/statistics/3USE_MT_ADULT.shtml

Webster, C. D., Douglas, K. S., Eaves, D., & Hart, S. D. (1997). *HCR-20: Assessing risk for violence* (Version 2). Burnaby, BC: Mental Health Law and Policy Institute, Simon Fraser University.

Westefeld, J. S., Range, L. M., Rogers, J. R., Maples, M. R., Bromley, J. L., & Alcorn, J. (2000). Suicide: An overview. *The Counseling Psychologist, 28*, 445–510.

World Health Organization (2006). *Preventing suicide: A resource for counsellors*. Geneva, Switzerland: WHO Press.

CHAPTER 12

Screening, Assessment, and Intervention for Intimate Partner Violence in Integrated Care

HEATHER THOMPSON

Intimate partner violence (IPV), also known as domestic violence, is a pervasive problem in this country that is both deadly and costly. The total estimated annual medical and mental health costs related to IPV exceed $5.8 billion (Centers for Disease Control and Prevention, 2003). Chronic physical health concerns are associated with IPV, and survivors often utilize medical care more often than those who have not experienced IPV (Nicolaidis & Touhouliotis, 2006). In response to this epidemic, the health care profession has called for routine screening and management of IPV in medical settings (Edwardsen, Morse, & Frankel, 2006; Sugg, 2006). The purpose of this chapter is to provide practical IPV screening, assessment, and crisis intervention recommendations for behavioral health professionals (BHPs) in integrated care (IC) settings. A continuous case study about IPV will be presented throughout this chapter.

IPV Case Study: Keera

Keera, an African American mother in early adulthood, was diagnosed by her obstetrician with postpartum depression after the birth of her first child. At the time, Keera reported having trouble sleeping, feeling edgy and agitated, losing her appetite, and worrying about her son, Marcus.

She scheduled a follow-up appointment with her obstetrician to check in about the postpartum symptoms and to discuss birth control options. During the appointment, Keera mentioned that she is feeling better but still feels overwhelmed. She wants to avoid "adding to the stress at home" by accidentally getting pregnant again. She mentioned that her husband, whom she married when she found out she was pregnant, has a temper, and she thinks that his "dark moods" are "agitating" the baby. She blamed his recent "anger problems" on being newly married and a new father. The obstetrician asked if she would like to meet with a BHP to discuss her recent transition to motherhood, and Keera agreed.

Case Questions

- What are your beliefs about individuals who stay in abusive relationships?
- How might your values and beliefs influence your work with Keera?
- What would you do if you were Keera's BHP?

IPV is often conceptualized as a pattern of threats and physical, sexual, emotional, or psychological abuse that is committed by one intimate partner against another (Family Violence Prevention Fund [FVPF], 2004). Estimates of IPV range from 3.4 to 8.7 million reported cases annually (Gelles, 1995; Straus, 1999). In the United States each year, women survive approximately 4.8 million physical assaults and rapes, and men endure approximately 2.9 million physical assaults by intimate partners (Tjaden & Thoennes, 2000). In 2005, 1,510 deaths resulted from IPV; 78% of those victims were female, and 22% were male (Tjaden & Thoennes, 2000). IPV occurs in both opposite-sex and same-sex relationships. Available research, although limited, indicates that IPV in same-sex relationships occurs at a similarly high rate as opposite-sex relationships (Renzetti, 1992), though the rate of IPV between same-sex male relationships is greater than that of same-sex female relationships (Tjaden & Thoennes, 2000). Although females experience more abuse (Tjaden & Thoennes, 2000), it is recommended that both females and males be assessed for IPV (FVPF, 2004).

Female survivors of IPV have a significantly greater rate of reporting physical health problems than those who are not in abusive relationships, including complaints of chronic pain, headaches, gastrointestinal problems, and sexually transmitted infections (R. Campbell, Sefl, & Ahrens, 2003; Tjaden & Thoennes, 2000; Trabold, 2007). Mental health issues associated with IPV include depression, anxiety (Felitti, 1991), substance abuse (McCauley et al., 1995) post-traumatic stress disorder (PTSD; Golding, 1999), low self-esteem (R. S. Thompson et al., 1998), and feelings of shame

(J. C. Campbell, 2002). Children who are exposed to violence between intimate partners in the home are at risk for a multitude of developmental concerns that include emotional, behavioral (Litrownik, Newton, Hunter, English, & Everson, 2003), and interpersonal (Kitzmann, Gaylord, Holt, & Kenny, 2003) issues. For many of these children, exposure to violence begins in the womb. In a comparison of multiple studies on the prevalence of IPV during pregnancy, Gazmararian et al. (1996) found that the majority of studies reported estimates ranging from 3.9% to 8.3%. IPV during pregnancy is a risk factor for low birth weight (McFarlane, Parker, & Soeken, 1996) and postnatal depression (Ludermir, Lewis, Valongueiro, de Araújo, & Araya, 2010).

Practice Recommendations

The utilization of health care services is greater for survivors of IPV than for those who have not experienced it (Ross, Walther, & Epstein, 2004). Despite the prevalence, less than 3% of cases of IPV are identified by PCPs (R. S. Thompson et al., 1998), and only 1% to 15% of patients are ever asked about experiences with IPV by their PCP (Gelles & Straus, 1988; McCauley et al., 1995; Straus, Gelles, & Steinmetz, 1980; Straus & Smith, 1993). PCPs may be hesitant to conduct an initial screening for IPV for fear of offending their patients (Jonassen & Mazor, 2003), however, studies have shown that patients do not feel offended when asked about IPV experiences (Caralis & Musialowski, 1997). Research also indicates that when screening is conducted in medical settings, it can be an effective way to identify patients who have experienced IPV (McFarlane, Christoffel, Bateman, Miller, & Bullock, 1991). With this information, health care professionals have called for increased screening and treatment for IPV (Murphy & Ouimet, 2008). BHPs in IC can address this call to action by advocating for a safety-related question in the self-completed patient inventory completed by new patients and during annual visits (e.g., Do you ever fear for your own safety or the safety of others while at home?). This would allow the practice to screen their entire population and identify patients for further screening. It also identifies those patients who may not have self-identified to the PCP or who have presented some of the indicators of IVP described in this chapter, and it gives the BHP an opportunity for follow-up screening and assessment. BHPs can also screen when there is reason to suspect IPV, can facilitate assessments and interventions, and can educate PCPs about the dynamics of IPV, indicators that a patient may be experiencing IPV, and sensitive screening procedures.

Table 12.1
Potential Indicators of IPV

- Physical injuries such as contusions, lacerations, fractures, or burns to the face, chest, or abdomen
- Bite marks, burns, and patterns of injury not consistent with the patient's reported diagnosis
- Oral, pharyngeal, vaginal, or anal trauma
- Somatic complaints such as chronic pain, headache, abdominal pain, pelvic pain, back pain, dyspareunia, fatigue, and insomnia
- Mental health issues such as substance abuse, anxiety, depression, disordered eating, suicide attempts, low self-esteem, and insomnia
- An overly attentive or possessive partner who insists on being present during the entire visit
- Delays in getting treatment for injuries, missed appointments, frequent use of the emergency room, and sudden increase or decrease in office visits

Screening

An adapted list of indicators that may warrant screening is provided in Table 12.1.

It should be noted that the FVPF (2002) maintains that IPV is such a significant health care concern that patients should be screened routinely regardless of the presence of indicators of abuse. PCPs may need to implement a policy that patients be seen individually in order to complete an IPV screen, before allowing friends and family members to participate in the visit (R. S. Thompson et al., 1998).

When screening for IPV, PCPs and BHPs must be cognizant of patients' privacy, immigration status, language barriers, cultural values and perceptions of abuse, homophobia, and fears related to child custody. There are discrepancies among states about reporting mandates, so BHPs need to become familiar with their state's particular directives. BHPs should explain the confidential nature of their conversations with patients, as well as the limitations of confidentiality. For example, state laws require that BHPs make a report to child protective services if a child has been maltreated or neglected as a result of IPV, regardless of the intentionality of the perpetrator (FVPF, 2004). Many states, however, do not require the abuse of a competent adult to be reported. A few states require that medical personnel report abuse of a competent adult if it is the result of criminal conduct or if the injury was caused by a weapon such as a firearm or knife (Scalzo, 2006). See the National Center for the Prosecution of Violence Against Women (NCPVAW) for information on state reporting laws related to IPV (Scalzo, 2006).

As is the case with suicide screening, questions about IPV experiences can be asked on a continuum of directness. Gender-neutral language, such as the use of the word *partner* as opposed to *spouse*, is recommended when screening for IPV. Be aware that when screening for IPV with survivors in same-sex relationships, in addition to disclosing the abuse or violence in their intimate relationship, survivors are faced with the task of "coming out" about their sexual identity, which may be difficult for some. It is a misperception that IPV in same-sex relationships is less dangerous or traumatic for the survivor because the playing field is leveled when the size and strength of the perpetrator is similar to that of the survivor (Tesch, Bekerian, English, & Harrington, 2010). Screening questions for IPV may include the following:

- Stress can sometimes lead to health problems. How are things at work? How are things at home?
- How does your partner express anger or frustration?
- What happens when you and your partner fight?

Validate, normalize, and communicate hope to the patient if he or she reveals that IPV is currently occurring in his or her relationship, and then further assess the patient's experiences with IPV.

- Intimate partner violence happens more often than you might expect. You are not alone, and you do not deserve the abuse.
- Intimate partner violence can affect your physical health and safety. Can you tell me about the worst fight?

More specific questions may include:

- Has your partner ever
  - yelled at you?
  - demeaned or humiliated you?
  - threatened you or your children?
  - destroyed your property?
  - tried to control your activities?
  - hurt your pets?
  - pushed or hit you?
  - forced an unwanted sexual experience?
  - attempted to choke or strangle you?
  - threatened you with a weapon?
  - hurt you with weapon?

Avoid clustering the questions (e.g., "Does your partner force sex, strangle you, or threaten you with a weapon?") because patients typically will not address all aspects of a multilayered question. Reflections of feelings, thoughts, and experiences, and empowering and normalizing statements should be interwoven into the overall assessment process so the patient does not feel interrogated. If a patient reports a recent experience of IPV with a current intimate partner, an assessment of his or her immediate safety is necessary. Trust the patient to determine the degree of danger in his or her relationship. The FVPF (2002) recommended asking the following questions for immediate safety concerns:

- Are you in immediate danger?
- Where is your partner at the moment?
- How do you feel about going home with your partner today?

It may be appropriate to call the police or security if the patient indicates that he or she is afraid to leave with his or her partner. If the patient chooses not to disclose experiences with IPV, the BHP can use the initial screening as an opportunity to communicate support and compassion for the patient, which may increase the likelihood of the patient seeking information or services in the future. The screening experience may be the patient's first interaction with someone who is willing to speak openly about IPV and may also be the first time the patient has received the message that he or she is not alone and that the abuse is not his or her fault.

Brief screening revealed that Keera's and James's "worst fight" happened 2 months ago when James was laid off from work. He was intoxicated, and he yelled at her, smashed objects in their house, slapped her, pushed her down, and physically restrained her when she tried to get away. Keera maintained that she does not feel like she is in immediate danger. James is not at the doctor's office with her.

Assessment

An initial screen that is positive for IPV should be followed by a more thorough assessment of the patient's safety. The severity of violence can be assessed with the use of instruments such as the Revised Conflict Tactics Scales (Straus, Hamby, Boney-McCoy, & Sugarman, 1996), Severity of Violence Against Women Scale (Marshall, 1992), or the Index of Spouse Abuse (D. W. Campbell, Campbell, King, Parker, & Ryan, 1994). A clinical interview can also be useful in assessing immediate danger; the duration, frequency, and severity of the abuse; and whether there is harm to children, self, or others.

Clinical interview questions may include the following:

- When did the abuse begin?
- How often does the abuse happen?
- Has the abuse become more harmful since the first time?

Specific probes aimed at assessing the severity of the abuse may include the following:

- Have you ever been hospitalized because of a fight?
- Has your partner ever stalked or harassed you?
- Has your partner ever hurt you with a weapon?
- Has your partner ever prevented you from leaving when you wanted to?
- Does your partner threaten to commit suicide?
- Has your partner threatened or hurt your children?
- Have your children ever intervened in a fight? Have your children ever been accidentally injured during a fight with your partner?

A suicide and homicide assessment should be conducted if the patient reports any of the following: an escalation in the frequency and severity of the abuse, the use of weapons, stalking, being held against his or her will, or if suicidal and/or homicidal threats have been made (FVPF, 2004). Survivors of severe and frequent IPV may feel they have no control over the abuse, ability to predict it, or means of protecting themselves or their children. Suicide or homicide may seem like the only option available to ending the violence. A brief suicide and lethality assessment may include questions such as the following:

- Risk of suicide by the survivor of IPV:
  - Have you ever felt like you didn't want to go on living?
  - Have you thought about suicide in the past?
  - Have you ever attempted suicide?
  - Are you thinking about killing yourself?
  - Do you have a plan?

- Risk of homicide by the survivor of IPV:
  - How do you perceive your options for protecting yourself from the abuse?
  - How do you perceive your options for protecting your children from the abuse?
  - Have you ever thought about killing your partner?
  - Have you ever attempted to kill your partner?
  - Have you thought about how you would do it?
  - Do you have a plan?

After the initial screening, a more thorough safety assessment revealed that the physical abuse began when Keera was pregnant with their son, Marcus: James would grab, shake, and push her and pull her hair. She attributed this behavior to his difficulty adjusting to married life and being a father. He has become more hostile since he was laid off 2 months ago and has been drinking more than usual. She reported that he has not threatened or hurt her with a weapon, hurt her to the point that she needed to be hospitalized, stalked her, restricted her ability to come and go as she pleases, threatened to kill himself, threatened to kill her, or hurt Marcus. A brief suicide and homicide assessment revealed that she does not feel suicidal or homicidal. She maintained that she is not happy in the relationship, but her father was absent for much of her life, and she wants to at least try to raise Marcus with James.

Crisis Intervention

Typically, the identification of patients in the medical setting who are currently experiencing IPV is followed by referral to IPV service providers (Nicolaidis & Touhouliotis, 2006). However, the BHP in the medical setting can extend the provision of services to patients who are experiencing IPV by validating and supporting patients, helping patients develop safety plans, offering psychoeducation about IPV, referring to outside professionals, following up with the patient, and documenting encounters.

Safety Plans

Safety plans, or self-management plans (Nicolaidis & Touhouliotis, 2006), are a commonly endorsed form of intervention with survivors of IPV. BHPs use safety plans to help survivors identify risks and anticipate future danger so they may plan accordingly to minimize victimization (Witte & Kendra, 2010). Safety planning should be done in a way that honors the survivor's ability to make choices about his or her safety, and it should acknowledge and expand upon safety strategies that the survivor already uses to minimize risk (Nicolaidis & Touhouliotis, 2006). A discussion about safety planning may be initiated by asking the following:

- How do you know when your partner is getting ready to be abusive?
- What specific things do you do to try to keep yourself (and your children) safe when the abuse starts?
- Who have you told about your abuse, if anyone?
- Who could you depend on to help you in a crisis?
- Where could you go to be safe during a cooling-off period?
- What items would you need to take with you if you needed to leave for a period of time?
- What is the best way to get out of your home in a hurry?
- What, if any, potential weapons are present where you live?

In general, safety plans include (a) identification of cues such as shifts in mood, certain facial expressions, particular speech patterns, threats, and substance use (Witte & Kendra, 2010) that indicate the potential for violence; (b) identification of people to call in a crisis; (c) enlistment of neighbors who will contact the police during violent episodes; (d) escape routes; (e) safe refuges; and (f) escape kits that include essential items (i.e., money, keys, social security cards, birth certificates, driver's license, bank account numbers, insurance policies, immunization records, and clothing; Lawson, 2003). Safety plans provide survivors with much more than a concrete behavioral plan for safety: They empower survivors to regain control. For example, the decision to hang keys by the door and place a purse on the floor below the keys in preparation for a quick exit is one way for survivors to regain control in an abusive relationship. McFarlane et al. (2004) created a safety checklist in both English and Spanish that includes essential items for an escape kit. A copy of the Safety-Promoting Behavior Checklist is available in McFarlane et al. (2004). The FVPF (2004) created a thorough tool for comprehensive safety planning (see Appendix H, p. 44).

These are both comprehensive visual aids for safety planning that may assist the BHP and the survivor in designing a personalized safety plan. When creating a safety plan with a survivor, the BHP needs to explore ways to prevent the plan, or other psychoeducatior.al materials, from falling into the hands of the perpetrator.

Safety planning may also include conversations about how to deal with the emotions that may come up as a result of having broken the cycle of silence related to experiences with IPV. Breaking the silence about abuse may stir up intense feelings, realizations, and a certain degree of cognitive dissonance. An emotional safety plan may address these feelings through the identification of relaxing diversions, tension-reducing exercises, healing rituals, physical recreation activities, social support, and spiritual support.

Psychoeducation

Survivors may be empowered by psychoeducation provided by the BHP about the dynamics of IPV. Two helpful resources, an adapted copy of Walker's (1984) cycle of violence and a violence wheel of power and control, may be found at http://www.domesticviolence.org. Having a framework to conceptualize a seemingly unpredictable and uncontrollable person provides a degree of power to a survivor whose only other explanation may be "I am the problem," "I deserve it," or "If only I'd do better." Psychoeducation may communicate to the survivor, "You are not alone," "This is a wide-spread epidemic," and "It is not your fault."

Survivors should also be aware that leaving an abusive relationship is likely to be challenging. It is often the most dangerous time because violence is likely to escalate when the perpetrator realizes he or she is losing control and power over the survivor. Regardless of the survivor's decision to stay or leave, provide validation and support with the hope that thoughts of change may be sparked and will be acted on weeks, months, or even years later.

Information on protective orders should be provided. Civil orders of protection can be obtained in every state in the United States. Protection orders temporarily protect the plaintiff and the plaintiff's children by prohibiting contact from the person who is the threat. Community organizations that specialize in treatment and advocacy for people affected by IPV should have a court advocate who can help the survivor navigate the legal process.

Referrals

BHPs should maintain a current list of support services for survivors of IPV. That list should include information on local services such as shelters, IPV support groups, children's services, transitional housing, legal and advocacy services, law enforcement, and clergy. Survivors should know that a crisis telephone hotline is available to them 24 hours a day. It is also important to know which service providers offer bilingual services. National support services are included in Table 12.2.

Referral to IPV services in the community is recommended when BHPs encounter patients who are experiencing IPV. Mental health professionals in the field of IPV may assist survivors with in-depth career, educational, and basic life skills education needed to maintain independence. IPV or community counseling services may be recommended to address cognitive and behavioral processes, empower the survivor, and facilitate the healing transformation from survivor to thriver. Counseling services may also be helpful in addressing the depression, anxiety, PTSD, or drug and alcohol abuse that may be associated with experiencing psychological and physical violence from an intimate partner.

Documentation

The BHP should encourage the PCP to document IPV in the event that the survivor decides to go to court. Documentation should include the name of the alleged perpetrator and his or her relationship to the survivor

Table 12.2
Intimate Partner Violence Support Services

- American College of Emergency Physicians: http://www.acep.org
- American Academy of Family Physicians: http://www.aafp.org
- American Congress of Obstetricians and Gynecologists: http://www.acog.org
- American Academy of Pediatrics: http://www.aap.org
- Centers for Disease Control and Prevention (intimate partner information): http://www.cdc.gov/ncipc/dvp/fivpt/spotlite/home.htm
- Family Violence Prevention Fund: http://www.fvpf.org
- Futures Without Violence: www.futureswithoutviolence.org
- Stop Abuse for Everyone (SAFE): http://www.safe4all.org/
- U.S. Department of Justice: http://www.ojp.usdoj.gov/vawo/

(Thompson et al., 1998). A description of injuries should be provided (color of bruises, texture, size, and location on the body) as well, and with the survivor's consent, photographs should be taken to supplement the written description of the injuries (FVPV, 2002).

Follow-up

Arrange for a follow-up meeting with the patient and obtain a safe phone number to reach the patient. It is important to take safety issues into consideration when trying to contact patients. For instance, BHPs may ask, "Is it safe to call you at this number? What is a safe way for me to contact you? What days and times of the day are safe to call you?" (FVPF, 2004).

During the crisis intervention it is communicated to Keera by the BHP that she is in no way responsible for the abuse. Her decision to stay in the relationship is respected, her desire to take an active role in her family planning is reinforced, and her efforts to protect herself and her son are commended. Appropriate psychoeducation is interwoven throughout conversations with Keera with the hopes that it will empower her by removing unknowns about IPV and presenting predictable patterns: IPV is a crime punishable by law; violence often begins or escalates during pregnancy; children exposed to IPV are at risk for developmental and behavioral problems; stress and substance abuse can lead to more frequent and hostile episodes of violence; periods of contrition between hostile outbursts become shorter and the violence tends to escalate over time; promises to reform are often forgotten; abuse can include intimidation, humiliation, threats, isolation, and sexual coercion; and the violence is likely to escalate when/if the survivor leaves.

A safety plan is suggested to empower Keera by bolstering her control and preparedness in case of an emergency. Keera identifies both her mother and James's mother as significant support people in her life. Both women live within a 30-mile radius of her home. Keera identifies her sister as an additional support person who lives 6 hours away. Keera maintains that all three women are aware of James's "anger problems." She believes she can depend on these women for basic needs and emotional support if she needed a "cooling-off period" from James. Keera does not want to call the police because she is afraid that getting him arrested might jeopardize his chances of getting another job. She does not want her neighbors to know about the abuse. She does, however, agree to approach her mother and James's mother about picking Marcus up from the house if it appears that James is likely to become violent.

Keera identifies several physical, emotional, and behavioral indicators that James's hostility is escalating. She maintains that there are firearms in the house. She decides to remove the ammunition. She does not think James will notice because he does not hunt anymore. If James asks, she will say she is concerned for Marcus. She believes that removing the ammunition will not jeopardize her safety.

Keera agrees to pack an overnight bag with essential items such as cash, social security cards, birth certificates, marriage license, and medications. She declines to meet with an advocate about a protective order or go to a shelter in a undisclosed location; however, she agrees to call the shelter "just in case" to find out more about the services it offers. She places the call from the office phone and has a private conversation with the house manager at the local shelter. She also accepts information about local support services for adults who are affected by someone else's substance abuse and information on mental health professionals in the community who provide counseling with sliding-scale fees.

Keera is reminded that intense feelings and cognitive dissonance may arise after having disclosed the inner workings of an abusive relationship. This is normalized, and Keera is encouraged to uphold her commitment to come back for a follow-up session. Coping strategies are identified to help ameliorate the discomforting thoughts and feelings that may be stirred up by the session. Safe calling procedures and times to call are identified, and a follow-up appointment is scheduled.

Conclusion

Debilitating mental health issues such as depression, anxiety, PTSD, and substance abuse are associated with experiences with IPV (Golding, 1999; Lown & Vega, 2001; M. P. Thompson et al., 1999). Survivors of IPV are also more likely to have chronic physical health concerns and utilize medical care more often than individuals who have not experienced IPV (Nicolaidis & Touhoulitiotis, 2006). Many health care organizations, including the American Medical Association, American Academy of Family Physicians, American Academy of Pediatrics, American College of Emergency Physicians, and the American Congress of Obstetricians and Gynecologists, have called for routine screening and management of IPV (Murphy & Ouimet, 2008). BHPs have the advantage of specialized education and training related to working with individuals in crisis. Furthermore, BHPs possess the clinical sensitivity to make screening and assessment therapeutic by creating a safe and nonjudgmental space for patients to feel heard and validated (Westefeld et al., 2000). Also within BHPs' professional purview is crisis intervention, which may include safety planning, psychoeducation, referral, follow-up, and documentation.

References

Campbell, D. W., Campbell, J. C., King, C., Parker, B., & Ryan, J. (1994). The reliability and factor structure of the index of spouse abuse with African-American battered women. *Violence and Victims, 9,* 259–274.

Campbell, J. C. (2002). Health consequences of intimate partner violence. *Lancet, 359,* 1331–1336.

Campbell, R., Sefl, T., & Ahrens, C. (2003). The physical health consequences of rape. *Women's Studies Quarterly, 31,* 90–103.

Caralis, P., & Musialowski, R. (1997). Women's experiences with domestic violence and their attitudes and expectations regarding medical care of abuse victims. *South Medical Journal, 90,* 1075–1080.

Centers for Disease Control and Prevention. (2003). *Costs of intimate partner violence against women in the United States.* Atlanta, GA: National Center for Injury Prevention and Control.

Edwardsen, E. A., Morse, D. S., & Frankel, R. M. (2006). Structured practice opportunities with a mnemonic affect medical student interviewing skills for intimate partner violence. *Teaching and Learning in Medicine, 18*(1), 62–68.

Family Violence Prevention Fund. (2004). *National consensus guidelines: On identifying and responding to domestic violence victimization in health care settings.* San Francisco, CA: Author. Retrieved from http://endabuse.org/userfiles/file/Consensus.pdf

Felitti, V. J. (1991). Long-term medical consequences of incest, rape, and molestation. *Southern Medical Journal, 84,* 328–331.

Gazmararian, J., Lazorick, S., Spitz, A., Ballard, T., Saltzman, L., & Marks, J. (1996). Prevalence of violence against pregnant women. *Journal of the American Medical Association, 275,* 1915–1920.

Gelles, R. J. (1995). *Violence toward men: Fact or fiction?* Report prepared for the American Medical Association, Council on Scientific Affairs, Family Violence Research Program, University of Rhode Island.

Gelles, R. J., & Straus, M. (1988). *Intimate violence.* New York: Simon & Schuster.

Golding, J. M. (1999). Intimate partner violence as a risk factor for mental disorders: A meta-analysis. *Journal of Family Violence, 14*(2), 99–132.

Jonassen, J. A., & Mazor, K. M. (2003). Identification of physician and patient attributes that influence the likelihood of screening for intimate partner violence. *Academic Medicine, 78,* S20–S23.

Kitzmann, M. K., Gaylord, N. K., Holt, A. R., & Kenny, E. D. (2003). Child witnesses to domestic violence: A meta-analytic review. *Journal of Consulting and Clinical Psychology, 71*(2), 339–352.

Lawson, D. M. (2003). Incidence, explanations, and treatment of partner violence. *Journal of Counseling and Development, 81,* 19–32.

Litrownik, A. J., Newton, R., Hunter, W. M., English, D., & Everson, M. D. (2003). Exposure to family violence in young at-risk children: A longitudinal look at the effects of victimization and witnessed physical and psychological aggression. *Journal of Family Violence, 18*(1), 59–73.

Lown, E. A., & Vega, W. A. (2001). Intimate partner violence and health: Self-assessed health, chronic health, and somatic symptoms among Mexican American women. *Psychosomatic Medicine, 63*(3), 352–360.

Ludermir, A. B., Lewis, G., Valongueiro, S. A., de Araújo, T. B., & Araya, R. (2010). Violence against women by their intimate partner during pregnancy and postnatal depression: A prospective cohort study. *The Lancet, 376*(9744), 903–910.

Marshall, L. L. (1992). Development of the Severity of Violence Against Women Scale. *Journal of Family Violence, 7,* 103–121.

McCauley, J., Kern, D., Kolodner, K., Dill, L., Schroeder, A., DeChant, H., & Deroeatis, L. R. (1995). The "battering syndrome": Prevalence and clinical characteristics of domestic violence in primary care internal medicine practices. *Annals Internal Medicine, 123,* 737–746.

McFarlane, J., Christoffel, K., Bateman, L., Miller, V., & Bullock, L. (1991). Assessing for abuse: Self-report versus nurse interview. *Public Health Nursing, 8,* 245–250.

McFarlane, J., Malecha, A., Gist, J., Watson, K., Batten, E., Hall, I., & Smith, S. (2004). Increasing the safety-promoting behaviors of abused women. *American Journal of Nursing, 104*(3), 40–50.

McFarlane, J., Parker, B., & Soeken, K. (1996). Physical abuse, smoking, and substance use during pregnancy (prevalence, interrelationships and effects on birthweight). *Journal of Obstetric Gynecologic and Neonatal Nursing, 25,* 313–320.

Murphy, S. B., & Ouimet, L. V. (2008). Intimate partner violence: A call for social work action. *Health and Social Work, 33*(4), 309–314.

Nicolaidis, C., & Touhouliotis, V. (2006). Addressing intimate partner violence in primary care: Lessons from chronic illness management. *Violence and Victims, 21,* 101–115.

Renzetti, C. M. (1992). *Violent betrayal: Partner abuse in lesbian relationships.* Newbury Park, CA: Sage.

Ross, J., Walther, V., & Epstein, I. (2004). Screening risks for intimate partner violence and primary care settings: Implications for future abuse. *Social Work in Health Care, 38*(4), 1–23. doi:10.1300/J010v38n04_01

Scalzo, T. P. (2006). *Reporting requirements for competent adult victims of domestic violence.* The National Center for the Prosecution of Violence Against Women, American Prosecutors Research Institute. Retrieved from http://www.usmcmccs.org/famadv/restrictedreporting/Natioinal%20Domestic%20Violence%20Reporting%20Requirements.pdf

Straus, M. A. (1999). The controversy over domestic violence by women: A methodological, theoretical, and sociology of science analysis. In X. B. Arriaga & S. Oskamp (Eds.), *Violence in intimate relationships* (pp. 17–44). Thousand Oaks, CA: Sage.

Straus, M. A., Gelles, R. J., & Steinmetz, S. K. (1980). *Behind closed doors: Violence in the American family.* New York: Doubleday/Anchor.

Straus, M. A., Hamby, S. I., Boney-McCoy, S., & Sugarman, D. (1996). The Revised Conflict Tactics Scale (CTS2). *Journal of Family Issues, 17,* 283–316.

Straus, M. A., & Smith, C. (1993). Family patterns and primary prevention of family violence. In M. A. Straus & R. J. Gelles (Eds.), *Physical violence in American families: Risk factors and adaptations to violence in 8145 families* (pp. 507–525). New Brunswick, NJ: Transaction.

Sugg, N. (2006). What do medical providers need to successfully intervene with intimate partner violence? *Journal of Aggression, Maltreatment and Trauma*, *13*(3–4), 101–120.

Tesch, B., Bekerian, D., English, T., & Harrington, E. (2010). Same-sex domestic violence: Why victims are more at risk. *International Journal of Police Science and Management*, *12*(4), 526–535.

Thompson, M. P., Kaslow, N. J., Kingree, J. B., Puett, R., Thompson, N. J., & Meadows, L. (1999). Partner abuse and posttraumatic stress disorder as risk factors for suicide attempts in a sample of low-income, inner-city women. *Journal of Traumatic Stress*, *12*(1), 59–72.

Thompson, R. S., Meyer, B. A., Smith-DiJulio, K., Caplow, M. P., Maiuro, R. D., Thompson, D. C., & Rivara, F. P. (1998). A training program to improve domestic violence identification and management in primary care: Preliminary results. *Violence and Victims*, *13*(4), 395–410.

Tjaden, P., & Thoennes, N. (2000). Prevalence and consequences of male-to-female and female-to-male intimate partner violence as measured by the National Violence Against Women Survey. *Violence Against Women*, *6*, 142–161.

Trabold, N. (2007). Screening for intimate partner violence within a health care setting: A systematic review of the literature. *Social Work and Health Care*, *45*, 1–18.

Walker, L. E. (1984). *The battered woman syndrome.* New York: Springer.

Walker, L. E. (2000). *Battered woman syndrome.* New York: Springer.

Witte, T. H., & Kendra, R. (2010). Risk recognition and intimate partner violence. *Journal of Interpersonal Violence*, *25*(12), 2199–2216.

CHAPTER **13**

Integrated Care for Returning Members of the Military and Their Families

GLENDA C. SAWYER and ROBIN R. MINICK

Introduction

The White House's Policy Committee on Military and Veteran Families identified two critical service area initiatives in an effort to help military members and their families thrive during and after deployment: (a) increase behavioral health care services through prevention-based integrated services in the community and (b) build awareness among military families and communities that psychological fitness is as important as physical fitness (U.S. Department of Veterans Affairs, 2011a). To carry out these initiatives, the Service Members Counseling and Support Center (SMCSC) was established as part of an integrated behavioral health program embedded within an urgent care clinic located in a rural area of the southeastern United States. The SMCSC resides on a hospital campus and provides integrated services for all patients and a specialty service that accommodates the unique health needs of active-duty, National Guard, Reserve, and veteran military personnel and their families. This chapter will describe the programming that meets the needs of service members and their families, as well as highlight the reasons why this approach is necessary. It will also explore the behavioral health issues facing military service members and their families and present considerations for how to best serve this population in integrated care (IC) settings.

IC Approach With Military Personnel and Their Families

Mild traumatic brain injury and post-traumatic stress disorder (PTSD) are considered the signature injuries of combat soldiers returning from Iraq and Afghanistan (Jones, Young, & Leppma, 2010). A positive screening result for PTSD is correlated with high somatic symptom severity (Hoge, Terhakopian, & Castro, 2007). The PTSD Checklist Military version (PCL-M; U.S. Department of Veterans Affairs, 2011b) is a self-report screening of the 17 symptoms of PTSD in the *Diagnostic and Statistical Manual of Mental Disorders* (American Psychiatric Association, 2000) geared toward stressful military-related situations. The PTSD Checklist Civilian version (PCL-C; U.S. Department of Veterans Affairs, 2011b) can be used to screen for PTSD in any population and can be utilized for military personnel who have had multiple traumas with some taking place before or after their military service. The medical burden of PTSD encompasses a variety of physical health problems 1 year postdeployment. The overlapping symptoms commonly experienced by returning service members include intrusive memories, social detachment, insomnia, anger, and concentration problems (Jones et al., 2010). Combat exposure, which contributes significantly to 12-month onsets of PTSD and major depressive disorder, has been shown to have a direct effect on unemployment and job loss, separation or divorce from significant others, domestic violence, and substance abuse concerns. Consequently, long-term negative effects on both the individual's and the nation's mental, social, and economic health are profound (Prigerson, Maciejewski, & Rosenheck, 2002). Redeployed personnel who reported combat exposures had a threefold increase in new onset of self-reported symptoms of PTSD compared to "nondeployers" (Smith et al., 2008). Overall, military personnel returning from modern deployments are at risk for adverse long-term mental and behavioral health conditions and related impacts on psychosocial functioning (Maguen, Reger, & Gahm, 2010). Cognitive behavioral therapy for PTSD and the Seeking Safety approach when both PTSD and substance use disorders are present are effective (Najavitz, 2007). In addition, cognitive processing therapy and prolonged exposure therapy are two cognitive behavioral therapies that are currently being used by the military and U.S. Department of Veterans Affairs Medical Centers (VA) system that are gaining a significant evidence base for PTSD treatment efficacy (Sharpless & Barber, 2011). Training for behavioral health providers (BHPs) who work outside of the VA and who wish to learn more about these therapies is becoming more readily available.

Active-duty military, veteran, Reserve, and National Guard personnel and their family members are a part of every community. For this reason, for every National Guard member deployed, many individuals in a given community are directly affected. Current combat operations in Iraq (Operation Iraqi Freedom) and Afghanistan (Operation Enduring Freedom) have been lengthy for the all-volunteer forces and entail prolonged exposure to the stress of combat that has been compounded by the reexposure experienced during multiple deployments. A 2008 RAND report suggested that these two factors are leading to a high number of stateside military-related personnel now living in their home communities who struggle with mental and physical health issues (Tanielian et al., 2008).

Many military service members who do not wish, or in some cases may not be eligible, to receive services from the VA seek medical help from local primary care providers (PCPs). These PCPs ideally triage for mental health treatment referral to local BHPs or in-house BHPs who are part of the primary care practice's IC team. PCPs and BHPs play an increasingly important role in screening, assessing, and providing appropriate treatment for the many concerns facing military service members and their families. Ideally, PCPs, BHPs, law enforcement, and emergency medical service providers work together as a team to meet the needs of military families. These teams should strive to provide seamless short-term, situational, problem-solving services, along with psychoeducation to help military service members and their families understand the impact of stress, deployments, and reunification with their families following deployments.

National Guard and Reserve military members require additional consideration by IC practices that serve them. One noteworthy challenge in reaching National Guard members is their unit affiliation. Guard members do not always drill in, and are not always attached to, a unit near to their home. For example, NC Guard units drill soldiers from all across North Carolina. The service member's military occupation specialty determines his or her drill location, so military service members and their families are not necessarily attached to the local units in the communities in which they live. Thus, advertising the existence of programs cannot be done adequately via communication with the Guard units and needs to be supplemented with local media advertising to reach all community members.

Other unique concerns for Guard and Reserve units relate to differences between the Guard and active-duty soldiers. Guard and Reserve soldiers are not attached to military installations and live mostly as civilians. Their training is limited to one weekend a month—these soldiers spend only limited time with their peers and may not be able to build important bonds, putting them at risk for insufficient support systems. When deployed, they are often used to fill in vacant slots in other units of the Guard and may encounter potentially stressful situations if they are placed with unfamiliar soldiers and need to cross-train to perform duties other than their military occupation specialty. Sudden removal from work and home reduces time for adjustment, making the transition both into and back from deployment more difficult. IC practices with PCPs and BHPs who wish to be most effective with Guard and Reserve members must be aware of their unique challenges when assessing and planning treatment for them.

Service Member Counseling and Support Center

The following description of the SMCSC, located in a rural area of the southeastern United States, serves to give an example of a medical center with a fully integrated behavioral health program tailored for military service members and their families. A discussion of the ways in which the tenets and insights of this IC program may be applied in integrated primary care practices will follow.

In an effort to provide care to military service members and their families within their communities, the University of North Carolina at Chapel Hill, Odum Institute for Research in Social Science, provided financial start-up support to create the Citizen Soldier Support Program as part of the Department of Defense. The SMCSC was funded by the program and is part of the integrated behavioral health services within an urgent care center of a small regional hospital serving a mostly rural area. The purpose of this program is to provide behavioral health services to military veterans of Operation Enduring Freedom and Operation Iraqi Freedom and their families and significant others who are not attached to or living in proximity to military installations where many health-related and supportive services are easily accessible. The SMCSC supports a part-time BHP and a part-time physician extender (nurse practitioner) and provides financial aid for medications. Ultimately, the program exists to help service members and their families who do not engage in VA services to find a well-equipped, nonmilitary-related IC clinic to meet many of their physical and behavioral health needs, while assisting and encouraging those who need more intensive medical and/or behavioral health intervention to connect with the VA.

Services Provided by the SMSCS

1. Assisting local PCPs and BHPs in becoming TRICARE Prime providers, thereby enabling military families to obtain health care close to home with no co-pay
2. Counseling family members after loss of a service member
3. Assisting community organizations in becoming more sensitive to the military lifestyle and common behavioral health issues of military service members and their families
4. Welcoming deployed military back into the local community

5. Providing medication management and assistance for obtaining affordable medications
6. Assisting military members in enrollment and making referrals to help them obtain services from the local VA hospital and their community-based outpatient clinics when necessary
7. Assisting Veterans Officers and Disabled American Veterans advocates in obtaining services and documentation required to meet eligibility for VA benefits
8. Providing services for veterans' families, which are not provided via the VA

SMCSC Services and the Implications for IC Practices

Upon returning home, service members may experience feelings of hyper-vigilance, anxiety, and paranoia in places that were perceived as non-threatening prior to deployment to combat areas. The routine exercising of lifesaving skills (e.g., hypervigilance) in combat situations may be difficult for service members to suppress once they return to a civilian lifestyle; this can sometimes lead to discord in relationships, impulsivity, and high levels of stress, and therefore increases the risk of drug and alcohol use (Tanielian et al., 2008). Timely outreach to National Guard and Reserve members and veterans is therefore imperative at the community level, especially in light of regular delays with evaluations and claims processing at the VA.

Screening, assessment, counseling, medication management, and resource referral are the primary services delivered to military service members and their families through the SMCSC. This IC program is designed to improve the functioning and quality of life of military service members and their families and to restore a sense of normalcy, as opposed to focusing on pathology, as the mode of treatment for this population. BHPs provide brief counseling, which aims to improve the individual's functional capacity to adapt to a civilian life. Unfortunately, some service members are not connected to a physician in a primary care setting at their time of need because of a lack of medical insurance, because PCPs are not available in their community, or because they haven't established a medical home for themselves. As a result, military members often turn to urgent care centers or emergency departments for their primary care needs and complex health problems. Behavioral health services integrated into primary care practices, like those at the SMCSC, can provide these benefits to service members and their families:

1. Service members receive behavioral health care without having to walk into a "mental health" center or clinic, which helps to reduce stigma that may be especially apparent in a rural community.

2. Patients who present to IC practices may receive a behavioral health screening such as for PTSD or mild traumatic brain injury and immediate assessment and intervention, with attention to the relationship between their behavioral health and their presenting physical health needs. In contrast, most private behavioral health practices, as well as VA medical centers, may have waiting periods and may not utilize a biopsychosocial approach, making the IC practice more responsive to the overall needs of service members and their families.

3. The presence of a BHP whose programming is sensitive to the behavioral health needs of the military population can increase the overall sensitivity of all clinicians in the practice to the multifaceted needs of military service members. The BHP is able to provide on-the-spot medical resources for the patient in this setting.

4. Many of those presenting for services in local communities are uninsured and ineligible for VA benefits. Local provision of treatment helps to bridge gaps in treatment for those filing claims for authorization of VA benefits. BHPs in IC settings should be informed of health and benefits resources available to military service members to assist their patients in obtaining them.

The SMCSC staff, in the context of a specialty center, engages in a number of community programs and events that honor and support military service members and their families because outreach efforts assist service members in their readjustment to civilian life and help to draw them back into involvement in their communities. BHPs in primary care practices may wish to become knowledgeable about current events and homecoming and deployment routines in the communities of military service members to continually update their point of reference for working with these patients. This can be achieved by reading public announcements and staying informed by media coverage about military news and events in the practice's community. One way that BHPs can promote the IC services offered to military patients in their primary care practice is by contacting veterans' service officers in their local community and providing them with referral information that describes their capacity to serve this population. Veterans' service officers meet with service members in the community as advocates who assist with navigation of the system for attaining benefits for service members and their families. BHPs should also be aware that behavioral health care screenings are available to military service members and veterans and their families through the VA's Rural Health Initiative and the nonmedical National Guard Family Program.

Case Scenario

The following case scenario with "John" is an example that demonstrates the unique needs of military personnel who have returned home from deployment and how the urgent care center-based SMCSC helped to provide assessment and treatment services to address his needs.

John is a 28-year-old single, disabled, Caucasian male who currently lives alone in a small rural town. John had an incident that involved law enforcement and subsequent hospitalization after recently returning from his final combat duty; he served four deployments from 2003 to 2009 in the U.S. Army Corps to Fallujah and Ramadi, Iraq, during Operation Iraqi Freedom.

John's inpatient psychiatric stay was prompted by an event for which law enforcement was called to his home. A neighbor reported that John had discharged a firearm several times late one night. John told police that he was shooting because he saw al-Qaeda walking in the woods behind his house, and he wished he had a shell left for himself. He was also under stress because of an event that occurred 3 days prior to the shooting incident: High winds had blown a large tree onto his house, and he was experiencing extreme frustration in dealing with his insurance company over that matter. Adding to that stress and frustration, John discovered that the water in his home was being disconnected for reasons of nonpayment.

John experienced many symptoms consistent with major depression with psychotic features and severe PTSD, including sleep disturbance and nightmares, frequent anxiety attacks, hypervigilance, and flashbacks with dissociation and depersonalization. John's symptoms of severe depression, which had been present for 2 to 3 years, included feelings of hopelessness and worthlessness, anhedonia, passive suicidal thoughts, chronic headaches, chronic fatigue and weakness, difficulty concentrating, difficulty making decisions, memory problems (immediate, recent, and remote), and severe gastrointestinal disturbance and loss of appetite. In addition, John had been experiencing some level of irritability, a decreased need for sleep, racing thoughts, distractibility, increased goal-directed behavior, and likely a manic state. Psychotic episodes of auditory and visual hallucinations were also problematic for John.

After inpatient psychiatric evaluation, John was diagnosed with PTSD and bipolar disorder, recurrent, depressed, and severe, with psychotic features. He was also diagnosed with chronic neck, back, and knee pain; migraines; and possible traumatic brain injury. After being discharged from inpatient treatment, John was scheduled to follow up with the SMCSC for outpatient treatment with medication management and behavioral treatment for PTSD. John reported that his overall health was much worse than it was prior to deployment in his military service, and he rated his health as generally poor, with his health problems making it very difficult for him to work at any tasks around his home and impossible to attempt employment. He also reported extreme levels of difficulty in taking care of simple and routine things at home and in getting along with other people because of feelings of anxiety and depression. He had been fired from seven jobs for "going off" on others because of his chronic irritability, mood swings, and inability to deal with common workplace stressors. Avoidance was John's primary defense mechanism; John described secluding himself in order to regulate his aggressive behavior and to avoid panic attacks in public situations. He also stated that he drank several beers each night in order to sleep, which was regularly interrupted with nightmares related to combat. He also had dissociative experiences due to "blanking out" periods and/or traumatic brain injury. There was no history of traumatic events, psychiatric illness or treatment, or the physical health symptoms described above prior to his military service.

During his deployment to Iraq, John was exposed to or encountered the following: depleted uranium in old tanks near Camp Fallujah; garbage; human blood, body fluids, body parts, and dead bodies; industrial pollution; JP8 (jet propellant); smoke from burning trash and feces; solvents; vehicle exhaust fumes; asbestos (over a 4-week period); and excessive vibrations and loud noise from explosions. During all of his deployments, John experienced approximately 60 blasts and explosions within a 50-meter range that originated from rocket-propelled grenades, indirect fire, and mortar fire (it is noteworthy that he experienced 14 of these episodes in one single day while in Fallujah). He cannot recall aspects of one particular mortar fire that exploded just 6 feet away from him while he was in Fallujah in 2003.

John's completed PCL-M indicated the following: (a) He was severely bothered by trouble remembering important parts of stressful experiences from his past; trouble falling or staying asleep; feeling irritable or having angry outbursts; having difficulty concentrating; and feeling and acting "super alert" or watchful and on guard; (b) he was moderately to severely bothered by repeated, disturbing memories; thoughts; or images of stressful experiences from the past; having physical reactions like heart pounding, trouble breathing, or sweating when something reminded him of stressful experiences from the past; avoiding thinking about, talking about, or having feelings related to stressful experiences from the past; having a loss of interest in things that he used to enjoy; feeling distant or cut off from other people; and feeling emotionally numb or being unable to have loving feelings for those close to him; (c) he was moderately bothered by having repeated, disturbing dreams of stressful experiences from his past; avoiding activities or situations because they remind him of stressful experiences from the past; feeling as if his future will be cut short; and feeling jumpy or easily startled; and (d) he was mildly bothered by suddenly acting or feeling as if stressful experiences were happening again, as if he were reliving it, and feeling very upset when something reminded him of stressful experiences from his past.

The results of the Defense and Veterans Brain Injury Center's (DVBIC) Traumatic Brain Injury Screening tool (level one screening) (Schwab et al., 2006) indicated that John experienced over 60 blasts within range of 50 meters while in Iraq. In one day while he was in Fallujah, 32 mortars exploded near him; one mortar exploded approximately 6 feet away from him, which he believes caused the most damage, including hearing loss, memory impairment, confusion, balance problems, dizziness, and chronic headaches. Results from the DVBIC traumatic brain injury level one screening indicated the need for further neurological testing for traumatic brain injury. It also revealed that John's somatization symptoms were most likely associated with his long-term and combined depression and anxiety, and that his symptoms of gastritis were congruent with his consistent alcohol consumption.

While he was being evaluated, a consultation was requested with a gastrointestinal specialist and neurologist at the VA. Recovery classes were also offered daily to increase his insight into and understanding of his condition and to teach him new coping strategies. The BHP faxed John's medical records from the SMCSC and made an appointment for follow-up at the VA.

John had follow-up outpatient treatment sessions two times a week for 1 month with a BHP. This was followed by weekly treatment sessions for 3 months, along with monthly medication management appointments with the IC program's psychiatric nurse practitioner. Collaboration with the VA program led to further evaluation and treatment of John's gastrointestinal and neurological symptoms.

Overall, the integrated, seamless, and continuous system of care that John received allowed him to receive the medical and behavioral health care that he needed within his own community. This local and comprehensive health care experience helped John by addressing his physical and psychiatric health needs at the same time, thereby reducing his anxiety and increasing his sense of safety. John's relationship with the BHP, a principal member of his health care team, was essential to his evaluation and treatment process. His recovery was fundamentally enhanced by the establishment of a safe and trustworthy relationship with his BHP, who helped him navigate his integral behavioral and physical health care needs.

Case Study Discussion Questions

1. As his BHP, how would you begin working with John?
2. How would you address his potential traumatic brain injury and provide accommodations for cognitive impairments during therapy?
3. What strategies would you employ to address John's alcohol abuse?
4. How would you address depressive symptoms, anxiety, and hypervigilance within a trauma-focused cognitive behavioral treatment framework?
5. How would you help John manage his bipolar disorder and psychotic symptoms?

Creating a Successful Program

It is essential for IC practices to collaborate with each other and share resources to maximize the potential for optimal and united service delivery for target populations without duplication of services. Investing in and sustaining collaborative relationships with regional and local community partners are vital when serving the military population in IC settings. Emphasis should be placed on connecting with all possible service provider organizations, including those at both national and state levels.

IC practices that wish to serve this population should consider enrolling their BHPs with Military OneSource, which is managed and funded via Ceridian for the Department of Defense. As a Military OneSource affiliate, a BHP in an IC practice can reach more military service members and their families. Service members can call the Military OneSource toll-free number to obtain an appointment with an affiliate. Other items BHPs should consider in accommodating the needs of this population are incorporating screening tools such as the PCL into existing tool kits, educating providers about the behavioral health needs of service members and their families, providing brief interventions and therapy, and establishing linkage to outside referrals, including the VA, as appropriate.

Conclusion

IC is a model of health care delivery that infuses behavioral health into an individual's primary health care. BHPs and their IC practice team members who are educated about and aware of the unique challenges facing military service members and their families can strive to meet the needs of this population in an effective way. When treating military service members and their families in an IC setting, a stepped-care approach that helps people from the point at which they need it—from screenings, to brief intervention and education, to counseling and a referral for specialty mental health when necessary—works well when coupled with knowledge of local resources and insights about the aspects of living in a community as a former or active service member. BHPs can employ brief, solution-focused therapies that infuse hope. IC practices serve veterans and the military population, as they assist in removing the stigma of mental illness and the inclination to treat those who have served our country in life-threatening situations from a standpoint of pathology. The entire therapeutic process is normalized for military service members and their families, making it seem possible for them to return to preservice levels of functioning and wellness. Programs like the SMCSC have focused on treating military service members and their families as a specific population, but they have also purposed to provide inspiration and ideas about how other practices, such as primary care practices, might successfully serve this population in their communities and health care systems.

Discussion Questions

1. How would you support your agency or workplace in being more accessible and welcoming to active-duty, retired, and veteran service members and their families?
2. Where can you go to learn about successful treatment modalities for serving military personnel?
3. What local resources are available to support treatment outcomes for military members seeking help for physical and mental or behavioral problems and for support in reintegrating back into civilian life?
4. How can the theories and practices of IC inform the evolving response to helping those who have served our country with their behavioral and mental health needs? How would you work simultaneously with those who provide assessment and treatment of their physical conditions and needs?
5. In what other venues and with what partners can mental and behavioral health providers contribute to the cognitive and emotional wellness of active-duty or veteran military service members and their families?

Resources for Working With Veterans in IC

http://maps.servicelocator.org/military/select_state.aspx
www.va.gov/opa/militaryfamilies.asp

http://armytimes.com/news/2011/01/army-guard-reserve-suicide-rate-sees-big-spike-011911w/
www.whitehouse.gov:keywords:militaryfamilies

References

American Psychiatric Association. (2000). *Diagnostic and statistical manual of mental disorders* (Rev. 4th ed.). Washington, DC: Author.

Hoge, C. W., Terhakopian, A., & Castro, C. A. (2007). Association of posttraumatic stress disorder with somatic symptoms, health care visits and absenteeism among Iraq war veterans. *American Journal of Psychiatry, 164,* 150–153.

Jones, D. K., Young, T., & Leppma, M. (2010). Mild traumatic brain injury and posttraumatic stress disorder in returning Iraq and Afghanistan war veterans: Implications for assessment and diagnosis. *Journal of Counseling and Development, 88*(3), 372–376.

Maguen, S. L., Reger, B. A., & Gahm, G. A. (2010). The impact of reported direct and indirect killing on mental health symptoms in Iraq war veterans. *Journal of Traumatic Stress, 23*(1), 86–90.

Najavitz, L. M. (2007). Seeking Safety: An evidence-based model for substance abuse and trauma/PTSD. In K. A. Witkiewitz & G. A. Marlatt (Eds.), *Therapist's guide to evidence-based relapse prevention: Practical resources for the mental health professional* (pp. 141–167). San Diego: Elsevier Press.

Prigerson, H. G., Maciejewski, P. K., & Rosenheck, R. A. (2002). Population attributable fractions of psychiatric disorders and behavioral outcomes associated with combat exposure among U.S. men. *American Journal of Public Health, 92*(1), 59–63.

Schwab, K. A., Baker, G., Ivins, B., Sluss-Tiller, M., Lux, W., & Warden, D. (2006). The Brief Traumatic Brain Injury Screen (BTBIS): Investigating the validity of a self-report instrument for detecting traumatic brain injury (TBI) in troops returning from deployment in Afghanistan and Iraq. *Neurology, 66*(5)(Supp. 2), A235. Retrieved from http://www.dvbic.org/Providers/TBI-Screening.aspx

Sharpless, B. A., & Barber, J. P. (2011). A clinician's guide to PTSD treatments for returning veterans. *Professional Psychology, Research and Practice, 42*(1), 8–15.

Smith, T. C., Ryan, M. A., Wingard, D. L., Slymen, D. J., Sallis, J. F., & Kritz-Silverstein, D. (2008). New onset and persistent symptoms of post-traumatic stress disorder self-reported after deployment and combat exposures: Prospective population based U.S. military cohort study. *BMJ, 336*(7640), 366–371.

Tanielian, T., Jaycox, L. H., Schell, T. L., Marshall, G. N., Burnam, M. A., Eibner, C., & the Invisible Wounds Study Team. (2008). *Invisible wounds of war: Summary and recommendations for addressing psychological and cognitive injuries.* Retrieved from *www.rand.org/pubs/monographs/2008/RAND_MG720.1.pdf*

U.S. Department of Veterans Affairs. (2011a). *Joining forces: Veterans and military families, meeting America's commitment.* Retrieved from http://www.va.gov/opa/militaryfamilies.asp

U.S. Department of Veterans Affairs. (2011b). *National Center for PTSD: PTSD checklist (PCL).* Retrieved from http://www.ptsd.va.gov/professional/pages/assessments/ptsd-checklist.asp

PART III

Helping Integrated Care
Professionals Thrive

CHAPTER **14**

Supervision for the Integrated Behavioral Health Provider

KEELY S. PRATT and ANGELA L. LAMSON

Supervision at best involves "face-to-face ongoing dialogues between a supervisor and supervisee where goodwill prevails; the learning is mutual and intense; the power relations are transparent; and the emphasis is on meeting standards of the profession, ensuring the well-being of clients served by the supervisory participants." (Fine & Turner, 2002, p. 229)

Introduction

Inherent in integrated care (IC) are novel circumstances that present opportunities for innovation in the collaborative provision of care for patients and families; however, it is rare for innovation to occur without complication. Although it is fortunate that many behavioral health professionals (BHPs) (e.g., counselors, marriage and family therapists, psychologists, and social workers) are trained by their respective programs about the importance of consulting with other professionals, few are trained on how to provide true collaborative care and work within the context of a team. In a medical setting, BHPs are members of multidisciplinary teams and need to learn the application of ethical codes, documentation, and treatment protocols. Supervision is a valuable tool that helps BHPs navigate these novel and unfamiliar territories in health care settings. This chapter will describe the process of choosing a supervisor, provide a list of elements that must be considered when developing a supervision contract, offer a template for crafting a practice model document that will assist with assessing fidelity to one's practice while maximizing consistency and productivity in the supervision process, and outline details about the potential dynamics of supervision that may arise in the various levels of clinical collaboration.

Review of Related Research

Supervision has long been an integral component of behavioral health programs, although there exists only limited research regarding BHP supervision in health care settings (Edwards & Patterson, 2006; Thomasgard & Collins, 2003). BHPs are trained within their individual academic programs (i.e., marriage and family therapy, psychology, social work, counseling, and substance abuse and rehabilitation counseling), all abiding by respective professional codes of conduct and ethics (see Table 14.1). In addition, each BHP training program has different access to and involvement in health care settings based on the scope of practice and the ability to bill for services. Therefore all BHPs have different levels of experience in providing IC services in medical settings. A substantial amount of literature describes clinical models of providing IC (McDaniel, Hepworth, & Doherty, 1992; Patterson, Peek, Heinrich, Bischoff, & Scherger, 2002; Robinson & Reiter, 2007), but to date there is no text in existence, and only one article (Edwards & Patterson, 2006), that details the supervision process of BHPs in health care settings. Edwards and Patterson (2006) suggested that supervision with BHPs in IC settings should focus on the following topics: (a) understanding medical culture, (b) locating the trainee in the treatment system, (c) investigating the biological and health issues, and (d) being attentive to the self-of-the-therapist. We agree with

Table 14.1
Supervision Resources for Respective BHP Professions

Profession	Professional Home	Supervision Standards Referenced in Ethic Codes
Marriage and family therapy/medical family therapy	American Association for Marriage and Family Therapy	See Principle IV Website: www.aamft.org
Counseling	American Counseling Association	See Section F Website: www.counseling.org
Social work	National Association of Social Workers	See Section 3.01 Website: www.naswdc.org
Psychology	American Psychological Association	See Standard 7 Website: www.apa.org

these recommendations and believe that some additional elements would ensure that BHPs are ready for success in the medical context, regardless of the degree of collaboration present in each setting. Three additional features that further support a successful IC supervisory relationship include (a) developing a detailed supervision contract between the BHP and his or her supervisor, (b) documenting the practice model including its strengths and challenges, and (c) structuring supervision according to the level of collaboration involved in clinical care (see Table 14.1).

The Contract

The details of supervision should be negotiated and described at the outset in a supervisor–supervisee contract, also known as informed consent (Atkinson, 2002). This contract should minimally detail the logistics of supervision, such as the supervisor's and supervisee's contact information, the length of supervision (i.e., 6 months, 1 year, etc.), the location and time of supervision, payment, cancellation and no-show policy, emergency procedures, and the frequency of contact. Some professionals, specifically those in marriage and family therapy, may expand on this and describe their supervision style or philosophy. In addition, the contract should clearly define ways in which electronic information may be shared between patient and BHP or between BHP and supervisor, including defining the content that can be shared in e-mail and electronic health records, and specifying those who have access and signing privileges to such information. Furthermore, it is common for supervisors to have supervisees describe goals they would like to accomplish over the course of supervision, providing a baseline for the end-of-semester evaluation. An example goal might be, "I would like to increase my exposure to chronic-pain patients and their providers by participating in the pain clinic at least once a week, and I hope to enhance my awareness and cultural sensitivity to those who suffer from this condition." The evaluation metrics (self-report measure and evaluation of the supervisee by supervisor and vice versa) should be determined and included as part of the contract to ensure that both supervisors and supervisees are aware of evaluation criteria. Examples of supervisor–supervisee evaluations include the Supervisory Styles Index (Long, Lawless, & Dotson, 1996) and the Basic Skills Evaluation Device (Nelson & Johnson, 1999).

Documentation of Practice Models

A valuable exercise is for supervisees to complete a preinternship self-evaluation, which some supervisors refer to as the "building your home project" (Lamson & Meadors, 2007). Anecdotal evidence suggests that this project facilitates supervisee self-awareness and provides an avenue by which supervisors can address supervisees' readiness to begin internship.

The "building your home project" is composed of the following components: (a) exploring the biological, psychological, social, and spiritual
experiences of BHPs and how these have influenced their biases, beliefs,
and values (Edwards & Patterson, 2006); (b) documenting their philosophy of therapy (e.g., nature of one's therapeutic assessment, process by
which goals are established, adjustments that may need to be considered
in their treatment modality based on the level of integration within their
practice); (c) describing common techniques that are used as part of their
practice model (e.g., using pedigrees or genograms and scaling questions,
externalizing the illness); and (d) assessing their level of effectiveness
with patients and multidisciplinary providers (e.g., disseminate surveys
to patients, evaluate health care outcomes of patients, and appraise the
cost-effectiveness or health care utilization of IC). Although it is suggested
that this information be documented in writing as a way for supervisees
to reflect on previous iterations, some supervisors may choose to simplify
the process by discussing the aforementioned topics during the first and
last supervision sessions. Anecdotal evidence suggests that this process is
highly valued by BHPs working within IC practices.

Levels of Clinical Supervision
Doherty, McDaniel, and Baird (1996) detailed the different levels of collaboration in clinical care, which range from minimal collaboration (level
one) to close collaboration in a fully integrated site (level five). Each level
of care has unique supervision challenges, such as adherence to treatment
protocols, documentation protocols, emergency procedures, and ethical
standards. Awareness of these challenges can help supervisors adjust their
methods to best meet the needs of the supervisees.

Level one. In settings where there is minimal contact between BHPs and
primary care providers (PCPs), as is typical in a level one clinical care model,
supervision should focus on the clinical concerns of patients. Supervision
would follow a more traditional mental health treatment format (e.g.,
50-minute sessions), with sessions likely to be held in a separate office from
the medical setting. In this arrangement, the focus is on helping the supervisee build clinical skills, strengthen collaborative relationships with PCPs,
and determine how to best obtain appropriate releases of information. The
ethics by which the BHP abides at this level are more easily navigated in relation to his or her professional home (e.g., American Association for Marriage
and Family Therapy, American Psychological Association, American
Counseling Association, etc.) because the BHP is less likely to interface with
other health care professionals on a regular basis, and it would be rare for his
or her notes to be shared with other providers. In level one care, the BHP's
emergency contact is most commonly the site supervisor.

Level two. Supervision in a level two context involves discussions with a BHP who has more frequent access to and contact with PCPs. In this type of setting, it would be appropriate for the supervisor to make on-site visits to conduct live supervision and to meet the PCPs with whom the BHP interacts. In level two, BHPs need to be aware of differences between their profession's ethical code and the ethical codes of their collaborators (i.e., American Medical Association, American Nurses Association). Supervisors and BHPs should discuss how information will be communicated and shared among professionals. In coordinated not colocated care (Blount, 2003), the BHP is not working within the IC setting. In most cases, therefore, documentation will be executed according to the BHP's professional home (i.e., mental health agency), and the BHP's site supervisor would be the emergency contact.

Level three. Supervision for BHPs that are part of a level three collaboration is more complex because of the colocation of BHPs and other health care providers. BHPs may have a supervisor from their university with whom to discuss patients' concerns, as well as an additional designated site supervisor (e.g., the "go-to" personnel member who typically manages the protocol and operations of the unit) at their place of practice. As in level two collaboration, it will be important for BHPs to be well versed in the ethical codes of their profession and those of their on-site colleagues and supervisors. The supervision contract should clearly state the appropriate supervisor with whom BHPs should consult in a given emergency situation (e.g., treating a suicidal client vs. reporting child abuse). The logistics of supervisor–provider–patient protocol concerning emergency procedures needs to be defined for all stakeholders before the BHP begins internship.

Levels four and five. BHPs who participate in level four and level five contexts benefit most from having an on-site supervisor (although it may not be necessary for the supervisor to be on-site all of the time, depending on the requirements of one's profession). Supervisors and BHPs should meet for at least 1 hour per week in a formal clinical supervision meeting, and in addition, BHPs should have access to impromptu supervision for urgent matters. Effective clinical supervision includes diagnostic and therapeutic skill building, case conceptualization, an increase in supervisees' self-awareness (Bernard, 1979), ethics, crisis management, documentation, patient outcomes, and how to effectively collaborate with PCPs (Lanning, 1986). An on-site supervisor is ideal in level four and level five clinical collaboration for BHPs because of the complexities inherent in working with multidisciplinary team members. It is especially important for BHPs who are working with PCPs in level four and level five settings to talk with their supervisors about professional boundaries. Other common supervisory issues that are addressed in these contexts include (a) helping BHPs learn how to introduce themselves to patients (e.g., "Hello, my name is _____, and I am a part of your health care team. Some of the services that I provide here include _____."), (b) describing how to conduct effective and efficient mental health assessments, (c) explaining how to concisely communicate relevant mental health information to the PCP, (d) role-playing how to provide effective brief treatment (i.e., 15- to 20-minute sessions compared to 50-minute sessions), and (e) demonstrating how to effectively document progress notes in the electronic health record.

Case Analysis

Jamee is a BHP at the Adolescent and Young Adults Clinic. The clinic operates within a level four collaborative context, with colocated BHPs and PCPs. Jamee is supervised by a licensed and approved supervisor from her professional home, who also provides clinical services in the same clinic (note: the supervisor does not share the same patient caseload as the supervisee). Jamee's supervisor and the respective PCP, with whom she is working, sign all of her patient-related documentation within the electronic health record.

Tia, an African American 16-year-old adolescent, came to the clinic complaining of abdominal pain. She was greeted by the nurse-manager, who initiated the standard laboratory tests. Shortly after Tia's lab tests were collected, the attending nurse escorted Tia to an exam room where she was greeted by Jamee, who introduced herself as a BHP and described her role as part of the health care team. Next, Jamee administered the Patient Health Questionnaire for Adolescents (PHQ-9A; Richardson et al., 2010) and the Pediatric Quality of Life Inventory (PedsQL; Varni, Seid, & Rode, 1999). Jamee asked Tia about her family and school and about what life changes may have occurred since her last visit to the clinic. Tia described her relationship with her boyfriend and stated that he was very possessive and often became jealous, especially when she spent time with friends. As soon as Jamee completed the psychosocial history, she returned to her office and scored the mental health assessments. Results indicated that Tia scored within the moderate range for depressive symptoms and indicated that she was experiencing suicidal ideation.

Jamee then consulted with her on-site supervisor about Tia's suicidal ideation. Her supervisor suggested assessing for a past history of suicide, if she has a suicide plan, and her intent to complete the plan. Jamee's supervisor demonstrated how to conduct a suicide assessment and discussed potential treatment options. For instance, if Tia indicated suicidal ideation without a plan, she was to complete a safety contract with Tia noting three people who could provide immediate support and whom Jamee could contact. Tia would also be asked to create a list of five healthy coping techniques that she could use to avoid hurting herself. Jamee consulted with the PCP about her plan of action in relation to Tia's treatment before her medical examination was to be conducted. The PCP informed Tia that her laboratory tests resulted in a positive trichomoniasis, an infection caused by a microscopic parasite *Trichomonas vaginalis*. Trichomoniasis is one of the most common sexually transmitted infections. Tia's PCP explained the positive trichomoniasis culture and discussed the medication needed to treat this condition.

After the exam, the PCP told Tia that her partner would need to be notified of her condition and that Jamee, the BHP, could assist in this matter. Jamee entered the exam room after the PCP left and proceeded to create a plan with Tia by which Tia could notify her boyfriend of her condition and inform him that he would need to address this issue, if relevant, with all of his sexual partners. After which, Tia reported that she had been concerned for months that he may have been cheating on her. She admitted to Jamee that her concern about this matter had caused her to lose sleep and weight and then stated, "It would just be better if I wasn't around anymore." Jamee explored Tia's evident distress and determined that she did not have a plan to end her life. Jamee, then, worked with Tia to develop a safety contract and provided her with appropriate contact information in case of an emergency. Jamee and Tia's PCP decided to ask Tia to return for a follow-up visit in 1 week to check her progress.

Jamee debriefed with her supervisor following the visit. She shared a copy of Tia's safety plan with her supervisor, and together they documented the session within Tia's medical record. Finally, Jamee sent her electronic notes about Tia's case to the PCP and supervisor for review and approved signature.

Conclusion

BHPs must learn to navigate within the complex environment of IC, especially those who are students, interns, and new professionals. Supervision that is tailored to the level of clinical collaboration in a BHP's given practice setting can provide a tailored structure for the supervision process that may not have otherwise existed. In addition, supervisor–supervisee considerations should include developing a contract, addressing self-of-provider issues, and discussing practice models. New clinical innovation models, such as IC, punctuate the need to further develop training methods to best equip the next generation of BHPs to work in collaborative settings. The next generation of BHPs must learn from their supervisors how to extend treatment through a continuum of care options and recognize that movement toward IC will require supervisors and supervisees to be acutely aware of the complex dynamics in patient care and provider-to-provider relationship dynamics.

Discussion Questions

1. How might supervision differ based on the level of clinical care and collaboration at your site?
2. What additional training, education, or supervision may be needed in order to provide best clinical care for the diverse patient populations you are working with?
3. What self-of-therapist issues need to be addressed during supervision sessions in order to best maximize the treatment practices for your patients and setting?
4. What space accommodations or changes in protocol would be necessary in order to facilitate the best outcome for supervision in a collaborative care or IC system or setting?
5. Where would you go to find the ethical standards and guidelines for supervision that are most relevant to your work context?
6. What evaluation metrics or feedback system would you use to increase the likelihood of success in your provision of collaborative care or IC?

References

Atkinson, B. J. (2002). Informed consent form. In C. L. Storm & T. C. Todd (Eds.), *The reasonably complete systemic supervisor resource guide* (pp. 11–15). Lincoln, NE: Allyn and Bacon.

Bernard, J. M. (1979). Supervisor training: A discrimination model. *Counselor Education and Supervision, 19*, 60–69.

Blount, A. (2003). Integrated primary care: Organizing the evidence. *Families, Systems, and Health, 21*, 121–134.

Doherty, W. J., McDaniel, S. H., & Baird, M. A. (1996). Five levels of primary care/behavioral healthcare collaboration. *Behavioral Healthcare Tomorrow, 5*(5), 25–28.

Edwards, T. M., & Patterson, J. E. (2006). Supervising family therapy trainees in primary medical settings: Context matters. *Journal of Marital and Family Therapy, 32*(1), 33–43.

Fine, M., & Turner, J. (2002). Collaborative supervision: Minding the power. In T. C. Todd & C. L. Storm (Eds.), *The complete systemic supervisor: Context, philosophy, and pragmatics* (pp. 229–240). Lincoln, NE: Allyn and Bacon.

Lamson, A. L., & Meadors, P. (2007). Building your home project. In D. Linville, K. M. Hertlein, & associates, (Eds.), *The therapist's notebook for family health care* (pp. 225–232). New York: Haworth Press.

Lanning, W. (1986). Development of the Supervisor Emphasis Rating Form. *Counselor Education and Supervision, 25*, 191–196.

Long, J., Lawless, J., & Dotson, D. (1996). Supervisory Style Index: Examining supervisees' perceptions of supervisor style. *Contemporary Family Therapy, 18*, 191–201.

McDaniel, S. H., Hepworth, J., & Doherty, W. J. (1992). *Medical family therapy.* New York: Basic Books.

Nelson, T. S., & Johnson, L. N. (1999). The Basic Skills Evaluation Device. *Journal of Marital and Family Therapy, 25,* 15–30.

Patterson, J., Peek, C. J., Heinrich, R. L., Bischoff, R. J., & Scherger, J. (2002). *Mental health professionals in medical settings: A primer.* New York: Norton.

Richardson, L. P., McCauley, E., Grossman, D. C., McCarty, C. A., Richards, J., Russo, J. E., … Katon, W. (2010). Evaluation of the Patient Health Questionnaire-9 Item for detecting major depression among adolescents. *Pediatrics, 126,* 1117–1125.

Robinson, P. J., & Reiter, J. T. (2007). *Behavioral consultation and primary care: A guide to integrating services.* New York: Springer.

Thomasgard, M., & Collins, V. (2003). A comprehensive review of a cross-disciplinary, case-based peer supervision model. *Families, Systems, and Health, 21*(3), 305–319.

Varni, J. W., Seid, M., & Rode, C. A. (1999). The PedsQL: Measurement model for the Pediatric Quality of Life Inventory. *Med Care, 37,* 126–139.

CHAPTER 15

Leadership in Integrated Care

JOHN J. SHERLOCK

When your leadership is noticed, and your expertise is appreciated, frankly, you become indispensible to the integrated care practice, and that feels good.

—Experienced behavioral health provider

Thus far, the chapters in this text have described the diverse role and responsibilities of behavioral health providers (BHPs) who work in integrated care (IC) settings. In this chapter, the description will continue to build with the added function of leadership; it is unlikely that BHPs hold executive titles or are considered "in charge." Leadership is not about holding a particular position of authority in an organization, however, and this chapter will describe how to lead *without* authority.

The first part of this chapter will outline the reasons why effective leadership is an integral component to the success of IC practices. Next, relational leadership theory (Graen & Uhl-Bien, 1995) and its application to IC practices will be explored, followed by a list of the key concepts of emotional intelligence (EI; Goleman, 1995) and a description of how BHPs can hone their EI skills to become effective collaborators within IC settings. Finally, this chapter concludes with recommendations for BHPs in the area of leadership for success in an IC environment. It should be noted that in addition to the relevant literature on leadership, collaboration, and EI, the author will also share information assembled from conversations held with experienced BHPs who work in various types of IC settings.

Why Leadership Is Essential to IC

IC is an exciting development in health care. However, it involves significant change for all of the stakeholders, in particular the patients, primary care providers (PCPs), and BHPs. Research has consistently shown that unsuccessful change initiatives are directly related to a lack of leadership (Caldwell, 2003; Chreim, Williams, Janz, & Dastmalchian, 2010; Kotter, 1995; Senge, 1993). Most people are familiar with the traditional resource-based structure of an organization, in which the "leader" gives the orders and determines how resources will be allocated. In many modern organizations, that structure is being replaced with a knowledge-based one, in which organizational members are equally engaged in building a "learning organization," and generating new knowledge about how to best function is made a priority (Senge, 1993). This knowledge-based configuration is particularly applicable to the IC setting because there is no preexisting formula for how IC must operate. Every part of the IC team, including office staff, PCPs, BHPs, and other health professionals, contributes ideas about how to create a successful IC setting. Research on the concept of change has shown that successful leadership in a learning organization involves the investment of time for stakeholders to find common ground and to build credibility and trust (Chreim et al., 2010).

Relational Leadership Theory

The relational focus is one that goes beyond a unidirectional leader-and-follower relationship to one that recognizes leadership wherever it occurs (Hunt & Dodge, 2000). Although it has been understood from the earliest studies that leadership involves relationship-oriented behavior (Stogdill & Coons, 1957), the term *relational leadership* is somewhat recent (Murrell, 1997; Uhl-Bien, 2003, 2005). When relationship-oriented behaviors were discussed in the early literature about leadership, the focus was on an individual in a position of authority (i.e., "the leader"). More recently, the leadership literature is increasingly giving attention to the concept of dispersed leadership, which can occur at any level of the organization (Bryman, 1996; Caldwell, 2003). Relational leadership theory is one that not only assumes this dispersed view of leadership but also shifts the focus from the individual to the process of relating (Uhl-Bien, 2006). The theory purports that leadership is something that develops within the relationships between two or more individuals rather than something that an individual possesses. In the absence of a restricting conceptualization and practice of leadership as requiring a "boss at the top," a profound relational dynamic is allowed to develop throughout the organization (Uhl-Bien, 2006).

It is important to distinguish relational leadership theory from those leadership theories that focus on the interpersonal influence (one-way or reciprocal) of individuals in a relationship (Graen & Uhl-Bien, 1995; Hollander, 1978) rather than the relationship itself. Thus, a relational perspective on leadership identifies the basic unit of analysis in leadership research as relationships, not individuals (Uhl-Bien, 2006). From a relational leadership theory perspective, organizational members engage and interact via relational dialogue to construct knowledge systems together (Drath, 2001; Uhl-Bien, 2006). In this way, relational leadership characterizes leadership as a shared responsibility. Murrell (1997) described relational leadership this way: "Leadership is a social act, a construction of 'ship' as a collective vehicle to help take us where we as a group, organization or society desire to go" (p. 35). Relational leadership approaches consider leadership relationships more broadly than traditional manager–subordinate dyads, and the interactions among them as more of an interactive process of individuals who are collaborators. Thus, the objective of relational leadership theory research is to better understand the relational dynamics and social processes that compose leadership and organizing (Uhl-Bien, 2006).

It is a fair statement that IC introduces a new social order within health care with novel experiences for patients, office staff, PCPs, and BHPs. All of the BHPs interviewed for this chapter mentioned that the IC environment in which they worked had evolved over time. Several described how more informal interactions and patterns of behavior became routine over time. Leadership can emerge out of everyday practices and interactions among organizational members. In this environment, the locus of relational leadership is not in top managers and the compliance of followers, but rather in the interactions that constitute the social structure (Uhl-Bien, 2006). Although relational leadership may seem promising, the question remains whether traditional primary care environments will embrace this approach. There is certainly evidence that BHPs could find themselves in an IC environment where the PCPs consider themselves the "bosses at the top" with a traditional autocratic leadership style. Such environments are very unlikely to reap the full benefits of an IC approach; how to identify, and avoid working in, these environments will be discussed later in this chapter. Clearly, the group of BHPs interviewed for this chapter is not representative of a scientific sample, but the conversations did yield some valuable information. The BHPs all described their IC environments as ones where the PCPs really wanted to achieve the full potential of IC, valued the skills of the BHPs, and displayed a more participative leadership style. Their descriptions are not to suggest, however, that ego issues and power dynamics may not exist in some environments. Collaborative skills and EI will be key components in the emergence of successful relational leaders in the IC setting, as further discussed in the following sections.

Collaboration

As attention turns to the relational processes by which leadership is produced and enabled, the concept of collaboration becomes important (Uhl-Bien, 2006). Doherty, McDaniel, and Baird (1996) identified five different levels of collaboration within the IC environment, ranging from operating in separate facilities with infrequent communication to a fully integrated system with regular collaborative team meetings. Ideally, those IC models with higher levels of collaboration involve shared decision making between PCPs and BHPs, *excellent communication, and egalitarian team processes grounded in the respect of individual team members* (Bluestein & Cubic, 2009). Cox (2011) described *collaboration as a process of social interaction*, which has as its foundation that each individual is responsible for the group's success and achievement of a common goal. Individuals who are adept at building relationships are more likely to succeed in collaboration; they share time, perspective, and experiences with others with whom they work through open communication.

Individuals hold different titles in the IC setting, and each team member brings a particular skill set and expertise. It is through the development and sharing of these unique skills in a collaborative effort that the potential to produce positive outcomes in unique ways are not otherwise ordinarily achievable (Cox, 2011). From an IC perspective, the goal of collaboration should be to provide the most clinically effective and cost-efficient care possible to the patient. When BHPs and PCPs agree on collaboration in theory, they should be aware that collaboration will still require some individual effort. Those efforts may involve communicating needs and concerns, asking questions about needs and concerns, and, importantly, listening. To foster collaboration, therefore, relational leaders need to employ EI.

Emotional Intelligence: Key to Collaboration

Although relational leadership theory and collaboration both place an emphasis on interactions among individuals, most people can identify individuals who are effective versus ineffective in their interactions with others. Strong relational leaders foster collaboration through more than just a charming personality. Slater (2005) asserted that those who are successful in developing collaborative work cultures are "able to manage, rather than deny, their emotional selves" (p. 330).

According to research conducted by Goleman (1995), EI appears to be one of the most important variables in determining one's ability to be successful in a career. Goleman, Boyatzis, and McKee (2002) conceptualized EI as consisting of the following four domains.

Domain 1: Self-awareness. This domain includes the competencies of emotional self-awareness, accurate self-assessment, and self-confidence. It involves recognizing one's emotions and their effects on oneself and others. This does not suggest that people with high EI must detach emotions from their actions; rather, their emotions need to be understood and managed appropriately (Cox, 2011).

Domain 2: Self-management. This domain includes the competencies of emotional self-control, adaptability, initiative, and optimism. When individuals try to collaborate with others, occasional conflict is inevitable. Individuals with high levels of EI can become aware and recognize what is happening inside them (Kunnanatt, 2004).

Mastery of Domains 1 and 2 is what Goleman et al. (2002) described as "personal competence" and requires listening to one's self, becoming aware of one's emotional state and one's potential positive and negative impact on others, and then behaving in the way that best achieves the desired outcome (see Domain 4, relationship management).

Domain 3: Social awareness. This domain includes empathy, political awareness (power dynamics), and sensitivity to verbal and nonverbal cues from individuals and groups. Individuals with high EI are aware of not only their own emotions but those of others as well and have a keen sense of others' moods.

Domain 4: Relationship management. This last domain of EI includes persuasion and conflict management and collaboration. People with high EI facilitate problem solving and conflict resolution and enhance the overall performance of collaborative teams (Cox, 2011).

Goleman et al. (2002) referred to mastery of EI Domains 3 and 4 as "social competence," which fundamentally relates to how one deals with relationships. Social competence plays an important role in the context of the previous discussion of relational leadership and collaboration. Those individuals who possess both personal competence and social competence interact with others in ways that quickly establish trust and foster cooperation.

Fortunately, BHPs typically possess a high level of EI. Measures of EI in samples of BHPs were shown to be higher than in heterogeneous comparison groups (Easton, Martin, & Wilson, 2008; Martin, Easton, Wilson, Takemoto, & Sullivan, 2004). Just as one's EI skills contribute to effective interactions with patients in a clinical practice, EI skills can be a tremendous asset to effective collaboration with colleagues in an IC environment. Ultimately, EI improves one's ability to be socially effective and can lead to improved collaborative outcomes (Cox, 2011).

Seven "Next Step" Leadership Recommendations

The following recommendations for BHPs support the goals of relational leadership, EI, and collaboration with other practicing BHPs to promote success in behavioral health programs.

1. *Overcome your disdain for the business side of IC.* One may not have the inclination, time, or money to pursue an advanced degree in business, but BHPs must acquire at least basic business literacy in order to be effective (O'Donohue, Cummings, & Cummings, 2009). Becoming familiar with the work of Guerin (2008), who provided basic business essentials related to finance, information technology, contracts (including leases), marketing, and business plans, would be helpful. Therefore, it is also recommended that BHPs build a network of trusted professionals who have business expertise in various areas.

2. *Have the right mind-set going into an IC setting.* The BHPs with whom I spoke all noted that working in an IC environment is different—in some ways remarkably different—from treating clients in a stand-alone behavioral health care practice. Notably, because efficiency is a hallmark of primary care, there's a need to quickly assess, diagnose, and treat presenting problems in an IC setting (Bluestein & Cubic, 2009). Also, frequent interruptions are more common than in a traditional behavioral health care setting. Evidence from EI research indicates that attitudes have a bearing on a clinical atmosphere and are often expressed, either overtly or covertly (Goleman et al., 2002). Therefore, BHPs will need to adopt an attitude of understanding and patience for interruptions and other efficiency practices, which are part of what is required to provide the overall quality of care. Although the interviewed BHPs reported that moving from private practice to an IC environment required an adjustment from private practice routines, they expressed that the change offered a unique and exciting challenge, resulting in a high level of overall care for the patient.

3. *Commit to learning about the world of primary care medicine.* To collaborate and communicate effectively with others, BHPs should use language that will be understood by others (Slater, 2005). Bluestein and Cubic (2009) stressed the value of BHPs developing a basic understanding of primary care medicine, just as they would develop basic business literacy. BHPs should gain a general understanding of primary care terminology and the basics of primary care practice without formal medical training. In addition to seeking out print and Internet resources, the interviewed BHPs recommended networking in order to learn more about the world of primary care, as in seeking out consultations with and opportunities to shadow nurses, staff, and other BHPs who work with PCPs. In addition, BHPs should seek opportunities to attend continuing education classes on the subject of health care. Bluestein and Cubic recommended developing

the ability to write succinct one- to two-paragraph updates that are jargon free and emphasize assessment results and treatment recommendations. In addition, the BHPs highlighted how PCPs typically want immediate feedback. Therefore, BHPs will not have the luxury of taking several days to conceptualize cases before reporting back to the PCP. Same-day concrete recommendations and consultations that incorporate behavioral health and health factors are integral to aligning the behavioral health programming to the pace of primary care (O'Donohue, Byrd, Cummings, & Henderson, 2005).

4. *Be visible.* When considering collaboration with PCPs, BHPs will find it helpful to make themselves known in the area, including providing information about their credentials and the types of services they could offer to an IC practice. BHPs may wish to send out a short letter of introduction, visit a practice, or attend health care networking events to introduce themselves to PCPs. When BHPs are beginning work in a practice, staying visible and learning how the practice functions in terms of daily logistics, values, routines, and leadership are integral first steps (Robinson & Reiter, 2007). The BHPs interviewed emphasized the importance of being visible in an IC practice by joining the activity of the practice rather than waiting in their office for referrals. They also recommended that BHPs seek out formal and informal interactions with the nursing and office staff, as they often interact more frequently with patients than do PCPs. Other suggestions were to join as many meetings with PCPs in attendance as possible with the goal of finding opportunities to contribute. When consulting with PCPs, one BHP suggested an approach of "gently interjecting" ideas, which was supported by another BHP who suggested using mild language, such as "You might want to think about …"

5. *Pick your battles.* The courage to speak out is an EI competency based on self-confidence and integrity (Slater, 2005). As Doherty et al. (1996) noted, even at the higher levels of integration between BHPs and PCPs, there are still likely to be some unresolved tensions. Ethical responsibility and patient care should not be compromised for the sake of being an IC team member. BHPs must differentiate between appropriate times for compromise and those that necessitate holding one's ground via constructive disagreement (Bluestein & Cubic, 2009). Critical skill development will yield competent judgment about clinical care, a knowledge of one's ethical boundaries, and an understanding of one's role on the team. Early on, BHPs should spend some time learning the nuances of the IC environment before engaging in debate with team members. BHPs should be clear about ethical boundaries and responsibilities, find colleagues for consult, and keep the phone number at hand for the ethics consultant in their professional organization. One BHP said her measure for how far to go with

constructive disagreement with colleagues is determined by the extent to which the issue could impact a patient's health.

6. *Do your homework before entering an IC arrangement.* It is certainly possible to have an encounter with a PCP who is interested in striking up some form of collaboration with you primarily for "appearance" purposes, but who is not truly committed to creating an IC culture and approach to treatment. It is also a possibility that interested physicians are not knowledgeable about the variety of services a BHP can provide beyond traditional colocated, scheduled therapy sessions. If this scenario exists, BHPs need to work to expand and add flexibility to the preexisting ideas that others have about IC programming. Same-day appointments, on-the-spot interventions, warm handoffs, and conjoint sessions are examples of common IC behavioral health services (O'Donohue et al., 2005) that PCPs may not have considered. BHPs should spend time getting to know the PCP's motives in pursuing a collaborative arrangement before committing. They should ask PCPs about what a typical day might look like and whether they plan to make "cold" or "warm" patient transfers, and they should ask, "How will your practice be different after I have been here for a year?" It will be helpful to become familiar with Doherty et al.'s (1996) five levels of primary care–behavioral health care collaboration in order to aid the conversation and as a way to inform about the breadth and depth of services possible in IC.

7. *Have a letter of agreement that includes an exit clause.* The numerous levels of potential BHP–PCP collaboration preclude the creation of a definitive list of items to be included in a letter of agreement. If a BHP is colocating his or her practice with a PCP, for example, then the agreement should specify the schedule of the hours the BHP is expected to be onsite, the cost and size of the space, and the office resources and technology available to the BHP. Often, BHPs are hesitant to enter into collaboration with a PCP because of the uncertainty about how to terminate the business relationship if necessary. For this reason, when entering into a collaborative relationship with a PCP, the BHP should be clear about performance expectations and evaluation criteria. Although BHPs may be hesitant to broach the "exit clause" issue with the PCP, they should be reassured that termination language is common in most business agreements and is prudent business practice. Here again, networking with other BHPs who work in an IC environment, and building relationships with professionals such as attorneys, will afford the BHP more insight about the various ways that letters of agreements can be crafted.

Conclusion

It was the intent of this chapter to serve as a reinforcement of the message delivered in previous chapters that IC is much more than the physical movement of a traditionally trained BHP into a primary care setting. It requires changes not only in provider skill sets but also in the way that patient care is conceptualized. It is helpful to remember that many, if not most, PCPs are still rookies in regard to integrating behavioral health into primary care settings and will be dealing with a great deal of change. BHPs, therefore, must be willing to embrace a leadership role rather than expect to walk into a fully functioning and perfectly performing IC system (Rollins, 2009). Ultimately, leadership skills grounded in relational theory and EI will help BHPs navigate this exciting new landscape in health care.

Discussion Questions

1. In what ways do you consider yourself a relational leader? How do you see your leadership abilities helping your effectiveness in the IC environment?
2. What do you see as the biggest leadership challenge to the BHP working in the IC environment? What is the best way to meet this challenge?
3. As you consider your own career as a BHP, do you view the opportunity to work in an IC environment with enthusiasm or concerns—or both? Explain.
4. Consider the four primary domains of EI. In which one are you strongest? How might you leverage this strength in an IC environment? What is your weakest domain? How can you develop this dimension of your EI?
5. Draft a short letter of introduction that you might send to a PCP in your area to begin a potential collaboration to provide integrated primary care–behavioral health services in a primary care practice.

References

Bluestein, D., & Cubic, B. (2009). Psychologists and primary care physicians: A training model for creating collaborative relationships. *Journal of Clinical Psychology in Medical Settings, 16*, 101–112. doi:10.1007/s10880-009-9156-9

Bryman, A. (1996). Leadership in organizations. In S. R. Clegg, C. Hardy, & W. Nord (Eds.), *Handbook of organization studies* (pp. 276–292). London: Sage.

Caldwell, R. (2003). Models of change agency: A fourfold classification. *British Journal of Management, 14*(2), 131–142.

Chreim, S., Williams, B. E., Janz, L., & Dastmalchian, A. (2010). Change agency in a primary health care context: The case of distributed leadership. *Health Care Management Review, 35*(2), 187–202.

Cox, J. D. (2011). Emotional intelligence and its role in collaboration. *Proceedings of the American Society of Business and Behavioral Sciences, 11*(1), 435–445.

Doherty, W. J., McDaniel, S. H., & Baird, M. A. (1996, October). Five levels of primary care/behavioral healthcare collaboration. *Behavioral Healthcare Tomorrow*, 25–28.

Drath, W. (2001). *The deep blue sea: Rethinking the source of leadership.* San Francisco: Jossey-Bass and Center for Creative Leadership.

Easton, C., Martin, W. E., & Wilson, S. (2008). Emotional intelligence and implications for counseling self-efficacy: Phase II. *Counselor Education and Supervision, 47*, 218–232.

Goleman, D. (1995). *Emotional intelligence: Why it can matter more than IQ.* New York: Bantam.

Goleman, D., Boyatzis, R., & McKee, A. (2002). *Primal leadership: Learning to lead with emotional intelligence.* Boston: Harvard Business School Press.

Graen, G., & Uhl-Bien, M. (1995). Relationship-based approach to leadership: Development of leader-member exchange (LMX) theory of leadership over 25 years; Applying a multi-level multi-domain perspective. *The Leadership Quarterly, 6*(2), 219–247.

Guerin, L. (2008). *Wow, I'm in business: A crash course in business basics.* Berkeley, CA: NOLO.

Hollander, E. P. (1978). *Leadership dynamics: A practical guide to effective relationships.* New York: Free Press.

Hunt, J., & Dodge, G. E. (2000). Leadership déjà vu all over again. *The Leadership Quarterly Review of Leadership, 11*(4), 435–458.

Kotter, J. P. (1995). Leading change: Why transformation efforts fail. *Harvard Business Review, 73*(2), 59–67.

Kunnanatt, J. T. (2004). Emotional intelligence: The new science of interpersonal effectiveness. *Human Resource Development Quarterly, 15*(4), 489–495.

Martin, W. E., Easton, C., Wilson, S., Takemoto, M., & Sullivan, S. (2004). Salience of emotional intelligence as a core characteristic of being a counselor. *Counselor Education and Supervision, 44*, 17–30.

Murrell, K. L. (1997). Emergent theories of leadership for the next century: Toward relational concepts. *Organizational Development Journal, 15*(3), 35–42.

O'Donohue, W. T., Byrd, M. R., Cummings, N. A., & Henderson, D. A. (Eds.). (2005). *Behavioral integrative care: Treatments that work in the primary care setting.* New York: Brunner-Routledge.

O'Donohue, W. T., Cummings, N. A., & Cummings, J. L. (2009). The unmet educational agenda in integrated care. *Journal of Clinical Psychology in Medical Settings, 16*, 94–100. doi:10.1007/s10880-008-9138-3

Robinson, P. J., & Reiter, J. T. (2007). *Behavioral consultation and primary care: A guide to integrating services.* New York: Springer.

Rollins, J. (2009). Reconnecting the head with the body. *Counseling Today Online.* Retrieved from http://www.counseling.org/Publications/Counseling TodayArticles.aspx?AGuid=604ad846-3804-41a1-9d8c-d7a79302f887

Senge, P. (1993). Transforming the practice of management. *Human Resource Development Quarterly, 4*(1), 4–32.

Slater, L. (2005). Leadership for collaboration. *International Journal of Leadership in Education, 8*(4), 321–333.

Stogdill, R. M., & Coons, A. E. (1957). *Leader behavior: Its description and measurement.* Columbus: Ohio State University Press.

Uhl-Bien, M. (2003). Relationship development as a key ingredient for leadership development. In S. Murphy & R. Riggio (Eds.), *The future of leadership development* (pp. 129–147). New Jersey: Lawrence Erlbaum.

Uhl-Bien, M. (2005). Implicit theories of relationships in the workplace. In B. Schyns & J. R. Meindl (Eds.), *Implicit leadership theories: Essays and explorations* (pp. 103–133). Greenwich, CT: Information Age Publishing.

Uhl-Bien, M. (2006). Relational leadership theory: Exploring social processes of leadership and organizing. *The Leadership Quarterly, 17,* 654–676.

CHAPTER **16**

Integrated Care Policy

BENJAMIN F. MILLER and ANDREA AUXIER

Health care policy is an important topic that is rarely sufficiently covered in graduate training for behavioral health providers (BHPs). This is in part because policy itself is a moving target, often ill defined and frequently confused with politics and advocacy. Any BHP entering the professional workforce should have attained a basic foundation in policy; that is, an understanding of policy in general, how it impacts one's chosen profession, and the ways it can be affected. Unfortunately, most graduate students are not educated about policy in their programs; it is often relegated to and learned via real-life experience, postgraduation. Case in point, answer this question: What is the difference between Medicaid and Medicare? This distinction matters because health care policy requires a basic understanding of the larger system and our role within that system. You may be asking, "How does this have anything to do with behavioral health and primary care?" The answer is simple: It has everything to do with how the two are integrated. A complication arises when considering the integration of behavioral and physical health care, or integrated care (IC), as there are two distinct health care policy systems that must be differentiated before a discussion can begin about how policy can be changed to bring them together. Grasping the details of behavioral health policy is certainly a challenge, one that is compounded by the need to acquire an understanding of the medical, or physical, side of the health care policy equation in order to get to the heart of IC policy.

From the time the writing of this chapter began to the time of publication, health care reform may or may not have happened, and few of us will understand the finer details of what that really means or how it will actually impact patients and providers. This ambiguity is mainly due to the multifaceted nature of health care reform and the difficulty inherent in appreciating it as health care. The intention of this chapter, then, is to provide relevant background information so that BHPs can develop a basic framework for understanding how legislation drives policy, which, in turn, impacts practice. There is a small caveat: The specifics in this chapter are subject to change, because health care is not a static construct. Rather it is dynamic and perpetually influenced by market forces, scientific developments, and patient demographics. Health care is additionally affected by the never-ending quest for money to sustain it and must compete with other national priorities for funding (e.g., military).

The Big Picture

Policy has two definitions:

1. (a) prudence or wisdom in the management of affairs, (b) management or procedure based primarily on material interest, and
2. (a) a definite course or method of action selected from among alternatives and in light of given conditions to guide and determine present and future decisions, (b) a high-level overall plan embracing the general goals and acceptable procedures especially of a governmental body.

Although these are dictionary definitions, for this chapter a slightly different definition that defines *policy* as a verb will be adopted, as policy is conceptualized as an organized movement in a specified direction. In health care, advocacy often shapes the direction and movement of policy. Different groups may advocate for different policies; all want movement, though possibly in different directions. Sometimes the implementation of one policy helps one group while unintentionally, or even intentionally, thwarting another. This has historically happened to health care, as it has grown to become a morass of competing interests and beliefs about policy and conflicting business interests. The results have created a "chasm" between the existing health care system and the desired system (Institute of Medicine, 2001).

Dispensing With Dualism

The separate treatment of mind and body exists throughout health care. This separation is apparent in the language we use to describe how health care is delivered (behavioral health vs. physical health), in how we set up our funding streams to pay for them, in the relative value we place on them through our policies and reimbursement models, and in the places people are supposed to obtain help for each. It seems that this artificial dichotomy exists at every level, except in actual people.

Much has been written about the need for a change in the way mind health and body health are separated. Integration efforts across the country are usually made based on the case that aside from integration simply making logical clinical sense, it is the right thing to do and results in better overall health outcomes (Butler et al., 2008; Collins, Hewson, Munger, & Wade, 2010). In this chapter terms will be introduced such as *outcomes* and *sustainability*, and it may be a surprise to learn that despite the growing body of literature supporting integration as sound clinical practice, our policies have not quite caught up with the evidence base. To understand IC, one must first understand the largest platform of health care delivery in the country: primary care.

Primary Care

Primary care is defined as the provision of collaborative, accessible health care services by clinicians who are accountable for addressing a large majority of personal health care needs, developing a sustained partnership with patients, and practicing from a biopsychosocial systems perspective in the context of family and community (Starfield, 1998; Starfield, Shi, & Mackino, 2005). As the largest platform of health care delivery in the country, primary care is the cornerstone of health care (Green, Fryer, Yawn, Lanier, & Dovey, 2001). Although the benefits of primary care have been discussed in great detail elsewhere (Starfield, 1998; Starfield & Shi, 2002; Starfield et al., 2005), a few fundamentals that are worth mentioning are listed below:

1. Primary care is not a medical specialty.
2. Primary care is made up of family medicine, pediatrics, geriatrics, and internal medicine.
3. Primary care is often the first line of entry for patients into health care.

As with most aspects of health care, ultimately much of the delivery of primary care is determined by how services are financed.

Medicaid Versus Medicare

Medicaid is a state and federal program used to provide medical care to people who are disabled, indigent families who have dependent children, and low-income older people (Mechanic, 1999). Depending on the relative economic position of states, the federal government matches state expenditures under the guidelines of the program. To receive federal funds, states must include certain eligible groups and services.

Because Medicaid programs are unique to each state, there are 50 unique and different systems of eligibility, benefits, and payment structures for primary care and mental health. When one considers the state-by-state model for Medicaid, systematic change is nearly impossible.

Medicaid mental health coverage in most states is included as one of the "optional" service categories. State Medicaid agencies classify an "optional service" as one that they may or may not choose to provide. Unfortunately, from a policy point of view, optional services are often the first thing to be cut during lean financial times. Mental health funding is therefore often a casualty of a state's decision to cut funds.

Medicaid waivers are another example of a variation in Medicaid that introduces a level of complexity for IC. A Medicaid waiver requests that rules and regulations for Medicaid included in Section 1115 and Section 1915 of the Social Security Act are eliminated for that state (Kautz, Mauch, & Smith, 2008). Waivers were created to allow states to modify and be creative in how they address health issues. In the past, states have chosen to use waivers to "carve out" mental health services into a managed care structure. When mental health benefits are carved out from primary care benefits, they are essentially managed and delivered by another system, resulting in difficulties in reimbursing for mental health services in primary care (Kathol, Butler, McAlpine, & Kane, 2010; Kautz et al., 2008). Although most individuals who have Medicaid should theoretically make use of community health centers (CHCs) for the majority of their health care, many are often seen and treated in primary care. This occurs for a number of reasons, including failure to meet diagnostic requirements that would qualify them for entry into the community mental health center (CMHC) system, the stigma associated with mental health treatment, or personal preference to be treated in one facility versus two.

When Medicaid is contrasted with Medicare, the differences in state funding versus federal funding for health care are exposed. Technically, Medicare is a government-run program that provides care for people who are 65 years old and older. There are several different types of Medicare (A, B, C, and D), all of which represent unique aspects of health care. For example, Medicare Part D subsidizes the cost of prescription drugs for the eligible population. We will not cover Medicare a great detail in this chapter, as it is a federally run and funded program and has less variability than Medicaid.

Federally Qualified Health Center

In 1965, President Johnson launched a "War on Poverty" (Adashi, Geiger, & Fine, 2010). That year, two CHCs were opened in Massachusetts and

Mississippi with the hope of reducing or eliminating health disparities for racial and ethnic minority groups and the economically disadvantaged. The CHCs were to become part of a national public "safety net" that would not only provide services to individuals but also focus on taking care of the health care needs of target populations through expanded services and collaboration with other health care agencies. Safety net systems were originally developed with the intention of providing health care services to low-income and Medicaid populations who could not access services elsewhere. In most communities, safety net systems are composed of public hospitals and clinics, and CHCs, that collectively care for the health needs of an entire population—often at an economic loss—while providing teaching sites for academic institutions (Katz, 2010).

The impetus for the evolution of the safety net system has been twofold: philosophical and pragmatic. On the philosophical side, CHCs originated in response to a national need to improve health care delivery to the neediest patients with the most limited access to those services. As a result, CHCs continue to be driven by a mission to care for the underserved, which often means developing protocols for expanded services, making staffing decisions to hire providers who can provide culturally competent care, and embracing a multidisciplinary team approach that often includes BHPs, dental providers, pharmacists, health educators, and case managers, in addition to medical providers. Many centers offer coordinated disease prevention programs with a focus on health maintenance. The core values of CHCs are remarkably similar to those of the Patient-Centered Medical Home, a national health care reform effort that promises to improve quality of care while reducing costs through a focus on team-based care and information-technology-driven performance measurement.

The centers receive partial funding through the Public Health Service Act and are administered by the Health Resources and Services Administration. Today, CHCs are often referred to as Federally Qualified Health Centers (FQHCs). FQHCs are nonprofit health care providers that must adhere to certain requirements in order to qualify for designation from the Bureau of Primary Health Care and the Centers for Medicare and Medicaid Services. To qualify for designation, a center must provide sliding-fee scales to uninsured patients and must agree to see all patients, regardless of their ability to pay. An FQHC must be governed by a board of directors and provide access to services for patients who make up a medically underserved population or to those living in medically underserved areas. The Rural Health Clinic Services Act of 1977 first described the core services expected to be provided by FQHCs, including those provided by clinical psychologists and clinical social workers (when providing the diagnosis and treatment of mental illness).

Collectively, the centers are responsible for meeting the health care needs of approximately 20 million Americans, which is 5% of the U.S. population (Adashi et al., 2010). Of these 20 million people, 35% have Medicaid, 25% have Medicare or private insurance, and 40% are uninsured. Enhanced Medicaid reimbursements for medical visits help offset the costs of providing services to such a large percentage of uninsured individuals. On the downside, though, restrictions on billing for additional services, whether medical or behavioral, diminish the effectiveness of the enhanced reimbursements. Seven out of 10 patients live below the poverty line, and over half identify as being from a minority group. Because most FQHCs are located in geographical areas targeting traditionally medically underserved groups, many are in remote locations where no other health care is available. Nevertheless, 43% of medically underserved areas continue to lack an FQHC site.

Community Mental Health Centers

Up to this point, this chapter has focused a great deal on primary care in the public delivery system and the limitations and insufficiencies of changing health care policy. Here, the publically funded mental health system, known as community mental health, will be discussed. A brief explanation of the history and current role of community mental health in health care will help emphasize the challenges of integration and in moving policy.

In 1963, President Kennedy signed the Mental Retardation Facilities and Community Mental Health Centers Construction Act. The act established funding for CMHCs, with a focus on providing mental health services in communities rather than in hospitals. Generally speaking, CMHCs rely on four funding streams: Medicaid, private insurance and sliding-scale payments for patients who are either uninsured or underinsured, and block grants. A block grant is a sum of money granted by the Department of Health and Human Services to a regional government with only general provisions for the way it must be spent. Like an FQHC, a CMHC must provide the core services described in the Public Health Service Act, which are as follows:

- outpatient services, including specialized outpatient services for children, older people, individuals who are chronically mentally ill, and residents of the CMHC's mental health service area who have been discharged from inpatient treatment at a mental health facility;
- 24-hour-a-day emergency care services;
- day treatment or other partial hospitalization services or psychosocial rehabilitation services; and

- screening for patients being considered for admission to state mental health facilities to determine the appropriateness of such admission.

For more information about CMHCs, visit www.cms.gov/ CertificationandComplianc/03_CommunityHealthCenters.asp.

Patient Protection and Affordable Care Act

In 2010, the federal Patient Protection and Affordable Care Act (PPACA) was passed with the hope of expanding health insurance to 34 million Americans by 2019, mostly through the expansion of the eligibility requirements for Medicaid (Office of the Actuary). However, of the 57 million uninsured people in the United States, 23 million will remain uninsured under PPACA, including undocumented immigrants and those citizens who are eligible for coverage but who, for various reasons, do not enroll. On the positive side, the expansion of Medicaid will mean that fewer people will be treated who do not have insurance, which translates to a reduced cost burden on the system.

On the negative side, PPACA reduces Medicaid hospital funding by $20 billion by the year 2020. Federal law requires that hospital emergency rooms provide or arrange for emergency care to all patients, regardless of ability to pay. As a result, hospital emergency room staffs end up treating a "disproportionate share" of Medicaid and uninsured individuals. A $20 billion loss is expected to impact hospitals' ability to care for these individuals at greater relative numbers than private hospitals. Theoretically, less funding will be required to care for these patients, because many of them will be eligible for insurance under PPACA. However, it is still too early to tell how things will balance out in the end. An additional obstacle that remains, one that is both politically charged and financially difficult, exists in how the United States provides services to undocumented immigrants. Under PPACA, the number of patients treated in CHCs is expected to grow by 20 million by 2015. Table 16.1 lists recent CHC appropriations.

Despite financial incentives, the challenges faced by CHCs are many. Centers are often tasked with finding ways to provide services to the growing number of uninsured individuals while facing regular budget cuts to state Medicaid programs. Second, money that is appropriated does not always actually become available. In addition, reimbursement practices are currently geared to incentivize specialty, not primary care, services. Given the remote geographic locations of these centers, specialty services are many times either unavailable or inaccessible for patients, especially for those who are uninsured.

Table16.1
Recent Appropriations

Bush administration	$2.1 billion by 2008
Obama administration: American Recovery and Reinvestment Act (ARRA) of 2009	$2 billion
National Health Service Corps (NHSC)	$300 million to recruit and place health care professionals in health professional shortage areas
	$47.6 million for medical and dental training programs
Patient Protection and Affordable Care Act 2010	$12.5 billion for community health center and NHSC expansion
	$230 million Title III grant program for community-based teaching programs
	Title IV grant program for residency training (amount to be determined)

Problematic Policies and Integration

The barriers to providing behavioral health services can be particularly daunting, yet it is not uncommon for patients with psychiatric conditions to seek mental health care in primary care practices (Cwikel, Zilber, Feinson, & Lerner, 2008), and roughly 40% of premature deaths in the United States can be attributed to behavioral health factors that could have been addressed in primary care settings (McGinnis, Williams-Russo, & Knickman, 2002; Mokdad, Marks, Stroup, & Gerberding, 2004). Examples of conflicting policies for integration are most apparent when primary care offices try to bill for integrated services. First, there is the problem of determining which providers can bill for behavioral health services. Primary care practices often encounter problems with reimbursement for behavioral health services delivered by primary care providers, as they are not considered to be experts in that field. Bills are often rejected, prompting the physician to use a secondary physical health diagnosis for billing purposes when the treatment is actually for a behavioral health condition (Kautz et al., 2008). Of course, misrepresenting a diagnosis can lead to confusion, as the medical record may not be consistent with the actual diagnosis and reason for treatment. These policies continue to place restrictions on the type of provider who can provide certain services and either limit payment to doctoral-level licensed psychologists entirely or provide lesser payment to professionals from other mental health disciplines.

Although the Health Insurance Portability and Accountability Act presented a consistent format for health care billing, and the set of Current

Procedural Technology (CPT) codes help keep condition classification consistent, there is *no standard set of credentialing guidelines* for providers for the use of CPT codes. Medicaid, which is driven by decisions at the state level, and private insurers have varying standards on the types of providers who can deliver and bill certain services (Bachman, Pincus, Houtsinger, & Unutzer, 2006). State by state, and insurer by insurer, variation on who pays for whom and what, makes it difficult for primary care practices and staff to translate requirements into effective billing practices for integration. Often added to this variation is the complex process of choosing CPT codes that correspond accurately with a diagnosis and the appropriately credentialed provider, leading to the possibly of billing errors and a lack of financial compensation for services.

As described earlier, many states have *carved out systems* whereby behavioral health services have been excised from the list of allowable billable services in a primary care setting, presumably under the rationale that mental health needs should be treated in a mental health setting. *Fee-for-service reimbursement* policies continue to pay for certain services such as assessments and therapy but are much more restrictive of other behavioral health services offered in primary care settings. Well-meaning developments such as the advent of health and behavior billing codes intended to capture services for patients with medical conditions affected by behavior, but in the absence of any psychiatric condition, they fail to capture the significant amount of services provided to those patients who do not qualify for these codes because they also have a comorbid psychiatric condition.

Finally, *same-day billing restrictions* make it impossible to bill for two services on the same day; when patients receive a behavioral health service on the same day as a medical one, practices cannot bill for both services. In integrated systems that are aspiring to treat the whole person, this restriction is problematic. On a related note, FQHCs cannot receive any additional reimbursement from Medicaid for *any* behavioral health service, because the Medicaid rate is a flat per-patient rate regardless of the number or types of services rendered during a particular visit.

Does Policy Matter?

Policy is often considered someone else's responsibility. In reality, policy is everyone's responsibility because it affects all of us. Health care change is a moving target of decoding, deciding, and prioritizing what needs to be done to adequately address the health needs of the public. On some days, the target is access; other days, it is controlling cost. Regardless of the priority, health care policy should always be about improving quality of care to thereby improve people's health. The variables are constantly changing, requiring systems to change in order to accommodate them.

Unfortunately, systems do not change easily, as they tend toward homeostasis and balance. *Homeostasis* is a term that is most often used to discuss biological organisms, but the description is also relevant to policy. Systems are constantly barraged by actions that threaten homeostasis by perturbing them and creating an imbalance. Systems then become unsettled and resist change by modifying themselves through attempts to achieve homeostasis. Like any system, policy systems change continuously in response to internal and external perturbation. The changes are generally modest, so the level of disruption is hardly noticeable within the operating system. Transformational changes of the magnitude we are discussing in this chapter, however, require novel reorganization, in essence, a redesign of the entire system.

Bateson (1979) suggested that changes that merely reorganize systems without core changes in operation and organization are known as first-order changes. These types of changes are familiar to health care (e.g., covering a new procedure or medication, or managed care not requiring preauthorization for the first set of visits for mental health care). However, there are some shifts that demand new rules for governing and that reorder the operation of systems. These shifts that are more than mere accommodations are classified as second-order change. IC can present either first- or second-order changes to health care systems. The colocation of a BHP in primary care, in which the BHP provides only traditional mental health services following a private practice model, represents a first-order change. In contrast, a second-order change occurs when the rules of operation are reordered by integrating systems of care in ways that necessitate a reworking of how practices operate and how systems organize and finance care.

The rules and organization of our health care model include fragmentation and ineffectiveness as an unfortunate by-product of its design (Institute of Medicine, 2001, 2006). This is most prominently seen in the separation between the behavioral health and the physical health systems of care (Kessler & Stafford, 2008; Regier et al., 1993). Convincing arguments for the inclusion of behavioral health as part of primary care have been made for the past 30 years (Blount, 1998; deGruy, 1996). Although the health care system has explicitly acknowledged those arguments, it continues to operate in a manner that perpetuates fragmentation. In short, the health care system maintains homeostasis without responding to the perturbations beyond modest first-order change. The perturbations in this system have managed to disrupt the dichotomy of mental and physical health systems and clinical care delivery. Research demonstrates the inseparability of, and need and demand for, merging mental and physical health systems together (Blount, 2003; Butler et al., 2008; Craven & Bland, 2006).

Because the research is very modest and linear, however, momentum has failed to develop and have a significant impact on policy. Ironically, the clinical excellence and innovative spirit of mental health providers has resulted in the creation of a variety of IC practice types, which has actually made it difficult to standardize any of the associated variables to a degree to which they can easily lend themselves to measurement. Consequently, because mental health providers cannot measure IC consistently across the variety of practice types, a solid evidentiary base for its effectiveness is still lacking.

The Example of Mental Health Parity

A practical example of first-order policy change in action is the Paul Wellstone and Pete Domenici Mental Health Parity and Addiction Equity Act of 2008. Its purpose is to offer equity between mental health and medical/surgical insurance coverage. The elimination of lifetime limits on the number of mental health services that can be accessed is the most significant change found in the bill. From a coverage perspective, the bill is an important step toward equity in treating mental health and medical conditions. Unfortunately, however, following the Act, nothing was done to change the health care system providing the care or the rules that govern that system of care; the delivery and organization remain unchanged.

Mental Health Parity, on both state and federal levels, has accomplished a great deal in the past 15 years. This substantial accomplishment should be hailed as a great achievement, and the leaders who are working toward parity should be applauded for their efforts. But despite the plethora of bills passed, meetings held, and papers written, comprehensive system change has yet to occur. Behavioral health and physical health continue to operate with two different sets of rules. Parity, for all that it has accomplished, has not changed the rules of the larger system or reorganized and restructured a new system of care.

Direction

There is a good deal of recent literature calling for specific policy change to accommodate integration (Blount et al., 2007; Kautz et al., 2008; Kessler, Stafford, & Messier, 2009). However, a substantial increase in research supporting a new system for delivery of care that addresses both mental health and physical health is still needed. This research base should not simply address one disease or one specific technique, but broadly examine multiple aspects of integration that include clinical outcomes and functions, operational descriptions, and financial impact (Peek, 2008). Preliminary metrics have been offered to help increase the type of data collected for IC (Miller, Mendenhall, & Malik, 2009), but the field remains behind other medical fields in terms of substantial evidence.

Increased IC research aside, future BHPs should ask, "What can I do to help influence the future of this emerging field?" In an attempt to simplify the complexity of changing health care policy, we developed three simple approaches BHPs can take to begin to impact policy for IC:

1. *Understanding the issue.* Before people can begin to impact policy, they need to thoroughly understand the issue. For example, anyone wishing to begin to make an impact on financial polices in IC will first need to know the specifics of payment in terms of who pays for what, who, where, and how.
2. *Explaining the issue.* When developing a document for a policy that explains the issue, people need to keep the message succinct and focused.
3. *Offering a solution.* Simply explaining the issue clearly is insufficient for moving policy. People need to be prepared to offer practical solutions to guide the process.

From what you have read in this chapter, answer the following questions:

1. Does any of this make sense to me, and if not, am I willing to learn more so that it does?
2. Do I still want to go into this field given all the obstacles?

If the answer is yes to both of these questions, welcome to becoming involved in the dialogue, learning, and momentum that surrounds IC.

Conclusion

Policy change requires a basic understanding of health care and the BHP's ability to articulate and advocate clearly. There is no better time or place to learn the basics of health care policy than early on in training and education. It is hoped that this chapter has given a solid introduction of the intricacies of health care delivery in this country, particularly as they apply to developing and sustaining integrated systems. This chapter described how CHCs are models for the integrated philosophy, while expressing a realistic summary of the obstacles they face. Also outlined were several new and significant health care policy shifts that allow for a renewed sense of optimism for potential innovation, despite the challenges. Namely, both the recently enacted PPACA and President Obama's 2011 budget (www.whitehouse.gov/omb/budget/Overview/) open a window of opportunity for the redesign of health care delivery that supports integration.

When one considers the potential advances in health care that could transpire as a result of treating the whole person, there is cause for excitement. Will we take advantage of the opportunities to move policy, or will we idly watch as policy shifts without us? Will our policy advocacy be momentous enough to produce substantial change? Policy does not change on its own. It requires the collective efforts of people at all levels of training and with differing expertise. Ultimately, we decided to write this chapter in a graduate-level text because we trusted that some of those who read it would be moved into thinking about how they can contribute to making IC a part of standard health care delivery for everyone.

Discussion Questions

1. If you could design an ideal health care system, what would it look like?
2. Do you think that CHCs have an obligation to provide care for individuals who are in the country illegally? Why or why not?
3. Can you think of another example of first-order change versus second-order change?
4. What are some advantages and disadvantages of a single-payer health care system?

References

Adashi, E. Y., Geiger, H. J., & Fine, M. D. (2010). Health care reform and primary care: The growing importance of the community health center. *New England Journal of Medicine, 362*(22), 2047–2050. doi:10.1056/NEJMp1003729

Bachman, J., Pincus, H. A., Houtsinger, J. K., & Unutzer, J. (2006). Funding mechanisms for depression care management: Opportunities and challenges. *General Hospital Psychiatry, 28*(4), 278–288. doi:10.1016/j.genhosppsych.2006.03.006

Bateson, G. (1979). *Mind and nature: A necessary unity.* New York: Dutton.

Blount, A. (Ed.). (1998). *Integrated primary care: The future of medical and mental health collaboration.* New York: Norton.

Blount, A. (2003). Integrated primary care: Organizing the evidence. *Families, Systems, and Health, 21*(2), 121–133.

Blount, A., Kathol, R., Thomas, M., Schoenbaum, M., Rollman, B. L., O'Donohue, W. T., & Peek, C. J. (2007). The economics of behavioral health services in medical settings: A summary of the evidence. *Professional Psychology: Research and Practice, 38*, 290–297.

Butler, M., Kane, R. L., McAlpin, D., Kathol, R. G., Fu, S. S., Hagedorn, H., & Wilt, T. J. (2008). *Integration of mental health/substance abuse and primary care No. 173* (Prepared by the Minnesota Evidence-Based Practice Center under Contract No. 290-02-0009; AHRQ Publication No. 09-E003). Rockville, MD: Agency for Healthcare Research and Quality.

Collins, C., Hewson, D. L., Munger, R., & Wade, T. (2010, May). *Evolving models of behavioral health integration in primary care.* New York: Milbank Memorial Fund.

Craven, M., & Bland, R. (2006, May). Better practices in collaborative mental health care: An analysis of the evidence base. *Canadian Journal of Psychiatry*, *51*(Suppl. 1).

Cwikel, J., Zilber, N., Feinson, M., & Lerner, Y. (2008). Prevalence and risk factors of threshold and sub-threshold psychiatric disorders in primary care. *Social Psychiatry and Psychiatric Epidemiology*, *43*(3), 184–191.

DeGruy, F. (1996). Mental health care in the primary care setting. In M. S. Donaldson, K. D. Yordy, K. N. Lohr, & N. A. Vanselow (Eds.), *Primary care: America's health in a new era* (pp. 285–311). Washington, DC: Institute of Medicine.

Green, L. A., Fryer, G. E., Jr., Yawn, B. P., Lanier, D., & Dovey, S. M. (2001). The ecology of medical care revisited. *New England Journal of Medicine*, *344*(26), 2021–2025.

Institute of Medicine. (2001). *Crossing the quality chasm: A new health system for the 21st century*. Washington, DC: National Academy Press.

Institute of Medicine. (2006). *Improving the quality of health care for mental and substance-use conditions*. Washington, DC: National Academy of Sciences.

Kathol, R. G., Butler, M., McAlpine, D. D., & Kane, R. L. (2010). Barriers to physical and mental condition integrated service delivery. *Psychosomatic Medicine*, *72*(6), 511–518. doi:10.1097/PSY.0b013e3181e2c4a0

Katz, M. H. (2010). Future of the safety net under health reform. *Journal of the American Medical Association*, *304*(6), 679–680. doi:10.1001/jama.2010.1126

Kautz, C., Mauch, D., & Smith, S. A. (2008). *Reimbursement of mental health services in primary care settings*. Rockville, MD: Center for Mental Health Services, Substance Abuse and Mental Health Services Administration.

Kessler, R., & Stafford, D. (Eds.). (2008). *Primary care is the de facto mental health system*. New York: Springer.

Kessler, R., Stafford, D., & Messier, R. (2009). The problem of integrating behavioral health in the medical home and the questions it leads to. *Journal of Clinical Psychology in Medical Settings*, *16*(1), 4–12. doi:10.1007/s10880-009-9146-y

McGinnis, J. M., Williams-Russo, P., & Knickman, J. R. (2002). The case for more active policy attention to health promotion. *Health Affairs*, *21*(2), 78–93. doi:10.1377/hlthaff.21.2.78

Mechanic, D. (1999). *Mental health and social policy: The emergency of managed care*. Englewood Cliffs, NJ: Prentice Hall.

Miller, B. F., Mendenhall, T. J., & Malik, A. D. (2009). Integrated primary care: An inclusive three-world view through process metrics and empirical discrimination. *Journal of Clinical Psychology in Medical Settings*, *16*, 21–30.

Mokdad, A. H., Marks, J. S., Stroup, D. F., & Gerberding, J. L. (2004). Actual causes of death in the United States, 2000. *Journal of the American Medical Association*, *291*(10), 1238–1245. doi:10.1001/jama.291.10.1238

Peek, C. J. (2008). Planning care in the clinical, operational, and financial worlds. In R. Kessler & D. Stafford (Eds.), *Collaborative medicine case studies: Evidence in practice*. New York: Springer.

Regier, D. A., Narrow, W. E., Rac, D. S., Manderscheid, R. W., Locke, B., & Goodwin, F. (1993). The de facto U.S. mental health and addictive disorders service system: Epidemiologic Catchment Area prospective. *Archives of General Psychiatry*, *50*, 85–94.

Starfield, B. (1998). *Primary care: Balancing health needs, services, and technology.* New York: Oxford University Press.

Starfield, B., & Shi, L. (2002). Policy relevant determinants of health: An international perspective. *Health Policy, 60*(3), 201–218. doi:S0168851001002081 [pii]

Starfield, B., Shi, L., & Mackino, J. (2005). Contributions of primary care to health systems and health. *The Milbank Quarterly, 83,* 457–502.

CHAPTER 17

An Outcome and Clinical Research Focus in an Integrated Care Patient-Centered Medical Home

RODGER KESSLER

Introduction

Collaborative or integrated primary care (referred to as integrated care [IC] in this chapter) is driven by bright people who are invested in resolving the historic mind-body split in health care. These professionals work in a variety of clinical settings, where they create and become involved in activities and projects in an effort to improve individual patient care that does not often translate to efficiencies for population-based approaches to health behavior counseling (Green, Cifuentes, Glasgow, & Stange, 2008). This chapter focuses on changes to the clinical, organizational, and financial worlds of mental health, substance abuse, and health behavior services as described by Peek (Patterson, Peek, Heinrich, Bischoff, & Scherger, 2002). Professionals who work in IC settings experience roles with more fluidity, where patients' varied and overall health needs can be met in one place. Although IC is a wonderful development for health care delivery, it is rife with challenges.

Currently, IC professionals' efforts are not carefully described, and their practice is infrequently built on evidence-based outcomes (Miller, Kessler, & Peek, 2011). In addition, lacking are common procedures for identifying patients' needs and how they might be assessed or treated. These shortcomings are not surprising, as there is no common language by which to describe, define, measure, or capture information about IC practice. To illustrate, please operationally define integration, collaborative mental health, coordinated care, colocated care, behavioral medicine, or primary care behavioral health (PCBH). How are they the same or similar, and how do they differ?

Without a clear and agreed-on language that can be used to evaluate effectiveness, compare practice efforts, or provide data, changes in a health care policy and financing system that has historically marginalized the efforts of IC professionals will not be supported. The individualization of integration efforts across practices is currently an obstacle to changing health care provision, policy, and financing to incorporate IC.

There has been limited research into these deficiencies and how best to address them; the research that has been conducted has suffered from constraints. Some of the weaknesses of IC research to date include lack of a clear agenda, lack of single disease-focused research, limited research funding, reliance on methodology that does not generalize and often excludes capturing results of the patients seen in IC settings, and funding for research that is conducted by people and organizations who are not aware of these issues (Kessler & Glasgow, 2011).

Analysis of the existing gaps in IC research suggests that for IC to mature as a field, a focus on goals that would diminish current limitations is needed. The following are some of these goals:

- a common language by which to describe and measure;
- a systematic definition and description of the tasks and the people who perform them, along with a description of the patients who are receiving care and the expected outcomes;
- the employment of a population-based focus;
- interactions between the clinical, organizational, and financial dimensions of care;
- the identification of a primary-care-based continuum of populations, and implementation of evidence-based services to persons with mental health, substance abuse, and health behavior needs;
- a consistent method of identifying those in need and protocols for how to proceed after identification;
- an agreed-on set of measures and metrics consistent with the language;
- a method of capturing and communicating that which is measured;
- a financing system based on agreed-on performance and outcome metrics;
- a bottom-up, practice-based research system that can answer questions important to patients, clinicians, funders, and policy and decision makers; and

- a research system that supports and funds research that is based on rigor and rapid learning systems, as these are approaches that work well in practices, are easily implemented, and involve patient participation.

The remainder of this chapter will elaborate on these limitations and give examples of potential solutions. For those who want to delve further into these issues, please see the list of references, in which greater detail of these efforts can be found. Table 17.1 summarizes the key gaps and examples of responses by IC practices around the country. Examples of this author's work are ample because of his experience in thinking about solutions and working in an IC environment. The examples are not meant to be exacting but rather intended to stimulate ideas, criticism, and the reader's creative responses. However, it cannot be more strongly stated: The gaps are real and must be addressed in order to move the field of IC further as an integral part of the larger health care system.

Table 17.1
Gaps and Examples of Responses

Definition and Description	Examples of Responses
Population focus	Obesity and diabetes screening
Clinical, organizational, and financial worlds	Electronic health record (EHR), dashboards, and project team conversation and planning
Continuum of populations and services	Kessler and Miller (2009) graphic (see Table 17.2)
Method for identification and intervention	Identification: Body mass index and blood glucose level Intervention: Health behavior lifestyle planning and correlated medical management
Common language to describe and measure	Peek paradigm case
Measures and metrics	Dimensions of the paradigm case
Capturing and communicating	Collaborative Interdisciplinary Research Program in Diabetes, Endocrinology, and Metabolic Diseases (R24), and EHR
Financing	DIAMOND initiative in Minnesota, and Vermont single-payer project
Research infrastructure	Collaborative Care Research Network
Research support system	National Institutes of Health Clinical Center

Common Language

Peek told the story of the formation of the Electrical Congress in the late 1800s. At the time there were many scientists around the world who were working with elements of electricity, but they had no common way to describe their experiments, compare results, or communicate with each other. In response, they formed the Electrical Congress, which generated common language and definitions of volts, ohms, and watts. Members decided that with these agreements, they could communicate and measure with common processes and discuss the results in mutually understandable terms. Thus, the basis for the science and field of electricity was created as they moved from the preempirical to the empirical (Peek, 2011).

Peek also illustrated the importance of common language another way. In his example, he suggested that if you are going to build something, you might need a piece of lumber. The clerk at the store needs to know precisely the dimensions and the type and grade of wood desired. Such specificity will produce about the same result, no matter which lumberyard cuts your wood, because the shared language eliminates ambiguity and uncertainty (Peek, 2011).

Earlier in this chapter, IC was described in several ways. In fact, if a group of practitioners were gathered and asked to define IC in as many ways as possible, the result would include a fairly broad set of descriptors, thereby substantiating the notion that the term IC does not really describe anything distinct and specific. In fact, integrated practices can have very little resemblance to one another, aside from this descriptive phrasing.

IC professionals have been in the same position as electricians before the creation of their congress, and they found similar difficulty in practicing their trade without a universally shared language and understanding. It is encouraging, however, that IC professionals are on their way to finding solutions and are on the cusp of a larger movement. Peek, a specialist in the integration of medicine and mental health care (please read his work for further study), has adopted a methodology from the field of descriptive psychology, called the "paradigm case formulation" (Ossorio, 2006), to ask the following questions of collaborative care: If you absolutely knew a practice was a collaborative care practice, how would you know? What are the core elements? If you knew a practice was not practicing collaborative care, what key elements would be missing? Using this process, along with panels of national experts in collaborative care, Peek developed the Collaborative Care Lexicon (Peek, 2011), which identifies the key elements, and their parameters and clauses, that allow for the determination of where a practice exists on a continuum of collaborative care. A brief description of the overarching key elements of Peek's (2011) paradigm case formulation of collaborative care follows:

- *A team:* There is a composition of clinicians, collaborative care training, proximity, role clarification, and unity of mission and culture to serve patients.
- *Shared population and mission:* The team treats the same population and/or an identified subset based on factors such as disease, age, and so on. The behaviorist operates within the parameters of primary care, referring to behavioral health specialists as needed such as when patients require wraparound services that are outside of the primary care treatment format.
- *Using a clinical system:* Practices consider collaboration for population-level screening methods, unified care plans, daily clinical routines, attention to patient culture, identified team roles and goals, shared medical records, and team-based decision making that is inclusive of patient input.
- *Support by an office and financial system:* Clinics have operations and processes that are clear, effective, and efficient and sustainable financial models that support IC.
- *Continuous quality improvement and effectiveness measurement:* There is an ongoing collection of data to be used to improve clinical, financial, and operational outcomes.

The Broad Needs of PCBH

What is the purpose of PCBH? Who is its target? In response to these questions, one may have thought about behavioral health providers (BHPs) providing mental health care to patients in a primary care practice. This concept is absolutely true but only part of the overall picture of PCBH. Peek's "three worlds" theory suggests that when organizations deliver clinical care, every clinical activity has corresponding organizational and financial dimensions (Patterson et al., 2002). For example, if a BHP holds a group session for patients with diabetes in the evening, it may generate greater patient participation than if it were held during work hours, but it also requires organizational accommodation for scheduling staff time, checking patients in, and entering information in the record differently. The financial considerations include determining if two copayments and two separate billings are necessary when a mental health clinician and physician are both working with the group.

The new reality for mental health clinicians is their role as a three worlds clinician, those who simultaneously consider the clinical, organizational, and financial issues of patient care in an IC setting (Kessler & Miller, 2009a). This change from the traditional mental health clinician's role, in which patients would see clinicians in their offices for sessions, has a profound impact on the way BHPs practice today and in the future.

There is in fact a broad range of primary care patient need, supported by estimates that 50% to as many as 70% of primary care visits are for psychosocial concerns (Gatchel & Oordt, 2003; Patterson et al., 2002; Robinson & Reiter, 2007). Table 17.2 outlines the range of behavioral health needs that can be addressed in IC.

Population Focus

Most of a BHP's typical graduate training focuses on treating an individual, couple, family, or group (Strosahl, 2005). However, contemporary health care reform—specifically the creation of the "patient-centered medical home"—has a population focus. A number of questions can be asked in relation to population focus in an IC setting:

- How can professionals in an IC setting think universally and organize care with a focus of responsibility to the population of patients in a practice?
- What is the best way to translate evidence about the best treatments for different populations of patients into treatment?
- What are the needs of older patients, patients with chronic medical diseases or depression, or those who fall into more than one of these categories? What is the best way to provide treatment to meet their needs?
- What needs exist for patients whose care should be coordinated with other providers or community agencies?
- What should be done for patients who need more behavioral and mental health treatment than can be provided in the primary care setting?

The Range of Need graphic in Table 17.2 demonstrates the kinds of activities BHPs might choose to participate in to address the differing presentations and needs of patients. In a fully integrated practice, every subpopulation of patients would receive treatment regardless of their medical provider, day of the week, or time of the day. Everyone presenting with the need can expect to be treated based on his or her level of need.

Patient Identification for BHP Assessment and Treatment, and Data Collection to Monitor for Desired Outcome and Determine Additional Need for Care

BHPs are trained to assess need and choose interventions for individual patients. Primary care settings present BHPs with patients who have a variety of complex needs. With a population focus, consider the scenario of BHPs working in a practice that serves 15,000 patients. Epidemiology supports that a third to a half or more of these patients have a mental health, substance abuse, or health behavior need (Gatchel & Oordt, 2003; Patterson et al., 2002; Robinson & Reiter, 2007). Three worlds clinicians must consider how to identify those patients, determine appropriate treatment, and decide how best to provide services in a way that is organizationally and financially sensible.

Data are necessary for identifying which patients, chosen from the whole population served by a practice, will most likely need further attention. BHPs need to be able to use data about populations to activate data-driven and evidence-driven interventions; that is, to determine which patients would benefit from a particular type of service, along with the development of a protocol for responding to patient needs both as an organization and as individual clinicians. It is imperative for BHPs to compare the intended outcomes of their treatment efforts to the actual outcome. Collecting data about results can be accomplished through measurement of clinical, organizational, and financial effectiveness. For an accurate comparison of different treatment approaches over time, agreed-on measures and metrics that are collectible during care and serve clinical, organizational, and research needs are necessary.

Measures and Metrics

Peek provided a common language set or categories that allow us to discuss collaborativeness. Metrics and measures further clarify terms used to discuss collaboration. Consider the example of XXX, an element of the paradigm case method. In this example, BHPs find general agreement that in a conversation about collaborative care, XXX should be discussed. Elsewhere, this author proposed a set of metrics to translate each of Peek's elements into statements that define the element, or metric. In this case, the metric for XXX is YYY. The statement, then, is about YYY. But to calculate the metric, the math that defines the statement must be established. So in addition to a metric, a measurement of the metric is needed. In this example, to compute the amount of XXX there is a numerator of A and a denominator of B. Thus, an element, its metric, and the method for computing the measure are created.

This is consistent with other aspects of medicine. A good example is in type 2 diabetes treatment. To assess the effectiveness of treatment for type 2 diabetes, people check blood sugar levels to see if they fall within an acceptable range, consistent with evidence-supported recommendations. A metric used to measure acceptability is hemoglobin A1C (Ha1c). The computation and measure of Ha1c is achieved by finding a numerator of XXX and a denominator of YYY, producing a standard measure of blood sugar. Because blood sugar's metric and measurement is universally accepted, and there are a vast number of patients with measured A1C levels to compare, standards have been able to be established for whether

Table 17.2
Range of Need for Collaboration in the Patient Centered Medical Home (Kessler & Miller, 2009)

	Severe Mental Health/Substance Abuse Management	Identification and Treatment of Mental Health and Substance Abuse	Comorbid Medical and Psychological Presentations	Medical Presentations Which Need Behavioral Treatment
Primary Care Functions	Manage pharmacology; coordinate w/ community providers; crisis management	Identification; motivational interviewing; brief intervention; pharmacology, refer to mental health/subsance abuse	Identification; patient education, co-treatment w/mental health, monitor activation and adherence (e.g., chronic medical disorders, non-adherence)	Identification; education; referral for consultation and co-treatment (e.g., primary insomnia, gastrointestinal, headache)
Primary Care Mental Health Clinician	Crisis intervention; communication w/ outside speciality care providers	Treatment of depression/anxiety; co-treatment w/ PCP; evidence-based treatment; medication monitoring	Psyhoeducation; motivational interviewing; behavioral activation	Health behavior change; psychoeducation; evidence-based treatment
Three Worlds of Healthcare (Peek, 2007)				
Clinical	Regular visits; pharmacology, assess medical comorbidity; communication w/ outside provider; crisis management	Identify and utilize evidence-based treatment protocol for screening and treatment/ co-treatment	Identification; implement clinical protocol; monitor medical functions	Identification; motivational interviewing; co-treat

Operational	Procedure for standard visits; welcoming environment; coordination mechanisms; information sharing	Standard screening; evidence-based protocol; referral; scheduling	Screening; evidence-based protocol; co-treatment protocol; referral scheduling; electronic health record	Identification; communication; electronic health record; referral; scheduling; data collection/sharing use
Financial	Regular office schedule; minimize ER visits; maintain consistent attendance at appointments; minimize physician time for case management	Consistent screening, identification, referral and scheduling; brief treatment protocol; optimal pharmacology management	TX comorbid; reduce ineffective medical visits, speciality referrals, and unhelpful pharmacy	Appropriate evidence-based intervention; limit pharmacy that is ineffective for prolonged use; enhance patient self-activation and reduce office and specialty care usage

Source: Kessler, R., & Miller, B. F. (2009b, March). *Model: Range of need for collaboration in the patient centered medical home.* Paper presented at the National Medical Home Summit, Philadelphia, PA. Retrieved from www.ehcca.com/presentations/medhomesummit2/kessler_2a.pdf

treatment is effective. In fact, in just about any evidence guideline concerning type 2 diabetes, Ha1c is a standard measure. Practitioners can record the measure in the patients' electronic health records (EHRs) so that the measures can be displayed and compared over time and offer a clinical picture of diabetic status.

Capturing and Communicating: The EHR, Data Extraction, and Dashboard Problem

Consider the following scenario: A BHP who is ahead of the curve conducts assessments based on a set of measures for each of her patients. Every couple of months she readministers some of the assessments to track progress. Each time, she enters the data into the "free text" area in her practice's EHR. Clinically, this scenario demonstrates how the BHP collects and uses data to make comparisons and to check progress. She can refer to the information at any point during treatment and as needed. In a collaborative care environment, though, the BHP's and physician's colleagues need to have access to the patient data without sifting through free text areas of the patient's EHR record. There are several considerations related to communication via the EHR:

- What collaboration exists or is needed in planning and executing treatment?
- How do assessment results relate to evidence about what type, frequency, and length of treatment should be provided?
- Organizationally, how are the measures selected and documented?
- How was the individual selected for treatment?
- How can the PCBH and medical treatment be coordinated for efficiency and best patient care?
- How do different clinicians' patients and performance compare? (If the clinical record is on paper, a comparison can be very difficult. If the data are in a free text area of the patient record of the EHR, they may not be easily retrievable.)
- What are the financial costs of providing different types of treatment?
- Is there more efficient care if there is greater or lesser communication between PCBH and medical providers?
- What happens to overall use and cost of the care provided?

For metrics and measures to be used effectively, information and data need to be collected, stored, easily accessed, and presentable to those who will access them. Therefore, the task of three worlds collaborative care clinicians is to involve themselves in institutional records policies, development and changes in EHRs, and communication about how data are generated, shared, and used for action.

Following is an example of the way measures were once recorded. In one of our early collaborative care practices, after patients' referral, a standard measure of depression, anxiety, and substance use was administered to patients and the results were collected on paper by the PCBH clinician. The PCBH clinician then scored the measures and entered the scores into the clinical notes as part of the body of the note for the physician to review at some point in the future. The positive aspects of this process included that the measures were selected because of their utility in primary care and took little time to collect, evidence-based treatment recommendations were associated with measurement-level results, and results were entered into the EHR. The negative aspects included that the measures had no bearing on the physician referral, there was no use of the evidence-associated treatment recommendations, and there was no collaboration on the basis of measurement. Furthermore, the measures that were recorded on paper were stashed in a file, retrospective, and the measures were rarely used to track progress. Moreover, the measures were not easily retrievable, living in free text or narrative areas within the patient record rather than in their own retrievable field in the EHR. This type of documentation offers very limited value for the clinician at the individual patient or collective patient level and for comparative or evaluative purposes.

Financing

PCBH Clinicians as Implementation and Dissemination Scientists

IC is a rapidly growing construct, and although the number of resources and training opportunities are expanding, we still know very little about it. Questions remain about cost considerations, how many clinicians should be present in a practice, whether more collaborativeness improves outcomes of care, the elements of the different models of IC and which have the greatest effect, and the impact of collaborative care on overall health care costs.

Glasgow, Vogt, and Boles (1999) suggested that effectiveness for various population-based health promotion interventions is not that which is discovered as the result of a randomized controlled trial where all variables are controlled and one condition is targeted. Glasgow et al. instead proposed that a different discovery approach is needed because traditional research has actually been shown to yield little practice benefit to busy clinic settings where routine patients present with a variety of chronic conditions and health behavior changes are needed. Rather than randomized controlled trials, then, IC clinicians can use a "RE-AIM" evaluation approach to determine the efficacy of chosen interventions. Research can be targeted to examine the effects on the patient population in terms of the intervention's impact on these five RE-AIM dimensions: reach, effectiveness, adoption, implementation, and maintenance. Rapid learning is supported by RE-AIM when it is used to determine which interventions and methods are effective in the real world of health care. Also beneficial are peer consultation and learning from what others have discovered in their own IC settings. Collaborative care is just beginning to adopt this method of research and discovery.

Family and internal medicine and pediatrics have been consulting with one another for years. As this chapter was written, six collaborative care practices under the auspices of the Collaborative Care Research Network (see www.aafp.org/online/en/home/clinical/research/natnet/get-involved/ccrn-info.html) are responding to the following questions: what types of patients attend collaborative care, what types of patients decline to participate, and when a physician makes a referral, how often is treatment initiated? Answers to these questions have the potential to provide valuable insight into the ways in which collaborative care professionals can best serve patients.

Conclusion

Collaborative care is emerging from its adolescence and entering its adulthood as a field. It is time for all clinicians to be the creators of the science of IC, implement it in our practices, and disseminate what is learned. IC has not yet demonstrated that it has made up its mind on whether it will be a part of the problem or the solution. In these early days, there is too much that is slick and looks good on the outside but has little depth beneath the surface. Rigor and attention are needed by three worlds clinicians to create three worlds practices. It is imperative that clinicians ask the questions that will shape how we think and what we do and will generate the data to which we need to respond and that we need to evaluate.

Discussion Questions

1. In the emerging field of IC, what is the importance of having a common language? Explain a few integrated concepts or practices that could benefit from a common language.
2. Which one of the five elements in Peek's Collaborative Care Lexicon do you think would be the most challenging to implement and why?

3. As a three worlds clinician in a practice that utilizes colocated planned sessions, how should a BHP who wants to provide brief patient encounters in exam rooms strive to make operational changes in his or her clinical practice? How do financial expectations factor into this scenario?

4. How can a BHP begin to explore the development of a system for the collection of data to track clinical outcomes of treatment that is both operationally and financially sensible?

References

Gatchel, R. J., & Oordt, M. S. (2003). *Clinical health psychology and primary care: Practical advice and clinical guidance for successful collaboration.* Washington, DC: American Psychological Association.

Glasgow, R. E., Vogt, T. M., & Boles, S. M. (1999). Evaluating the public health impact of health promotion interventions: The RE-AIM framework. *American Journal of Public Health, 89*, 1322–1327.

Green, L. A., Cifuentes, M., Glasgow, R. E., & Stange, K. C. (2008). Redesigning primary care practice to incorporate health behavior change: Prescription for health round-2 results. *American Journal of Preventive Medicine, 35*(5S), S347–S349. doi:10.1016/j.amepre.2008.08.013

Kessler, R., & Glasgow, R. E. (2011). A proposal to speed translation of healthcare research into practice: Dramatic change is needed. *American Journal of Preventive Medicine, 40*(6), 637–644.

Kessler, R., & Miller, B. F. (2009a, October). *A framework for collaborative care.* Paper presented at the meeting of the Collaborative Care Research Network Research Development Conference, Denver, CO.

Kessler, R., & Miller, B. F. (2009b, March). *Model: Range of need for collaboration in the patient centered medical home.* Paper presented at the National Medical Home Summit, Philadelphia, PA. Retrieved from www.ehcca.com/presentations/medhomesummit2/kessler_2a.pdf

Miller, B. F., Kessler, R., & Peek, C. J. (2011). *A National Agenda for Research in Collaborative Care: Papers from the Collaborative Care Research Network Research Development Conference* (AHRQ Publication No. 11-0067). Rockville, MD: Agency for Healthcare Research and Quality. Retrieved from http://www.ahrq.gov/research/collaborativecare/

Ossorio, P. G. (2006). Some conceptual-notational devices. In P. G. Ossorio (Ed.), *The behavior of persons: The collected works of Peter. G. Ossorio* (Vol. V). Ann Arbor, MI: Descriptive Psychology Press.

Patterson, J., Peek, C. J., Heinrich, R., Bischoff, R., & Scherger, J. (2002). *Mental health professionals in medical settings: A primer.* New York: W. W. Norton.

Peek, C. J. (2011). A Collaborative Care Lexicon for asking practice and research development questions. In *A National Agenda for Research in Collaborative Care: Papers from the Collaborative Care Research Network*

Research Development Conference (AHRQ Publication No. 11-0067). Rockville, MD: Agency for Healthcare Research and Quality. Retrieved from http://www.ahrq.gov/research/collaborativecare/

Robinson, P. J., & Reiter, J. T. (2007). *Behavioral consultation and primary care: A guide to integrating services.* New York: Springer.

Strosahl, K. D. (2005). Training behavioral health and primary care providers for integrated care: A core competencies approach. In W. T. O'Donohue, M. R. Byrd, N. A. Cummings, & D. A. Henderson (Eds.), *Behavioral integrative care: Treatments that work in the primary care setting (pp. 15–52).* New York: Brunner-Routledge.

CHAPTER **18**

Preparing Graduate Students for Careers in Integrated Care

SUSAN DENNY, ERIC M. PITTS,
JENNIFER M. HARDIN, and RUSS CURTIS

It has often been pointed out that in healthcare it is 20 years after the proven effectiveness of a treatment before it is fully adopted. In this point of view, it will be 10 more years before integrated care is mainstream. (Cummings, O'Donohue, & Cummings, 2009, p. 36)

The majority of this text has been written by professionals, researchers, and academics, all of whom are interested in advancing the integrated care (IC) field. The primary purpose of this final chapter is to summarize and, in some areas, to elaborate on how to best prepare graduate students for work in IC practices. To ensure that the information provided in this chapter is developmentally appropriate, the authors asked three recent master's-level graduates to assist. Susan, Eric, and Jennifer earned their master's of science degree in clinical mental health counseling and completed internships in the same IC practice during different semesters. The students were asked to keep a record of their experiences throughout their internship experiences by documenting their activities and describing the challenges and rewards of working in an IC setting.

The IC practice in which the students interned is a family medical practice and residency program that is partially funded by the University of North Carolina Medical School. This practice includes three professional behavioral health providers (BHPs) who work full-time alongside physicians, medical residents and interns, pharmacists, nurses, and office staff. The practice also contracts with a licensed psychiatrist for one half day per week. The three BHPs include a licensed psychologist with a PhD in clinical psychology, a licensed clinical social worker with a master's degree in social work, and a licensed professional counselor with a master's degree in psychology. To qualify to serve an internship with this practice, the students needed to have performed exceptionally well in their core classes, successfully completed their semester-long practicum experience, and received positive letters of recommendation from faculty and practicum site supervisors. These BHP interns worked 40 hours per week during the 15-week semester and received a minimum of 1 hour per week of site supervision from their approved site supervisor, as well as 3 hours per week of group supervision from their university faculty supervisor. During the university group supervision, students played audiotaped segments of their counseling/consultation sessions (with signed consent from patients), in which they received oral and written feedback from the faculty supervisor and their peers. Typical intern duties at this IC practice include the following:

Daily tasks:

- providing individual counseling;
- consulting with doctors (faculty, residents, and interns) and other staff (e.g., dietician, triage nurses, and psychiatrist);
- conducting depression protocol: making regular phone calls to patients who were diagnosed with depression to support their treatment and medication compliance, monitor their symptoms, and help them initiate and maintain self-care action plans;
- documenting clinical notes in the electronic medical record; and
- responding to e-mail or snail mail related to patient issues and concerns.

Other responsibilities:

- having monthly peer consultation with BHPs working in other practices;
- attending behavioral health didactics: 1-hour seminars conducted by BHPs to educate medical professionals about key behavioral health issues and strategies (e.g., motivational interviewing, communicating test results);
- creating information sheets and brochures for patients;
- maintaining and updating the intern manual and revising the depression protocol procedures as needed; and

- keeping notes of their experiences, including the frustrations, challenges, surprises, and rewards of working within an IC practice.

The intern's notes were compiled and reviewed by the last author, who is one of their university faculty supervisors, and organized according to Strosahl's (2005) six core competencies for IC professionals: (a) clinical skills, (b) practice management skills, (c) consultation skills, (d) documentation skills, (e) team performance skills, and (f) administrative skills. A description of each competency, with student comments and recommendations for how BHP educators can best prepare students for IC careers, follows.

The Six Core Competencies of IC Providers

Clinical Skills

To become effective clinicians within IC settings, BHPs must be competent in conducting brief functional assessments and providing brief treatment that draws on patients' strengths and is culturally and developmentally appropriate. Learning and acquiring clinical skills can be unnerving for BHPs-in-training, especially when working within the fast-paced and dynamic IC environment.

> Susan, BHP intern: When I first started, I didn't like that everything was so new to me, that I felt like a burden to the team. Seeing patients felt much more like a learning experience for me as opposed to a helping experience for them. I was apprehensive about my work in an IC setting because I knew I would have clients with physical illnesses, and I was afraid I would not fully understand how these issues impacted patients' mental health. I chose to deal with my apprehensions by acknowledging my areas of growth, accepting myself for who I am as a BHP intern, and preparing the best I could.

Implicit in Susan's note is initial performance anxiety, which is not an unusual feeling for interns. This is considered to be especially true for the new generation of graduate students (Twenge, 2007). But what is noteworthy about the aforementioned statement is Susan's desire to be proactive and self-directed in learning what she needs to feel more competent as a BHP. Indeed, Susan appears to possess a high internal locus of control (Rotter, 1966). Thus, the first step in training students to work in IC is to make them aware that this type of work requires BHPs who are confident and comfortable taking initiative (Serrano, 2009).

> Jennifer, BHP intern: My first impression of integrated care was pleasant discomfort, a mix of warm welcome and intimidating

knowledge and status [of doctors]. However, the ever-flowing stream of people [staff and patients] offered an extroverted counselor's ideal work environment.

To date there are no quantifiable personality profiles of IC professionals conducted using standardized instruments, and it is hoped that anyone with motivation and drive to work in IC, regardless of personality, can succeed. But Jennifer's statement suggests that one must be at ease with having frequent interactions with many people throughout the day. Both of these BHP intern statements also speak to feelings of initial intimidation about interning in an IC setting. The following recommendations are based on the last author's 10 years of experience in supervising IC interns and are proposed to enhance students' clinical skills.

First, introduce all students to IC in their first semester so they can begin to understand the IC culture and how it can serve to reach many patients who would otherwise never seek counseling services (Aitken & Curtis, 2004). Make students aware that prevention and the use of comprehensive care to draw on the strengths of patients has been the battle cry of mental health for over 50 years, to little or no avail; that is, until now, with the emergence of IC (Cummings et al., 2009). Inviting experienced BHPs to speak to students in introductory classes and giving students the opportunity to shadow BHPs at IC practices reinforces this message.

Second, in the assessment and diagnosis classes, it is advisable for students to take several personality indicators so they can begin to assess their own strengths and become aware of the challenges they personally may face when working in the IC field. Anecdotal evidence suggests that students benefit from taking and interpreting the following tests: (a) a representation of the five-factor model of personality (www.personalitytest. net/ipip/ipipneo1.htm), (b) the Jung Typology Test (www.humanmetrics. com), (c) a multiple intelligence survey (http://surfaquarium.com/MI/ inventory.htm), (d) the rosebush projective technique (see Ray, Perkins, & Oden, 2004), (e) instruments used within the field of positive psychotherapy (www.authentichappiness.sas.upenn.edu/register.aspx), and (f) the eco-map (see Curry, Fazio-Griffith, & Rohr, 2008). All of these instruments take little time to complete and are particularly good catalysts for increasing self-awareness. Once students complete the instruments, score them, and review their results, they should then be given numerous opportunities to interpret them in role-play situations, with instructor supervision. Allowing only 20 minutes to interpret test results keeps the assignment manageable and prepares students to work within a brief assessment framework.

Third, in the counseling theories and techniques class, in which traditional therapies are taught (e.g., cognitive behavioral therapy), make certain to introduce, discuss, and role-play motivational interviewing (Miller & Rollnick, 1991), solution-focused brief therapy (De Shazer, 1991), and positive psychotherapy (i.e., mindfulness, acceptance; see Seligman, 2011). Students should be given the opportunity to role-play each of these strategies with fellow classmates. To best prepare students for IC practices, it advisable to have students role-play, taking a turn for 15 to 20 minutes as the counselor, so every student has the opportunity to practice counseling in a safe environment under instructor supervision. Case scenarios should be provided so students do not feel pressured to talk about their own personal experiences, although, when appropriate, students can be invited to share personal experiences if they wish. Typically, students will talk about the stress of graduate school and how it affects their work and relationships; it is important for the instructor to remind students that they are being evaluated and that it is imperative that they share only "appropriate classroom role-play material" and that other personal issues should be saved for their own personal counseling. Anecdotal evidence indicates that students' ability to follow these rules can be an indicator of their maturity, professionalism, and readiness to work in IC practices.

Fourth, regularly facilitate discussion about the current paradigm of IC and the purpose of brief population-based counseling and how it can reach a larger percentage of the population than that served by the current specialty mental health system. In other words, get students to consider where they learned about counseling and how their preconceived notions affect their perceptions of how to best reach and help people. The media often depicts counseling with a psychoanalytic perspective, and it is not uncommon for beginning students to consider that theoretical orientation to be the norm. Challenging this notion early in graduate students' programs increases their awareness about the different theoretical perspectives that can be employed to help people obtain their goals, including brief, strengths-based counseling as is commonly used in IC settings.

Practice Management Skills

Practice management skills include the ability to manage time wisely in an effort to provide quality services to many people throughout the day (Robinson & Reiter, 2007). To do this, BHPs must learn to become adept at conducting brief 20- to 30-minute sessions, in addition to holding brief consultations with primary care providers (PCPs), to meet the needs of the high volume of patients seen in IC practices.

> Susan, BHP intern: In the first weeks, I had to remind myself to slow down, listen, and use appropriate interventions with each client. It was easy to want to skip rapport building and move directly to implementing techniques.

Students working in IC practices will have to be willing and able to provide brief assessment and therapy, but these should not be at the expense of building and maintaining good working relationships with patients. Regardless of the type of system in which one works (e.g., IC, mental health agency, psychiatric hospital), the patient–BHP relationship is a powerful agent for change (Budd & Hughes, 2009). The challenge for BHPs is to determine the ways in which the BHP–patient relationship can be fostered and maintained within a fast-paced IC environment.

> Jennifer, BHP intern: It is definitely challenging building and maintaining relationships with all staff—nurses, doctors, and administrators—while scheduling the depression protocol, counseling, and documentation of consultations.

> Eric, BHP intern: During the initial intake, assess for the basics first, keep it simple. During intake I asked patients to report about their sleep, appetite, energy, and mood. These are the mental health vitals, and when they become problematic, people suffer.

As discussed in the previous chapters, a brief assessment should be functional, with a focus on patients' most pressing concerns. As Eric indicated, sleep, appetite, energy, and mood are commonly problematic for patients seen in IC settings. Conducting brief assessments can be challenging, especially if a patient is particularly talkative or presents in crisis. One way to overcome these challenges to brief assessments is for BHPs to gently place some parameters on what they are seeking. For instance, the BHP could say, "Michelle, Dr. Hasan mentioned you are feeling anxious. In a couple of paragraphs, can you tell me more about what you're experiencing?" In this statement the BHP sends the message that he or she wants to hear more from the patient but that it needs to be brief. Anecdotal evidence suggests that this statement helps patients stay focused and speak more succinctly when explaining their issues.

It can be helpful for BHPs to organize the information obtained during the assessment into the following domains: emotions, thoughts, behaviors, and physiology (Boffey, 1993). For example, if a patient complains of increasing anxiety, she may talk about how her heart races and she begins to sweat and feel nauseated when driving her car. These symptoms are causing her to call in sick from work and avoid other obligations, which in turn increases her anxiety and causes her to feel hopeless about her future. In this scenario, the BHP can organize the information in a way that is comprehensive yet manageable. The information could be organized as follows: *emotions:* anxious and depressed; *thoughts:* "I'm losing control," "I'm going crazy"; *behavior:* avoiding work and other obligations; and *physiology:* racing heart, nausea, and sweating. Anecdotal evidence suggests that presenting a summary to patients in this format compartmentalizes the issue, which makes the problem seem less overwhelming. In addition, summarizing the assessment into the four domains helps patients and PCPs learn and/or remember how thoughts, emotions, behaviors, and physiology are all intertwined, thereby illuminating the importance of developing a comprehensive treatment plan that includes cognitive behavioral strategies and medication, among other things.

> Eric, BHP intern: As your intern duties and caseload increases, free time becomes increasingly rare. So, if you have a little extra time before your next session or consult and you are trying to decide whether to plan a little bit longer or take the time to center yourself and become relaxed and focused, I would encourage the latter. Both you and your patient benefit when you do what is needed to stay relaxed.

To ensure good practice management, interns need to find "breathing moments" throughout the day to maintain their sense of peace and focus. Everyone in the practice will benefit from an intern who keeps self-care in mind throughout the day. BHP educators can reinforce this type of practice by beginning each class with a brief (i.e., 5 minutes) relaxation exercise and by asking students at random times during class to stop, breathe, and relax before returning to the topic or activity at hand. This should be a part of every class until it becomes habit for students. The hope is that it will help students maintain a productive and satisfying work schedule while reducing the risk of burnout.

See vignettes 1 through 6 in the *Integrated Care in Action* video for demonstrations of effective clinical and practice management skills.

Consultation Skills

Consultation skills are critical in IC settings because a key ingredient to successful IC practices is effective communication between PCPs and BHPs. BHPs should be skilled at providing concise and cogent information to PCPs without needless "psycho-jargon." Jennifer expressed this sentiment as follows:

> Jennifer, BHP intern: I feared that what I had to say would be a bother rather than helpful. I had to learn how to be concise and gain confidence with the importance of mental health information in case conceptualization for medical professionals. I had to recognize that I, too, was a professional with wisdom and expertise to offer.

The SOAP note (Weed, 1964) is the most common way to document treatment plans in IC practices. This type of note is composed of the *subjective* experience of the client (e.g., "I'm feeling anxious when driving."), the *objective* observations of the BHP and PCP (e.g., patient seems concerned, voice was shaking throughout the interview), the *assessment* (e.g., patient meets criteria for panic disorder with agoraphobia), and the *plan* (e.g., PCP will prescribe 20 mg of Paxil taken once per day [qd] and will be taught relaxation skills to be practiced twice a day [bid]). Once the information is compiled, Serrano (2009) recommended that the BHP consult with the PCP by first communicating the assessment and plan (of the SOAP note), followed by other pertinent information, if needed. Thus, a BHP in this scenario would say to a PCP during consultation, "Based on my assessment, the patient appears to be experiencing intense anxiety symptoms that were triggered by witnessing a car accident 2 weeks ago. I will teach her a mindfulness-based relaxation exercise and follow up with her by phone every week for the next several weeks. It does appear to me that she could benefit from medicine as well. She reports having taken 20 mg of paroxetine qd with 0.5 mg of lorazepam as needed the last time she experienced similar symptoms and said that it helped. What are your thoughts?" Observing IC supervisors in consultation with PCPs is one way BHP interns can begin to home the skill of "curbside" consultations.

> Susan, BHP intern: Be honest about your clinical skills. I felt over-whelmed at times, which I knew was normal, but I let my clients know when I needed to consult with my supervisor. The patients appreciated the honesty, and I got to learn the best way to handle situations that were unfamiliar to me.

Willingness to admit the need for supervision is a sign of maturity, one that is often evident in more experienced clinicians and is a welcomed trait in new supervisees (Loganbill, Hardy, & Delworth, 1982). Susan's statement indicates her desire to learn and willingness to be both vulnerable and genuine within the counseling relationship. These qualities are attributes of personal strength, ones that will ultimately strengthen the patient–BHP relationship (Budd & Hughes, 2009). Educators can reinforce the need for supervision by giving students a model by which they can regularly evaluate themselves to determine the areas in which they might need to seek supervision. One such model, the discrimination model, was created by Bernard (1979) and further enhanced by Lanning (1986). Introducing this model of supervision to students early in their master's and doctoral programs can help them become aware of the main areas to be cognizant of while working with patients and supervisors. The model is composed of the following components: (a) counseling skills, (b) cognitive counseling skills (i.e., generating hypotheses, conceptualizing cases, diagnosing), (c) self-awareness (i.e., awareness of intra- and interpersonal experiences when working with patients), and (d) professional behavior (i.e., general timeliness, accurate documentation, respectful and facilitative communication with all staff and patients).

It is not uncommon for beginner-level clinicians to focus solely on counseling skills, eschewing the other pertinent areas of counselor competence. By introducing this model and addressing issues within its components when conducting supervision, educators can help students become more comfortable seeking help for the inextricably linked intra- and interpersonal issues that arise when providing patient care. Following this model also prevents students and supervisors from falling into the trap of using supervision strictly for case consultation. Good clinical supervision should help BHPs-in-training develop clinical and personal skills on multiple levels.

See vignette 8 of the *Integrated Care in Action* video for a demonstration of an effective BHP–PCP consultation.

Documentation Skills

Creating pertinent and concise notes that highlight the patient's presenting concerns, assessment results, and a tentative treatment plan is necessary for effective documentation. From the following comments, it is clear that students were initially intimidated by this task, underscoring the importance of the introduction of SOAP notes early in training programs.

> Jennifer, BHP intern: When writing my first note, I carefully reviewed the intern's manual for clarity and instruction. It may have taken the better part of an hour for ONE note! Ha! When consulting with my first doctor, I prepared for several minutes to ensure a clear, concise, and valuable inquiry and response. I felt the need to earn the respect of physicians in order to continue to support the validity, value, and professionalism of counselors. I was surprised by the acceptance and support.

> Eric, BHP intern: One of the best ways to improve documentation skills is to request to see sample notes from the IC supervisor. It may be weeks before an intern begins seeing patients, but that does not mean that an intern has to wait until then to begin to practice documentation. In the weeks before I began seeing patients, I got a head start by requesting to see sample notes from my supervisor. I also used shadow sessions (sessions that I observed with my supervisor) to begin practicing documentation.

Jennifer's and Eric's comments about documentation reinforce the notion that it behooves BHP educators to provide sample SOAP notes, as well as case scenarios for which SOAP notes should be completed and discussed by the students, in all of their graduate classes (see Cameron & turtle-song, 2002). Serrano (2009) said this type of exercise is critical in developing future BHPs' case conceptualization skills. Once students become comfortable documenting in the SOAP note format, they can then begin role-playing case presentations to hone their skills in providing brief yet cogent assessment and treatment plan recommendations.

Team Performance Skills

A team player in an IC practice builds relationships with all members of the staff and is willing to help in any capacity. Team players are also visible (i.e., don't retreat to an office between visits) and seek opportunities to collaborate with other staff members.

> Jennifer, BHP intern: Building relationships with the entire staff helped me feel like I had a role and purpose. In addition, accolades from PCPs speaking of the benefit and help of behavioral health and from clients in crisis who were afforded a few minutes after a doctor's visit to "unload" also gave me confidence that behavioral health is a tremendous asset to a primary care clinic.

> Eric, BHP intern: The residents, PCPs, nurses, and other staff took the behavioral team seriously, and this helped me recognize my value within IC.

A key theme in both of these statements is the need to build relationships and be an active member of the team. It is important for BHPs-in-training to recognize that although their expertise is valued, they must also be willing to be visible and help with all practice-related duties, including but not limited to conducting case management, billing, providing documentation, creating brochures, analyzing data, consulting, and providing counseling services.

Administrative Skills

Administrative skills necessary for BHPs to be successful in an IC setting include adherence to ethical standards, documentation of patient sessions and consults in a timely manner, and maintenance of good work habits (e.g., showing up on time, following up with PCP and patient recommendations, staying late when needed).

> Jennifer, BHP intern: Keeping up with several clients and consults can be difficult. Strive to follow up with doctors and/or clients within a 24-hour window. I kept a notepad that had information about who I had spoken with and who I needed to follow up with and tried to do this within 2 to 3 days, according to the request. If it was a case management item, I tried to give forewarning that it may take a couple days, but I usually handled it within a 24-hour window.

It can be an unwelcome reality for some BHPs-in-training to recognize that agencies and practices must prioritize billing for services and generating income. Anecdotal evidence suggests that many master's-level students do not enter the field with dreams of making big salaries, and some students express disdain for the financial side of the field. It can be helpful for BHP educators to discuss these issues in class and explain that BHPs are providing valuable services that need to be reimbursed accordingly for the practice to continue to offer services.

Conclusion

The opening quote of this chapter foretells that the integration of behavioral and primary medical health care is expected to be the norm in the near future. IC's emphasis on comprehensive prevention and tertiary care, coupled with its philosophy of strengths-based patient involvement in treatment, is leading to the rapid rise of IC from grassroots agencies to state and federal policy and is quickly disassembling the artificial walls that separated mental and physical health care. Thus, there is a growing impetus for behavioral health educators to begin training their students to work effectively within this new and exciting health care paradigm. In closing, consider one last quote from Susan, a recent graduate and future IC professional:

> The health care professionals working in my integrated care practice were concerned for the overall well-being of their patients, and this internship experience allowed me the opportunity to provide patients with much-needed counseling and education. For many of these patients, it was the first time they had ever worked with a mental health professional.

Discussion Questions

1. Identify your own strengths and challenges for each of the components of Bernard's (1979) discrimination model of clinical supervision.
2. Create a SOAP note from the following case scenario: Jordan is a 51-year-old White male who has come to see his PCP for the following symptoms: inability to concentrate, irritability, "memory problems," and general exhaustion. He reports that these symptoms have lasted for the past 2 years, and he has been using increasing amounts of caffeine to "get through the day" and complete his responsibilities at work and home. He also reports that he does not sleep well at night and has a hard time staying awake during the day. There is no family history of alcohol or illicit substance use, but he admits to drinking 8 to 10 beers per week. He

was diagnosed with dysthymia in his early 30s but said none of the medication worked, which is when he started increasing his caffeine and alcohol intake. He says that he is ready to make changes if it will help but admits that he feels a little hopeless about the situation.

3. Do you view yourself as more extroverted or introverted? How might your answer impact your work in IC?

4. What might you do to increase health care providers' perceptions of the value of behavioral health services for patients?

5. How might you begin a discussion with a PCP about the possibility of joining his or her practice?

References

Aitken, J. B., & Curtis, R. (2004). Integrated health care: Improving client care while providing opportunities for mental health counselors. *Journal of Mental Health Counseling, 26*(4), 321–331.

Bernard, J. (1979). Supervisor training: A discrimination model. *Counselor Education and Supervision, 19*(1), 60–68.

Boffey, D. B. (1993). *Reinventing yourself: A control theory approach to becoming the person you want to be*. Chapel Hill, NC: New View.

Budd, R., & Hughes, I. (2009). The dodo bird verdict—controversial, inevitable and important: A commentary on 30 years of meta-analyses. *Clinical Psychology and Psychiatry, 16*, 510–522.

Cameron, S., & Turtle-Song, I. (2002). Learning to write case notes using the SOAP format. *Journal of Counseling and Development, 80*, 286–292.

Cummings, N. A., O'Donohue, W. T., & Cummings, J. L. (2009). The financial dimension of integrated behavioral/primary care. *Journal of Clinical Psychology in Medical Settings, 16*, 31–39. doi:10.1007/s10880-008-9139-2

Curry, J. R., Fazio-Griffith, L. J., & Rohr, S. N. (2008). My solar system: A developmentally adapted eco-mapping technique for children. *Journal of Creativity in Mental Health, 3*(3), 233–242.

De Shazer, S. (1991). *Putting difference to work*. New York: Norton.

Lanning, W. (1986). Development of the supervisor emphasis rating form. *Counselor Education and Supervision, 25*, 191–196.

Loganbill, C., Hardy, E., & Delworth, U. (1982). Supervision: A conceptual model. *Counseling Psychologist, 10*(1), 3–42.

Miller, W. R., & Rollnick, S. (1991). *Motivational interviewing: Preparing people for change*. New York: Guilford Press.

Ray, D. C., Perkins, S. R., & Oden, K. (2004). Rosebush fantasy technique with elementary school students. *Professional School Counseling, 7*, 277–282.

Robinson, P. J., & Reiter, J. T. (2007). *Behavioral consultation and primary care: A guide to integrating services*. New York: Springer.

Rotter, J. B. (1966). Generalized expectancies for internal versus external control of reinforcement. *Psychological Monographs, 80*(1), 1–28. doi:10.1037/h0092976

Seligman, M. E. P. (2011). *Flourish: A visionary new understanding of happiness and well-being.* New York: Free Press.

Serrano, N. (Producer). (2009, June 1). *Advanced supervision* [Audio podcast]. Retrieved from http://itunes.apple.com/bw/podcast/primary-care-behavioral-health/id268585478

Strosahl, K. (2005). Training behavioral health and primary care providers for integrated care: A core competencies approach. In W. O'Donohue, M. Byrd, N. Cummings, & D. Henderson (Eds.), *Behavioral integrative care: Treatments that work in the primary care setting* (pp. 15–52). New York: Routledge.

Twenge, J. M. (2007). *Generation me: Why today's young Americans are more confident, assertive, entitled—and more miserable than ever before.* New York: Free Press.

Weed, L. L. (1964). Medical records, patient care and medical education. *Irish Journal of Medical Education, 6,* 271–282.

Index